CUSTOMER SERVICE

Skills for Success

CUSTOMER SERVICE

Skills for Success

4th Edition

Robert W. Lucas
Webster University, Orlando, Florida

Boston   Burr Ridge, IL   Dubuque, IA   Madison, WI   New York   San Francisco   St. Louis
Bangkok   Bogotá   Caracas   Kuala Lumpur   Lisbon   London   Madrid   Mexico City
Milan   Montreal   New Delhi   Santiago   Seoul   Singapore   Sydney   Taipei   Toronto

CUSTOMER SERVICE: SKILLS FOR SUCCESS

Published by McGraw-Hill, a business unit of The McGraw-Hill Companies, Inc., 1221 Avenue of the Americas, New York, NY, 10020. Copyright © 2009 by The McGraw-Hill Companies, Inc. All rights reserved. Previous editions © 2005, 2002, and 1996. No part of this publication may be reproduced or distributed in any form or by any means, or stored in a database or retrieval system, without the prior written consent of The McGraw-Hill Companies, Inc., including, but not limited to, in any network or other electronic storage or transmission, or broadcast for distance learning.

Some ancillaries, including electronic and print components, may not be available to customers outside the United States.

This book is printed on acid-free paper.

3 4 5 6 7 8 9 0 WCK/WCK 0 9

ISBN 978-0-07-354544-8

MHID 0-07-354544-9

Vice president/Editor in chief: *Elizabeth Haefele*
Vice president/Director of marketing: *John E. Biernat*
Sponsoring editor: *Natalie J. Ruffatto*
Developmental editor: *Kristin Bradley*
Marketing manager: *Keari Bedford*
Lead media producer: *Damian Moshak*
Media producer: *Benjamin Curless*
Director, Editing/Design/Production: *Jess Ann Kosic*
Project manager: *Christine M. Demma*
Production supervisor: *Mark A. S. Dierker*
Designer: *Srdjan Savanovic*
Photo research coordinator: *Lori Kramer*
Media project manager: *Janean A. Utley*
Cover design: *George Kokkonas*
Interior design: *Kay Lieberherr*
Typeface: *10/12 Times New Roman*
Compositor: *Aptara*
Printer: *Quebecor World Versailles Inc.*
Credits: The credits section for this book begins on page 288 and is considered an extension of the copyright page.

Library of Congress Cataloging-in-Publication Data

Lucas, Robert W.
    Customer service : skills for success / Robert W. Lucas. — 4th ed.
      p. cm.
    Includes index.
    ISBN-13: 978-0-07-354544-8 (alk. paper)
    ISBN-10: 0-07-354544-9 (alk. paper)
    1. Customer services. I. Title.
HF5415.5.L83 2009
658.8'12—dc22   2007045960

The Internet addresses listed in the text were accurate at the time of publication. The inclusion of a Web site does not indicate an endorsement by the authors or McGraw-Hill, and McGraw-Hill does not guarantee the accuracy of the information presented at these sites.

www.mhhe.com

Personal Biography

ROBERT (BOB) W. LUCAS

Bob Lucas holds dual roles as president of *Creative Presentation Resources*—a creative training and products company—and founding managing partner for *Global Performance Strategies,* LLC—an organization specializing in performance-based training, consulting services, and life-planning seminars.

Bob has extensive experience in human resources development, management, and customer service over the past three decades in a variety of organizational environments. This background gives him a real-world perspective on the application of theory he has studied and used for several decades. He is certified in a variety of programs from various national and international training organizations.

Bob focuses on assisting organizations and individuals in developing innovative and practical strategies for improved workplace performance. His areas of expertise include presentation skills, training and management program development, train-the-trainer, interpersonal communication, adult learning, customer service, and employee and organizational development.

Currently, Bob serves on the board of directors for the Central Florida Safety Council. Additionally, he is a former president of the Central Florida Chapter of the American Society for Training and Development, and served on the board for the Metropolitan DC and Suncoast chapters of that organization.

In addition to giving regular presentations to various local and national groups and organizations, Bob serves as an adjunct faculty members for Webster University. In that position, he teaches organizational and interpersonal communication, diversity, and Introduction to Training and Development.

Listed in the *Who's Who in the World, Who's Who in America,* and *Who's Who in the South and Southeast* for a number of years, Bob is also an avid writer. Published works include *The Creative Training Idea Book; Inspired Tips and Techniques for Engaging and Effective Learning; The BIG Book of Flip Charts; How to Be a Great Call Center Representative; Customer Service Skills and Concepts for Success; Job Strategies for New Employees; Communicating One-to-One; Making the Most of Interpersonal Relationships; Coaching Skills: A Guide for Supervisors; Effective Interpersonal Skills; Training Skills for Supervisors;* and *Customer Service: Skills and Concepts for Business.* Additionally, he has been a contributing author for the *Annual: Developing Human Resources* series by Pfeiffer & Company since 1992 and to the HRHandbook by HRD Press.

Bob has earned a Bachelor of Science degree in Law Enforcement from the University of Maryland and a Master of Arts degree with a focus in Human Resources Development from George Mason University in Fairfax, Virginia. He also completed a Master of Arts program in Management and Leadership at Webster University.

Brief Contents

Contents

Preface

IS CUSTOMER SERVICE IMPORTANT?

While there may be those that argue customer service is nothing more than basic, common sense, it has become increasingly clear that it is, in fact, vital to the success of any business. Don't believe us? Just ask Mona Shaw.

Shaw, a 75-year-old retired Air Force nurse, was attempting to switch her cable and phone service to another provider. After a missed appointment, an unauthorized phone number change, and a series of shabbily handled customer service interactions, Shaw's frustration escalated. When the manager she requested an audience with went home for the day without seeing her, Shaw returned with her husband's hammer and proceeded to destroy computer monitors and phones. When police were summoned, she agreed to set her hammer down . . . she just did so with force and directly on top of a phone.

While this story is extreme, her plight highlights exactly why customer service is the lifeblood of successful companies. As technology changes, the solutions to customer problems are becoming increasingly complex. The result is an environment in which Customer Service Representatives (CSRs) are walking the fine line between technology solutions that cannot be resolved instantaneously and the historically proven need to treat customers with respect and care. Walking that fine line is exactly why *Customer Service: Skills for Success* is essential reading for anyone fortunate enough to impact customers on a regular basis.

What makes the fourth edition of *Customer Service: Skills for Success* unique to the market is the understanding that at the core of all workflow and technological changes is common courtesy that cannot be ignored. This edition focuses specifically on emerging technologies and the globalization of customer service workflows without losing sight of what is fundamentally important in the first place . . . the customer.

In addition to helping students cope with the changing landscape of customer service professions, we recognize that, like the industry itself, streamlining is a necessity. We have streamlined the text in an effort to communicate pertinent information in a time-efficient model.

As our global community evolves, customer service models must be adaptable to meet changing needs. This understanding is at the core of *Customer Service: Skills for Success*. The text and ancillary materials do more than just provide a how-to for CSRs. The supplements give students a skill set that will allow them to adapt and change as rapidly as the businesses they work for. Ultimately, the goal of this book is to provide students with the skills they will need to thrive in the real world.

NOT THE SAME OLD CUSTOMER SERVICE TEXTBOOK

Customer Service: Skills for Success uses a variety of activities and example to gain and hold readers' interest while providing additional insights into the concepts and skills related to customer service.

The text begins with a macro view of what customer service involves today and provides projections for the future then focuses on specific skills and related topics.

http://abcnews.go.com/GMA/story?id=3750705&page=1

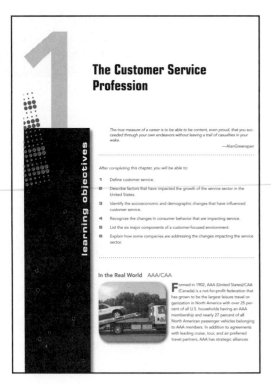

1

The Customer Service Profession

The true measure of a career is to be able to be content, even proud, that you succeeded through your own endeavors without leaving a trail of casualties in your wake.

—Alan Greenspan

learning objectives

After completing this chapter, you will be able to:

1 Define customer service.

2 Describe factors that have impacted the growth of the service sector in the United States.

3 Identify the socioeconomic and demographic changes that have influenced customer service.

4 Recognize the changes In consumer behavior that are impacting service.

5 List the six major components of a customer-focused environment.

6 Explain how some companies are addressing the changes impacting the service sector.

In the Real World AAA/CAA

Formed in 1902, AAA (United States)/CAA (Canada) is a not-for-profit federation that has grown to be the largest leisure travel organization in North America with over 25 percent of all U.S. households having an AAA membership and nearly 27 percent of all North American passenger vehicles belonging to AAA members. In addition to agreements with leading cruise, tour, and air preferred travel partners, AAA has strategic alliances

---

The 4th Edition of *Customer Service: Skills for Success* contains 10 chapters divided into three parts, plus the Appendix, Glossary and Bibliography. The sections focus on different aspects of customer service: (1) The Profession (2) Skills for Success, and (3) Building and Maintaining Relationships. Along with valuable ideas, guidance, and perspectives, readers will also encounter interviews of real-world service providers and case study scenarios and activities to help you apply concepts learned to real-world situations in order to challenge your thinking on the issues presented.

Each chapter starts with behavioral-based **Learning Objectives** to direct your focus and to help you measure your end of chapter success in grasping the concepts presented. You will also find a **quote** from a famous person to prompt your thinking related to the chapter topic and the text focus.

As you explore the chapter material readers will find many helpful tools to enhance their learning experience and assist them in transferring their new knowledge to the workplace. These include:

An opportunity to do a short **Self-Assessment** of current skills and knowledge levels before even reading the first page. This is done through a series of brief questions related to providing customer service that readers can score themselves. If the responses are incorrect, you can use the areas missed to focus in on specific chapters as you read the book. For those areas where you get the answers right, you can use chapters which discuss them as a reinforcement.

Pretests called **Quick Preview** are provided at the beginning of each chapter to allow readers to check their topic knowledge. Answers to the questions are provided at the end of the chapter.

with world-known organizations like Disney and Hertz Corporation. AAA and CAA have over 38,000 full-time employees in 1,100 offices who serve over 50 million members in the United States and Canada.

AAA sponsors the AAA Foundation for Traffic Safety, the School Safety Patrol Program throughout the United States, and many other safety initiatives. AAA provides services to its members. The organization is also one of the largest travel publishers in the world, distributing nearly 166 million copies of travel-related materials annually.

Chief among the benefits to AAA members is the roadside assistance program for stranded motorists. Each year AAA/CAA dispatches emergency road service to more than 29 million stranded motorists. In addition to roadside assistance, AAA offers travel agency services to anyone who visits one of the local AAA offices. There, they can purchase luggage and other travel products, make reservations for car rentals, hotels, and transportation, or book a cruise. AAA also offers many other free and discounted services exclusively to members, including insurance (for example, travel, automobile, life, home-owners, and travelers), national and international travel assistance, free maps and tour guides, car buying services, credit cards and financial services, and automobile-related maintenance services.

A key to AAA's success has been its focus on member responsiveness, quality service, and the trust that have been established through over a century of dedication to members, the community, and the United States and Canada. In recent years, AAA has automated many of its functions by establishing service kiosks in malls and other locations and has a state-of-the-art call center that dispatches emergency road service and helps members maximize use of membership benefits.

For more information about this organization visit www.aaaexchange.com/Main/.

Quick Preview

Before reviewing the content of the chapter, respond to the following statements by placing a "T" for true or an "F" for false on the rules. Use any questions you miss as a check-list of material to which you will pay particular attention as you read through the chapter. For those you get right, congratulate yourself, but review the sections they address in order to learn additional details about the topics.

____ 1. The concept of customer service evolved from the practice of selling wares in small general stores, off the back of wagons, or out of the home.

____ 2. The migration from other occupations to the service industry is a recent trend and started in the late 1970s.

____ 3. One of the reasons for the shift from manufacturing to customer service is that society has changed.

____ 4. As more women have entered the workforce, the demand for personal services has increased.

____ 5. Advances in technology have created a need for more employees in manufacturing businesses.

____ 6. Workers in the United States have more disposable income now than at any other time in history.

____ 7. As a result of deregulation in a variety of industries, competition has slowed.

____ 8. Quality customer service organizations recruit, select, and train qualified people.

____ 9. Customers are happy when they receive quality and quantity as promised.

5

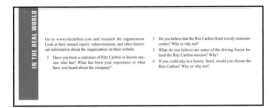

In the Real World sections, placed at the beginning of many of the chapters, provide insights into customer service in a variety of well-known businesses, industries, and organizations. These candid snapshots provide an overview of how successful businesses provide products and services and succeed in a highly competitive global world.

Work It Out activities throughout the chapters challenge readers knowledge and provide an opportunity for individual and/ or small group work on a specific topic or issue.

At the end of each chapter is a **Chapter Summary** and **Chapter Review Questions**, along with **Key Terms and Concepts** to bring together the key elements and issues encountered in the chapter.

Face to Face exercises are customer service scenarios in which readers assume the role of a specified employee and use information provided to determine how they would handle a customer service issue.

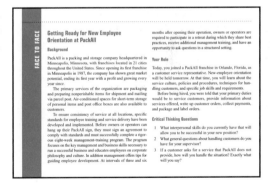

Search It Out activities at the end of skill-building chapters provide the opportunity to use research skills on the Internet. In each chapter, explore the Internet to obtain a variety of customer service facts, figures, and related information to use in group activities, presentations or discussions. Visit the Website especially designed by McGraw-Hill for *Customer Service: Skills for Success* at www.mhhe.com/lucas09.

Participate in **Collaborative Learning** activities where readers and one or more of their peers can actually work through a customer service issue with the instructor to practice your skills and find answers to various questions.

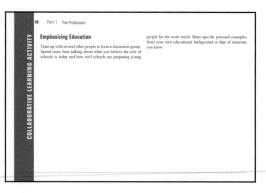

Planning to Serve activities provide a roadmap for planning strategies and identifying techniques that you can be used from the book to provide superior customer service in the future.

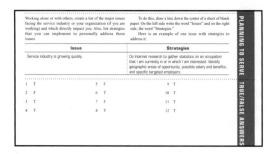

Use the **Reader Satisfaction Survey** found in the **Appendices** section of the text to provide the author with feedback.

THE CUSTOMER SERVICE TEXT THAT GIVES YOU MORE

STUDENT RESOURCES

Online Learning Center (OLC)—Student Content: A separate section of the McGraw-Hill Web site has been reserved for students and instructors. This section contains online practice tests, additional learning exercises, and other World Wide Web links to stimulate your research efforts. Visit www.mhhe.com/lucas09.

Spanish Translations: Spanish speaking readers can take advantage of the **Spanish Translations** of the glossary of key terms and online quizzes.

Student Study Guide: The **Student Study Guide** includes worksheets, practice tests, and supplemental learning materials so students can reinforce their learning of the chapter concepts. The Student Study Guide is organized by chapter and learning outcome to assist students in understanding each chapter's goals and objectives. This guide is available in both a print version or as part of the online enhanced cartridge.

INSTRUCTOR RESOURCES

Online Learning Center (OLC)—Instructor Content: The instructor's side of **Online Learning Center (OLC)** serves as a resource for instructors and has several features that support instructors in the creation of lessons. Included on the OLC are the Instructor's Manual (IM), which is organized by each chapter's learning objectives and includes page references, PowerPoint Slides that include additional instructor teaching notes, the Asset Map and other valuable materials.

Instructor's Manual: The **Instructor's Manual** outlines course materials, additional in-class activities, and support for classroom use of the text. It has been organized by learning objectives to give instructors not only a basic outline of the chapter, but to assist in all facets of instruction. For every question posed in the text, the IM provides a viable answer. The text page numbers provide easy reference for instructors. In addition, the instructor's manual guides instructors through the process of integrating supplementary materials into lessons and assignments. The instructor's manual also includes sample syllabi, video notes, and student success insights. Ultimately, this will be an instructor's greatest advantage in using all materials to reach all learners.

Test Bank: Every chapter provides a series of test questions, available in our Test Bank. Questions are organized by Learning Objective and Bloom's Taxonomy. A Test Table aligns questions with the content and makes it easy for you to determine the questions you want to include on tests and quizzes.

Asset Map: We know that instructors' time is valuable. To help you prepare, we have created an **Asset Map**. The Asset Map identifies by chapter, learning objective, and page number, exactly which supplements are available for you to use. Visit our Web site at www.mhhe.com/lucas09 to preview how the Asset map can help!

Power Points: Power Point slides created specifically for instructors include additional teaching notes and are tied directly to Learning Objectives. Each slide also includes a text page reference for your convenience.

Sample Syllabi: Six and sixteen week syllabi are provided in order to tailor content to different learning programs.

Customer Service DVD: These brand new videos were created exclusively to accompany *Customer Service: Skills for Success,* 4/e. Each video matches to chapter content to offer real-world examples of customer service theories.

BASIS FOR CONTENT

This book draws from my more than three plus decades of real-world experience in customer service environments, management, and human resource development. I have worked in sales, retail management, and service functions for a number of organizations; I am a performance consultant working with client organizations in many different industries; and I have been the president of my own e-commerce retail company—Creative Presentation Resources (www.presentationresources.net)—since 1994. I have taught at numerous colleges and universities through the Master's level for over a decade. I deal with customer issues and needs everyday and know that the techniques described in this book work. While there are some research and theoretical sections in the chapters, much of the information is derived from personal experience, research, and reflections of actual customer service encounters experienced by others.

Whether you are new to the service profession and have no base of customer service knowledge, or are more experienced and wish to enhance your knowledge and skills, *Customer Service: Skills for Success* and accompanying ancillary materials can provide a catalyst for their success.

I am confident that this book will assist you reaching your goal to become a better service provider.

Bob Lucas

Acknowledgments

Throughout the years, my wife, friend, and life partner, M.J., and my mother, Rosie, have sacrificed much as I have dedicated time and effort to developing tools such as this book to help others grow. Their support and love have been an invaluable asset in helping me reach my goals and are much appreciated.

A special note of appreciation also goes to Natalie Ruffatto and Kristin Bradley, and the entire McGraw-Hill editorial team, for their expert guidance and support. Their efforts were essential in helping to create this book and add many new features to enhance its value.

Preparing any project of the length and depth of this book requires much assistance. No one person can bring together all the necessary knowledge, expertise, and insights to capture the essence of a topic.

It is with deepest gratitude to all of the following experts who took the time to read through many draft pages of the manuscript for *Customer Service: Skills for Success* and provide valuable insights, guidance, and suggestions for improvement. Without them, the final product would have proven to be of far less value to its users.

Brenda Dupras
The Saulter School

Matthew Graham
Andover College

Elizabeth D. Hall
Tidewater Technical College

DeAnn Hurtado
Sinclair Community College

Mark King
Indiana Business College

Judith Rozarie
Gibbs College

Dee Shields
Indiana Business College

Henry Tarbi
Year Up

Special thanks also to the following educators who reviewed previous editions and offered suggestions, critique, and guidance in the refinement of the book content and format.

A. Murlene Asadi
Scott Community College

Blake Beck
Idaho State University

Claudia Browning
Mesa Community College

Gary Corona
*Florida Community College
at Jacksonville*

Margaret A. Fisher
*Florida Community College
at Jacksonville*

Linda Harris
Florida Metropolitan University

Heidi Hutchins
Gateway Community College

Lea Ann Kremer
McCann School of Business & Technology

Albert Mastromartino
Sir Sanford Fleming College

John Moonen
Daytona Beach Community College

Jacqueline Nicholson
Holyoke Community College

Shelly Rex
York Technical Institute

Paul Ricker
*Broward Community College—
North Campus*

Carl Stafford
Manchester Community College

Kathleen Wachter
University of Mississippi

Joyce Walsh-Portillo
Broward Community College

Michael Wierzbicki
Scottsdale Community College

Callie P. Williams
*Florida Community College
at Jacksonville*

Richard Williams
Nashville State Community Collee

CUSTOMER SERVICE

Skills for Success

The Profession

CUSTOMER SERVICE INTERVIEW   Stephen A. Tanzer

Steve is a founding partner of a human resources consulting and training company that regularly works with a variety of industrial and government organizations.

Steve's business background crosses many industries and market segments. He started with a Fortune 500 telecommunications company, where he served the needs of national customers. Later, he functioned as a human resources performance improvement consultant, interfacing with customers at the most senior level in the entertainment, travel, ecommerce, telecommunications, aerospace, IT, manufacturing, and processing industries.

Over the past decade Steve's responsibilities have expanded to include international customers. He regularly deals with issues ranging from obvious language differences to the less obvious cultural, business process, and protocol variations.

STEPHEN A. TANZER, Managing Partner, Global Performance Strategies LLC

I consider anyone who has the position of working with internal and external customers as a professional. This recognition places a higher level of expectation of skills and abilities on them. They must possess strong professional, interpersonal, and communication skills in such areas as verbal and written communication, presentations, problem solving, negotiation, telephone communication, business etiquette, stress management, and cultural and international awareness/experience (e.g., diversity, language, protocol).

1   What are the personal qualities (communication skills etc.) that you believe are essential for anyone working with internal and external customers? Please explain.

2   What do you see as the most rewarding part of working with customers? Why?

The opportunity to work with diverse people, helping to solve their problems and deliver excellent customer satisfaction is a key reward. This work is extremely satisfying for professionals, as it allows them to use their total package of skills, knowledge, and abilities. Each day is also so different because every customer is unique, with differing needs and wants.

3 **What do you believe that the biggest challenges are in working with customers? Why?**

Determining what the real customer issues or needs are and then finding the right solution to resolve these. Many times the customers do not know these themselves and this can lead to frustration on their part. A skilled professional will know how to help the customer determine the real issue/need and help to meet that need to the customer's satisfaction.

4 **What role does technology play in your job when working with customers and how have you seen this change since you started in the workplace?**

Technology can be either an effective business tool to enhance the customer experience or a curse if and when it is not used appropriately.

There are two sides when you look at the technology question. The first is how the company deploys its technology. This seems to be where most customers have an issue. Faced with multitiered menus to select from, long hold times, and in many cases hang-ups or "all our agents are busy, now call back later" announcements. All of this leads to the company being perceived as not customer-focused.

The other side is the training and effective use of the technology on the part of the customer service representative. This is a dual responsibility—on the part of the company to effectively train and update the employee on its use, and on the part of the employee to use the equipment as trained.

Unfortunately, there seems to be a trend in American business where technology is being used to cut costs, leaving the customer to bear the burden of the issues defined above.

5 **What issues (e.g., changing demographics, technologies, customer needs/values) do you see evolving related to dealing with customers in the future and why do you think these are important?**

As the world of business changes, so must those who work in customer service. Business has been on the journey of globalization for the past decade plus.

This change brings about new demographics and customer needs that must be met by those who have primarily served single markets (e.g., the United States).

To serve these new customers, service professionals must grow their knowledge and skills to meet these new markets. New language skills, cultural knowledge for the markets being served, protocol, and etiquette are some of the new "knowledge and skills" that service providers must learn. Those who commit themselves will find great success and new satisfaction as a customer service professional. Those who do not adapt will be one of the statistics of "former" customer service professionals and will not find any satisfaction in their work.

6 **What advice related to customer service do you have for anyone seeking a career in customer service–related fields?**

Research, research, research. Customer service work is hard. Not everyone can do it! Do your research before becoming a customer service representative. Call centers are perhaps the number one work place where customer service representatives are employed. Statistics show that call centers can have turnover rates in the 50 to 125 percent range—meaning that those percentages of their customer service representatives leave during the year. Many do so because the work is not what they expected, it was too hard, or the stress level was higher then they could manage.

The one thing that all customers have in my experience is the expectation of quality service. Failure to deliver this will result in a short-lived relationship between you and your customers. Long-term business today is based upon the "total experience" that the customer has with your organization. From sales to delivery to customer service; only the best will result in the customer being a customer tomorrow.

Take classes, develop your knowledge and skills, love what you do, and do it well. Your ability to develop your skills and keep them sharp will make you shine among your peers and allow you to be successful and enjoy your work.

The Customer Service Profession

*The true measure of a career is to be able to be content, even proud, that you suc-
ceeded through your own endeavors without leaving a trail of casualties in your
wake.*

—Alan Greenspan

. . . .

After completing this chapter, you will be able to:

1   Define customer service.

2   Describe factors that have impacted the growth of the service sector in the
     United States.

3   Identify the socioeconomic and demographic changes that have influenced
     customer service.

4   Recognize the changes in consumer behavior that are impacting service.

5   List the six major components of a customer-focused environment.

6   Explain how some companies are addressing the changes impacting the service
     sector.

. . . .

In the Real World Service—American Automobile Association/ Canadian Automobile Association (AAA/CAA)

Formed in 1902, AAA (United States)/CAA
(Canada) is a not-for-profit federation that
has grown to be the largest leisure travel organization in North America with over 25 percent of
all U.S. households having an AAA membership
and nearly 27 percent of all North American
passenger vehicles belonging to AAA members.
In addition to agreements with leading cruise,

tour, and air preferred travel partners, AAA has strategic alliances with world-known organizations like Disney and Hertz Corporation. AAA and CAA have over 38,000 full-time employees in 1,100 offices who serve over 50 million members in the United States and Canada.

AAA sponsors the AAA Foundation for Traffic Safety, the School Safety Patrol Program throughout the United States, and many other safety initiatives. AAA provides services to its members. The organization is also one of the largest travel publishers in the world, distributing nearly 166 million copies of travel-related materials annually.

Chief among the benefits to AAA members is the roadside assistance program for stranded motorists. Each year AAA/CAA dispatches emergency road service to more than 29 million stranded motorists. In addition to roadside assistance, AAA offers travel agency services to anyone who visits one of the local AAA offices. There, they can purchase luggage and other travel products, make reservations for car rentals, hotels, and transportation, or book a cruise. AAA also offers many other free and discounted services exclusively to members, including insurance (for example, travel, automobile, life, homeowners, and travelers), national and international travel assistance, free maps and tour guides, car buying services, credit cards and financial services, and automobile-related maintenance services.

A key to AAA's success has been its focus on member responsiveness, quality service, and the trust that have been established through over a century of dedication to members, the community, and the United States and Canada. In recent years, AAA has automated many of its functions by establishing service kiosks in malls and other locations and has a state-of-the-art call center that dispatches emergency road service and helps members maximize use of membership benefits.

For more information about this organization visit www.aaa.com.

See activity based on this section on page 29.

Quick Preview

Before reviewing the content of the chapter, respond to the following statements by placing a "T" for true or an "F" for false on the rules. Use any questions you miss as a checklist of material to which you will pay particular attention as you read through the chapter. For those you get right, congratulate yourself, but review the sections they address in order to learn additional details about the topics.

_____ 1. The concept of customer service evolved from the practice of selling wares in small general stores, off the back of wagons, or out of the home.

_____ 2. The migration from other occupations to the service industry is a recent trend and started in the late 1970s.

_____ 3. One of the reasons for the shift from manufacturing to customer service is that society has changed.

_____ 4. As more women have entered the workforce, the demand for personal services has increased.

_____ 5. Advances in technology have created a need for more employees in manufacturing businesses.

_____ 6. Workers in the United States have more disposable income now than at any other time in history.

_____ 7. As a result of deregulation in a variety of industries, competition has slowed.

_____ 8. Quality customer service organizations recruit, select, and train qualified people.

_____ 9. Customers are happy when they receive quality and quantity as promised.

Answers to Quick Preview can be found at the end of the chapter.

customer service
The ability of knowledgeable, capable, and enthusiastic employees to deliver products and services to their Internal and external customers in a manner that satisfies Identified and unidentified needs and ultimately results In positive word-of-mouth publicity and return business.

_____ **10.** To determine whether delivery needs are being met, organizations must examine industry standards, customer expectations, capabilities, costs, and current and projected requirements.

_____ **11.** There are six key components that can be identified in a customer service environment.

_____ **12.** An organization's "culture" is what the customer experiences.

. . . .

●° 1 DEFINING CUSTOMER SERVICE

service industry
A term used to describe businesses that are engaged primarily in service delivery. Service sector is a more accurate term, since many organizations provide some form of service to their customers even though they are primarily engaged in research, development, and manufacture of products.

product
Something produced or an output by an individual or organization. In the service environment, products are created to satisfy customer needs or wants.

customer-focused organization
A company that spends energy and effort on satisfying internal and external customers by first identifying customer needs, then establishing policies, procedures, and management and reward systems to support excellence in service delivery.

Concept: Customer-focused organizations determine and meet the needs of their internal and external customers. Their focus is to treat everyone with respect and as if they were special.

Many attempts have been made to define the term **customer service.** However, depending on an organization's focus, such as retailing, medical, dental, industry, manufacturing, or repair services, the goals of providing customer service may vary. In fact, we often use the term **service industry** as if it were a separate occupational field unto itself. In reality, most organizations provide some degree of customer service. For the purposes of this text, _customer service_ is defined as the ability of knowledgeable, capable, and enthusiastic employees to deliver **products** and services to their internal and external customers in a manner that satisfies identified and unidentified needs and ultimately results in positive word-of-mouth publicity and return business. By doing these things, organizations can truly become **customer-focused organizations** (see Figure 1.1).

Many organizations specialize in providing only services. Examples of this type of company are banks and credit unions, consulting firms, Internet service providers, utility companies, call centers, brokerage firms, laundries, plumbing and electrical companies, transportation companies, and medical or dental facilities. Some organizations provide both products and services. Examples are businesses such as car dealerships, retail stores and manufacturers that have support services for their products, supermarkets, theaters, and restaurants.

FIGURE 1.1

Customer-Focused Organizations

customer relationship management (CRM)
Concept of identifying customer needs: understanding and influencing customer behavior through ongoing communication strategies in an effort to acquire, retain, and satisfy the customer. The ultimate goal is customer loyalty.

Some common characteristics for customer-focused organizations are:

- They have internal customers (for example, peers, coworkers, bosses, subordinates, people from other areas of their organization) and/or external customers (for example, vendors, suppliers, various telephone callers, walk-in customers, other organizations, others not from within the organization).
- Their focus is on determining and meeting the needs of customers while treating everyone with respect and as if they were special. Information, products, and services are easily accessible by customers. Policies are in place to allow employees to make decisions in order to better serve customers.
- Management and systems support and appropriately reward employee efforts to serve customers.
- Reevaluation of the way business is conducted is ongoing and results in necessary changes and upgrades to deliver timely, quality service to the customer.
- Build relationships through **customer relationship management (CRM)** programs.

The term **service sector** as used by the Census Bureau and the Bureau of Labor Statistics in their reports and projections typically includes:

Transportation, communication, and utilities

Wholesale trade

Retail trade

Finance, insurance, and real estate

Other services (including businesses such as legal firms, barbershops and beauty salons, personal services, housekeeping, and accounting)

Federal government

State and local governments

In addition, there are people who are self-employed and provide various types of services to their customers and clients.

Before distribution systems were modernized, peddlers went from house to house, particularly in rural areas, to deliver merchandise or services. Doctors often went to the sick person's home and made house visits. *How do these methods of delivery differ from those used today? Do you think the ones used today are better? Why or why not?*

THE CONCEPT OF CUSTOMER SERVICE

The concept or practice of customer service is not new. Over the years, it has evolved from a meager beginning into a multibillion-dollar, worldwide endeavor. In the past when many people worked on farms, small artisans and business owners provided customer service to their neighbors. No multinational chain stores existed. Many small towns and villages had their own blacksmith, general store, boardinghouse (hotel), restaurant, tavern, barbershop, and similar service-oriented establishments owned and operated by people living in the town (often the place of business was also the residence of the owner). For people living in more rural areas, peddlers of kitchenware, medicine, and other goods made their way from one location to another to serve their customers and distribute various products. Further, to supplement their income, many people made and sold or bartered products from their homes in what came to be known as **cottage industries.** As trains, covered wagons, and stagecoaches began to cross the country, they carried vendors and supplies in addition to providing transportation. During that whole era, customer service differed from what it is today by the fact that the owners and chief executive officers (CEOs) were also motivated frontline employees working face-to-face with their customers. They had a vested interest in providing good service and in succeeding.

When industry, manufacturing, and larger cities started to grow, the service industry really started to gain ground. In the late 1800s, as the mail services matured, companies such as Montgomery Ward and Sears Roebuck introduced the mail-order catalog to address the needs of customers. In rural areas, the population grew and expanded westward, and service providers followed.

POST–WORLD WAR II SERVICE

After World War II, there was a continuing rise in the number of people in the United States in service occupations. According to an article published by the Bureau of Labor Statistics, "At the conclusion of the war in 1945, the service industry accounted for only

service sector
Refers to organizations and individuals involved in delivering service as a primary product.

cottage industries
Term adopted in the early days of customer service when many people started small business in their homes or cottages and bartered products or services with neighbors.

CUSTOMER SERVICE SUCCESS TIP

Educate yourself on the service profession in general and your organization in particular. Focus on trends, improvements, and enhancements being made by other similar organizations, and developing skills that add value to your organization.

FIGURE 1.2

From Pre–WW II
Occupations to Service
Occupations

Typical Former Occupations	Typical Service Occupations
Farmer	Salesperson
Ranch worker	Insurance agent
Machinist	Food service
Engineer	Administrative assistant
Steelworker	Flight attendant
Homemaker	Call center representative
Factory worker	Repair person
Miner	Travel professional
Tradesperson (for example, watchmaker)	Child care provider
Railroad worker	Security guard

10 percent of nonfarm employment, compared to 38 percent for manufacturing. In 1982 services surpassed manufacturing as the largest employer among major industry groups. From 2000–2010 virtually all nonfarm wage and salary employment growth is expected to be in the service-producing sector, accounting for a net increase of 8.9 million jobs."[1]

THE SHIFT TO SERVICE

service economy
A term used to describe the trend in which businesses have shifted from primarily production and manufacturing to more service delivery. As part of the evolution, many organizations have developed specifically to provide services to customers.

Today, businesses have changed dramatically as the economy has shifted from a dependence on manufacturing to a focus on providing timely, quality service. The age of the **service economy** has been alive and strong for some time now. Tied to this trend has been the development of international quality standards by which effectiveness is measured in many multinational organizations.

Because of the multinational nature of business in this century, many companies choose to use outsourcing for certain job functions, one of which may be the customer service function. This will be discussed later in this chapter.

As shown in Figure 1.2, since the end of World War II, people have moved from other occupations to join the rapidly growing ranks of service professionals.

2   GROWTH OF THE SERVICE SECTOR

Concept: Technology has affected jobs in the following ways: quantity of jobs created, distribution of jobs, and quality of jobs. The service sector is projected to have the largest job growth.

According to the U.S. Bureau of Labor Statistics, there are employment demands in many occupations (see Figure 1.3). "The long-term shift from goods-producing to service-providing employment is expected to continue. Service-providing industries are expected to account for approximately 18.7 million of the 18.9 million new wage and salary jobs generated over the 2004-14 period. This all comes as employment in the goods-producing industries has been relatively stagnant since the early 1980s. Overall, this sector is expected to decline 0.4 percent."[2]

[1]M. Toosi, "Consumer Spending: An Engine for U.S. Job Growth," *Monthly Labor Review,* U.S. Department of Labor, Bureau of Labor Statistics, Washington, D.C., November 2002, p. 12.

[2]Tomorrow's Jobs, U.S. Bureau of Labor Statistics. www.bls.gov/oco/oco2003.htm.

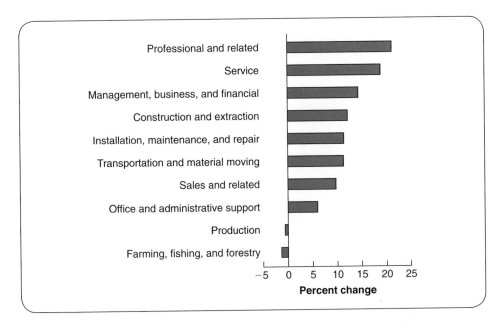

FIGURE 1.3   **Percent Change in Total Employment by Major Occupational Groups, Projected 2004–2014**

The impact of these numbers can be seen as technology replaces many production line workers, and increasing numbers of service jobs are created. This comes about because, as greater numbers and greater varieties of goods are produced, more service people, salespeople, managers, and other professionals are needed to design and market service delivery systems that support those products. Technology-related service jobs such as those of database administrators, computer support specialists, computer scientists, computer engineers, and systems analysts are expected to continue to grow at a rapid pace.

According to the Bureau of Labor Statistics, growth will continue in service sectors:

- Professional and related occupations will grow the fastest and add more new jobs than any other major occupational group: a 21.2 percent increase in the number of professional and related jobs is projected (6 million new jobs). About three-quarters of the job growth will come from three groups of professional occupations—computer and mathematical occupations, health care practitioners and technical occupations, and education, training, and library occupations;

- Employment in service occupations is projected to increase by 5.3 million, or 19 percent, the second largest numerical gain and second highest rate of growth among the major occupational groups. Food preparation and serving–related occupations are expected to add the most jobs among the service occupations, 1.7 million. However, health care support occupations are expected to grow the fastest, 33.3 percent, adding 1.2 million new jobs;

- Workers in management, business, and financial occupations plan and direct the activities of business, government, and other organizations. Their employment is expected to increase by 2.2 million, or 14.4 percent. The numbers of preschool and child care center/program educational administrators and of computer and information systems managers will grow the fastest, by 27.9 percent and 25.9 percent, respectively;

- Transportation and material moving workers transport people and materials by land, sea, or air. The number of these workers should grow 11.1 percent, accounting for 1.1 million additional jobs;

- Sales and related occupations are expected to add 1.5 million new jobs by 2014, growing by 9.6 percent. The majority of these jobs will be among retail salespersons and cashiers, occupations that will add 849,000 jobs combined;
- Office and administrative support occupations is expected to grow by 5.8 percent, adding 1.4 million new jobs by 2014. Customer service representatives will add the most new jobs, 471,000. Desktop publishers will be among the fastest growing occupations in this group, increasing by 23.2 percent over the decade. However, because of rising productivity and increased automation, office and administrative support occupations also account for 11 of the 20 occupations with the largest employment declines;
- Among all occupations in the economy, computer and health care occupations are expected to grow the fastest over the projection period (see Figure 1.4). In fact, health care occupations make up 12 of the 20 fastest growing occupations, while computer occupations account for 5 out of the 20 fastest growing occupations in the economy;
- The occupations with the largest numerical increases cover a wider range of occupational categories than do those occupations with the fastest growth rates (see Figure 1.5).

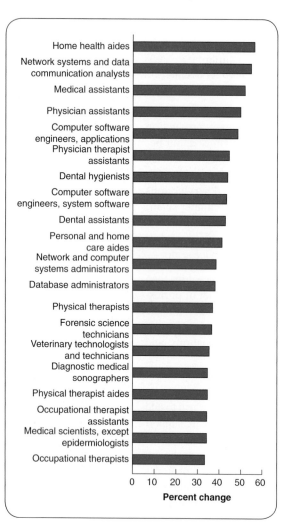

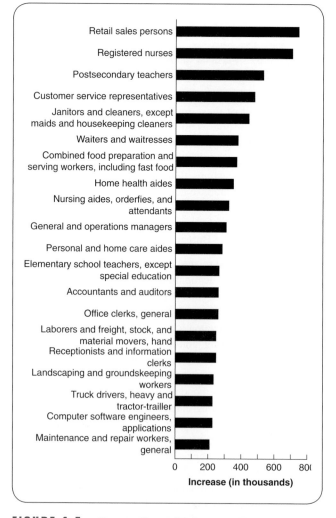

FIGURE 1.4   **Percent of Change in Employment in Occupations Projected to Grow**

FIGURE 1.5   **Occupations with Largest Numerical Increases in Employment**

TAKE A MOMENT TO LIST SOME OF THE CHANGES YOU HAVE PERSONALLY WITNESSED IN THE BUSINESS WORLD DURING YOUR LIFETIME. Are these changes for better or worse?

With these changes in mind, what do you—or would you—do to improve service quality as a customer service professional in your chosen industry or position?

IMPACT OF THE ECONOMY

According to leading economists, today's economy is affecting jobs in three ways: (1) overall quantity of jobs created; (2) the distribution of jobs among industries, occupations, geographic areas, and organizations of different sizes; and (3) the quality of jobs, measured by wages, job security, and opportunities for development.

Quantity of Jobs Being Created   A variety of factors, including prevailing interest rates and consumer demand, typically cause companies to evaluate how many people they need and which jobs will be established or maintained. In addition, the advent of technology has brought with it the need for many new technical skills in the areas of computer hardware and software operation and maintenance. At the same time, technology has created an opportunity for organizations to transfer tasks previously performed by employees to automation.

telecommuting
A trend seen in many metropolitan areas and government offices. To reduce traffic, pollution, and save resources (e.g., rent, telephone, and technology systems) many organizations allow employees to set up home offices and from there electronically communicate and forward information to their corporate offices.

Distribution of Jobs   Two parallel trends in job development are occurring. The first comes about from the need for employees to be able to have regular access to personal and professional networks and to engage in collaborative exchanges. This trend means that more jobs are likely to develop in major metropolitan areas, where ease of interaction with peers and suppliers, high customer density, and access to the most current business practices exist. Training and technology resources are also available in these areas. Access to technology resources helps ensure continued learning and growth of employees and also aids organizations in achieving their goals and objectives.

The second trend in job development arises from the ease of transmission and exchange of information by means of technology. It is called **telecommuting.** Employees can now work from their homes or satellite office location. Government agencies, technology-focused organizations, and many companies with large staffs in major metropolitan areas that experience traffic congestion (for example, Los Angeles, Boston, Chicago, and Washington, D.C.) often use telecommuting to eliminate the need for employees to travel to work each day. According to the U.S. Department of Labor, 20.7 million persons usually do some work at home as part of their primary job. From an industry perspective, workers employed in professional and business services, in

Today, many employees work from their homes all or part of the time. Telecommuting, as this is called, is used frequently by companies in large cities, such as Los Angeles, to decrease travel time. *Do you think you would need different skills or abilities to telecommute? Why or why not?*

downsizing
Term applied to the situation in
which employees are terminated.

financial activities, and in education and health services are among the most likely to work at home.[3] The telephone, fax, and computer modem make it possible to provide services from almost any remote location. For example, telephone sales and product support services can easily be handled from an employee's home if the right equipment is used. To do this, a customer calls a designated 800 number and a switching device at the company dispatches the call to an employee working at home. This is seamless to the customer, who receives the service needed and has no idea where the call originated. This also makes it easier for many companies to outsource some functions, thus saving money by relocating those jobs to geographical areas worldwide where wages and benefits may be less competitive. You will learn more about technology in customer service in Chapter 9.

Quality of Service Jobs   Since the late 1990s there has been increasing economic growth, low interest rates, and new job opportunities. Unemployment rates reached a historic low, then went up. However, as the social and workplace demographics continue to shift and people move around in our mobile society, job security has been affected and it is likely that competition for desired jobs will continue to become much more intense. This has become evident as the unemployment and interest rates have risen since the early years of the twenty-first century. Employees who obtain and maintain the better customer service jobs that provide good working conditions, security, and benefits will be better educated, trained, and prepared. They will also be the ones who understand and have tapped into the concept of professional networking. Networking is the active process of building relationships inside and outside the organization through meetings, interactions, and activities that lead to sound interpersonal relationships and sharing of resources. Practices such as joining and becoming actively involved in committees and boards of governors or directors will prove to be invaluable. Many good books have been published on the subject. The Internet (for example, Amazon.com, Barnes&Noble.com, and Borders.com) can lead to such resources.

3   SOCIETAL FACTORS AFFECTING CUSTOMER SERVICE

Concept: Many factors caused the economic shift from manufacturing to service. Increased technology, globalization of the economy, deregulation, and many government programs are a few factors. You will read about these and others in the following paragraphs.

The economies of America and many other countries are being dramatically changed by the forces that are shaping the world. Demographic shifts in population, constant technological change, globalization, deregulation of industries, geopolitical changes, increases in the number of white-collar workers, socioeconomic program development, and more women entering the workplace are some of the major shifts that continue to occur each year in the U.S. and around the world.

You may wonder what, exactly, caused the economic shift from manufacturing to service. Some of the more important factors are discussed in the following sections.

SHIFTS IN THE POPULATION AND LABOR FORCE

According to the U.S. Department of Labor, "The U.S. civilian noninstitutional population is expected to increase by 23.9 million over the 2004–14 period, at a slower rate of growth than during both the 1994–2004 and 1984–94 periods. Additionally the youth population,

[3]Tomorrow's Jobs, U.S. Bureau of Labor Statistics. www.bls.gov/oco/oco2003.htm.

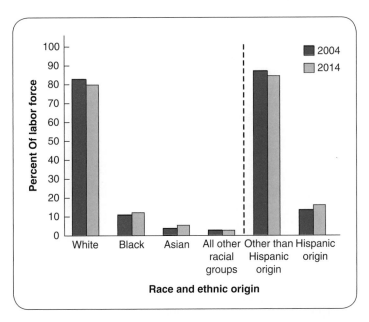

FIGURE 1.6   **Percent of Labor Force by Race and Ethnic Origin, 2004 and Projected 2014**

aged 16 to 24, will grow 2.9 percent over the 2004–14 period. As the baby boomers continue to age, the group aged 55 to 64 will increase by 36 percent or 10.4 million persons, more than any other group. The group aged 35 to 44 will decrease in size, reflecting the birth dearth following the baby boom generation.

"Continued growth will mean more consumers of goods and services, spurring demand for workers in a wide range of occupations and industries. The effects of population growth on various occupations will differ. The differences are partially accounted for by the age distribution of the future population."[4]

Since the size of the labor force is the most important factor related to the size and makeup of the available pool of workers, the figures according to the Labor Department will potentially continue to shift based on race and ethnic origin, (see Figure 1.6) and will have the following impact on the U.S. labor force between 2004–2014:

- The civilian labor force is projected to increase by 14.7 million, or 10 percent, to 162.1 million.
- The male labor force is projected to grow by 9.1 percent, compared with 10.9 percent for women.
- The youth labor force, aged 16 to 24, is expected to slightly decrease its share of the labor force to 13.7 percent.
- The primary working age group, between 25 and 54 years old, is projected to decline from 69.3 percent of the labor force in 2004 to 65.2 percent.
- Workers 55 and older, on the other hand, are projected to increase from 15.6 percent to 21.2 percent of the labor force between.
- The U.S. workforce will become more diverse by 2014 (see Figure 1.7).
- White, non-Hispanic persons will continue to make up a decreasing share of the labor force, falling from 70 percent in 2004 to 65.6 percent.
- White, non-Hispanics will remain the largest group in the labor force.

[4]Tomorrow's Jobs, U.S. Bureau of Labor Statistics. www.bls.gov/oco/oco2003.htm.

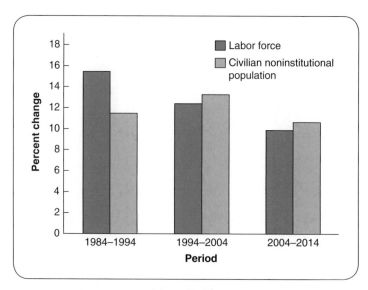

FIGURE 1.7 **Percent Change in the Population and Labor Force 1984–1994, 1994–2004, and Projected 2004–2014**

- Asians are projected to account for an increasing share of the labor force, growing from 4.3 to 5.1 percent.
- Hispanics are projected to be the fastest growing of the four labor force groups, growing by 33.7 percent.
- Hispanics will continue to constitute a larger proportion of the labor force than will blacks, whose share will grow from 11.3 percent to 12.0 percent.[5]

INCREASED EFFICIENCY IN TECHNOLOGY

The development and increased sophistication of machines and computers have caused an increase in production and quality. Two side effects have been an increased need for service organizations to take care of the technology and a decrease in manufacturing and blue-collar jobs.

An advantage of this change is that machines can work 24 hours, seven days a week with few lapses in quality, no need for breaks, and without increases in salary and benefits. This makes them extremely attractive to profit-minded business and corporate shareholders. Although technology can lead to the loss of some jobs, technological advances in the computer and telecommunications industry alone have created hundreds of service opportunities for people who monitor and run the machines and automated services. Everything from 800 numbers and telemarketing to shopping and service via the Internet, television, and telephone has evolved and continues to expand.

A major factor driving implementation of technology-based service is that, according to the 2000 U.S. Census figures, 50.5 percent of U.S. households have and use Internet access. This is up from 26.2 percent in 1998. Additionally, on an average day, 41 percent of online Americans (60 million adults) use search engines and 52 percent of Internet users are sending and receiving email on any given day.[6]

The value of technology is that much of it can be used in remote locations. This allows employees to work independently from home (telecommuting). No longer do organizations

CUSTOMER SERVICE SUCCESS TIP

Knowledge is power. Learn as much about as many software packages and pieces of equipment used by your organization as possible. Stay abreast of emerging technology trends in your industry. Volunteer to attend training and to work on committees tasked with identifying and implementing new service technology.

---

[5]Tomorrow's Jobs, U.S. Bureau of Labor Statistics. www.bls.gov/oco/oco2003.htm.
[6]Pew Internet and American Life Project. www.pewinternet.org-pdfs-PIP_SearchData_1105.pdf.

have to have a brick-and-mortar workplace. Because of the affordability of current technology, which allows workers to do their jobs "virtually" instead of commuting to a common workplace, many customer-service oriented jobs are done in a home instead of an office.

Globalization of the Economy Beginning in the 1960s, when worldwide trade barriers started to come down, a variety of factors have contributed to expanded international cooperation and competition. This trend has been termed **globalization,** with many companies focusing on **business-to-business (B2B)** initiatives, as well as individual consumers. Since the 1960s, advances in technology, communication, and transportation have opened new markets and allowed decentralized worldwide access for production, sales, and service. To survive and hold onto current market share while opening new gateways, U.S. firms need to hone the service skills of their employees, strengthen their quality, and look for new ways of demonstrating that they can not only meet but exceed the expectations of customers. All of this means more competition and the evolution of new rules and procedures that they have not been able to obtain in the past. Sometimes the deciding factor for the customer on whether to purchase a foreign or domestic product will be the service you provide.

For many customer service jobs, skill in using technology will increase your value as a source of information for current and future customers. *How can you keep abreast of changes in technology?*

At some point, many companies make staffing and/or production decisions based on bottom-line figures. When this happens, companies can, because of recent changes in the law, take their production or call center functions "offshore" (**outsourcing**) to other countries (Mexico, India, etc.), and in doing so, companies save money on production costs, wages, benefits, etc. This is becoming more and more common in technology-oriented companies.

DEREGULATION OF MANY INDUSTRIES

Over the years, we have witnessed the deregulation of a number of industries (airlines and the telephone and the utility industries in the later 1990s to the early 2000s). **Deregulation** is the removal of government restrictions on an industry. The continuing deregulation of major U.S. public services has caused competition to flourish. However, deregulation has also brought major industry shakeups, sometimes leading to breakdowns in service quality in many companies. These events have created opportunities for newly established companies to step in with improvements to close the gaps and better serve customers.

GEOPOLITICAL CHANGES

Events such as oil embargoes, political unrest, and conflicts and wars involving various countries have reduced U.S. business access and competition within some areas of the world (for example, Cuba, Vietnam, Iran, Iraq) while some countries have free access in those areas. These circumstances not only limit access to product, manufacturing, and distribution channels but also reduce the markets to which U.S. businesses can offer products and services. For example, every closed port or country border has a negative effect on travel industry professionals, such as reservationists, air transport and manufacturing employees, tour guides, and border-area retail businesses.

globalization
The term applied to an ongoing trend of information, knowledge, and resource sharing around the world. As a result of a more mobile society and easier access to transportation and technology, more people are traveling and accessing products and services from international sources than ever before.

business-to-business (B2B)
Refers to a business-to-business customer service.

outsourcing
Refers to the practice of contracting with third-party companies or vendors outside the organization (usually in another country) to deliver products and services to customers or produce products.

deregulation
Occurs when governments remove legislative or regulatory guidelines that inhibit and control an industry (e.g., transportation, natural gas, and telecommunications).

Other positive and negative historical changes have occurred that—like it or not—have affected the way companies do business and will continue to do so into the twenty-first century. The passage of the **North American Free Trade Agreement (NAFTA)** made it possible for many U.S.-based companies to relocate and send jobs across borders (outsourcing) in order to find less expensive labor forces, increase profits, and avoid unions. The demise of the Soviet Union and the political and economic chaos that ensued as companies jockeyed to establish business relationships with the Commonwealth of Independent States (CIS) has also had an impact. The unexpected resignation from office on the eve of the new millennium by Russian President Boris Yeltsin, and the successor he handpicked to finish his term, added political fuel that continues to have long-standing effects. Whether these effects will be positive or negative remains to be seen; however, if there is a return to **Cold War** practices by Russia and the United States, the economies of many countries will certainly be impacted in a variety of ways. Further events, such as trade agreements with China and the thawing of relations with Vietnam in the past decade, have opened new political and economic doors. The shift in relations with Iran, Iraq, Afghanistan, and several other nations as the result of human rights violations, violence, terrorism, and military-related actions have created obstacles to international trade and commerce in a variety of ways.

Geopolitical events such as these will lead to more multinational mergers and a need for better understanding of diversity-related issues by employees and managers.

With increased ease of transportation and communication, companies cannot afford to ignore international competitors. For years, American firms viewed Japan as their chief economic and business rival. Now other countries are challenging Japan (Taiwan, Korea, Vietnam, China, and India) and are becoming firmly entrenched in the marketplace. An example of this was the introduction of the South Korea–made KIA car line into the U.S. market in the 1990s, which continues to make headway into a sagging auto manufacturing market for U.S automobile makers. Although many Pacific Rim countries experienced severe economic setbacks during the 1990s—from inflation and a variety of political factors—these countries have traditionally been strengthened through adversity.

North American Free Trade Agreement (NAFTA)

A trade agreement entered into by the United States, Canada, and Mexico among other things to help eliminate barriers to trade, promote conditions of fair trade across borders, increase investment opportunities, and promote and protect intellectual property rights.

Cold War

A period of military, economic, and political tension and competition between the United States and the former Soviet Union that lasted from the 1940s through the 1990s.

INCREASE IN THE NUMBER OF WHITE-COLLAR WORKERS

With the movement out of factories and mines and off the farm, more people find themselves working at a traditional nine-to-five office job or providing service on a variety of work shifts (telephone and technical support centers). This trend has led to the creation of new types of service occupations. Office workers need to have someone clean their clothes, spruce up their homes (inside and out), care for their children, do their shopping, run their errands, and feed their families. In effect, the service phenomenon has spawned its own service trend.

MORE WOMEN ENTERING THE WORKFORCE

The fact that more women are in the workplace means that many of their traditional roles in society have shifted, out of necessity or convenience, to service providers such as cleaners, cooks, and child care providers. The tasks previously handled by the stay-at-home wife and mother are now being handled by the employees of various service companies.

WORK IT OUT 1.2

Personal Exposure to the Global Trend

TO HELP YOU RECOGNIZE THE IMPACT THIS GLOBAL TREND HAS ON YOU AND YOUR FAMILY AS CONSUMERS, THINK ABOUT ALL THE PRODUCTS YOU OWN (FOR EXAMPLE, CAR, CLOTHING, MICROWAVE OVEN, TELEVISION, COMPUTER, FAX MACHINE). List five major products along with their country of origin (you can find this on the warranty plate along with the product's serial number, usually on the back or bottom of the product).

As a matter of fact, the Department of Labor has published statistics showing that the number of women in the workplace, in all age groups, continues to grow more rapidly than the number of men. As a result, women's share of the workplace is projected to increase from about 47 percent in 2000 to approximately 48 percent in 2010.[7]

As women have become a larger part of the workforce, they have slowly seen their income levels rise compared to those of their male counterparts. Younger female workers have seen this occur by larger margins. According to the U.S. Bureau of Labor Statistics, "The difference between women's and men's earnings was much larger than among younger workers. For instance, among workers aged 45 to 54, women earned 75 percent as much as men. By comparison, among workers 25 to 34 years old, women earned 89 percent as much as men, and among 16–24-year-olds, the earnings ratio rose to 93 percent."[8] The direct impact of this trend related to service is that many women often have more disposable income as consumers.

A MORE DIVERSE POPULATION IS ENTERING THE WORKFORCE

As with the entrance of women into the workforce, the increase in numbers of people from different cultures entering the workforce will have a profound impact on the business environment. Not only are the members of this expanded worker category bringing with them new ideas, values, expectations, needs, and levels of knowledge, experience, and ability, but as consumers themselves, they bring a better understanding of the needs of the various groups that they represent.

According to the U.S. Department of Labor, "By 2014, the Hispanic labor force is expected to reach 25.8 million, due to faster population growth resulting from a younger population, higher fertility rates, and increased immigration levels. Despite relatively slow growth, whites will remain the largest group, composing 80.2 percent of the labor force. Blacks will constitute 12.0 percent of the labor force. Asians will continue to be the fastest growing race group, climbing to 5.1 percent of the labor force."[9] Further," Foreign-born legally admitted immigrants, refugees, and temporary resident workers' share of the U.S. workforce continues to grow. In 2006, foreign-born

[7]H. N. Fullerton Jr., and M. Toosi, "Labor Force Projections to 2010: Steady Growth and Changing Composition," *Monthly Labor Review,* U.S. Department of Labor, Bureau of Labor Statistics, Washington D.C., November 2001, p. 21.

[8]2004–14 Employment Projections. U.S. Bureau of Labor Statistics, ftp://ftp.bls.gov/pub/news.release/History/ecopro.12072005.news.

[9]2004-2014 Employment Projections, U.S. Bureau of Labor Statistics, ftp://bls.gov/pub/news.release/History/ecopro.12072005.news.

workers made up 15.3 percent of the U.S. civilian labor force age 16 and over, up from 14.8 percent in 2005. Hispanics comprised about 50 percent of the foreign-born labor force compared with about 7 percent of the native-born labor force. About 22 percent of the foreign-born workforce was Asian compared with about 1 percent of the native-born workforce. One in 5 persons in the foreign-born labor force was non-Hispanic whites, compared with nearly 4 of 5 in the native-born labor force."[10]

You will explore these trends, and other diversity factors, further in Chapter 8.

A population made up of women, ethnically different people, older people, and those with other diverse characteristics, make a better understanding of various groups essential for service success. *How can you improve your own knowledge of different groups so that you can better serve?*

MORE OLDER WORKERS ENTERING THE WORKFORCE

Think about the last time you went to a fast-food restaurant or a retail store like McDonald's, Wendy's, Burger King, Wal-Mart, Big Kmart, or Target. Did you notice the number of people serving and assisting you who seemed to be older than people you usually see in those roles? This relatively new phenomenon is the result of a variety of social factors. The most significant factor is that the median age of people in the United States is rising because of the aging of the "baby boom" generation (those born between 1946 and 1964).[11]

From a workplace perspective, this means that more of the people in this age group will stay in the workplace or return once they leave (see Figure 1.8). This may be caused by pure economic necessity, since many people may have not prepared adequately for retirement and cannot be certain that the Social Security system will support them. Some people return to the workplace for social reasons—they miss the work and/or the opportunity to

FIGURE 1.8

2004–2014 Employment Projections

CUSTOMER SERVICE SUCCESS TIP

Diversity is here to stay. Learn about different cultures, gender issues, age groups, religions, ability issues, and other factors that each person brings to the workplace so that you can effectively interact with and maximize the potential of others.

> In 2014, baby-boomers will be age 50 to 68 years, and this age group will grow significantly over the 2004–14 period. The labor force will continue to age:
>
> - The number of workers in the 55-and-older group projected to grow by 49.1 percent, nearly 5 times the 10 percent growth projected for the overall labor force.
> - The 55-and-older age group, is projected to gain share of the labor force, from 15.6 percent to 21.2 percent.
> - Youths—those between the ages of 16 and 24—will decline in numbers and lose share of the labor force, from 15.1 percent in 2004 to 13.7 percent in 2014.
> - Prime-age workers—those between the ages of 25 and 54—also will lose share of the labor force, from 69.3 percent in 2004 to 65.2 percent in 2014.
>
> Source: 2004-14 Employment Projections, U.S. Bureau of Labor Statistics, ftp://ftp.bls.gov/pub/news.release/History/ecopro.12072005.news

[10]Labor Force Characteristics of Foreign-Born Workers Summary, U.S. Bureau of Labor Statistics, www.bls.gov/news.release/forbrn.nr0.htm.
[11]See www.sba.gov/aboutba/sbastats.html for more information.

interact with others and feel useful. Whatever the reason for the desire or willingness of older workers to reenter the workforce, many organizations have realized that they often have an admirable work ethic. Also, since there are not enough entry-level people in the traditional pool of younger workers (because of smaller birth rates during the 1970s), companies are actively recruiting older workers.

INCREASED NUMBER OF SMALL BUSINESSES

The law defines a small business as "one that is independently owned and operated and is not dominant in its field of operation."

Nationally, these small businesses make up more than 70 percent of all businesses. They may be run by one or more individuals, can range from home-based businesses to corner stores or construction contractors, and often are part-time ventures with owners operating more than one business at a time.

A 2004 report from the **Small Business Administration's (SBA)** Office of Advocacy states that there are 24.7 million businesses in the U.S., and that small companies with fewer than 500 employees represent 99.9 percent of the 24.7 million businesses, since the most recent data show there are just 17,000 large businesses.

The Center for Women's Business Research (CWBR) states that one in 11 adult women is an "entrepreneur," and that nearly half of all privately held U.S. businesses are 50 percent or more woman-owned. The CWBR also states that 10.6 million firms are at least half owned by women, and that "these firms employ 19.1 million people and generate nearly $2.5 trillion in sales. Between 1997 and 2004, the number of companies 50% or more women-owned increased at nearly twice the rate of all companies—as did employment rates."[12]

GROWTH OF E-COMMERCE

The last decade of the twentieth century was witness to unimagined use of the personal computer and the Internet by the average person. By 2003, e-commerce sales topped 12.5 billion dollars, which was a 27.8 percent increase from the previous year. Almost any product is available at the click of a mouse, press of a key, or voice command. Consumers regularly "surf the net" for values in products and services without ever leaving their homes or office. This new way of accessing goods and services through technology has been termed **e-commerce.**

Armed with a password, site addresses, and credit cards, shoppers use this virtual marketplace to satisfy needs that they likely did not know they had before logging onto their computer and connecting with the Internet. And, with so many options available for just a small investment of time, they can comparison-shop simply by changing screens. No wonder the twentieth century saw the establishment of more millionaires and billionaires than any of its predecessors. The creators and owners of the most innovative sites and products can provide products and services worldwide without ever physically coming into contact with a customer, and yet can amass huge reserves of money. Examples of these success stories are eBay (an online auction service) and Amazon.com (an online book and product seller and auction line), which have become household names and are used by millions of shoppers yearly.

[12]A Stew of Small Biz Stats. www.businessweek.com/smallbiz/content/may2006/sb20050502.489185.htm.

ethical dilemma 1.1

With all the competition for customer service jobs in your organization, you are concerned that you might not be able to get a promotion that you feel you deserve. You have heard that there are three other employees for a job opening for which you want to apply. You know all three people and their work habits. Each has a "skeleton in the closet" related to performance issues in the past of which you are aware, but your supervisor is not. Your supervisor will be screening applicants soon.

1. Should you inform your supervisor of what you know to ensure that she makes an educated choice based on qualifications? Why or why not?
2. What could be the potential result of any action that you take about this issue? See possible responses at the end of the chapter.

Small Business Administration (SBA)
United States governmental agency established to assist small business owners.

e-commerce
An entire spectrum of companies that market products and services on the Internet and through other technology, and the process of accessing them by consumers.

● 4 CONSUMER BEHAVIOR SHIFTS

Concept: Americans are enjoying increasing amounts leisure time and have more disposable income as they age. The income and wealth of people in other countries is also rising and they are pursuing life and leisure activities at a record pace.

DESIRE FOR BETTER USE OF LEISURE TIME

Nowadays, many Americans and workers of other developed nations are enjoying increasing amounts of leisure time (see Figure 1.9). In the United States, many workers now have more disposable income and as a whole are growing older. Numerous reports have found that the number of millionaires is growing around the world with countries like China, Russia, India, and Singapore leading the charge to produce more high-net-worth individuals.[13] Those individuals who do not have cash readily available are not impeded in their effort to enjoy life. They are setting new records of credit spending in their pursuit of life and leisure activities.

The 2000 Census shows that four in ten households earn in excess of $50,000 per year. Additionally, three in ten black households have achieved middle- and upper-income status. These factors have heightened a desire to relax, enjoy children and grandchildren, and do other things that people value—they want to use their free time in more personally satisfying ways (see Figure 1.9). To accomplish this, they now rely more heavily on service organizations to maintain their desired lifestyle. Examples of some of the services tapped by members of today's society are personal grocery shopping services, lawn services, car wash/care, dog walkers, laundry pickup and delivery, and executive book summaries that condense current business publications to a three- or four-page synopsis of key points.

CUSTOMER SERVICE SUCCESS TIP

If your goal is to ultimately have your own service-oriented business, start planning today. Take college courses on business-related topics, network with others in your industry through professional groups like the International Customer Service Association (ICSA), and conduct research on how to start a small business effectively through the Small Business Association.

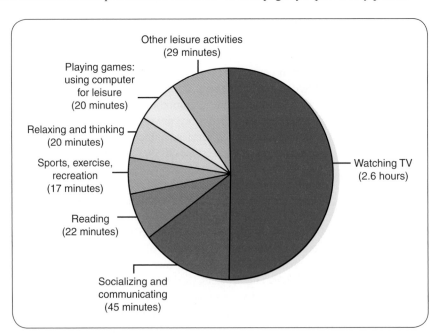

FIGURE 1.9   **Leisure Time on an Average Day**

[13]*11th Annual World Wealth Report,* Merrill Lynch and Capgemini. www.ml.com/index.asp?id=7695_7696_8149_74412_79272_79918.

EXPECTATION OF QUALITY SERVICE

Most customers expect that if they pay a fair dollar, in return they will receive a quality product or service. If their expectations are not met, customers simply call or visit a competing company where they can receive what they think they paid for. An example of the power of the consumer was the spending of billions of dollars by the U.S. government and businesses to ensure that the so-called **Y2K bug** did not debilitate computer systems at the stroke of midnight on December 31, 1999. Had preventive measures not been taken to fix a programming oversight made decades ago, there would have been a monumental consumer outcry as services shut down across the country and world. Another example of consumer clout was the initiatives to shore up the electrical grid system following the 2003 blackout because of public and political outrage.

The expectation of quality service that most consumers have also creates a need for better-trained and better-educated customer service professionals. Not only do these professionals need up-to-date product information, but they also need to be abreast of current organizational policies and procedures, what the competition offers, and the latest techniques in customer service and satisfaction.

Y2K bug
The term applied to a programming error made in many software packages that would cause a computer to fail to recognize the year 2000 at midnight on December 31, 1999. In instances where the oversight occurred, computers would cease to function at that hour. Billions of dollars were spent to correct the error worldwide.

ENHANCED CONSUMER PREPARATION

Customers today are not only more highly educated than in the past, they are also well informed about the price, quality, and value of products and services. This has occurred in part through the advertising and publicity by companies competing for market share and by the activities of consumer information and advocacy groups that have surfaced. As Syms, a discount-clothing store, used to tout in its advertising, "An informed consumer is our best customer." That advertising campaign was based on the belief that if you shop around and compare quality and costs, you will come back to Syms. This type of strategy sends a message that "we have nothing to hide" and invites customer confidence.

Armed with knowledge about what they should receive for their money, consumers make it extremely difficult for less-than-reputable businesspeople to prosper or survive. With consumers now on the defensive and ready to fight back, all business owners find that they have to continually prove the worth of their products and services. They must provide customer satisfaction or face losing customers to competitors.

5   THE CUSTOMER SERVICE ENVIRONMENT

Concept: In this section the six components that make up a service environment and contribute to customer service delivery are discussed. Use these factors to ensure that a viable customer service environment is the responsibility of every employee of the organization—not just the customer service representatives.

COMPONENTS OF A CUSTOMER SERVICE ENVIRONMENT

Let's take time to examine the six key components of a **customer service environment,** which will illustrate many factors that contribute to customer service delivery:

1. The customer
2. Organizational culture
3. Human resources

**customer service
environment**
The environment made up of and influenced by various elements of an organization. Examples are delivery systems, human resources, service, products, and organizational culture.

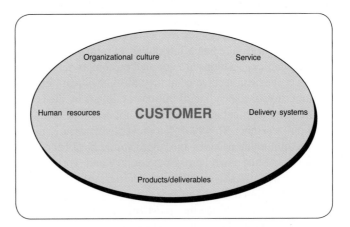

FIGURE 1.10   **Components of a Customer-Focused Environment**

4. Products/deliverables
5. Delivery systems
6. Service

What goes into the making of quality customer service? This is discussed in the following sections.

The Customer   As shown in Figure 1.10, the key component in a customer-focused environment is the customer. All aspects of the service organization revolve around the customer. Without the customer, there is no reason for any organization to exist. And, since all employees have customers, either internal or external, there must be a continuing consciousness of the need to provide exceptional, enthusiastic customer service. As Karl Albrecht and Ron Zemke say in their book *Service America,* "If you're not serving the customer, you'd better be serving someone who is." This is true because if you aren't providing stellar support and service to internal customers, external customers usually suffer.

INTERNAL CUSTOMERS

internal customers
People within the organization who either require support and service or provide information, products, and services to service providers. Such customers include peers, coworkers, bosses, subordinates, or people from other areas of their organization.

Many people in the workplace will tell you that they do not have "customers." They are wrong. Anyone in an organization has customers. They may not be traditional customers who come to buy or use products or services. Instead, they are **internal customers** who are coworkers, employees of other departments or branches, and other people who work within the same organization. They also rely on others in their organization to provide services, information, and/or products that enable them to do their jobs.

Recognizing this formidable group of customers is important and crucial for on-the-job success. That is because, in the internal customer chain, an employee is sometimes a customer and at other times a supplier. At times, you may call a coworker in another department for information. Later that same day, this coworker may call you for a similar reason. Only when both parties are acutely aware of their role in this customer-supplier relationship can the organization effectively prosper and grow to full potential.

Who Are My Internal Customers?

TAKE A FEW MINUTES TO THINK ABOUT YOUR CURRENT OR-GANIZATION OR SELECT ANY ORGANIZATION WITH WHICH YOU HAVE BEEN ASSOCIATED AND CREATE TWO LISTS: one of your internal customers and another of your suppliers. Then compare your lists to see which customers also act as suppliers and help you better serve the external customers of your organization.

EXTERNAL CUSTOMERS

External customers may be current or potential customers or clients. They are the ones who actively seek out, research, and buy, rent, or lease products or services offered by your organization. This group can involve business customers who purchase your product to include with its own for resale. It can also involve an organization that acts as a franchise or distributor. Such an organization buys your products to resell or uses them to represent your company in its geographic area.

Organizational Culture   Without the mechanisms and atmosphere to support frontline service, the other components of the business environment cannot succeed. Put simply, **organizational culture** is what the customer experiences. This culture is made up of a collection of subcomponents, each of which contributes to the overall service environment. The impact of culture on customer satisfaction is discussed further in Chapter 2.

Human Resources   To make the culture work, an organization must take great care in recruiting, selecting, training and retaining qualified people—its **human resources.** That's why, when you apply (or applied) for a job as a customer service professional, a thorough screening process will be (or was) used to identify your skills, knowledge, and aptitudes. Without motivated, competent workers, any planning, policy, and procedure change or systems adaptation will not make a difference in customer service.

Many organizations go to great lengths to obtain and retain the "right" employees who possess the knowledge, skills, and competencies to professionally serve customers (see Figure 1.11). Employees who are skilled, motivated, and enthusiastic about providing service excellence are hard to find and are appreciated by employers and customers. As noted earlier, organizations now rely on all employees to provide service excellence to customers; however, they also maintain specially trained "elite" groups of employees who perform specific customer-related functions. Depending on their organization's focus, these individuals have a variety of titles (for example, a customer service representative in a retail organization might be called a *member counselor* in an association, but these employees often perform similar functions).

Products/Deliverables   The fourth component of a service environment is the product or **deliverable** offered by an organization. The product or deliverable may be a tangible item manufactured or distributed by the company, such as a piece of furniture, or a service available to the customer, such as pest extermination. In either case, there are two potential areas of customer satisfaction or dissatisfaction—quality and quantity. If your customers receive what they perceive as a quality product or service to the level that they expected, and in the time frame promised or viewed as acceptable, they will likely be happy. On the other hand, if customers believe that they were sold an inferior product or given an

external customers
Those people outside the organization who purchase or lease products and services. This group includes vendors, suppliers, and people on the telephone, or others not from the organization.

organizational culture
Includes an element of an organization that a customer encounters.

human resources
Refers to the employees of an organization.

deliverables
Products or services provided by an organization.

TAKE A MINUTE TO THINK ABOUT CUSTOMER SERVICE. external customers?
In what ways do organizations typically provide service to

FIGURE 1.11

Typical Titles and Functions Performed by Customer Service Personnel in Organizations

Receptionist/Front Desk Clerk

Employees performing this function in organizations have the primary role of meeting, greeting, and offering initial assistance to customers and visitors. This is a crucial role that starts setting the tone for how others view the organization. Whether in a doctor's or attorney's office, gym, car dealership, homeless shelter, or office building, these frontline service representatives are the standard bearer for an organization and should be adequately trained and empowered to assist those with whom they come into contact.

Customer Service (CS)/Member Support Clerk

This is typically an entry-level position requiring strong organizational ability, an ability to follow instructions, listen, and manage time, and a desire to help. A key function is clerical support, which includes filing, researching information, typing, and similar assignments.

Customer Service (CS) Representative/Member Counselor

This position is an entry-level position into the customer service field (although many people have years of experience in the job). Since these employees interact directly with customers and potential customers, they need strong interpersonal (communication, conflict management, listening) skills as well as a desire to help others, a fondness for working with people, a knowledge of organizational products and services, and thorough understanding of what a CS representative does. Key functions include interacting face-to-face or over the telephone with customers, receiving and processing orders or requests for information and services, responding to customer inquiries, handling complaints, and performing associated customer contact assignments.

Data Entry/Order Clerk

The data entry/order clerk is an entry-level position requiring knowledge of personal computers and software, ability to work on repetitive tasks for long periods of time, and an eye for accuracy. Key functions include verifying and batching orders received from customer service representatives for input by computer personnel. In organizations that have personal computer systems connected by networks, data entry/order clerks enter data, and generate and maintain reports.

Senior Customer Service (CS) Representative/Member Counselor

This position is usually staffed by personnel with experience as a CS representative. A position like this one requires a person with a sound understanding of basic supervisory skills, since job duties may include providing feedback, training, and support and administering performance appraisals to other representatives or counselors.

Service Technicians or Professionals

This group provides many different types of services and carries a variety of titles (for example, air-conditioning technologist, plumber, automotive specialist, office equipment technician, law enforcement officer, firefighter, or sanitation worker). Each specialized area requires specific knowledge and skills.

(continued)

FIGURE 1.11
(continued)

Inbound/Outbound Telemarketing Specialist

Customer service representatives may perform some or all of the functions of this job, but often specially hired or trained employees fill the position. They make and receive phone calls with the intent of promoting or selling company products or services. In many organizations these employees are full-time or part-time sales personnel whose job is to use the telephone to call customers or potential customers or receive orders or questions from customers. Employees in these positions need strong self-confidence because of the number of rejections to offers and irate calls they receive, sound verbal communication and listening skills, positive attitude, good knowledge of sales techniques, ability to handle people who are upset, and a desire to help others through identification and satisfaction of needs. Key functions include placing and/or receiving calls, responding to inquiries with product and service information, asking for and recording orders, and following up on leads and requests for information.

Call Center Quality Analyst

People in this position typically screen incoming and outgoing calls to ensure quality, customer service, and adherence to the policies and procedures of the organization. They also give feedback to representatives' supervisors to assist in the development of performance improvement goals.

Counter and Rental Clerk

These employees work in a variety of organizations receiving orders for services such as repairs, car and equipment rentals, dry cleaning, and storage. They are typically responsible for estimating costs and accepting payments and in some cases completion of rental agreements.

Other Functions

In addition to these positions, many organizations have supervisor, manager, director, and vice president positions in most of the job areas indicated or in the service area as a whole. The existence of higher-level positions provides opportunities for upward advancement and learning as experience is gained.

inferior service or one that does not match their expectations, they will likely be dissatisfied and could take their business elsewhere. They may also provide negative word-of-mouth advertising for the organization.

Delivery Systems   The fifth component of an effective service environment is the method(s) by which the product or service is delivered. In deciding on **delivery systems,** organizations examine the following factors.

Industry standards: How is the competition currently delivering? Are current organizational delivery standards in line with those of competitors?

Customer expectations: Do customers expect delivery to occur in a certain manner within a specified time frame? Are alternatives acceptable?

Capabilities: Do existing or available systems within the organization and industry allow for a variety of delivery methods?

Costs: Will providing a variety of techniques add real or perceived value at an acceptable cost? If there are additional costs, will consumers be willing to absorb them?

Current and projected requirements: Are existing methods of delivery, such as mail, phone, and face-to-face service meeting the needs of the customer and will they continue to do so in the future?

delivery systems
The method(s) used by an organization to provide services and products to its customers.

CUSTOMER SERVICE SUCCESS TIP

To gain a better perspective of the scope of service jobs and salaries for the profession, visit the Salary Wizard section at www.monster.com.

THINK ABOUT ORGANIZATIONAL STRATEGIES AIMED AT RECRUITING AND TRAINING SERVICE EMPLOYEES. What are some things you have heard or read about that companies are doing to attract, hire, and keep qualified employees?

Service   Stated simply, service is the manner in which you and other employees treat your customers and each other as you deliver your company's product(s) or other deliverables. Effective use of the techniques and strategies outlined later in this book is required in order to satisfy the needs of your customers.

6   ADDRESSING THE CHANGES

Concept: All customer-based organizations must provide excellence in service and an environment in which customer needs are identified and satisfied.

With all the changes, developing strategies for providing premium service that will capture and hold loyal customers has become a priority for most organizations. All customer-based organizations have one focus in common—they must provide service excellence and an environment in which customer needs are identified and satisfied—or perish.

learning organizations
A term used by Peter Senge in his book *The Fifth Discipline* to describe organizations that value knowledge, education, and employee training. They also learn from their competition, industry trends, and other sources, and they develop systems to support continued growth and development in order to remain competitive.

To this end, organizations must become **learning organizations,** a term made popular by author Peter Senge in his book *The Fifth Discipline.* Basically, a learning organization is one that uses knowledge as a basis for competitive advantage. This means providing ongoing training and development opportunities to employees so that they can gain and maintain cutting-edge skills and knowledge while projecting a positive can-do customer-focused attitude. A learning organization also ensures that there are systems that can adequately compensate and reward employees on the basis of their performance. In such an organization, systems and processes are continuously examined and updated. Learning from mistakes, and adapting accordingly, is crucial. In the past, organizations took a reactive approach to service by waiting for customers to ask for something or by trying to recover after a service breakdown. Often, a small customer service staff dealt with customer dissatisfaction or attempted to fix problems after they occurred. In today's economy, a proactive approach of anticipating customer needs is necessary and becoming common. To excel, organizations must train *all* employees to spot problems and deal with them before the customer becomes aware that they exist. Every employee must take personal responsibility for customer care. If a service breakdown does occur, managers in truly customer-focused organizations should empower employees at all levels to do whatever is necessary to satisfy the customer. For this to happen, management must educate and train staff members on the techniques and policies available to help serve the customer. They must then give employees the authority to act without asking first for management intervention in order to resolve customer issues. This concept, known as **service recovery,** is described in detail in Part Three, "Building and Maintaining Relationships."

service recovery
The process of righting a wrong or correcting something that has gone wrong involving provision of a product or service to a customer. The concept involves not only replacing defective products, but also going the extra step of providing compensation for the customer's inconvenience.

As many organizations move toward a more quality-oriented, customer-focused environment, developing and fine-tuning policies, procedures, and systems to better identify customer needs and meet their expectations will be crucial. Through a concerted effort to perfect service delivery, organizations will be able to survive and compete in a global economy. More emphasis must be placed on finding out what the consumer expects and going beyond those expectations. Total customer satisfaction is not just a buzz phrase; it is a way of life that companies are adopting in order to gain and maintain market share. As a customer service professional, it is your job to help foster a customer-oriented service environment.

business-to-business (B2B) 15
Cold War 16
cottage industries 6
customer-focused organization 6
customer relationship management (CRM) 6
customer service 6
customer service environment 21
deliverables 23
delivery systems 25
deregulation 15
downsizing 12
e-commerce 19
external customers 23
globalization 15
human resources 23

internal customers 22
learning organizations 26
North American Free Trade
 Agreement (NAFTA) 16
organizational culture 23
outsourcing 15
product 6
service economy 8
service industry 6
service recovery 26
service sector 7
Small Business Administration (SBA) 19
telecommuting 11
Y2K bug 21

Either on your own or in discussion with someone else review what you have learned in this chapter by responding to the following questions:

1 What is service?
2 Describe some of the earliest forms of customer service.
3 What are some of the factors that have facilitated the shift to a service economy?
4 What have been some of the causes of the changing business environment in recent decades?
5 Describe the impact of a company's culture on its success in a customer-focused business environment.

6 What role does the human resources element of the customer service environment play in customer satisfaction?
7 What two factors related to an organization's products or deliverables can lead to customer satisfaction or dissatisfaction?
8 When organizations select a delivery method for products or services, where do they get information on the best approach to take?
9 What are the six key components of a customer service environment?
10 Why are many organizations changing to learning organizations?

Searching the Web for Salary and Related Information

To learn more about the history, background, and components of customer service occupations, select one of the topics below, log on to the Internet, and gather additional research data. One valuable site is the U.S. Department of Labor at http://stats.bls.gov.

Report your findings to your work team members, peers, or students depending on the setting in which you are using this book.

Research the projected salaries and benefits for customer service providers in your industry or in one that interests you.

Develop a bibliographic listing of books and other publications on topics introduced in this chapter. The resources should be less than five years old.

You can do this by going to sites such as:

www.amazon.com
www.bn.com
www.glencoe.com/ps
www.mhprofessional.com

Find the websites of at least three companies that you believe have adopted a positive customer service attitude and are benefiting as a result. Select any issue raised in this chapter and research it further.

Note: A listing of websites for additional research on specific URLs is provided on the Customer Service website at **www.mhhe.com/lucas09**.

Emphasizing Education

Team up with several other people to form a discussion group. Spend some time talking about what you believe the role of schools is today and how well schools are preparing young people for the work world. Share specific personal examples from your own educational background or that of someone you know.

Getting Ready for New Employee Orientation at PackAll

Background

PackAll is a packing and storage company headquartered in Minneapolis, Minnesota, with franchises located in 21 cities throughout the United States. Since opening its first franchise in Minneapolis in 1987, the company has shown great market potential, ending its first year with a profit and growing every year since.

The primary services of the organization are packaging and preparing nonperishable items for shipment and mailing via parcel post. Air-conditioned spaces for short-term storage of personal items and post office boxes are also available to customers.

To ensure consistency of service at all locations, specific standards for employee training and service delivery have been developed and implemented. Before owners or operators can hang up their PackAll sign, they must sign an agreement to comply with standards and must successfully complete a rigorous eight-week management-training program. The program focuses on the key management and business skills necessary to run a successful business and educates employees on corporate philosophy and culture. In addition management offers tips for guiding employee development. At intervals of three and six months after opening their operation, owners or operators are required to participate in a retreat during which they share best practices, receive additional management training, and have an opportunity to ask questions in a structured setting.

Your Role

Today, you joined a PackAll franchise in Orlando, Florida, as a customer service representative. New-employee orientation will be held tomorrow. At that time, you will learn about the service culture, policies and procedures, techniques for handling customers, and specific job skills and requirements.

Before being hired, you were told that your primary duties would be to service customers, provide information about services offered, write up customer orders, collect payments, and package and label orders.

Critical Thinking Questions

1   What interpersonal skills do you currently have that will allow you to be successful in your new position?

2   What general questions about handling customers do you have for your supervisor?

3   If a customer asks for a service that PackAll does not provide, how will you handle the situation? Exactly what will you say?

SERVICE—AAA/CAA

1 **What have you experienced or heard about AAA/CAA?**

2 **From a customer perspective, what do you believe are the strengths of this organization? Why? Weaknesses? Why?**

3 **How do you feel that AAA compares to some of its major competitors (e.g. State, Farm, All State, and American Express)?**

4 **As a consumer, do you plan to use AAA/CAA services in the future? Why or why not?**

Go to www.aaa.com and research the organization. Look at their historical and other information about the organization on their website.

Working alone or with others, create a list of the major issues facing the service industry or your organization (if you are working) and which directly impact you. Also, list strategies that you can implement to personally address these issues.

To do this, draw a line down the center of a sheet of blank paper. On the left side write the word "Issues" and on the right side, the word "Strategies."

Here is an example of one issue with strategies to address it:

Issue	Strategies
Service industry is growing quickly.	Do Internet research to gather statistics on an occupation that I am currently in or in which I am interested. Identify geographic areas of opportunity, possible salary and benefits, and specific targeted employers.

1	T	5	F	9	T
2	F	6	T	10	T
3	T	7	F	11	T
4	T	8	T	12	T

Ethical Dilemma 1.1 Possible Answers

1 Should you inform your supervisor of what you know to ensure that she makes an educated choice based on qualifications? Why or why not?

This is a touchy Issue. If their performance (or lack of it) is affecting you, other employees, the organization, and customers, then you should probably approach your supervisor in a confidential manner to inform her of what is going on. The downside of taking such action is that your supervisor might question your timing and motives for doing so, especially since there are three different people involved and you have not come forward earlier.

2 What could be the potential result of any action that you take about this issue?

In such situations, when you witness inappropriate activities or behavior of others that impacts the organization, you should discreetly point it out to them, and if necessary, to someone in charge. It is unwise to save such information for an opportune time in which you can use it in retaliation or to gain personally. This could affect how they, your supervisor and peers view you and could impact trust in the future, thus negatively impacting your future opportunities.

Contributing to the Service Culture

The most important single ingredient in the formula of success is knowing how to get along with people.

—Theodore Roosevelt

After completing this chapter, you will be able to:

1 Explain the elements of a service culture.

2 Define a service strategy.

3 Recognize customer-friendly systems.

4 Implement strategies for promoting a positive service culture.

5 Separate average companies from exceptional companies.

6 Identify what customers want.

DILEMMA SUMMARY

In the Real World Health Care—Johns Hopkins Institutions

According to their website, "The Johns Hopkins Institutions is a collective name for the university and the Johns Hopkins Health System. The Johns Hopkins University includes nine academic and research divisions, and numerous centers, institutes, and affiliated entities while Johns Hopkins Medicine is a governing structure for the university's School of Medicine and the health system, coordinating their research, teaching, patient care, and related enterprises."

Originally founded as America's first research hospital in the late 1800s, Johns Hopkins has grown and expanded its corporate and academic scope tremendously. Researchers and staff members from Johns Hopkins have made tremendous contributions in the area of medicine, physics, arts, business, and many other disciplines over the decades. Some of the significant developments include:

- Development of the artificial sweetener saccharine
- Formation of the American Historical Society
- Pioneering the use of rubber gloves and antiseptic practice in operating rooms
- Development of the blood clotting agent heparin
- The invention of a chlorination system for water treatment
- Creation of the first supersonic ramjet engine
- Creation of cardiopulmonary resuscitation (CPR), used to save heart attack victims
- Development of a medical school with stipulation that men and women students would be treated equally
- Identification of the first effective treatment for sickle-cell anemia
- Development of a low-cost land mine detector

The organization has added 1,000 people per year to its payroll since 1999 and contributes over $7 billion dollars a year to the economy In its home state of Maryland, It was the first American research university founded for the express purpose of expanding human knowledge and putting that knowledge to work for the good of humanity. Working with many countries and governments, Johns Hopkins is pioneering research in the treatment of AIDS, cancer, and many other life-threatening diseases.

To facilitate positive customer service and deal effectively with the current and future patients, vendors, and clients, Johns Hopkins implements a number of service strategies. For example, in October 2006 during National Customer Service Week, their Information Technology Department established a webpage (http://it.jhu.edu/etso/customerservices/appreciation.html) and celebrated customer service week, giving the following reasons given for doing so:

- Boost morale, motivation, and teamwork.
- Reward staff for a job well done throughout the year.
- Raise awareness of the importance of customer service.
- Thank other subunits/departments for their support.
- Let customers know about the university's commitment to customer satisfaction.

In recent years the organization formulated a Business Process Improvement Committee to address many quality and performance concerns. As a result, efforts were streamlined and enhanced, ultimately leading to cost savings and improved quality of service. Each employee goes through extensive training that stresses things like the following service excellence standards:

- *Customer relations.* How we interact with customers face-to-face and over the phone.
- *Self management.* How we meet personal and organizational standards.
- *Teamwork.* How we work together to meet our customers' needs.
- *Communication.* How we use words, tone, and body language to send and receive messages.
- *Ownership and accountability.* How we take care of our environment.
- *Continuous performance improvement.* How we improve the safety and quality of our services.

For additional information about this organization, visit www.johnshopkins.edu/index1.html on the Internet.

See activity based on this section on page 57.

Quick Preview

Before reviewing the chapter content, respond to the following questions by placing a "T" for true or an "F" for false on the rules. Use any questions you miss as a checklist of material to which you will pay particular attention as you read through the chapter. For those you get right, congratulate yourself, but review the sections they address in order to learn additional details about the topic.

_____ **1.**   Service cultures include such things as policies and procedures.

_____ **2.**   To remain competitive, organizations must continually monitor and evaluate their systems.

_____ **3.**   Advertising, service delivery, and complaint resolution are examples of customer-friendly systems.

_____ **4.**   To better face daily challenges and opportunities in the workplace, you should strive to increase your knowledge, build your skills, and improve your attitude.

_____ **5.**   Some of the tools used by organizations to measure service culture include employee focus groups, mystery shoppers, and customer lotteries.

_____ **6.**   By determining the added value and results for me (AVARFM), you can develop more personal commitment to service excellence.

_____ **7.**   Use of "they" language to refer to management when dealing with customers helps demonstrate your commitment to your organization and its culture.

_____ **8.**   Communicating openly and effectively is one technique for working more closely with customers.

_____ **9.**   Even though you depend on vendors and suppliers, they are not your customers.

_____ **10.**   Business etiquette dictates that you should return all telephone calls within four hours.

_____ **11.**   Your job of serving a customer should end at the conclusion of a transaction so that you can switch your attention to new customers.

_____ **12.**   Customers want value for their money and effective, efficient service.

Answers to Quick Preview can be found at the end of the chapter.

··

1   DEFINING A SERVICE CULTURE

Concept: Many elements contribute to a service culture.

service culture
A service environment made up of various factors, including the values, beliefs, norms, rituals, and practices of a group or organization.

What is a **service culture** in an organization? The answer is that it is different for each organization. No two organizations operate in the same manner, have the same focus, or provide management that accomplishes the same results. Among other things, a culture includes the values, beliefs, norms, rituals, and practices of a group or organization. Any policy, procedure, action, or inaction on the part of your organization contributes to the service culture. Other elements may be specific to your organization or industry. A key point to remember about service culture is that you play a key role in communicating the culture of your organization to your customers. You may communicate through your appearance, your interaction with customers, and your knowledge, skill, and attitude. Culture also encompasses your products and services, and the physical appearance of the organization's facility, equipment, or any other aspect of the organization with which the customer comes into contact. Unfortunately, many companies are top-down–oriented (with upper management at the top of their hierarchy and

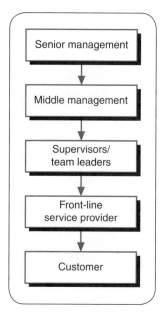

FIGURE 2.1 **Typical Hierarchical Organization**

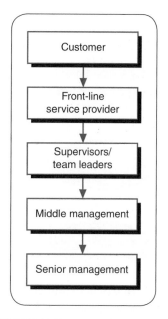

FIGURE 2.2 **Customer-Centric Organization**

customers as a final element or afterthought) or product-centered and view customers from the standpoint of what company products or services they use (Figure 2.1). Successful organizations are customer-centered or **customer-centric** and focus on individual needs (Figure 2.2).

An organization's service culture is made up of many facets, each of which affects the customer and helps determine the success or failure of customer service initiatives (Figure 2.3). Too often, organizations overpromise and underdeliver because their cultural and internal systems (*infrastructure*) do not have the ability to support customer service initiatives. For example, suppose that management has the marketing department develop a slick piece of literature describing all the benefits of a new product or service provided by a new corporate partner. Then a special 800 number or website is set up to handle customer responses, but no additional staff is hired to handle the customer calls or current service providers are not given adequate information or training to do their job. The project is likely doomed to fail because adequate service support has not been planned and implemented.

In the past, organizations were continually making changes to their product and service lines to try to attract and hold customers. Often this has been their primary approach to customer satisfaction. Now, many major organizations have become more customer-centric and stress relationships with customers. They realize that it is cheaper, and smarter, to keep current customers rather than subscribe to a revolving door approach of continually trying to attract new customers to replace the ones that they lost to competitors. Advertising campaigns often reflect this new awareness as companies try to communicate that they are focused on their customers. The following are some familiar slogans used by companies in their promotional materials:

"Like a good neighbor"—State Farm Insurance

"When you're here, you're family"—Olive Garden Restaurants

"You're in good hands"—Allstate Insurance Company

"It's your store"—Albertsons Grocery Stores

customer-centric
A term used to describe service providers and organizations that put their customers first and spend time, effort, and money identifying and focusing on the needs of current and potential customers. Efforts are focused on building long-term relationships and customer loyalty rather than simply selling a product or service and moving on to the next customer.

FIGURE 2.3

Elements of a Service Culture

Many elements define a successful organization. Some of the more common are shown here.

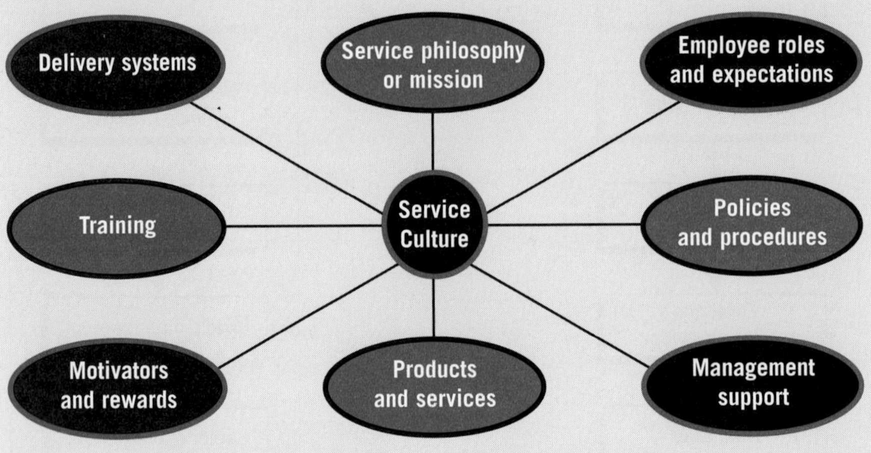

Service philosophy or mission: The direction or vision of an organization that supports day-to-day interactions with the customer.

Employee roles and expectations: The specific communications or measures that indicate what is expected of employees in customer interactions and that define how employee service performance will be evaluated.

Delivery systems: The way an organization delivers its products and services.

Policies and procedures: The guidelines that establish how various situations or transactions will be handled.

Products and services: The materials, products, and services that are state of the art, competitively priced, and meet the needs of customers.

Management support: The availability of management to answer questions and assist front-line employees in customer interactions when necessary. Also, the level of management involvement and enthusiasm in coaching and mentoring professional development.

Motivators and rewards: Monetary rewards, material items, or feedback that prompts employees to continue to deliver service and perform at a high level of effectiveness and efficiency.

Training: Instruction or information provided through a variety of techniques that teach knowledge or skills, or attempt to influence employee attitude toward excellent service delivery.

SERVICE PHILOSOPHY OR MISSION

mission
The direction or focus of an organization that supports day-to-day interactions with customers.

service philosophy
The approach that an organization takes to providing service and addressing the needs of customers.

Generally, an organization's approach to business, its **mission** or its **service philosophy,** is driven from the top of the organization. Upper management, including members of the board of directors, when appropriate, sets the vision or tone and direction of the organization. Without a clearly planned and communicated vision, the service ethic ends at the highest levels. This is often a stumbling block where many organizations falter because of indecision or dissension at the upper echelons.

Leadership, real and perceived, is crucial to service success. In successful organizations, members of upper management make themselves clearly visible to front-line employees and are in tune with customer needs and expectations.

Although it is wonderful when organizations go to the trouble of developing and hanging a nicely framed formal mission or philosophy statement on the wall, if it is not a functional way of life for employees, it serves little purpose.

EMPLOYEE ROLES AND EXPECTATIONS

In addition to some of the job responsibilities of service providers described in Chapter 1, many tasks and responsibilities are assigned to front-line service providers. Depending on your job, the size and type of your organization, and the industry involved, the **employee roles** and **employee expectations** may be similar from one organization to another, and yet they may be performed in a variety of different ways. Such roles and expectations are normally included in your job description and in your performance goals. They are updated as necessary during your tenure on the job. Where goals are concerned, you are typically measured against them during a performance period and subsequently rewarded or not rewarded, depending on your performance and your organization's policy.

RUMBA   For you and your organization to be successful in providing superior service to your external and internal customers, your roles and expectations must be clearly defined and communicated in terms of the following characteristics, sometimes referred to as **RUMBA** (**R**ealistic, **U**nderstandable, **M**easurable, **B**elievable, **A**ttainable).

Realistic   Your behavior and responsibilities must be in line with the reality of your particular workplace and customer base. Although it is possible to transfer a standard of performance from one organization, and even industry, to another, modifications may be necessary to fit your specific situation. For example, is it realistic that all customer calls must be handled within a specified time period? Many managers set specific goals in terms of "talk time" for their customer service representatives. Can every angry customer be calmed and handled in a two- to three-minute time frame? If not, then a standard such as this sets up employees for failure.

After a performance goal has been set for you, evaluate it fairly and objectively for a period of time (possibly 30 days). This allows time for a variety of opportunities to apply it. At the end of the specified trial period, if you think the goal is unrealistic, go to your supervisor or team leader and discuss modifying it. In preparation for this discussion, think of at least two viable alternatives to the goals. Also, recognize that performance goals are often driven by organizational goals that may be passed down from upper management. Although they might be modified, it may take some time for the change to come about, so be patient. Ultimately, if the goal cannot be modified, do your best to perform within the established standard so that your professional image does not suffer.

Understandable   You must have a sound understanding of your performance goals before you can act appropriately and effectively, just the way you need to understand how to do your job or how to communicate with others in the workplace. You should first try to participate in the establishment of your performance goals and those of your department or team. To do this, set up a meeting with your supervisor or team leader to discuss goals. Once goals are in place, you and everyone else affected must have a clear understanding of them so that you can effectively reach the assigned goal.

As part of the understanding step, you should apply all the skills covered in Chapters 3 and 4 related to giving and receiving information effectively. If you do not understand your goals and responsibilities, ask for clarification.

employee roles
Task assignments that service providers assume.

employee expectations
Perceptions about positive and negative aspects of the workplace.

RUMBA
An acronym for five criteria (realistic, understandable, measurable, believable, and attainable) used to establish and measure employee performance goals.

CUSTOMER SERVICE SUCCESS TIP

Meet with your supervisor to discuss your organization's service philosophy and mission statement and what your role is related to helping accomplish this.

Organizational Culture

THINK ABOUT YOUR OWN ORGANIZATION'S SERVICE CUL-TURE OR, IF YOU'RE NOT ACTIVELY WORKING AS A CUS-TOMER SERVICE PROFESSIONAL, THE CULTURE OF AN ORGANIZATION WITH WHICH YOU ARE FAMILIAR.

1. What do you believe the service philosophy of this organization to be? Why?
2. Are there things that make the organization unique? If so, what are they?

3. What factors (positive or negative) about employee performance in this organization stand out in your mind?
4. Are there factors about the culture that detract from effectiveness? If so, what are they?
5. If you were managing this organization, what service culture aspects would you change? Why?

---

service measurement
Techniques used by organizations to determine how customers perceive the value of services and products received.

ethical dilemma 2.1

Assume that your organizational philosophy states in part that your purpose is "to provide quality products at a competitive price in a low-pressure customer atmosphere." Even so, your supervisor establishes a goal that requires you to have "x" number of sales per shift as an outbound sales representative. This number is two more than the typical industry average for a salesperson during a work shift. You recognize that to achieve this goal, you will have to be more "persuasive" than you usually are when dealing with customers or than you feel comfortable in doing.
1. What ethical issue(s) do you face in this situation?
2. How might these impact service delivery?
3. How might this situation be addressed?
See possible responses at the end of this chapter.

Measurable   Can your performance be measured? The answer is yes. Typically, factors such as time, productivity, quantifiable results, revenue, and manner of performance (how you accomplish your job tasks in terms of following an established step-by-step formula) are used to determine your accomplishment of goals. In a production environment, or in certain sales environments, performance can be measured by reviewing the number of products made or sales completed. In a purely customer-focused environment, **service measurement** can be in terms of factors such as talk time on the telephone, number of customers effectively served, customer feedback surveys and satisfaction cards, and letters or other written correspondence—or, on the negative side, by customer complaints.

Whatever the measure, it is your responsibility to be sure that you know the acceptable level and do your best to perform to that level. If something inhibits your performance, or if organizational obstacles such as conflicting priorities, overburdening multiple assignments, policies, procedures, equipment, or other employees stand in your way, you should immediately discuss the difficulties with the appropriate authority.

Believable   For any goal to be attained, it must be believable to the people who will strive to reach it and to the supervisors or team leaders who will monitor it. The biggest issues in developing goals are to make them believable and to ensure that they make sense and tie in directly with the established overall departmental and organizational goals. Too often, employees are given assignments that are contrary to the ultimate purpose or mission of the organization.

Attainable   Given the right training, management support, and organizational environment in which the tools, information, assistance, and rewards are provided, you can attain your goals. The determining factor, however, is you and your attitude toward achieving agreed-upon levels.

Managers should always attempt to set up win/win situations in which you, your organization, and ultimately, the customer benefit from any service encounter. However, you should be aware that in the "real world" this does not always happen—systems break down. In such cases, it is up to you to ensure that service continues to be delivered to customers in a seamless fashion. They should not hear about internal problems, and quite honestly, the customers probably do not care about these problems. They should be able to expect that the products and services they paid for are delivered when promised, in the manner agreed upon, and without inconvenience to them. Anything less is unacceptable and is poor service.

Employee Roles in Larger Retail and Service Organizations

As customers have matured in their knowledge of service standards and what they expect of providers, they look for certain qualifications in those who serve. They gain knowledge from numerous sources that help them be more savvy in their dealings with businesses (for example, *Consumer Reports* magazine; Internet research; and television shows such as *20/20, Dateline,* and *60 Minutes*). Many times, these customers become sticklers about service and when they do not get the level of service they expect, they take their business elsewhere and/or take legal action. In some cases, they might give the organization a second chance by complaining. This benevolent initiative, allowing organizations to "fix themselves," is often done as a test. If you or your peers fail, several things can occur. You may not only lose a customer, but you may also "gain" an onslaught of negative word-of-mouth publicity that can irreparably damage an organization's image as a whole, and yours specifically.

Customers expect service employees to typically have at least the following qualifications and competencies in both large and small organizations:

- Broad general knowledge of products and service
- Interpersonal communication skills
- Technical expertise related to products sold and serviced
- Positive, customer-focused, "can-do" attitude
- Initiative
- Motivation
- Integrity
- Loyalty (to the organization, to products, and to customers)
- Team spirit
- Creativity
- Sound ethics
- Time management skills
- Problem-solving capability
- Conflict resolution skills

Such skills and capabilities are crucial, whether you are operating a cash register, polishing a car, handling a returned item, repairing a sink, questioning a crime witness or suspect, coaching an executive or technical manager (for example, a consultant who offers seminars on enhancing interpersonal skills), or dealing with a negative situation (for example, a shoplifter or disgruntled customer). If you fail to possess and/or exhibit any or all of these factors, the end result could be a breakdown in the relationship between you and your customer, with ultimately negative repercussions.

Employee Roles in Smaller Retail and Service Organizations

The growth of small businesses since the early 1990s has skyrocketed, especially women- and minority-owned businesses. Many small business entrepreneurs started out of necessity (because of layoffs or downsizing) or out of frustration caused by limitations within a larger structure (lack of promotion opportunity, low salaries, actual or perceived discrimination, poor management, or continual changes).

With this massive growth of sole proprietorships (one-owner businesses) and small businesses has come more choice for customers. This growth has also created problems for people making the transition from large to small organizations. This is because, in addition to having to possess all the qualifications and characteristics listed earlier, employees in small businesses perform greatly varied tasks. Typically, the human resources and technical systems they might call upon for support are limited. If something goes wrong, they cannot "bump the problem upstairs," nor can they obtain immediate, on-site assistance. This often causes customer frustration or anger.

The types of jobs that fall into this struggling category run the gamut of industries. Some examples are:

- Administrative assistant (freelance)
- Accountant
- Consultant
- Automotive mechanic
- Computer technician
- Salesperson
- Caterer
- Tailor
- Personal shopper
- Office support staff
- Hair stylist
- Masseuse/masseur
- Office equipment repairer
- Office cleaning staff
- Child care provider
- Gardener
- Electrician and plumber
- Electronics repairperson
- Visiting nurse or nurse consultant
- Driver
- Temporary worker

To stave off failure and help ensure that customer needs are identified and satisfied, owners and employees in such establishments must continually strive to gain new knowledge and skills while working hard to deliver a level of service equal to that offered by the bigger organizations. The public is generally unforgiving and, like elephants, they have long memories—especially when service breaks down.

If you work in this type of environment, look for opportunities to provide stellar service and really go out of your way to practice your people skills. Get back to the basics that you will learn more about in Chapters 3 to 5—listen, ask questions, provide feedback, communicate well—and do not miss an opportunity to let your customers know that they are special and that you are there to serve their needs.

Employee Roles in Nonprofit Organizations   Even though revenue generation is not the primary goal in nonprofit organizations, money is a significant force. Without donations, grants, and other fundraising efforts, such organizations cannot provide the crucial services and products and deliverables to their customer/client base (often lower-income and older people or others who have few other alternatives for attainment of needed items and services). In such organizations, administrators, staff and volunteers

---

The following qualifications and competencies are very helpful for anyone working In a nonprofit environment.

- Specific knowledge of the organization and products and services it provides
- Interpersonal communication skills
- Positive, customer-focused "can do" attitude
- Initiative
- Motivation to succeed
- Integrity
- Commitment to others
- Volunteer spirit
- Team orientation
- Sound ethical attitude
- Time management skills
- Problem-solving ability (ability to think "outside the box")
- Entrepreneur spirit (ability to work in an environment in which free thinking and creativity are encouraged and needed)

provide a wide degree of services and support. Unless these workers maintain a cheerful, positive, and professional attitude, revenue and service levels might plummet. They must never forget that everyone with whom they come into contact Is either a potential donor or recipient of products and services.

Policies and Procedures Although there are a lot of local, state, and federal regulations with which you and your organization must comply, many policies are flexible. For example, if you go to your bank to deposit a fairly large check that exceeds the maximum amount the bank will accept, the teller may inform you that there will be a seven-day hold put on the check until it clears the sender's bank. In this case, you might petition the branch manager and possibly get this period modified, since you are dealing with a "bank" policy.

Owners and employees in sole proprietorships must work hard to deliver service equal to that given by larger organizations. *How can an owner make his or her organization special or different?*

Many customers negatively meet organizational culture directly when a service provider hides behind "company policy" to handle a problem. The goal should be to policy customer requests and satisfy needs as quickly, efficiently, and cheerfully as possible. Anything less is an invitation for criticism, dissatisfaction, potential customer loss, and employee frustration.

Return policies in a retail environment are a case in point. Even though customers may not always be "right," they must be treated with respect and as if they are right in order to effectively provide service and generate future relationships. An effective return policy is part of the overall service process. In addition to service received, the return policy of an organization is another gauge customers use to determine where they will spend their time and money. The return statements shown in Figure 2.4 send specific messages about the organizational culture of both organizations. Notice the tone or service culture that radiates from each example. Think about your "gut" reaction as a customer when you read both policies.

Organizations often hang up fancy posters and banners touting such claims as, "The customer is always right," "The customer is No. 1," or "We're here to serve YOU!" But at the moment of truth, when customers come into contact with employees, they frequently hear, "Please take a number so we can better serve you," "I can't do that," or (on the phone) "ABC Company, please hold—CLICK." Clearly, when these things occur, the culture is not customer-focused and service has broken down. The important question for organizations is, "How do we fix our system?" The answer: make a commitment to the customer and establish an environment that will support that commitment. That's where you come in as a customer service professional. Through conscientious and concerned assistance to customers, the organization can form a solid relationship with the consumer through its employees.

PRODUCTS AND SERVICES

The type and quality of products and services also contribute to your organizational culture. If customers perceive that you offer reputable products and services in a professional manner and at a competitive price, your organization will likely reap the rewards of loyalty and positive "press." On the other hand, if products and services do not live up to expectations or promises, or if your ability to correct problems in products and services is deficient, you and the organization could suffer adversely.

Think about the two return policies in Figure 2.4

What is your reaction to policy example 1? Why?   What is your reaction to policy example 2? Why?

MOTIVATORS AND REWARDS

In any employee environment, people work more effectively and productively when their performance is recognized and adequately rewarded. Whether the rewards are in the form of monetary or material items, or a simple verbal pat on the back by the manager, most employees expect and thrive on some form of recognition.

As a way of managing your own motivation level, it is important to remember that there will be many times when your only motivation and reward for accomplishing a goal or providing quality service will come from you. The reality is that every time you do something well or out of the ordinary, you may not receive a financial or any other kind

FIGURE 2.4

Sample Return Policies

POLICY 1

To err is human, to return is just fine . . .

Already read the book? Pages printed upside down? The package arrived bruised, battered, and otherwise weary from the trip? Actually, the only reason you need to return an item bought from us is this: You're not satisfied . . .

Having the chance to talk with our customer helps us learn and improve our service. It is also an opportunity to demonstrate the [organization's name] customer policy: YOU'RE RIGHT!

POLICY 2

Return Policy

Returns must meet the following criteria:

1. Books must be received within thirty (30) days of the invoice date. Please allow one week for shipping.

2. Books must be received in salable condition. Damaged books will not be accepted for credit.

3. Refunds will not be made on videotapes and software unless they were defective at the time of purchase. Please notify [organization's name] of any such defects within ten (10) days of the invoice date.

Return Shipping Information

Returns must be shipped to [organization's name and full address].

Any returns not shipped to the above address will not be credited and FULL PAYMENT for shipping will be the responsibility of the shipper.

All charges incurred in returning materials, including customer's charges, if any, are the responsibility of the shipper.

Ensure that your returns are not lost or damaged.

Comments and Feedback

We value your opinion! If you need to return any of the enclosed material, please take a minute to let us know why. Your comments and suggestions will help us better meet your needs in the future.

of reward for it. On the other hand, many companies and supervisors go out of their way to recognize good performance. Many use public recognition, contests, games, employee activities (sporting or other events), financial rewards, incentives (gifts or trips), employee of the month or year awards, and a variety of other techniques to show appreciation for employee efforts. Whatever your organization does, there is always room for improvement and you should take time to make recommendations of your own on ways to reward employees.

MANAGEMENT SUPPORT

You cannot be expected to handle every customer-related situation that develops. In some instances, you will have to depend on the knowledge and assistance of a more experienced employee or your supervisor or manager and defer to his or her experience or authority.

A key role played by your manager, supervisor, and/or team leader is to provide effective, ongoing coaching, counseling, and training to you and your peers. By doing this, supervisors can pass on valuable information, guide you, and aid your professional development. Also, it is their job to be alert to your performance and ensure that you receive appropriate rewards based on your ability to interact effectively with customers and fulfill the requirements of your job. Unfortunately, many supervisors have not had adequate training that would enable them to provide you with the support you need. They were probably good front-line service providers, with a high degree of motivation, initiative, and ability. As a result, their management promoted them, often without providing the necessary training, coaching, and guidance to develop their supervisory skills. In other instances, they may be as overwhelmed with job responsibilities as you are. Even they may recognize the importance of coaching and intend to do so, they may simply not have the time.

If you find that you are not receiving the support you need, there are some things you should consider doing in order to ensure that you have the information, skills, and support to provide quality service to your customers.

Strive for Improvement   Customer service can be frustrating, and in some instances, monotonous. You may need to create self-motivation strategies and continue to seek fulfillment or satisfaction. By remaining optimistic and projecting a can-do image that makes customers enjoy dealing with you, you can influence yourself and others. Smile as an outward gesture of your "I care" philosophy. Many self-help publications and courses are available that can offer guidance in this area.

Look for ways to improve your skills and to raise the level of service you provide to your customer. Whether it is through formal training, mentoring, or simply observing positive service techniques used by others and mimicking them, work to improve your own skills. The more you know, the better you can assist customers and move your own career forward.

Look for a Strong Mentor in Your Organization   Mentors are people who are well acquainted with the organization and its policies, politics, and processes. They are well connected (inside and outside the organization), communicate well, have the ability and desire to assist you (the **mentee**), and are capable and experienced. Ask these people to provide support and help you grow personally and professionally. Many good books on the topic of mentoring are available. Figures 2.5 and 2.6 list some characteristics of a mentor and mentee.

mentors
Individuals who dedicate time and effort to befriend and assist others. In an organization, they are typically people with a lot of knowledge, experience skills, and initiative, and have a large personal and professional network established.

mentees
Typically less experienced recipients of the efforts of mentors.

Managing Customer Encounters

TAKE A FEW MINUTES TO RESPOND TO THE FOLLOWING QUESTIONS. Then your instructor may group you with others to discuss responses.

1. Have you ever witnessed or experienced a customer service situation in which a supervisor or manager became involved in an employee-customer encounter? If so, what occurred?

2. How do you feel the supervisor handled the situation?

3. Could the supervisor's approach have been improved? If so, how?

CUSTOMER SERVICE SUCCESS TIP

If your supervisor empowers you to make decisions, that means he/she trusts your ability to handle various issues. Do not take this trust lightly. Before taking action, stop, weigh alternatives, and then resolve the situation to the best of your ability in order to send a message of competency and professionalism.

As a service provider, think of customer situations in which you have to get approval from a supervisor or manager before making a decision or taking action to serve your customers. If you feel having to do so is causing a delay in serving your customers, approach your supervisor and suggest having decision-making authority given to you.

Some examples of possible empowerment situations include the following:

- *A cashier has to call a supervisor for approval of a customer's personal check.*
- *A cable television installer has to call the office for approval before adding an additional hookup for another room.*

Avoid Complacency   Anyone can go to work and just do what he or she is told. The people who excel, especially in a service environment, are the ones who constantly strive for improvement and look for opportunities to grow professionally. They also take responsibility or ownership for service situations. Take the time to think about the systems, policies, and procedures in place in your organization. Can they be improved? How? Now take that information or awareness and make recommendations for improvements. Even though managers have a key role, the implementation and success of cultural initiatives

When searching for someone to mentor you, look for these characteristics:

- Willingness to be a mentor
- Experience in the organization or industry and/or job you need help with
- Knowledgeable about the organization and industry
- Good communicator (verbal, nonverbal, and listening skills)
- Aware of the organizational culture
- Well connected inside and outside the organization

- Enthusiastic
- Good coaching skills and a good motivator
- Charismatic
- Trustworthy
- Patient
- Creative thinker
- Self-confident
- Good problem solver

FIGURE 2.5

Characteristics of an Effective Mentor

Since mentoring is a two-way process, you should make sure that you are ready to have a mentor. You should have the following characteristics:

- Willingness to participate, listen, and learn
- Desire to improve and grow
- Commitment to working with mentor
- Self-confidence
- Effective communication skills

- Enthusiasm
- Openness to feedback
- Adaptability
- Willingness to ask questions

FIGURE 2.6

Characteristics of a Successful Mentee

TAKE A FEW MINUTES TO THINK ABOUT AND RESPOND TO THESE QUESTIONS. Once you have responded, your instructor may form groups and have you share answers.

1. What type of skills training do you believe would be valuable for a customer service professional? Why?

2. What types of training have you had or do you need to qualify for a service position?

(practices or actions taken by the organization) rest with you, the front-line employee. You are the one who interacts directly with a customer and often determines the outcome of the contact.

Some people might throw up their hands and say, "It wasn't my fault," "Nobody else cares, why should I," or "I give up." A special person looks for ways around roadblocks in order to provide quality service for customers. The fact that others are not doing their job does not excuse you from doing yours. You are being paid a salary to accomplish specific job tasks. Do them with gusto and with pride. Your customers expect no less. You and your customers will reap the rewards of your efforts and initiative.

EMPLOYEE EMPOWERMENT

Employee **empowerment** is one way for a supervisor to help ensure that service providers can respond quickly to customer needs or requests. The intent of empowerment is a delegation of authority where a front-line service provider can take action without having to call a supervisor or ask permission. Such authority allows on-the-spot responsiveness to the customer while making service representatives feel trusted, respected, and like an important part of the organization. Empowerment is also an intangible way that successful service organizations reward employees. Often someone who has decision-making authority feels better about himself or herself and the organization.

TRAINING

The importance of effective training cannot be overstated. To perform your job successfully and create a positive impression in the minds of customers, you and other front-line employees must be given the necessary tools. Depending on your position and your organization's focus, this training might address interpersonal skills, technical skills, organizational awareness, or job skills, again depending on your position. Most important, your training should help you know what is expected of you and how to fulfill those expectations. Training is a vehicle for accomplishing this and is an essential component of any organizational culture that supports customer service.

Take advantage of training programs. Check with your supervisor and/or training department, if there is one. If you work in a small company or nonprofit organization, have a limited budget for training, or do not have access to training through your organization, look for other resources. Many communities have lists of seminars available through the public library, college business programs, high schools, chambers of commerce, professional organizations, and a variety of other organizations. The Internet also offers a wealth of articles and information. Tap into these to gain the knowledge

empowerment
The word used to describe the giving of decision-making and problem-resolution authority to lower-level employees in an organization. This precludes having to get permission from higher levels in order to take an action or serve a customer.

CUSTOMER SERVICE SUCCESS TIP (*continued*)

- *A computer technician cannot comply with a customer's request that she make a backup CD-ROM of her hard drive before running a diagnostic test because policy prohibits it.*
- *A call center service representative does not have the authority to reverse late payment charges on the account of a customer who explained that he was in the hospital for three weeks with surgery complications.*
- *A bank representative cannot waive returned check fees even though she acknowledges the bank created the error that resulted in bounced checks in the first place.*
- *An assistant cruise purser cannot correct a billing error until the purser returns from lunch.*
- *A volunteer coordinator must check with the director before allowing a worker to implement a new process that she recommends to expedite service delivery to a client.*

43

and skills you will need to move ahead. Also, your training and skill level will often determine whether you keep your job if your organization is forced to downsize and reduce staff.

2 ESTABLISHING A SERVICE STRATEGY

Concept: A service provider helps determine approaches for service success.

The first step a company can take in creating or redefining its service environment is to do an inspection of its systems and practices to decide where the company is now and where it needs to be in order to be competitive in a global service economy. The manner in which internal and external customer needs are addressed should also be reviewed.

As a service provider, you should do your part in determining needed approaches for service success. From the perspective of a customer service professional, ask yourself the following questions to help clarify your role:

- Who is my customer?
- What am I currently doing, or what can I do, to help achieve organizational excellence?
- Do I focus all my efforts on total customer satisfaction?
- Am I empowered to make the decisions necessary to serve my customer? If not, what levels of authority should I discuss with my supervisor?
- Are there policies and procedures that inhibit my ability to serve the customer? If so, what recommendations about changing policies and procedures can I make?
- When was the last time I told my customers that I sincerely appreciated their business?
- In what areas of organizational skills and product and service knowledge do I need additional information?

The best way to create a service culture is to get everyone in the organization involved in planning and brainstorming. Everyone should be encouraged to share ideas about how and where internal changes need to be made to be more responsive to customer needs. *How do you think these ideas can be shared most effectively?*

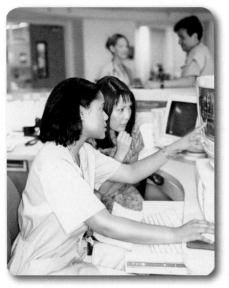

3 CUSTOMER-FRIENDLY SYSTEMS

Concept: System components are advertising, complaint resolution, and delivery systems.

A service culture starts at the top of an organization and filters down to the front-line employee. By demonstrating their commitment to quality service efforts, managers lead by example. It's not enough to authorize glitzy service promotional campaigns and send out directives informing employees of management's support for customer initiatives; managers must get involved. Further, employees must take initiative to solve problems and better serve the customer. They must be alert for opportunities and make recommendations for improvement whenever appropriate. Only in these situations can changes and improvements in the culture occur.

TYPICAL SYSTEM COMPONENTS

Part of the effectiveness in serving customers can be accomplished through policies and practices that say "We care" or "You're important to us." Some **customer-friendly systems** that can send positive messages are:

Advertising Advertising campaigns should send a message that products and services are competitive in price and that the quality and quantity are at least comparable to those of competitors. Otherwise, customers will likely go elsewhere. An advertisement that appears to be deceptive can cost the organization customers and its reputation. For example, if an advertisement states that something is "free" (a cup of coffee, a buy-one, get-one-free item, tire rotation, or a consultation) but somewhere in the advertisement (in small print) there are restrictions ("with a purchase of $20 or more," "while supplies last," "if you buy two new tires," or "if you sign a one-year contract)," then it may be viewed as deceptive. To prevent misunderstandings as a service provider, make sure that you point out such restrictions to customers when they call or ask questions. If you notice that an advertisement sounds a bit "tricky," inform your supervisor immediately. Possibly the ad was not proofread carefully enough before it was printed and/or aired. Remember, you have a vested interest in your organization's success. Take ownership.

Complaint or Problem Resolution The manner in which complaints or problems are handled can signal the organization's concern for customer satisfaction. If an employee has to get approvals for the smallest decisions, the customer may have to wait for a supervisor to arrive (a supermarket cashier has to call for a manager to approve a check for $10, and when the supervisor arrives, he or she doesn't even look at the check before signing and walking away). This can lead to customer and employee frustration and irritation and makes the organization, and the service provider, look inept.

As a service professional, you should make recommendations for improvement whenever you spot a roadblock or system that impedes provision of service excellence.

customer-friendly systems
Refers to the processes in an organization that make service seamless to customers by ensuring that things work properly and the customer is satisfied.

SERVICE DELIVERY SYSTEMS

Your organization must determine the best way to deliver quality products and service and to provide effective follow-up support. Everything you do in customer service is crucial. This includes the way information is made available to customers, initial contacts and handling of customer issues, sales techniques (hard sell versus relationship selling), order collection and processing, price quotations, product and service delivery, processing paperwork, invoicing, and follow-up. Customers should not have to deal with internal policies, practices, or politics. They should be able to contact you, get the information they need, make a buying decision, where appropriate, and have the product or service selected flawlessly delivered in a timely, professional manner. Anything less is poor service and may cost your organization in terms of lost business, customers, or reputation.

Customers also expect value for their money. Part of this is professional, easy-to-access service. For example, if you are in a retail organization and do not have an 800, 877, or 888 number with online customer support, extended hours of operation, top-quality merchandise, and effective resolution of problems, your customers may rebel. They can do this by complaining, speaking negative word-of-mouth publicity, writing letters to consumer advocacy groups (television or radio stations; Better Business Bureaus; local, state, and federal government agencies), and/or going elsewhere for their needs. Additionally, if your company's website is not kept up to date (or if your company has no web presence), or if the website is difficult to navigate, customers may go elsewhere. Customers want to quickly "click" for their information. Websites that are hard to navigate or that take a long time to load up will often be abandoned by customers.

There are many ways available for delivering service to customers. Two key factors involved in delivery are transportation modes (how products and services are physically delivered—by truck, train, plane, U.S. Postal Service, courier, and electronically) and location (facilities located centrally and easily accessible by customers). You will explore the use of technology in service delivery in detail when you read Chapter 9. The location can be crucial to nonprofit organizations and medical or dental care providers since many clients or patients do not have access to dependable transportation. They often have to depend on friends, family, and public transportation to access services and products.

Direct or Indirect Systems   The type of delivery system used (direct or indirect contact) is important because it affects staffing numbers, costs, technology, scheduling, and many other factors. The major difference between the two types of systems is that in a direct contact environment, customers interact directly with people, whereas in an indirect system their needs are met primarily with self-service through technology (possibly integrated with the human factor an in customer contact/call centers) integrated with Internet services.

service delivery systems
The mechanisms or strategies used by an organization to provide service to customers.

There is a delicate balance in selecting a **service delivery system.** This is because each customer is unique and has personal preferences. While many prefer a hands-off self-service approach, others resent it and often view it as a loss of caring. Many banks discovered this fact in recent years. They saw technology as a cost-saving strategy to deliver service. Branches were closed as money was spent to upgrade automated phone systems and add automatic teller machines (ATMs). Many customers rebelled. The result is that companies like Bank One are now increasing their branch locations and retrofitting their branches and ATMs. Washington Mutual touts a high-touch customer environment complete with free checking, comfortable waiting areas, and play areas for children. In addition, like many organizations, these companies use automated attendant phone systems that allow callers to speak or manually enter information with their telephone touchpad.

Figure 2.7 shows some ways by which organizations are providing service to customers and prospective customers.

Third-Party Delivery (Outsourcing)   In recent years, as companies strive to reduce costs, increase profit, and stay ahead of the competition, an interesting trend has occurred. Many companies are eliminating internal positions and hiring outside (third-party) organizations and individuals to assume eliminated and newly created roles (call center customer support functions, human resource benefits administration, accounting functions, and marketing). Many third-party providers and the jobs outsourced are located in India, Mexico, and a number of other developing nations where the labor supply is large and the cost of doing business is much lower. Major U.S. companies like American Express, Citigroup, Microsoft, and others have found this alternative to be a lucrative practice. They save millions of dollars in taxes and revenue by distributing call center and service functions outside the borders of the United States.

FIGURE 2.7

**Service Delivery
Systems**

Many industries are using technology to provide service that has traditionally been obtained by a customer going to a supplier and meeting face to face with an organization's representative. The following lists compare the traditional (direct) and technological (indirect) approaches.

Direct Contact	Indirect Contact
Face to face	800, 877, 888 number
Bank tellers	Automated teller machines or online banking
Reservationists (airlines, hotels)	Online computer reservations
Front desk staff (hotels)	On-screen, in-room television checkout and bill viewing
Ticket takers (theme parks)	Ticket scanners
Customer service representatives	Online viewing to provide balance or billing information (credit card companies)
Lawyers	Telephone tip lines or e-mail
Photo developers	Self-service film kiosk or Internet transmission of digital images
Supermarket clerks	Online ordering and delivery
Towing dispatchers	In-car navigation and notification systems
Receptionists	Self-service checkout cash registers

This practice of outsourcing (see chapter 1 for definition) provides multiple benefits while bringing with it some downsides. On the positive side, companies can save money by:

- Eliminating large ongoing salaries
- Reducing health benefits, retirement, and 401(k) payments
- Avoiding the need to purchase and update computers and equipment and a myriad of other equipment
- Bringing in new, fresh expertise and perspectives from outside the organization

And, on the negative side:

- Long-term employee expertise is lost.
- Employee loyalty to the organization suffers.
- The morale of the "survivors" (employees whose jobs were not eliminated) is adversely affected.
- Managing becomes more complex.
- Customers must deal with "strangers" with whom they cannot build a long-term relationship because their provider may be gone the next time they call or stop by.

Many organizations have adopted the practice of redesignating job positions as either part-time or shared (by two employees who are both part-time and therefore do not qualify for all benefits because of the number of hours they work). Another common strategy is to fill positions with "temporary" employees contracted through a temporary staffing agency. All of this is done in an effort to reduce rising employee costs (especially benefits) while providing the necessary customer support.

TOOLS FOR SERVICE MEASUREMENT

In a customer-oriented environment, it is important to constantly gauge service effectiveness. Organizations can use many ways to find out how well you and your peers are doing in serving customers. Once the results of organizational self-assessments are obtained, they will likely be shared with you and other employees in an effort to determine ways to reduce shortcomings and enhance strengths. If your supervisor fails to share such results, simply ask. Again, you have a vested interest in improvement and if he or she forgets to include you in the improvement loop—or intentionally omits you—you should take the initiative to demonstrate that you do care and are concerned with customer service delivery.

Here are some of the typical techniques or tools available for customer service data collection:

Employee focus groups.   In such groups, you and others might be asked to comment or develop ideas on various topics related to customer service or employee and organizational issues. Although you will be providing interesting and valuable insights from your own perspective, remember that your views may differ significantly from those of your customers. For this reason, if your ideas are not implemented, do not be discouraged. Overriding organizational and customer issues to which you are not privy may be the reason.

Employee opinion surveys.   Such surveys are often done yearly to gain employee perspectives on how well policies, procedures, management, technology, and other systems perform.

Customer focus groups.   Like the employee groups, these forums provide an opportunity to gather a group of customers (selected geographically, demographically by factors such as age, sex, race, income, or interests, or randomly from lists). Customer focus groups are brought together to answer specific questions related to some aspect of product or service.

Among other responsibilities, customer service professionals make a point of communicating their company's commitment to service in face-to-face interactions with customers. *What skills does a customer service representative need to create a positive service culture when talking with customers?*

Mystery shoppers.   These people may be internal employees or external consultants who pose as customers in on-site visits, over the telephone or online, to determine how well customers are being served.

Customer satisfaction surveys.   This type of survey can be written or orally administered. It could be something as simple as an employee or manager chatting with customers at a restaurant and gathering their feedback, or it could be something more formal. Customers are sometimes asked to complete a brief questionnaire at the end of their service transaction. Some organizations do follow-up telephone satisfaction surveys; others put their surveys on their website and encourage feedback. Customers are often enticed to participate in a survey through the use of gifts, prizes, and discounts.

Customer comment cards.   Many food service and hospitality businesses use these simple cards to get immediate reactions and comments from customers after a visit. They are also used in doctors' and dentists' offices, nonprofit organizations, government offices, and anywhere else where managers really care about what their customers and clients think.

Profit and loss statements or management reports. These reports are invaluable in spotting trends or dramatic changes in profits or losses that might indicate or lead to a service breakdown.

Employee exit interviews. These interviews are typically administered by the human resources or personnel department, or in smaller organizations, an officer or owner might informally ask questions of a departing employee. Such information can identify trends or concerns. Departing employees often feel that they have nothing to lose and will candidly provide valuable feedback about management practices, policies, and procedures, and a multitude of other organizational issues.

Walk-through audits. Create a checklist of service factors (for example, responsiveness, friendliness, and so on) for supervisors or managers to use as they walk through a store or service facility to view the operations from a customer's perspective.

On-site management visits. These visits provide firsthand observation of service practice and allow interaction between managers, employees, and customers. They are especially helpful when there are off-site workers (at construction sites or branch offices), or operations consulting projects, or in-home services, (such as plumbing). A side benefit of these types of visits is that they show the organization is committed to fulfilling the customers' needs.

Management inspections. As a follow-up to employee service delivery, many organizations often have supervisors or managers follow up on service performed by checking the work or asking the customers how they liked the service or product received (e.g., at a carwash after the cleaning of a vehicle). Sometimes, these checks are done over the telephone or via the Internet.

4 TWELVE STRATEGIES FOR PROMOTING A POSITIVE SERVICE CULTURE

Concept: To perform effectively as a customer service professional, you will need a plan.

Here are 12 strategies for service success.

1. ***Explore your organization's vision.*** By working to better understand the focus of the organization and asking yourself, "What's the added value and results for me?" (AVARFM), you can develop your own commitment to helping make the organization successful. An example of AVARFM might occur when a new policy is implemented that requires you to answer a phone by the third ring.

   A "mystery caller" system is in place as a means of monitoring compliance. Also, to each employee who meets the three-ring standard, rewards are given. You now have a reason or added value associated with compliance.

2. ***Help communicate the culture and vision to customers—daily.*** Customers have specific expectations. It does no good for the organization to have a vision if you do not help communicate and demonstrate it to the customer. Many companies place slogans and posters throughout the workplace or service area to communicate the vision. Although these approaches reinforce the message, a more effective means is for you to deliver quality customer service regularly. Through your attitude, language, appearance, knowledge of products and services, body language, and the way you communicate with your customers, they will feel your commitment to serve them. You will read more about techniques for presenting yourself professionally in later chapters.

3. ***Demonstrate ethical behavior.*** Ethical behavior is based on values—those of the society, organization, and employees. These values are a combination of beliefs, ideologies, perceptions, experiences, and a sense of what is right (appropriate) and wrong (inappropriate). Successful demonstration of ethical behavior is often determined by the values of the customer and how they perceive your behavior, and the customer often holds you and your organization to high standards. Thus, it is crucial for you to be aware of your words and actions so that you do not inadvertently send a negative ethical message to your customers.

How do you know which values your organization holds as important? Many times, they are communicated in an employee manual distributed during new hire orientation. Sometimes they are emblazoned on a plaque on the wall, possibly as part of the mission or philosophy statement or next to it. However, the reality test or "where the rubber meets the road" related to your organization's values comes in the day-to-day operational actions of you and your organization.

From an ethical standpoint, it is often up to you and your front-line peers to assess the situation, listen to your customers' requests, scrutinize your organizational policies and procedures, consider all options, and then make the "right" decision. This decision is fair—to your customer and your organization—and it is morally and legally right. A 1999 movie (*The Insider* with Al Pacino and Russell Crowe) epitomized the issues of ethical behavior. The movie is based on the true story of a tobacco industry insider who blew the whistle on his company, which publicly denied the harmful side effects of smoking. Even though the man stood to lose everything, possibly even his life, he acted out of conscience in an effort to help others. Another movie, *Erin Brocovich,* demonstrated what can happen if unethical behavior is not immediately caught and corrected by an organization. In that movie, Pacific Gas & Electric (PG&E) dumped chemicals into the soil and water of Hinkley, California, for years. They then covered up the pollution even though many of the local residents developed serious health problems and died. The company even paid medical bills for some residents to give the appearance of a good corporate neighbor. Ultimately, Erin was able to piece together the details while working for a small legal firm and a class-action lawsuit resulted in the largest class-action lawsuit payment in history at the time and severe damage to the reputation of PG&E.

As a front-line contact with customers, you will be asked a variety of questions about the company and its products. *What skills will you need and what information should you give customers in this situation?*

The key to ongoing customer relations is trust. Without it, you have no relationship and cannot win customer loyalty.

4. ***Identify and improve your service skills.*** Take an inventory of your interpersonal and customer service skills; use the strengths, and improve the weaker areas. By continually upgrading your knowledge and skills related to people, customer service, and products and services offered, you position yourself as a resource to the customer and an asset to the organization. There are a list of different websites offering various behavioral style surveys at www.mhhe.com/lucas09 if you wish to pursue learning more about yourself. Some sites periodically offer a shortened or beta test version of surveys they develop.

5. ***Become an expert on your organization*** As the front-line contact person with customers, you

are likely to receive a variety of questions related to the organization. Typical questions involve organizational history, structure, policies and procedures systems, products, or services. By being well versed in the many facets of the organization and its operation, related industry topics, and your competition, you can project a more knowledgeable, helpful, and confident image that contributes to total customer satisfaction.

6. ***Demonstrate commitment.*** As an employee with customer contact opportunities and responsibilities, you are the organization's representative. One mistake that many front-line employees (and many supervisors) make in communications with customers is to intentionally or unintentionally demonstrate a lack of commitment or support for their company and a sense of powerlessness. A common way in which this occurs is with the use of "they" language when dealing with customers. This can be in reference to management or policies or procedures, for example, "Mrs. Howard, I'd like to help but our policy says . . ." or "Mrs. Howard, I've checked on your request, but my manager (they) said we can't . . ."

   An alternative to using "they" language is to take ownership or responsibility for a situation by telling the customer what you can do, not what you cannot do. Customers are not interested in internal strife or procedures; they want to have their needs satisfied. To try to involve customers in situations that are out of their control and that do not concern them is unfair and unwise. Positive language and effort on your part can reduce or eliminate unnecessarily dragging the customer in. Here's one approach: "Mrs. Howard, I'm terribly sorry that you were inconvenienced by our mistake (policy or omission). What I can do to help resolve this situation is . . ."

7. ***Partner with customers.*** Customers are the reason you have a job and the reason your organization continues to exist. With that in mind, you should do whatever you can to promote a positive, healthy customer-provider relationship. This can be done in a number of ways, many of which will be addressed in detail in later chapters. Here are some simple techniques:

   - Communicate openly and effectively.
   - Smile—project a positive image.
   - Listen intently, and then respond appropriately.
   - Facilitate situations in which customer needs are met and you succeed in win/win situations helping accomplish organizational goals.
   - Focus on developing an ongoing relationship with customers instead of taking a one-time service or sales opportunity approach.

8. ***Work with your customer's interest in mind.*** Think to yourself, "If I were my customer, what type of service would I expect?" Then, set out to provide that service.

9. ***Treat vendors and suppliers as customers.*** Some customer service employees view vendors and suppliers as salespeople whose only purpose is to serve them. In fact, each contact with a vendor or a supplier offers a golden opportunity to tap into a pre-established network and potentially expand your own customer service base while providing better service to existing customers. People remember how they are treated and often act in kind.

10. ***Share resources.*** By building strong interpersonal relationships with coworkers and peers throughout the industry, you can develop a support system of resources. Sometimes customers will request information, products, or services that are not available through your organization. By being able to refer customers to alternate sources, you will have provided a service, and they are likely to remember that you helped them indirectly.

11. ***Work with, not against, your customers.*** Customers are in the enviable position of being in control. At no time in recent history has the cliché "It's a buyers market" been more true, and many consumers know it. To capitalize on this situation, many organizations have become very creative and proactive in their efforts to grab and hold customers. One large Colorado-based national supermarket, Albertson's, developed a series of commercials touting "Albertson's—it's your store" and stressing that corporate efforts were focused on customer satisfaction. Your efforts should similarly convey the idea that you are working with customers to better serve them.

12. ***Provide service follow-up.*** Providing follow-up is probably one of the most important service components. Service does not end when the service encounter or sale concludes. There are numerous follow-up opportunities to ensure that customer satisfaction was attained. This can be through a formal customer satisfaction survey or telephone callback system or through an informal process of sending thank-you cards, birthday cards, special sale mailings, and similar initiatives that are inexpensive and take little effort. Think of creative ways to follow up, and then speak to your supervisor about implementing them. These types of efforts reinforce service commitment to customers and let them know that you want to keep them as your customers.

5 SEPARATING AVERAGE COMPANIES FROM EXCELLENT COMPANIES

Concept: Ask questions to determine the service environment in a company in which you seek employment or are currently employed.

Whether you are currently working in an organization or are seeking employment, the following factors can demonstrate an organizations level of service commitment. They can be also used as a basis for questions you might ask supervisors or interviewers in order to determine what type of service environment exists:

- Executives spend time with the customers.
- Executives spend time talking to front-line service providers.
- Customer feedback is regularly asked for and acted upon.
- Innovation and creativity are encouraged and rewarded.
- Benchmarking (identifying successful practices of others) is done with similar organizations.
- Technology is widespread, frequently updated, and used effectively.
- Training is provided to keep employees current on industry trends, organizational issues, skills, and technology.
- Open communication exists between front-line employees and all levels of management.
- Employees are provided with guidelines and empowered (in certain instances, authorized to act without management intervention) to do whatever is necessary to satisfy the customer.
- Partnerships with customers and suppliers are common.
- The status quo is not acceptable.

6 WHAT CUSTOMERS WANT

Concept: Customers expect effective, efficient service and value for their money. Customers also expect certain common things that service providers can furnish.

Most customers are like you. And **what customers want** is value for their money and/or effective, efficient service. They also expect certain intangible things during a service encounter. Here are seven common things that customers want and expect if they are to keep doing business with you and your organization:

1. *Personal recognition.* This can be demonstrated in a number of ways (sending thank-you cards or notes or birthday cards, returning calls in a timely fashion, or taking the time to look up information that might be helpful even if the customer did not ask for it). A simple way to show recognition to a customer who enters your work area, even if you cannot immediately stop what you are doing to serve him or her, is to smile and acknowledge the person's presence. If possible, you might also offer the customer the option of waiting, having a seat, and so on.

2. *Courtesy.* Basic courtesy involves pleasantries such as "please" and "thank you," as there is no place or excuse for rude behavior in a customer service environment. Even though customers may not always be right, you must treat them with respect. If a situation becomes too intense and you find yourself "losing it," call upon someone else to serve that customer. This is especially important in stressful environments where customers are truly suffering and not likely to be in the mood for poor attitudes or delays (e.g., hospital waiting rooms, and doctors' or dentists' offices).

3. *Timely service.* Most people don't mind waiting briefly for service if there is a legitimate reason (as when you are waiting on another customer or obviously serving another customer on the phone), but they do not like to spend what they believe is undue amounts of time waiting to be served. Your challenge as a customer service professional is to provide prompt yet effective service. It is important to remember that customers value their time as much as you and your managers/bosses do. Work diligently to stay on schedule and at least explain when delays do occur so that the customer understands the reason for the wait (e.g., in a doctor's office when scheduled appointments are running behind because of a medical emergency or the doctor was delayed while in surgery). If extensive delays are likely to occur, offer the customer an option of possibly rescheduling. They probably will not want to, but the gesture of allowing them some decision in the situation is psychologically soothing in many cases.

4. *Professionalism.* Customers expect and should receive knowledgeable answers to their questions, service that satisfies their needs and lessens effort on their part, and service personnel who take pride in their work. You can demonstrate these characteristics by exemplifying the ethics talked about earlier, and the communication behaviors outlined in later chapters of this book.

5. *Enthusiastic service.* Customers come to your organization for one purpose—to satisfy a need. This need may be nothing more than to "look around." Even so, they should find a dedicated team of service professionals standing by to assist them in whatever way possible. By delivering service with a smile, offering additional services and information, and taking the time to give extra effort in every service encounter, you can help guarantee a positive service experience for your customer.

6. *Empathy.* Customers also want to be understood. Your job as a service provider is to make every effort to be understanding, and to provide appropriate service. To succeed, you must be able to put yourself in the customer's position or look at the need from the customer's perspective as much as possible. This is especially true when customers do not speak English well or have some type of disability that reduces their communication effectiveness. When a customer has a complaint or believes that he or she did not receive appropriate service, it is your job to calm or appease in a nonthreatening, helpful manner and show understanding.

what customers want
Things that customers typically desire but do not necessarily need.

Your Customer Expectations

NOW THAT YOU KNOW WHAT GOES INTO MAKING A CUS-TOMER ENVIRONMENT "CUSTOMER-FRIENDLY," THINK ABOUT YOUR OWN EXPECTATIONS WHEN YOU PATRONIZE A COMPANY. Share your answers with others in the class.

Drawing on your own experiences, list four or five expectations that you feel are typical of most customers.

---

feel, felt, found technique
A process for expressing empathy and concern for people and for helping them understand that you can relate to their situation.

A common strategy for showing empathy is the **feel, felt, found technique.** When using it, a service provider is demonstrating a compassionate understanding of the customer's issue or situation. For example, a customer is upset because the product desired is not in stock. A service provider might respond by saying: "Mr. Philips, I know how you *feel*. I've *felt* the same way when I had my heart set on a specific item. Many customers have actually *found* that the alternative product I described to you has the same features and performs several other functions as well."

7. ***Patience.*** Customers should not have to deal with your frustrations or pressures. Your efficiency and effectiveness should seem effortless. If you are angry because of a policy, procedure, management, or the customer, you must strive to mask that feeling. This may be difficult to do when you believe that the customer is being unfair or unrealistic. By suppressing your desire to speak out or react emotionally, you can remain in control, serve the customer professionally, and end the contact sooner. Some tips on managing difficult customers and your own stress levels will be addressed in Chapters 7 and 10. There is a chapter on stress management available at www.mhhe.com/lucas09.

SUMMARY

Professional customer service helps highlight and define service culture. Everything customers experience from the time they contact an organization in person, on the phone, or through other means, affects their perception of the organization and its employees. To positively influence their opinion, you must constantly be alert for opportunities to provide excellent service. Taking the time to provide a little extra effort can often mean the difference between total customer satisfaction and service breakdown.

....

KEY TERMS

customer-centric 33
customer-friendly systems 45
employee expectations 35
employee roles 35
empowerment 43
feel, felt, found technique 54
mentees 41
mentors 41

mission 34
RUMBA 35
service culture 32
service delivery systems 46
service measurement 36
service philosophy 34
what customers want 53

1   What are some of the key elements that make up a service culture?

2   How does management's service philosophy affect the culture of an organization?

3   How does RUMBA help clearly define employee roles and expectations? Why is each component important?

4   How can policies and procedures affect the customer's impression of customer service?

5   What questions should you ask yourself about your role as a service provider?

6   What are some indicators that a company has customer-friendly systems in place?

7   What are some of the tools used by organizations to measure their service culture?

8   What are some strategies for helping promote a positive customer culture?

9   What separates average organizations from excellent ones?

10   What are some typical things that customers want?

· ·

Customer Service and Organizational Culture

Log on to the Internet and research the mission statements of the following five organizations: (1) U.S. Department of Education, (2) USAA Educational Foundation, (3) Enterprise Rent-a-Car, (4) Starbucks Coffee, and (5) Florida Hospital. You can locate information by going to available search engines (Yahoo.com, Infoseek.com, google.com, AltaVista.com, Excite.com, or Ask.com) and typing in the name of the organization, then searching its site for "mission statement."

As you view each organizational mission statement, answer the following questions:

Are there shared values and beliefs evident in the different mission statements? If so, what are they?

As a customer/client, do you feel that the organization values you? Why or why not?

Does the focus of each mission statement seem to differ between types of organizations (e.g., government, nonprofit, not-for-profit, and for profit)? Why or why not?

If you were writing each mission statement, what would you add or delete?

Be prepared to share your findings at the next scheduled meeting.

· ·

Service Culture

Along with assigned group members, go on a field trip to several local organizations before your next class meeting. Use Figure 2.3, Elements of a Service Culture, as a guideline to determine the level and quality of the service culture of each organization visited. Take notes and be prepared to share your observations with other groups when you return to class. As part of your note taking, answer the following questions about each organization:

1   Did you notice any overt signs that indicated the organizations' cultural philosophy (mission or philosophy statements on walls)? If yes, what were they?

2   In what way was service delivered and how did the delivery indicate the organization's philosophy related to customer service?

3   What did the organization's products and services say about its approach to service (quality and quantity, availability, and service support)?

4   What evidence did you see of management support for the service initiatives being used by employees?

5   What indicators of motivators and rewards did you notice (employee of the month or year plaques, parking space for employee of the month, visible indicators of rewards on employees' clothes or uniforms, for example, items such as pins or buttons)?

6   Were there any indications that training of employees is occurring (employees have a consistent greeting or closing "Thanks for shopping at_____")?

You and Your New Job in Customer Service

In the following case study, you are a new employee and are excited and happy to begin your position in customer service with United Booksellers. Read about the company and your role in customer service, then answer the questions at the end of the case study.

Background

United Booksellers is the fifth-largest retailer of publications on the West Coast in the United States. It started 15 years ago as a family-owned bookstore in Seattle, Washington, and has grown to over 125 stores in seven states. The organization currently employs 3,000 employees, each of whom receives extensive customer service training before being allowed to interact with customers.

Recent issues of *Booksellers Journal* and *Publishers Select* magazine have heralded the quality service and friendly atmosphere of the organization. United Booksellers has been praised for the appearance of the facilities, helpfulness and efficiency of employees, wide selection of publications, and intimate coffee shops where patrons can relax and read their purchases over a hot cup of fresh cappuccino.

Your Role

As a new customer service professional with United Booksellers, you are excited about starting your job, which will require continual customer contact. As a child, you watched your siblings perform customer service functions at the local Burger Mania Restaurant and always thought you'd like to follow their lead. Since you like people, enjoy a challenge, don't get stressed out easily, and have hopes of moving into management, you anticipate that this job should be just right for you. In this position, you'll be expected to receive new publications from publishers, log in receipts, stock shelves, assist customers, and occasionally work as backup cashier.

Critical Thinking Questions

1 Are there indicators of United Booksellers' service culture? If so, what are they?

2 If you were an employee, in what ways would you feel that you could contribute to the organizational culture?

3 If you were a customer, what kind of service would you expect to receive at United Booksellers? Why?

To better understand the role of service providers in helping establish and maintain a positive service culture, think about what you read in this chapter. Also, think about factors related to service cultures in organizations with which you are familiar. Make a list of five to ten key culture elements. Beside these elements, create a list of strategies that you can/could take as a service provider to improve them if you worked in such an organization. Share your list with others in the class.

HEALTH CARE—Johns Hopkins Institutions

Think about what you read related to the Johns Hopkins organization at the beginning of the chapter and answer the following questions. Your instructor may have you work together and share ideas in a group.

What about the organization might help build customer/patient confidence? Why?

Would you feel comfortable being a patient in this hospital? Why or why not?

How does the Johns Hopkins approach to service and business compare to other health care organizations with which you are familiar?

1	T		5	F		9	F
2	T		6	T		10	F
3	T		7	F		11	F
4	T		8	T		12	T

Ethical Dilemma 2.1 Possible Answers

1   What ethical issue(s) do you face in this situation?

The supervisor is putting employees in the awkward position of either making their performance goal or facing punitive actions and losing potential rewards. Moreover, this practice can violate some basic principles of ethical behavior because it can damage trust between supervisors and employees and, ultimately, between customers and service providers and the organization. This practice also defeats the part of the organizational philosophy that states, "in a low-pressure customer atmosphere."

2   How might these affect service delivery?

The customer is likely to receive less than stellar service because front-line service providers are going to feel pressured to hurry their service delivery. Additionally, service providers will potentially resent the supervisor, policy, and organization for creating a stressful work environment and/or withholding rewards on the basis of circumstances not always created by the employees. In the long run, employees may act out through tardiness, absenteeism, and high turnover. This can lead to stressed-out supervisors and a revolving door problem of rotating employees who require ongoing training, increased costs, and loss of expertise to the organization.

3   How might this situation be addressed?

Supervisors should take a realistic look at the mission statement and philosophy of the organization. They should also benchmark against similar industry organizations to see what types of policies and procedures they use with similar service situations. Ultimately, they should work with employees to develop realistic standards for quality service delivery.

Employees should bring issues related to poor policies and procedures to their supervisor/team leader for discussion. They should take ownership of the issue rather than simply complaining to others about the stress and working conditions.

part two

Skills for Success

3 Verbal Communication Skills

4 Non-Verbal Communication Skills

5 Listening Skills

CUSTOMER SERVICE INTERVIEW   Holly Faries

Holly Faries works for CuraScript Specialty Distribution in Lake Mary, Florida. The company provides integrated delivery to safely and consistently distribute pharmaceuticals and medical supplies for administration in offices and clinics. Holly's responsibilities include designing, developing, and administering a call monitoring program for the organization. She monitors organizational processes to ensure that they are efficient and effective for customers. Holly also trains employees in the skills necessary to expertly provide services. As part of her job assignments, Holly works with approximately 120 employees (including sales reps, contract administrators, account receivable reps, customer support reps and warehouse agents) to ensure that they are providing the highest quality customer service to client physicians and clinics on a consistent basis.

With over 25 years of experience in the fields of sociology and psychology, Holly's strengths include gather-

HOLLY FARIES, Quality Assurance and Customer Experience Manager, CuraScript Specialty Distribution

ing detailed information, assessing work styles and preferences, and facilitating the generation of new input and ideas. As Holly supports individuals in maximizing their personal strengths and learning how to improve challenges, she teaches teams to create new ways to communicate and work together.

Holly's career has a clear foundation in customer service. In addition to her role within her organization, she is also the 2007 president of the Central Florida chapter of the International Customer Service Association (ICSA).

Throughout her career as both a consultant and part-time professor at several local colleges, Holly has worked with many organizations, including the Orange County (Florida) Public Library, Fiserv, Convergys, Siemens, and Mitsubishi.

1 **What are the personal qualities that you believe are essential for anyone working with customers in a call center environment?**

I believe that any true customer service professional needs to have the following qualities: patience; empathy; compassion; a love of people; a desire to help; a pleasant, polite & professional demeanor; and most of all, integrity—nothing matters more!

2 **What do you see as the most rewarding part of working with customers? Why?**

It is wonderful to be able to have the ability to serve and educate people. We can solve problems and most of all, make people happy! I always tell my reps that they have the power to make or break someone's day. That's a lot of power to be wielding! Make good use of it.

3 **What do you believe that the biggest challenges are in working with customers? Why?**

There are many challenges you will encounter when dealing with customers. All customers are different. That's what makes them so wonderful! Whenever you "assume" you know what a customer wants, you are setting yourself up for failure. The challenge is to be able to "keep it fresh." Don't get comfortable or be complacent. Always think of new ideas to do it better than the competitor. Ask yourself "What do I offer my customers that my competitor doesn't?" If you offer the same services at about the same price, what is to set you apart from your competitors? *The customer service you provide.* My competitors may have (whatever I sell) but they don't have me!

Realize that your customers have ever-changing wants and needs. Keep up with them or risk getting run over by your competition. It is easy for us to get in the habit of using "cookie cutter customer service" when we deal with customers day in and day out. Very often, we find ourselves delivering the same or similar message time after time. Customers basically ask us the same questions. Often, we not only deliver the *same* message, we also use the *same* style to communicate that message even though customers have different personalities. We forget that customers are people and people are different. We need to take a proactive approach to customer service and treat each customer as an individual. Anticipate your customers needs and remember—just because they didn't ask for something, doesn't

mean they didn't need it. *You* are the professional and an expert in your field.

Always be up-front and honest. Integrity is the key. It's in the "how." How you deliver the information is as important as what information you have to deliver.

4 **What role does technology play in your job when working with customers and how have you seen this change since you started in the workplace?**

I started in customer service at a time when we used microfiche and note cards as a file system! Of course, now we use computers and multiple software applications and database systems to keep track of our customers' orders. Thank goodness!

I started in a company with a one-line phone system to handle our calls. We never knew how long a customer waited before being taken care of. Nor did we have any idea of how many customers hung up and weren't even given the opportunity to be taken care of! We also had no idea how our customers were being treated by our reps. Now, of course, we have a variety of hardware and software systems to help us track and understand everything that happens to customers from the moment they enter our phone system to the moment they disconnect. We know how their calls were handled from start to finish.

5 **What future issues do you see evolving related to dealing with customers in your profession and why do you think these are important?**

Customer's expectations continually change; becoming more "demanding" as time goes by. They want things faster and better than it ever was. Being "good" isn't good enough anymore. "Going the extra mile" or "Going above and beyond" will soon become the standard level of service. I think this will be expected in every profession.

6 **What advice related to customer service do you have for anyone seeking a career in call center customer service?**

I believe you truly have to love what you do to be in this profession. You need to bring a passion for service with you. You need to be able to love working with people.

Verbal Communication Skills

Your most unhappy customers are your greatest source of learning.

—Bill Gates

. . . .

After completing this chapter, you will be able to:

1   Explain the importance of effective communication in customer service.

2   Recognize the elements of effective two-way interpersonal communication.

3   Avoid language that could send a negative message and harm the customer relationship.

4   Project a professional customer service image.

5   Provide feedback effectively.

6   Use assertive communication techniques to enhance service.

7   Understand key differences between assertive and aggressive behavior.

. . . .

In the Real World   Retail—Enterprise Rent-A-Car

Enterprise Rent-A-Car was started as Executive Leasing Company by Jack Taylor with an investment of $100,000 dollars and seven cars in the lower level of a St. Louis Cadillac dealership in 1957. The company was based on a simple philosophy: "Take care of your customers and employees *first*, and profits will follow."

By 1992 Enterprise had surpassed $1 billion in annual revenues and had nearly 10,000 employees in its work force. By 2006 Enterprise posted $9 billion in annual revenue and operated a total fleet of 878,000 vehicles with more than 64,000 employees. The company has locations within 15 miles of 90 percent of the U.S. population and operates 6,900 offices in the U.S.,

Canada, the United Kingdom, Ireland, and Germany. The company purchases millions of dollars worth of vehicles through local car dealerships.

The Enterprise mission is to fulfill the automotive and commercial truck rental, leasing, car sales, and related needs of customers. Employees continually strive to not only meet, but also exceed expectations for service, quality, and value. Long-term loyalty is crucial to Enterprise's success and is earned by being honest and fair and working to deliver more than promised.

Part of the organizational mission focuses on the fact that customer service is the driving force behind the business. As a result of their business philosophy, Enterprise has come to be known for commitment to service and has been recognized numerous times for its superior service. J.D. Power and Associates and Market Metrix have repeatedly named Enterprise Rent-A-Car number one in customer satisfaction in the car rental industry.

A key element of the Enterprise success is to provide a supportive environment in which employees can develop and have opportunity to grow professionally while being compensated for their successes and achievements.

To ensure that their ability to provide superior customer service is never compromised, Enterprise has created a unique customer service satisfaction measure. They use the Enterprise Service Quality index (ESQi) which is driven by two simple words: *completely satisfied*. Every month, customer satisfaction is measured with each local branch through telephone surveys of hundreds of thousands of customers. Each branch earns a ranking based on the percentage of its customers who say they were *completely satisfied* with their last Enterprise experience. They call that ranking "top box," and that's the standard of excellence they set when working with customers.

While many competitors have struggled, Enterprise has grown into the largest and most successful car rental company in America. It is one of the biggest customers of General Motors, Ford, and several other car manufacturers, buying more cars than any other company in the world.

Forbes magazine has consistently ranked Enterprise among the top 20 largest private companies in America. Standard and Poor's rates Enterprise as the most financially sound rental car company.

For additional information about this organization, visit www.enterprise.com on the Internet.

See activity based on this section on page 83.

Quick Preview

Before reviewing the chapter content, respond to the following questions by placing a "T" for true or an "F" for false on the rules. Use any questions you miss as a checklist of material to which you will pay particular attention as you read through the chapter. For those you get right, congratulate yourself, but review the sections they address in order to learn additional details about the topic.

_____ **1.** Feedback is not an important element in the two-way communication model.

_____ **2.** Customers appreciate your integrity, and they trust you more when you use language such as "I'm sorry" or "I was wrong" when you make a mistake.

_____ **3.** Phrases such as "I'll try" or "I'm not sure" send a reassuring message that you're going to help solve a customer's problem.

_____ **4.** When you use agreement or acknowledgment statements, customers can vent without their emotions escalating.

_____ 5. You should attempt to make a positive impression by focusing on the customer and his or her needs during your initial and subsequent contacts.

_____ 6. Having one prepared greeting and closing statement to use with all customers is a good practice.

_____ 7. When you are not certain of an answer, it is a good idea to express an opinion or speculate when something will occur if a customer asks.

_____ 8. An acceptable response to a customer's question about why something cannot be done is "Our policy does not allow . . ."

_____ 9. You should delay feedback whenever possible unless you're communicating in writing.

_____ 10. The appearance of your workplace has little effect on customer satisfaction as long as you are professional and help solve problems.

_____ 11. Assertive communication means expressing your opinions positively and in a manner that helps the customers recognize that you are confident and have the authority to assist them.

_____ 12. Assertiveness is another word for "aggressiveness."

Answers to Quick Preview can be found at the end of the chapter.

1   THE IMPORTANCE OF EFFECTIVE COMMUNICATION

Concept: You represent your organization, and customers will respond according to you and your actions.

As a customer service professional, you have the power to make or break the organization. You are the front line in delivering quality service to your customers. Your appearance, actions or inactions, and ability to communicate say volumes about the organization and its focus on customer satisfaction. For all these reasons, you should continually strive to project a polished, professional image and go out of your way to make a customer's visit or conversation with you a pleasant and successful one.

A key element in making your interactions with customers successful is to recognize how you tend to communicate. The easiest way to find out how you communicate is to ask those who know you best. Unfortunately, many people are leery about requesting feedback because of what they might hear. Conversely, most people have difficulty giving useful feedback because they either never learned how to do it or are uncomfortable doing it. In any event, try it. Ask a variety of people for their feedback because each person will likely have a different perspective.

2   ENSURING TWO-WAY COMMUNICATION

Concept: Two-way communication involves a sender and a receiver, who each contribute to the communication process. Part of the communication process is deciding which is the best channel to ensure clear message delivery.

As a customer service professional, you are responsible for ensuring that a meaningful exchange of information takes place. By accepting this responsibility, you can perform your job more efficiently, generate goodwill and customer loyalty for the organization, and provide service excellence. To facilitate this, you should be aware of all the elements of **two-way communication** and

two-way communication An active process in which two individuals apply all the elements of interpersonal communication (e.g., listening, feedback, positive language) in order to effectively exchange information and ideas.

the importance of each. Figure 3.1 shows a communication model that clarifies the process.

INTERPERSONAL COMMUNICATION MODEL

Environment. The environment (office, store, and group or individual setting) in which you send or receive messages affects the effectiveness of your message.

Sender. You take on the role of **sender** as you initiate a message with your customer. Conversely, when customers respond, they assume that role.

Receiver. Initially, you may be the **receiver** of your customer's message; however, once you offer feedback, you switch to the sender role.

Message. The **message** is the idea or concept that you or your customer wishes to convey.

Channel. The method you choose to transmit your message (over the phone, in person, by fax, by e-mail, or by other means) is the **channel**.

Encoding. **Encoding** occurs as you evaluate what must be done to effectively put your message into a format that your customer will understand (language, symbols, and gestures are a few options). Failing to correctly determine your customer's ability to decode your message could lead to confusion and misunderstanding.

Decoding **Decoding** occurs as you or your customer converts messages received into familiar ideas by interpreting or assigning meaning. Depending on how well the message was encoded or whether filters interfere, the received message may not be the one originally sent.

Two-way communication is the foundation of effective customer service. *How can you be sure that you are listening to the customer?*

sender
One of the two primary elements of a two-way conversation. Originates messages to a receiver.

receiver
One of the two primary elements of a two-way conversation. Gathers the sender's message and decides how to react to it.

message
A communication delivered through speech or signals, or in writing.

channel
Term used to describe the method through which people communicate messages. Examples are face to face, telephone, e-mail, written correspondence, and facsimile.

encoding
The stage in the interpersonal communication process in which the sender decides what message will be sent and how it will be transmitted along with considerations about the receiver.

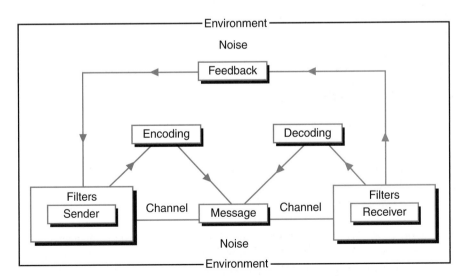

FIGURE 3.1   **Interpersonal Communication Model**

decoding
The stage in the interpersonal communication process in which messages received are analyzed by a receiver in an effort to determine the sender's intent.

feedback
The stage of the interpersonal communication process in which a receiver responds to a sender's message.

Feedback. Unless a response is given to messages received, there is no way to determine whether the intended message was received. **Feedback** is one of the most crucial elements of the two-way communication process. Without it, you have a monologue.

Filters. **Filters** are factors that distort or affect the messages you receive. They include, among other things, your attitude, interests, biases, expectations, education, beliefs, and values.

Noise **Noise** consists of physiological or psychological factors (your physical characteristics, level of attention, message clarity, loudness of message, or environmental factors) that interfere with the accurate reception of information.

3   AVOIDING NEGATIVE COMMUNICATION

filters
Psychological barriers in the form of personal experiences, lessons learned, societal beliefs, and values through which people process and compare information received to determine its significance.

noise
Refers to physiological or psychological factors (physical characteristics, level or attention, message clarity, loudness of message, or environmental factors) that interfere with the accurate reception of information.

global terms
Potentially inflammatory words or phrases used in conversation. They tend to inappropriately generalize behavior or group people or incidents together (e.g., always, never, everyone, everything, all the time).

Concept: Use positive words or phrases, rather than emphasize the negative.

You can squelch customer loyalty and raise customer frustration in a number of ways when communicating. Your choice of words or phrasing can often lead either to satisfaction or to confrontation, or it can destroy a customer-provider relationship. Customers do not want to hear what you can't do; they want to hear how you're going to help satisfy their needs or expectations. Focus your message on how you can work with the customer to accomplish needs satisfaction. Don't use vague or weak terminology. Instead of "I'm not sure …" or "I'll try … ," say "Let me get that answer for you …" or "I can do …"

Another pitfall to watch out for is the use of **global terms** (all-encompassing or inclusive expressions such as *always, never, everyone, all*). If your customer can give just one example for which your statement is not true, your credibility comes into question and you might go on the defensive. Suppose you say, "We always return calls in four hours," yet the customer has personally experienced a situation when that did not happen. Your statement is now false. Instead, phrase statements to indicate possible variances such as, "We attempt to return all calls within four hours" or "Our objective is to return calls within four hours." Be careful, too, about "verbal finger pointing," especially if your customer is already upset. This tactic involves the use of the word *you,* as in "You were supposed to call back to remind me" or "You didn't follow the directions I gave you." This is like pointing your finger at someone or using a patronizing tone to belittle them. People are likely to react powerfully and negatively to this type of treatment. See Figure 3.2.

4   COMMUNICATING POSITIVELY

Concept: A positive approach can produce positive results.

Just as you can turn customers off with your word choice, you can also win them over. Figure 3.3 contains some tips.

PLAN YOUR MESSAGES

You should think out everything from your greeting to your closing statements before you come into contact with a customer. Know what you want and need to say, avoid unnecessary details or discussion, and be prepared to answer questions about the organization, its products and services, and the customer's order.

Here are some words and phrases that can lead to trouble with your customers. Avoid or limit their use.

You don't understand.	You aren't listening to me.
You'll have to …	Listen to me.
You don't see my point.	I never said …
Hold on (or hang on) a second.	In my opinion …
I (we, you) can't …	What's your problem?
Our policy says (or prohibits) …	The word *problem*.
That's not my job (or responsibility).	Do you understand?
You're not being reasonable.	Are you aware …
You must (or should) …	The word *no*.
The word *but*.	Global terms (*always, never, nobody*).
What you need to do is …	Endearment terms (*honey, sweetie, sugar, and baby*).
Why don't you …?	
I don't know.	Profanity or vulgarity.
You're wrong or mistaken.	

FIGURE 3.2   Words and Phrases That Damage Customer Relationships

Some phrases can assist you in strengthening relationships with your customers. Such language reinforces your integrity and encourages customers to trust you. How do you or could you use these words? Which ones do you use the most?

Please.	You're right.
Thank you.	May I … ?
I can or will …	Have you considered …
How may I help?	I'm sorry (I apologize) for …
I was wrong.	*However, and,* or *yet* (instead of *but*).
I understand (appreciate) how you feel.	It's my (our) fault.
Situation, issue, concern (instead of *problem*).	Would you mind … ?
Often, many times, some (instead of *global terms*).	What do you think?
	I appreciate …
	Use of customer's name.

FIGURE 3.3   Words and Phrases that Build Customer Relationships

FOCUS ON THE CUSTOMER AS A PERSON

Strive to let customers know that you recognize them as individuals and appreciate their time, effort, patience, trust, and business. This is important. To deliver quality service effectively, you must deal with the human being before you deal with his or her needs or business concerns.

For example, if someone has waited in a line or on hold for service, as soon as this person steps up or you come back on the line, smile warmly, thank him or her for being patient, apologize for the wait, and ask what you can do to assist him or her. Often in such situations the service provider says something like "Next" (sounds canned and not customer-focused) or "Can I help the next person?" (better, but still goes straight to business without an apology or without recognizing the customer's inconvenience or wait). On the phone the service provider goes straight to, "This is Jean, how may I help you?" (with no recognition of the customer's inconvenience).

Another opportunity to focus on the customer occurs at the end of a transaction or call. If your organization does not have a standard parting comment to use with customers, simply smile and say something like, "Mr. Rinaldi, thank you for coming to (or calling) ABC Corporation. Please come back (or call) again." The key is that you must sound sincere. You may even want to modify your parting statement for subsequent customers so that it sounds more personal—and so the next person in line doesn't hear you parrot the same words with each customer.

Offer assistance.   Even if a problem or question is not in your area of responsibility, offer to help get answers, information, or assistance. Your customer will likely appreciate the fact that you went out of your way to help.

Be prepared.   Know as much as possible about the organization, its products and services, your job, and as appropriate, the customer. Also, make sure that you have all the tools necessary to serve the customer, take notes, and do your job in a professional manner. This allows you to deliver quality information and service while better satisfying customer needs and expectations.

Provide factual information.   Don't express opinions or speculate why something did or didn't, or will or will not, occur. State only what you are sure of or can substantiate. For example, if you are not sure when a delivery will take place or when a coworker who handles certain functions will return, say so, but offer to find the answer or handle the situation yourself. Don't raise customer expectations by saying, "This should be delivered by 7:30 tomorrow morning," or "Sue should be back from lunch in 10 minutes." If neither event occurs, the customer is likely to be irritated.

Be helpful.   If you cannot do something or don't have a product or service, admit it but be prepared to offer an alternative. Do not try to "dance around" an issue in an effort to respond in a manner that you feel the customer expects. Most people will spot this tentative behavior, and your credibility will suffer as a result. Do not insult your customer's intelligence by taking this approach. You and the organization will lose in the long run.

Accept responsibility.   Take responsibility for what you do or say and, if necessary, for actions taken by someone else that failed to satisfy the customer. Don't blame others or hide behind "they said" or "policy says" excuses. When something goes wrong, take responsibility and work to resolve the problem positively and quickly. If you don't have the authority needed, get someone who does, rather than refer the customer to someone else.

Take appropriate action.   You should take whatever action is necessary to satisfy the customer. Sometimes this may mean bending the rules a bit. In such cases, it may be easier to ask forgiveness from your supervisor than to explain why you lost the organization a good customer. If a request really cannot be honored because it is too extreme (a customer demands a free $100 item because he or she had to return one that did not work properly), explain why that specific request cannot be fulfilled and then negotiate and offer alternatives. In Chapter 7 you will find some suggestions for appropriate service recovery strategies.

CUSTOMER SERVICE SUCCESS TIP

No matter what type of organization you work for, look for ways to celebrate your customers and make them feel special and valued. This will return dividends of Increased customer satisfaction, higher levels of customer trust in the organization, and reduced stress for you because you will have fewer instances of unhappy customers with whom you have to deal.

Analyzing Your Verbal Communication Skills

TO HELP YOU DETERMINE HOW YOU SOUND TO OTHERS, TRY A BIT OF OBJECTIVE SELF-ANALYSIS. To do this, place a cassette recorder nearby, either at home or in the office, and leave it on for about 45 minutes to an hour while you interact with other people. Then play the cassette to hear what your voice sounds like when you communicate verbally with others. Be especially alert for verbal cues that send a negative message or seem to be misinterpreted by the other people involved. Also, listen carefully to the manner in which others respond to you. Do their words or voice tone seem different from what you expected? Did they seem to respond to your comments in a way that shows confusion, frustration, or irritation because of what you said or how you said it? If you answer yes to these questions, and this occurs several times on the tape, go back to the people involved in the conversation and ask them to help you interpret what's on the tape. You may find that your communication style is doing more to hurt than help in gathering information and building relationships with others.

GREET CUSTOMERS WARMLY AND SINCERELY

If appropriate, shake hands, smile often, and offer a sincere welcome, not the canned "Welcome to . . . ." Instead, use whatever your organizational policy dictates, such as, "Good morning/afternoon, welcome to . . . . My name is . . . . How may I assist (or help) you?"

Even on the telephone you should smile and verbally "shake your customer's hand," because your smile can definitely be heard in your voice. Be conscious of the need to sound approachable and receptive.

USE CUSTOMER-FOCUSED LANGUAGE

A mistake by many service providers is to communicate as if they are the important element of a transaction. In reality, it is the customer upon whom a message should be focused. The following examples show the difference in focus:

Provider-Centered

- As soon as I have time …
- I'll send out a form that we need you to complete and sign.
- Let me explain the benefits of this product.

Customer-Centered

- I'll take care of that right away.
- To make sure that we have all the information needed to ensure you the best service, once you get the form, please complete and sign it.
- As a savvy consumer, you'll appreciate the benefits of this product. May I explain?

MAKE CUSTOMERS FEEL WELCOME

Most people like to feel as if they belong, to be recognized as special, and to be seen as individuals. Know the customer's name when possible. Use it in greeting him or her, several times throughout the conversation, and when closing the encounter. Try to avoid using negative-sounding "you" messages as a primary means of addressing your customer. For example, instead of "You'll need to fill out this form before I can process your refund," try "Mr. Renaldi, can you please provide some information on this form while I start processing your refund? That way, we'll have you out of here quickly." The latter approach makes it sound as if you recognize customers as being important, respect their time, and are not

CUSTOMER SERVICE SUCCESS TIP

When the telephone rings, mentally "shift gears" before answering. Stop doing other tasks, clear your head of other thoughts, focus on the telephone, then cheerfully and professionally answer the call.

dictating to them. This can often mean the difference between a smile from your customer and a confrontation and demand to speak to a supervisor.

Many companies go out of their way to send the message of "family." For example, the Saturn automobile company advertisements tout that customers become part of the "Saturn family" once they buy a car from the company. Similarly, CarMax and several other national automobile chains go to great lengths to make the customer feel welcome and special. For example, they drape a huge ribbon over a newly purchased vehicle in a well-lit garage, available sales representatives gather with the customer to congratulate him or her on being part of the "family," and photographs are taken of this "special moment."

USE EYE CONTACT EFFECTIVELY

In addition to greeting the customer, make regular eye contact (normally no longer than three to five seconds at a time) and assume a positive approachable posture throughout your interaction with a customer. More discussion on the topics of eye contact and nonverbal communication appears in Chapter 4.

LISTEN CAREFULLY AND RESPOND APPROPRIATELY

Listening is the key element of two-way verbal communication. The manner in which you listen and respond often determines the direction of the conversation. When customers feel that they are not being listened to, their attitude and emotions can quickly change from amiable to confrontational. If necessary, review Chapter 5 for specific suggestions on effective listening.

BE SPECIFIC

Whenever you have to answer questions, especially details relating to costs, delivery dates, warranties, and other important areas of customer interest, give complete and accurate details. If you leave something out, possibly because you believe it isn't important, you can bet that the customer may feel it was important, and will be upset.

Examples   If deliveries are free, but only within a 50-mile radius, make sure that you tell the customer about the mileage policy. (The customer may live 51 miles away!) If a customer calls to ask for the price of an item and your quote does not include tax, shipping, and handling, say so. Give the total cost, so that there are no surprises when the customer drives to the store to make the purchase or orders from your website and ends up paying more.

USE POSITIVE "I" OR "WE" MESSAGES

"I" or "we" messages
Messages that are potentially less offensive than the word "you," which is like nonverbal finger pointing when emotions are high.

In addition to avoiding the "you" statements mentioned earlier, focus on what "I" or "we" can do for or with the customer. In addressing the customer, state the specific service approaches you will take, for example, "I'll handle this personally," as opposed to "I'll do my best" or "I'll try." Expressions like "I'll handle this personally" sound proactive and positive. **"I" or "we" messages** go a long way in subtly letting the customer know that you have the knowledge, confidence, and authority to help out.

USE "SMALL TALK"

Look for opportunities to communicate on a personal level or to compliment your customer. If you promptly establish a professional relationship with your customers, they are less likely to attack you verbally or complain. Listen to what they say. Look for specific things that you have in common. For example, suppose your customer mentions that she has just returned form Altoona, Pennsylvania, where she visited relatives. If you grew up in or near Altoona, comment about this and ask questions. By bonding with the customer, you show that you recognize the customer as more than a nameless face or a prospective sale.

One thing to keep in mind about **small talk** is that you must listen to your customer's words and tone. If it is obvious he or she is impatient or in a hurry, skip the small talk and focus on efficiently providing service.

USE SIMPLE LANGUAGE

Many interpersonal impartation decompositions can be ascribed to one singular customer service professional fallacy—that all customers can discern the significance of the employee's vernacular. Simply stated, *Many customer service professionals fail to use language their customers can understand.*

When dealing with customers, especially if you are selling or servicing in a technical field, use terms and explanations that are easily understood. Watch the customer's nonverbal body language for signs of confusion or frustration as you speak, and frequently ask for feedback and questions.

If you are on the telephone, listen for sounds of confusion or pauses that may indicate that the customer either did not understand something you said or has a question.

PARAPHRASE

To ensure that you get the message the customer intended to communicate, take time to ask for feedback. Do this by repeating to the customer the message you heard, but in your own words—**paraphrase.** An example would be, "If I understand the problem, Mrs. Hawthorne, you bought this item on June 28 as a present for your son. When he tried to assemble it, two parts were missing. Is that correct?"

ASK POSITIVELY PHRASED QUESTIONS

Sometimes the simplest things can cause problems, especially if someone is already irritated. To avoid creating a negative situation or escalating customer emotions, choose the wording of your questions carefully. Consider these two specific techniques.

The first is to find a way to rephrase any question that you would normally start with "Why?" The reason is that this word cannot be inflected in a way that doesn't come across as potentially abrasive, intrusive, or meddlesome. As with many experiences you have, the origin of negative feelings toward the word likely stem from childhood. Remember when you wanted to do something as a child and were told no? The word that probably came out of your mouth (in a whiney voice) was "Why?" This was a verbal challenge to the person who was telling you that you couldn't do something. And the response you probably heard was "Because I said so" or "Because I'm the mommy (or daddy), that's why." Most likely, you didn't like that type of response then, and neither did your customers when they were children. The result of this early experience is that when we hear the word *why,* it can sound like a challenge and can prompt a negative emotional reaction. To prevent this from occurring, try rewording your "Why" questions.

Look for opportunities to communicate in a friendly atmosphere. *Do you think a friendly conversation can facilitate working through a conflict or problem?*

small talk
Dialogue used to enhance relationships, show civility, and build rapport.

paraphrase
The practice of a message receiver giving back in his or her own words what he or she believes a sender said.

Examples

Instead of	Try
Why do you feel that way?	What makes you feel that way?
Why don't you like … ?	What is it that you don't like about … ?
Why do you need that feature?	How is that feature going to be beneficial to you?
Why do you want that color?	What other colors have you considered?

The second technique to consider regarding question phrasing is to ask questions that do not create or add to a negative impression. This is especially important if you have a customer who is already saying negative things about you, your product, or service, or the company. By asking questions that start with a negative word and trying to lead customers to an answer, you can be subtly adding fuel to an emotional fire.

For example, suppose your customer is upset because he ordered window blinds through the mail and did not get the color he wanted. He has called you to complain. You have asked a few questions to determine the color scheme of the room in which the blinds will be installed. You say, "Based on what you have told me, don't you think the color you received would work just as well?" Your customer now launches into a tirade. He probably thinks that you were not listening to him, were not concerned about his needs, and presumed you could lead him to another decision.

Here are some more examples of questions that could cause communication breakdowns, along with some suggested alternatives.

Examples

Instead of	Try
Don't you think … ?	What do you think … ?
Wouldn't this work as well?	How do you think this would work?
Couldn't we do … instead?	Could we try … instead?
Aren't you going to make a deposit?	What amount would you like to deposit?
Don't you have two pennies?	Do you have two pennies?
Shouldn't you try this for a week before we replace the part again?	How do you feel about trying it for a week to see how it works before we replace the part again?

ASK PERMISSION

Get customer approval before taking action that was not previously approved or discussed, such as putting a telephone caller on hold or interrupting. By doing so, you can raise the customers to a position of authority, boost their self-esteem, and empower them (to say yes or no). They'll likely appreciate all three. You'll learn more about telephone etiquette and effective usage in Chapter 9.

AGREE WITH CUSTOMERS

Like most other people, customers like to hear that they are right. This is especially true when a mistake has been made or something goes wrong. When a customer has a complaint or is upset because a product and/or service does not live up to expectations, acknowledge the emotion he or she is feeling and then move on and help resolve the issue. Defusing by acknowledgment is a powerful tool.

However, listen carefully for the level of emotion. If the customer is very angry, you may want to choose your words carefully. For example, suppose you have a customer who has called or returned to your store on four occasions to address a single problem with a product. She has been inconvenienced, has not gotten satisfaction in the previous encounters, and has spent extra time in an effort to correct the problem. When she calls or arrives, her voice tone and volume are elevated and she is demanding that you get a supervisor. In this situation, your best approach probably is to let her vent and describe the problem without interrupting, apologize as often as appropriate, and do everything you can to resolve the issue fairly (assuming that she has a legitimate complaint). You would not want to use a statement that could further enflame her.

Although phrases such as, "You sound upset Ms. O'Malley," or "I can understand how you feel" can help diffuse some tense situations, they can come across as patronizing and insincere when someone is really angry (such as in the above example). Instead of using such terminology, try looking for something she is saying that you can agree with. Also, remember that when customers get angry, raise their voices, and say certain things, they are not typically angry with you—they are frustrated and angry with the organization and/or system. Try not to become defensive or sound irritated, since this will likely only escalate the customer's emotions.

For example, suppose Ms. O'Malley says something like, "You people are a bunch of idiots. I've been coming in here for years and I always have problems. Why don't you hire someone with brains to serve your customers?" The normal human response would be to retaliate. However, think back on what happened when you were a child at the playground. When someone pushed you or called you a name and you responded with name-calling or pushed back, emotions escalated until someone either struck out or ran away crying. No one won. The relationship was damaged, possibly irreparably.

In the case of Ms. O'Malley, if you strike back with similar comments, neither of you will win. Moreover, you will likely lose a valued customer who will tell her story to many friends—and you will have to explain to your boss why you acted the way you did. Instead, try a defusing technique in which you seek something to agree upon. For example, you might reply, "I know this is frustrating, especially when it seems we haven't done a good job solving your problem." After this, assuming she doesn't launch back in with another tirade, you might then offer, "Let me help you take care of this right now." If she does verbally attack again, let her vent and then try another calm agreement response, followed by a second offer to assist. The key is to remain professional and in control of your emotions so that you can find a suitable resolution to the issue.

The value in this approach is that in letting Ms. O'Malley vent, you are discovering her emotions and possibly the history of the problem by listening actively. If you need more information, you can ask questions once you have defused her emotions and she calms down a bit. Typically, if you remain calm and objective and look for minor things with which you can agree, the customer will back off. Also, the customer may likely start to see that she is the one out of control and that you are being professional while trying to help her. If the customer truly wants the problem to be solved, she soon realizes that cooperation with you is necessary.

In many cases, if you resolve the customer's problem professionally, the customer will often apologize for his or her actions and words.

ELICIT CUSTOMER FEEDBACK AND PARTICIPATION

Make customers feel as if they are a part of the conversation by asking questions. Ask opinions, find out how they feel about what you're doing or saying, and get them involved by building **rapport** through ongoing dialogue. Acknowledge their ideas, suggestions, or information with statements such as, "That's a good idea (or suggestion or decision)." This will foster a feeling that the two of you are working together to solve a problem. The beauty of such an approach is that if the customer comes up with an idea and you follow through on it, he or she feels a sense of ownership and is less likely to complain later or feel bad if things don't work out as planned.

rapport
The silent bond built between two people as a result of sharing of common interests and issues and demonstration of a win-win, I care attitude.

CLOSE THE TRANSACTION PROFESSIONALLY

Instead of some parroted response used for each customer like, "Have a nice day," offer a sincere "Thank you" and encourage the customer to return in the future. Remember, part of a service culture is building customer loyalty.

ADDRESS PET PEEVES

Most people have something that bothers them about how others communicate or behave. These "hot buttons," or **pet peeves,** can lead to customer relationship breakdowns if you are not aware of what your pet peeves are and how you come across to others. By identifying and acknowledging your potential irritants, you can begin to modify your behavior in order to prevent problems with customers. You may also be able to avoid situations in which such behaviors are present or might manifest themselves and cause problems for you.

pet peeves
Refers to factors, people, or situations that personally irritate or frustrate a service provider and which, left unchecked, can create a breakdown in effective service.

Your customers also likely have a list of things that they dislike about service providers. If you exhibit one of their pet peeves while serving them, you could find yourself opposite a disgruntled person who is not afraid to voice his or her displeasure. They may even escalate their complaint to your supervisor or elsewhere.

Some typical behaviors that service providers exhibit, and that might bother customers, include:

Disinterest in serving

Excessive wait times

Unprofessional service provider appearance

Lack of cleanliness (environment or service provider)

Abruptly putting someone on telephone hold without their permission

Failing to answer telephone within four rings

Eating or chewing while dealing with a customer

Lack of knowledge or authority

Poor quality of service

Condescension (taking an air of superiority to the customer)

Rudeness or overfamiliarity (using first names without permission)

5   PROVIDING FEEDBACK

Concept: Your feedback could affect the relationship you have or are building with your customers. The effect may be positive or negative, depending on the content and delivery.

Feeling Special

THINK OF TIMES WHEN YOU HAVE BEEN PUT ON HOLD OR STOOD IN A LINE.

1. How did the service provider address you when it was your turn for service?

2. Did you feel special or did you feel like the next in a long line of bodies being processed? Why?

3. When the service provider simply picked up the phone and offered to assist you or shouted "Next" while you waited in line, what thoughts went through your mind about the provider and the organization?

4. What could service providers do or say to eliminate negative customer feelings in such situations?

Feedback is a response to messages a listener receives. This response may be transmitted verbally (with words) or nonverbally (through actions or inaction). Depending on the content and delivery, your feedback could positively or negatively influence your relationships with your customers. Figure 3.4 offers some tips on providing feedback effectively, and the two types of feedback are discussed in the following sections.

VERBAL FEEDBACK

The words you choose when providing feedback to your customers are crucial to interpretation and understanding. Before providing feedback, you should take into consideration the knowledge and skill level of your customer(s). This is part of the "encoding" discussed earlier in the "Interpersonal Communication Model" discussed earlier in this chapter. Failure to consider the customer could result in breakdowns in understanding. For example, if you choose words that are not likely to be part of your customer's vocabulary, because of the customer's education and/or experience, your message may be confusing. Also, if you use acronyms or technical terms (jargon or words unfamiliar to the customer), the meaning of the message could get lost. When providing **verbal feedback,** you should also be conscious of how your customer is receiving your information. If the customer's body language or nonverbal cues (gestures, facial expressions) or words indicate misunderstanding, you should pause, and take any corrective action necessary to clear up the confusion.

verbal feedback
The response given to a sender's message that allows both the sender and receiver to know that a message was received correctly.

FIGURE 3.4

Guidelines for Providing Positive Feedback

Here are 10 tips for effectively providing feedback:

1. When appropriate, give feedback immediately when communicating face to face or over the telephone.

2. Communicate in a clear, concise manner.

3. Remain objective and unemotional when providing feedback.

4. Make sure that your feedback is accurate before you provide it.

5. Use verbal and nonverbal messages that are in congruence (agree with each other).

6. Verify the customer's meaning before providing feedback.

7. Make sure that your feedback is appropriate to the customer's original message (active listening helps in getting the original message).

8. Strive to clarify feedback when the customer seems unclear of your intention.

9. Avoid overly critical feedback or negative language (as described in this chapter).

10. Do not provide feedback if it could damage the customer-provider relationship.

CUSTOMER SERVICE SUCCESS TIP

To check your perception of nonverbal cues received from others so that you can respond appropriately, use the following process:

1. *Identify the behavior observed. Example: "Mr. Warlinkowski, when I said that it would be seven to ten days before we could get your new sofa delivered to your home, your facial expression changed to what appeared to be one of concern."*

2. *Offer one or two interpretations. Example: "I wasn't sure whether you were indicating that the time frame doesn't work for you, or whether something else went through your mind."*

3. *Ask for clarification. Example: "Which was it?"*

By asking for clarification, you reduce the chance of having a dissatisfied customer. You also send a message that you are paying attention to the customer.

nonverbal feedback
Messages sent to someone through other than spoken means. Examples are gestures, appearance, and facial expressions.

assertiveness
Involves projecting a presence that is assured, confident, and capable without seeming to be aggressive or arrogant.

NONVERBAL FEEDBACK

Nonverbal feedback will be explored in depth in Chapter 4. Here are a few ways in which feedback can be given nonverbally.

Body Language   The ways in which you sit, stand, gesture, position your body (face-to-face or at an angle), or use facial expressions can all send positive or negative messages.

6   DEALING ASSERTIVELY WITH CUSTOMERS

Concept: Express ideas simply without weakening your position.

Your level of **assertiveness** is directly tied to your style of behavior. Some people are direct and to the point; others are calm and laid back. Neither style is better or worse than the other. What is important is to be able to recognize which style to call upon in various situations. You will explore behavioral styles in detail in Chapter 6.

Generally, assertive communication deals with expressing ideas positively and with confidence. An example would be to stand or sit erect, make direct eye contact, smile, listen empathetically, and then calmly and firmly nod and explain what you can do to assist the customer.

Figure 3.5 lists several examples of nonassertive and assertive language and behaviors. Additional resources are listed in the Bibliography.

The following list contains examples of nonassertive and assertive language and behaviors, along with tips for increasing your assertiveness.

Nonassertive	Assertive
• Poor eye contact while speaking.	• Look customer in the eye as you speak.
• Weak ("limp fish") handshake.	• Grasp firmly without crushing (web of your hand against web of the other person's hand).
• Use of verbal paralanguage (ah, um, you know).	• Stop, gather thoughts, speak.
• Apologetic in words and tone.	• Apologize if you make a mistake (I'm sorry, please forgive me), then take control and move on with the conversation.
• Soft, subdued tone.	• Increase volume, sound firm and convincing.
• Finger pointing; blaming others.	• Take responsibility; resolve the problem.
• Nervous gestures, fidgeting.	• Hold something; grasp a table or chair; fold your hands as you talk.
• Indecisive or unsure.	• Know your products and services. If possible, prepare a list of points, comments, or questions before calling or meeting with your customer(s).
• Rambling speech, not really stating a specific question or information.	• Think, plan, and then speak.

FIGURE 3.5   **Nonassertive and Assertive Behaviors**

Perceptions Are Reality

TO EMPHASIZE THAT DIFFERENT PEOPLE OFTEN HAVE DIFFERENT PERCEPTIONS OF WHAT THEY SEE, AND THE IMPORTANCE OF APPEARANCE, LOOK AT THE PHOTOGRAPHS OF THE PEOPLE BELOW. Honestly describe your reactions to and perceptions of each as asked below. Once finished, compare your responses to those of fellow students.

1. What are your perceptions?
2. Explain why you have these perceptions.
3. How might your perception affect your ability to effectively serve this person?

1. What are your perceptions?
2. Explain why you have these perceptions.
3. How might your perception affect your ability to effectively serve this person?

1. What are your perceptions?
2. Explain why you have these perceptions.
3. How might your perception affect your ability to effectively serve this person?

1. What are your perceptions?
2. Explain why you have these perceptions.
3. How might your perception affect your ability to effectively serve this person?

1. What are your perceptions?
2. Explain why you have these perceptions.
3. How might your perception affect your ability to effectively serve this person?

1. What are your perceptions?
2. Explain why you have these perceptions.
3. How might your perception affect your ability to effectively serve this person?

1. What are your perceptions?
2. Explain why you have these perceptions.
3. How might your perception affect your ability to effectively serve this person?

1. What are your perceptions?
2. Explain why you have these perceptions.
3. How might your perception affect your ability to effectively serve this person?

7   ASSERTIVE VERSUS AGGRESSIVE SERVICE

Concept: Assertive service is good for solving problems; aggressive service may escalate them.

Do not confuse assertive with aggressive service. Why is the distinction so important in customer service? What's the difference? The answer: Assertiveness can assist in solving problems; aggression can escalate and cause relationship breakdowns. Asserting yourself means that you project an image of confidence, are self-assured, and state what you believe to be true in a self-confident manner. Aggression involves hostile or offensive behavior, often in the form of a verbal or even physical attack. Aggressive people send messages verbally and nonverbally that imply that they are superior, or in charge. They often do this through behavior and language that is manipulative, judgmental, or domineering. An assertive person states (verbally and nonverbally), "Here's my position. What's your reaction to that?" An aggressive person sends the message, "Here is my position. Take it or leave it."

Obviously, the two modes of dealing with customers create very different service experiences. The manner in which you nonverbally or verbally approach, address, and interact with customers may label you as either assertive or aggressive. Consider the following interactions between a customer and a service provider:

Assertive Behavior Example

Customer (returning an item of merchandise): Excuse me, I received this sweater as a present and I'd like to return it.

Service Provider (smiling): Is there something wrong with it?

Customer (still smiling): Oh no. I just don't need another sweater.

Service Provider (still smiling): Do you have a receipt?

Customer (not smiling): No. As I said, it was a gift.

Service Provider (handing over a form): That's all right. To help me process your refund a bit faster for you, could you please provide a bit of information and sign this form?

Customer (not smiling): Does this mean I have to get out of line and then wait again? I've already been in line for 10 minutes.

Service Provider (smiling): Well, rather than delay the line, if you could step over to that table to fill out the form, and then bring it back to me, I'll take care of you. You won't have to wait in line again.

Customer (smiling): Okay, thanks.

In this example, the service provider is trying to assure the customer, through words and body language, that he or she is there to assist the customer.

Aggressive Service Example

Customer (returning an item of merchandise): Excuse me, I received this sweater as a present and I'd like to return it.

Service Provider (not smiling): What's wrong with it?

Customer (smiling): Oh nothing, I just don't need another sweater.

Service Provider (still not smiling): Do you have a receipt?

Customer (not smiling): No. As I said, it was a gift.

Service Provider (handing over a form): Well, our policy requires that you'll have to fill out this form since you don't have a receipt.

Customer (not smiling): Does that mean I have to get out of line and then wait again? I've already been in line for 10 minutes.

Improving Feedback Skills

To STRENGTHEN YOUR ABILITY TO PROVIDE FEEDBACK, WORK WITH TWO OTHER PEOPLE (ONE PARTNER AND ONE OBSERVER) TO PRACTICE YOUR SKILL IN DELIVERING FEEDBACK.

Select a topic for discussion (e.g., a vacation, career goals, or positive or negative customer experiences).

Spend 10 minutes talking about your selected topic with your partner.

During the conversation, you and your partner should use verbal and nonverbal feedback.

At the end of the 10 minutes, ask your partner, and then the observer, the following questions.

1. How did I do in providing appropriate verbal feedback? Give examples.
2. How did I do in providing appropriate nonverbal feedback? Give examples.
3. How well did I interpret verbal and nonverbal messages? Give examples.
4. What questions did I ask to clarify comments or feedback provided? Give examples.
5. What could I have done to improve my feedback?

Service Provider (not smiling): The line's getting shorter. It shouldn't take long. Next …

In this example, the service provider is not doing well on service delivery, nor is he or she projecting a positive image. The nonverbal and verbal messages convey an almost hostile attitude. This type of behavior can easily escalate into an unnecessary confrontation.

RESPONDING TO CONFLICT

Conflict should be viewed as neither positive nor negative. Instead, it is an opportunity to identify differences that may need to be addressed when dealing with your internal and external customers. It is not unusual for you to experience conflict when dealing with someone else. In fact, it is normal and beneficial as long as you stay focused on the issue rather than personalizing and internalizing the conflict. When you focus on the individual, or vice versa, conflict can escalate and can ultimately do irreparable damage to the relationship. Figure 3.6 describes various forms of conflict.

Conflict typically results when you and someone else disagree about something. The following are examples of five forms of conflict that might occur in your organization.

Between individuals. You and your supervisor (or another employee) disagree on the way a customer situation should be handled.

Between an individual and a group. You disagree about a new customer procedure created by your work team.

Between an individual and an organization. A dissatisfied customer feels that your organization is not providing quality products or services.

Between organizational groups. Your department has goals (for example, the way customer orders or call handling procedures are processed) that create additional requirements or responsibilities for members of another department.

Between organizations. Your organization is targeting the same customers to sell a new product similar to one that an affiliate organization markets to that group.

FIGURE 3.6   Forms of Conflict

CUSTOMER SERVICE SUCCESS TIP (continued)

Gestures. Use open gestures with arms and hands. Gesture with open palms, as opposed to pointing.

Eye contact. Maintain intermittent eye contact as you smile. Avoid squinting or glaring.

Win-win solutions. Work toward mutual understanding and the attainment of resolutions that allow the organization and the customer to succeed.

Aggressive behavior can lead to relationship failure. When someone verbally attacks another, the chances of emotions escalating and relationships failing increase significantly. How can you avoid aggressive behavior in a relationship?

Aggressive behavior can lead to relationship failure. When someone verbally attacks another, the chances of emotions escalating and relationships failing increase significantly. *How can you avoid aggressive behavior in a relationship?*

conflict

Involves incompatible or opposing views and can result when a customer's needs, desires, or demands do not match service provider or organizational policies, procedures, and abilities.

CAUSES OF CONFLICT

There are many causes of conflict. The following are some common ones.

Conflicting values and beliefs. These sometime create situations in which the perceptions of an issue or its impact vary. Since values and beliefs have been learned over long periods of time and are often taken personally at face value, individuals get very defensive when their foundations are challenged. For example, you have been taught that stealing is not only illegal, but also morally wrong. One of your coworkers regularly takes pens, paper, and other administrative supplies home for his child to take to school. His logic is that "they (the organization) are a big company and can afford it." You disagree.

Personal style differences. As you will read in Chapter 6, each person is different and requires special consideration and a unique approach in interactions. For example, your supervisor has a high D style, is very focused, and typically wants to know only the bottom line in any conversation. You have a high E style and find it difficult to share information without providing a lot of details in a highly emotional fashion. When the two of you speak, this can lead to conflict unless one or both of you are aware of the other's style and are willing to adapt your communication style.

Differing perceptions. People often witness or view an incident or issue differently. This can cause disagreement, frustration, and a multitude of other emotional feelings. For example, an employee (Sue) tells you that she is upset because a deadline was missed because another employee (Fred) did not effectively manage his time. Fred later commented to you that your supervisor pulled him off the project in question in order to work on another assignment. This resulted in his missing the original assignment deadline and a perception by Sue that he could not manage time.

Inadequate or poor communication. Any time there is inadequate communication, the chance for conflict escalates. For example, a coworker (Leonard) confides to you that he may have forgotten to tell a customer about limitations on your organization's return policy. As a result, when the customer brought a product back to return it, another coworker had to deal with a frustrated and angry customer.

Contrary expectations. When one party expects something not provided by another, conflict will likely result. For example, your company offers a 90-day parts-only warranty on equipment that you sell; however, when it breaks down within that period, the customer expects free service also. If that expectation is not met, you have to deal with conflict and the customer is potentially dissatisfied.

Inadequate communication. People generally like to know what to expect and do not want a lot of surprises from their supervisor. When they get mixed signals because of inconsistency, frustration and conflict could result. For example, your supervisor told the entire service staff that in the future, each employee would have an opportunity to earn bonuses based on how many customers they could convince to upgrade their membership in the organization. You believe that you have sold the most for the month, yet when you point this out to your supervisor, he tells you that the bonus applies only if you have high sales for two months in a row.

Goals that are out of sync with reality.   Frustration and resentment can result from misaligned efforts. For example, you have been working as a service technician for over a year and have learned that, on average, it takes about 1½ hours to install a new telephone line. Your supervisor regularly counsels you because you do not accomplish the feat within the goal of 1 hour.

Opposition over shared resources.   When two people or groups vie for the same resources, conflict usually results. For example, all monies for employee training are lumped into a central training budget in your organization. You have been requesting to go to a customer service training skills program for the past six months; however, you are told that there is only enough money to train people from the technical staff to learn new computer software.

Outcomes dependent on others.   Whenever you have two or more people, departments, teams, or organizations working jointly toward goal attainment, the potential for conflict exists. For example, your department receives customer orders over the telephone, and then forwards them to the fulfillment department for processing and order shipment. If the fulfillment process breaks down, a customer has your name and number, and he or she typically contacts you. If the customer is unhappy, it is you who has to placate him or her and spend time resolving the conflict.

Misuse of power.   Resentment, frustration, and retaliation often result when employees believe that their supervisor is abusing his or her authority or power. For example, you overhear your supervisor telling an attractive employee that unless certain sexual favors are granted, she will not receive a desired promotion.

There are various ways you can deal effectively with conflict. Figure 3.7 gives some guidelines.

SALVAGING RELATIONSHIPS AFTER CONFLICT

Managing conflict involves more than just resolving the disagreement. If you fail to address the emotional and psychological needs of those involved, you may find the conflict returning and/or severe damage to the relationship may occur.

Depending on the severity of the conflict and how it was handled at each step of the resolution process, it may be impossible to go back to the relationship as it was before the disagreement. The key to reducing this possibility is to identify and address conflicting issues as early as possible. The longer an issue remains unresolved, the more damage it can cause. Whenever possible, apply one or more of the following strategies to help protect and salvage the relationship(s) between you and your coworkers, supervisor, and customers.

- *Reaffirm the value of the relationship.*   You cannot assume that others feel the same as you or understand your intent unless you communicate it. Tell them how much you value your relationship. This is especially important when dealing with customers. Recall the statistics from Chapter 1 about how many dissatisfied customers typically tell others about the experience and damage can be done to the organizations reputation.
- *Demonstrate commitment.*   You must verbalize and demonstrate your desire to continue or strengthen your relationship. The way to do this with customers is through service recovery (see Chapter 1 for definition), which will be addressed in detail in Chapter 7.

FIGURE 3.7

Guidelines for Effective Conflict Management

Even though each situation and person you deal with will differ, there are some basic approaches that may help in resolution of disagreement(s). Try the following strategies.

- *Remain calm.* You cannot be part of the solution if you become part of the problem. If you are one of the factors contributing to the conflict, consider getting an objective third party to arbitrate; possibly a coworker or your supervisor.

- *Be proactive in avoiding conflict.* As a customer service representative for your organization, you must try to recognize the personalities of those with whom you come into contact daily. If you are dealing with coworkers or peers, try to identify their capabilities and the environments most conducive to their effectiveness. If you are interacting with a customer, use verbal and nonverbal techniques discussed here and in Chapter 4 to help determine the customer's needs. Approach each person in a fashion that can lead to win/win situations; do not set yourself or others up for conflict or failure.

- *Keep an open mind.* Be cautious in order to avoid letting your own values or beliefs influence your objectivity when working toward conflict identification and resolution. As you will read later, this can cause damage to your long-term relationship(s).

- *Identify and confront underlying issues immediately.* Because of the emotional issues often involved in dealing with problem situations, few people enjoy dealing with conflict. However, if you fail to acknowledge and confront issues as soon as they become known, tensions may escalate.

- *Clarify communication.* Ensure that you elicit information on the causes of the conflict and provide the clear, detailed feedback necessary to resolve the issue. This effort can sometimes test your patience and communication skills, but it is a necessary step in the resolution process.

- *Stress cooperation rather than competition.* One of your roles as a service provider is to ensure that you work toward common goals with your coworkers, supervisor, and customers. When one person succeeds at the expense of another's failure, you have not done your job. Encourage and develop teamwork and cooperation when dealing with others.

- *Focus resolution efforts on the issues.* Do not get caught up in or allow finger pointing, name calling, or accusations. Keep all efforts and discussions directed toward identifying and resolving the real issue(s). Stay away from criticizing or blaming others.

- *Follow established procedures for handling conflict.* It is easier to implement a process already in place than to have to quickly come up with one. That is why most customer service organizations have set customer complaint handling procedures.

- *Be realistic.* Because of behavioral styles, it is difficult for some people to "forgive and forget." You have to systematically help restore their trust. It can take a while to accomplish this, but the effort is well worth it.

- *Remain flexible.* A solid relationship involves the ability to give and take. It is especially crucial that you and the other people involved make concessions following conflict.

- *Keep communication open.* One of the biggest causes of conflict and destroyed relationships is poor communication.

- *Gain commitment.* You cannot do it all by yourself. Get a commitment to work toward reconciliation from any other person(s) involved in the conflict.

- *Monitor progress.* Do not assume that, because the conflict was resolved, it will remain that way. Deep-seated issues often resurface, especially when commitment was not obtained. With customers, be sure to do the follow-up that you have read about in earlier chapters.

Providing service that makes a customer feel special can lead to customer satisfaction and loyalty to you and your organization. By responding appropriately and in a positive manner (verbally and non-verbally), you will increase your likelihood of success. When additional information is needed, it is up to you to ask questions that will elicit useful customer feedback. You must then interpret and respond in kind with feedback that lets the customer know you received the intended message. You must also let your customers know that you'll take action on their needs or requests.

assertiveness 74
channel 63
conflict 77
decoding 64
encoding 63
feedback 64
filters 64
global terms 64
"I" or "we" messages 68
message 63

noise 64
nonverbal feedback 74
paraphrase 69
pet peeves 72
rapport 71
receiver 63
sender 63
small talk 69
two-way communication 62
verbal feedback 73

1   What are some things you can do as a customer service professional to project a positive image to the customer?

2   What element(s) of the interpersonal communication model do you believe are the most important in a customer service environment? Explain.

3   What are some strategies to use in order to avoid words or phrases that will negatively affect your relationship with your customer?

4   What are some of the tips outlined in this chapter for ensuring effective customer interactions?

5   What is feedback?

6   How can verbal feedback affect customer encounters?

7   Give some examples of nonverbal feedback and explain how they complement the verbal message and how they can affect customer interactions.

8   List at least five tips for providing positive feedback.

Search the Web for Information on Verbal Communication

Log on to the Internet to research topics related to verbal communication, such as those presented in this chapter. Use various search engines (Yahoo.com, Google.com, and Excite.com); your results will be different with each. Look for one or more of the following, print out pages you feel are helpful, and be prepared to share your findings with your peers in class. Some possible topics are:

Assertiveness
Conflict resolution

Interpersonal communication
Learning styles
Nonverbal feedback
Positive image
Questioning
Two-way communication
Verbal feedback

COLLABORATIVE LEARNING ACTIVITY

Role-Playing to Improve Verbal Communication

Find a partner and use the following role-plays to improve your verbal communication skills. After reading the scenarios, pick the two for which you want the most feedback. Next, take a moment to think about how each of you will play your part and then have a two- or three-minute dialogue centering on the situation.

For the four scenarios, alternate roles with your partner: each of you should role-play twice, and each of you will be the debriefer twice. If possible, videotape or audiotape the conversation. This will allow each of you to see or hear how you seem when you interact with others. After the role-play, discuss how each of you felt about the way the other person handled the situation. Each of you should ask the other these questions about your own performance:

What did I do well?

What did I not do so well?

What can I do to improve in the future?

Scenario 1

You are a customer service professional in a dry cleaner's shop. A customer who has been coming in for years stops by with a silk shirt that has a stain that, according to him, was not there before the most recent dry cleaning. He is upset because the garment is expensive and was to have been worn to a class reunion yesterday.

Scenario 2

You are a member services representative in an automobile club that provides maps, trip information, towing and travel services, and a variety of travel-related products. A member has stopped by to find out whether she can get a replacement membership card and assistance in planning an upcoming vacation.

Scenario 3

You are a counter clerk in a fast-food restaurant. It is lunchtime, and the restaurant is full of patrons. As you are taking an order from a customer, a second customer steps to the front of the line, interrupts the first customer, and demands a replacement sandwich because the one she received is not what she ordered.

Scenario 4

As a clerk in a local video rental store, you see many of the same patrons regularly and have a fairly good relationship with many of them. One of the regular customers has just come in to rent a video but is not sure what he wants. You must determine his needs and properly assist him. Be sure to ask probing, open-ended questions, phrased positively, to help you get the information you need.

FACE TO FACE

Seeking Information from a Client

Background

LKM Graphics has been in business in Norfolk, Virginia, for almost five years. The company employs 17 full-time employees in its graphic design department, a part-time administrative assistant, and three interns from Old Dominion University's graphic arts program. During a typical week, LKM prints 300,000 to 400,000 documents for businesses in the surrounding Tidewater metropolitan area. Most clients have 15 or fewer employees, although there are two active and ongoing government contracts with the Naval Operations Base, which is nearby. The owner of LKM, Linda McLaroy, hired you three years ago when you graduated from the graphic arts program. You are now one of the senior graphics account managers with the company and supervise four other team members.

Your Role

As a quality control measure, each month you are required to visit the clients assigned to your region. During those visits, you are to answer questions, deliver completed orders, verify customer satisfaction, collect feedback data, and look for new orders. On a recent visit to Brickman Bakery, you met the new office manager, Sylvia Greco. You had been told by a friend who works at Brickman's that Sylvia is considering closing her account with LKM Graphics and moving it to a competitor. Before joining Brickman's last month, she had been employed by another organization in the area and had developed a strong relationship with your competitor. Since she is comfortable with the competitor's operation and has friends there, she wants to maintain the relationship. You've also heard through the grapevine that Sylvia prefers to work with your competitor's account representative.

Critical Thinking Questions

1 Since you don't have a relationship with Sylvia, what will you do to get off to a solid start during your visit?

2 How should you approach Sylvia verbally and nonverbally?

3 What strategies among the ones discussed in this chapter can you use to find out where you and LKM stand in Sylvia's mind?

Using the content of this chapter as a guide, create a Personal Action Plan focused on improving your verbal communication skills when providing service to your customers. Begin by taking an objective assessment of your current verbal communication strengths and areas for improvement. Once you have identified areas that need improvement, set goals for improvement.

Start your assessment by listing as many strengths and areas for improvement as you are aware of. Share your list with other people who know you well to see if they agree or can add additional items. Keep in mind that you will likely be more critical of yourself than will others. Additionally, you may be sending messages that you are not aware of because of the way you currently communicate. For those reasons, keep an open mind when considering their comments.

Once you have a list, choose two or three items that you think need the most work and can add the most value when interacting with others. List these items on a sheet of paper along with specific courses of action you will take for improvement, the name of someone you will enlist to provide feedback on your behavior, and a specific date by which you want to see improvement. In regard to the date, keep in mind that research shows that it takes on average 21 to 30 days to see behavioral change; therefore, set a date that is at least in this range.

Verbal Communication Strength			Areas for Improvement

Top Three Items	Who Will Help	Date for Change	
1.			
2.			
3.			

- -

RETAIL—Enterprise Rent-A-Car

Think about what you read related to Enterprise Rent-A-Car at the beginning of the chapter and answer the following questions. Your instructor may have you work together and share ideas in a group.

1. Have you been a customer of Enterprise or known anyone who has? What has been your experience or what have you heard about the company?

2. Do you believe Enterprise is truly customer-centric? Why or why not?

3. What do you believe are some of the driving forces behind the Enterprise success? Why?

4. If you were going to rent a car this weekend, would you choose Enterprise? Why or why not?

- -

1	F	5	T	9	F
2	T	6	F	10	F
3	F	7	F	11	T
4	T	8	F	12	F

Ethical Dilemma 3.1 Possible Answers

1   Would you intervene? If so why or why not?

This is a touchy situation because you do not want to usurp your coworker or make it appear that there are differing standards of service provided within the organization. At the same time, your organization's reputation for effectiveness, efficiency, and customer service are all at stake and all employees represent and impact that reputation.

Since it seems that neither your organization nor the customer is at fault in this situation, you may want to intervene in order to deliver quality customer service and to prevent an emotional exchange between the customer and coworker.

2   If you decide to intervene, what would you say or do? Why?

You might say something like the following to the customer. "I'm sure my coworker is going to handle this, but since she had to step away, let me get your copy rather than keep you waiting and cause further inconvenience." By getting the copy, you have satisfied the customer, who has already waited two weeks and now had to make a trip to the office to get resolution of the issue. You have also potentially salvaged the organization's reputation and prevented any type of confrontation between the customer and your coworker.

Of course, you will likely now have to explain to your coworker why you intervened and gave a "free" copy. In that discussion, it is important to put your explanation in terms of how your efforts helped the coworker and sped up service to all customers, since the situation was resolved and the customer left satisfied without becoming emotional. Also, stress that it seemed that neither the organization nor customer was at fault and that you felt it important to deliver a high quality of service to the customer.

Note: To prevent possible future repeats of this type of situation, you may want to bring it up globally (without naming your coworker or pointing fingers) in your next staff meeting. Try to get some guidance on handling similar situations in the future.

Ethical Dilemma 3.2 Possible Answers

1   How would you react to or feel about your supervisor's position?

Depending on how you were reared and the values that were reinforced to you (e.g., personal from your parents and/or religious) the supervisor's stance might be a real demotivator for you and could lead to loss of respect or other feelings toward him/her.

On the other hand, you may share his/her views and reason that you are not harming anything by creating an excuse for failure to deliver to the customer as promised and that they will never know the difference. The downside of such logic is that should they find out the truth, your credibility and that of the organization is at stake and could result in lost business (from the customer and anyone else they tell the story to).

2   Would this cause any change in your relationship with your supervisor? Why or why not?

This is a personal decision that only you can make. In many cases, such behavior on the part of the supervisor could lead to suspicion (e.g., if he or she lies about this type of thing, what else might he or she lie about in the workplace). It could also lead to loss of trust in the supervisor's ability to lead and manage effectively. Additionally, if others find out about what the supervisor said, morale and effectiveness within the organization could suffer. There is likely some value in the adage "honesty is the best policy."

Nonverbal Communication Skills

The most important thing in communication is hearing what isn't said.
—Peter F. Drucker

After completing this chapter, you will be able to:

1   Define nonverbal communication.

2   Recognize various nonverbal cues and their effect on customers.

3   Explain the effect that gender has on communication.

4   Describe the effect of culture on nonverbal communication.

5   Identifying unproductive behaviors.

6   Use a variety of nonverbal communication strategies.

7   Demonstrate specific customer-focused nonverbal behavior.

In the Real World   Retail—Starbucks Corporation

According to the Starbucks website, they are " . . . the leading retailer, roaster, and brand of specialty coffee in the world, with more than 12,000 company-operated and licensed locations In North America, Latin America, Europe, the Middle East, and Asia Pacific."

Founded in 1971 in Seattle, Washington, Starbucks continues to flourish. A secret to Starbucks' success and expansion is the way the company addresses the needs of its customer markets. The format of the Starbucks stores can be varied from a full-size coffee shop to a small kiosk, with the differences being the array and amount of products stocked and offered. In addition, Starbucks continues to think outside the box and has signed licensing agreements with hotel chains, airports, food service companies, warehouse clubs, supermarkets, and a number of other venues that carry its products. In 1996 Starbucks and Dreyer's Grand Ice Cream Inc. formed a partnership to introduce Starbucks® Ice Cream and Starbucks Ice Cream bars. Starbucks Ice Cream quickly became the number one brand of coffee ice cream in the United States.

Overall, customers have responded favorably and the company's revenues reflect its success, with revenues for 2006 ($7.8 billion) up slightly over $1 billion from 2005 ($6.4 billion). In a 2006 customer satisfaction survey, customers were asked if they would recommend Starbucks to a friend or family member and 87 percent said that they were extremely satisfied or very likely to recommend to family and friends.

Service and treatment of employees are two cornerstones of any successful company. The Starbucks guiding principles from its mission statement, relating to creating a great work environment where people are treated with respect and dignity and developing enthusiastically satisfied customers, have helped form a culture that is prospering. It has also led to an environment that earned Starbucks a ranking on *Fortune* magazine's 100 Best Companies to work for in 2007, as one of the 100 Best Corporate Citizens by *Business Ethics* magazine, and in the Top 50 Companies for Diversity by *DiversityInc*.

For more information about Starbucks Corporation, go to www.starbucks.com.

See activity based on this section on page 110.

Quick Preview:

Before reviewing the chapter content, respond to the following questions by placing a "T" for true or an "F" for false on the rules. Use any questions you miss as a checklist of material to which you will pay particular attention as you read through the chapter. For those you get right, congratulate yourself, but review the sections they address in order to learn additional details about the topic.

_____ 1. It is possible for you to not send nonverbal messages.

_____ 2. By becoming knowledgeable about body language, you can use the cues you observe to accurately predict the meaning of someone's message.

_____ 3. By leaning toward or away from people as they speak, you can better communicate your level of interest in what they are saying.

_____ 4. Smiling may mean that someone agrees with what you say. Smiling may also mean that the person is listening.

_____ 5. The use of open, flowing gestures could encourage listening and help illustrate key points.

_____ 6. Taking the time to polish your shoes and clean and press your clothing can help in presenting a positive personal image.

_____ 7. Vocal qualities have little effect on the way others perceive you.

_____ 8. Pauses in your oral message delivery can nonverbally say, "Think about what I just said" or "It's your turn to speak."

_____ 9. The words you use can distort message meaning.

_____ 10. Spatial preferences are the same throughout the world.

_____ 11. People often draw inferences about you on basis of the appearance of your office.

_____ 12. The amount of time you allocate for meetings with people could nonverbally communicate your feelings about the importance of those people.

Answers to Quick Preview can be found at the end of the chapter.

1   WHAT IS NONVERBAL COMMUNICATION?

Concept: Nonverbal messages can contradict or override verbal messages. When in doubt, people tend to believe nonverbal messages.

The study of messages sent via nonverbal means has fascinated people for decades. The general public became aware of this subject when the books like *Body Language*[1] and several others were published over four decades ago. In *Body Language,* Julius Fast defined various postures, movements, and gestures by ascribing to them the unspoken messages that they might send to someone observing them (for example, defensiveness or accessibility). Since then, hundreds of articles, books, and research studies have explored the topic and expanded the knowledge on the subject.

nonverbal messages
Consist of such things as movements, gestures, body positions, vocal qualities, and a variety of unspoken signals sent by people, often in conjunction with verbal messages.

By being aware that you constantly send **nonverbal messages** to others and that it is impossible for you to *not* communicate, you can increase your effectiveness in customer encounters or anywhere you come into contact with another person. A significant fact to remember is that, according to a classic research study on how feelings are transmitted between two people during communication, nonverbal signals can contradict or override verbal messages.[2] This is especially true when emotions are high. In Dr. Albert Mehrabian's classic and often-referenced study, it was found that in communication between two people, 55 percent of message meaning (feelings) is extracted from nonverbal (facial and other body cues), 38 percent is taken from vocal cues, and 7 percent is received from the actual words used. (The various cues will be discussed in more detail later in this chapter.) This should not be construed to mean that your words are not important; they are just typically overridden by nonverbal cues. When in doubt about your message meaning, people tend to believe the nonverbal (facial and vocal) parts. Figure 4.1 illustrates the importance of the different types of cues.

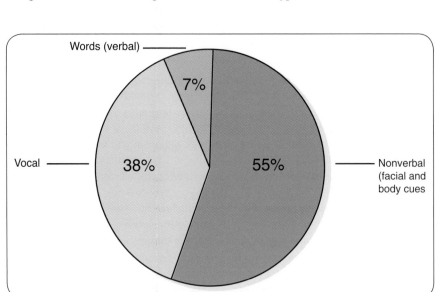

FIGURE 4.1   Communication of Feelings

[1]Julius Fast, *Body Language,* Pocket Books, New York, 1960.
[2]Albert Mehrabian, *Silent Messages: Implicit Communication of Emotions and Attitudes,* 2nd ed., Wadsworth Publishing, Belmont, Calif., 1981, pp. 75–80.

Although nonverbal cues carry powerful messages, it is important to understand that there is considerable room for misinterpretation of the cues used by different people. The skill of recognizing, assigning meaning, and responding appropriately to nonverbal messages is not exact. Human behavior is too unpredictable and the interpretation of nonverbal cues is too subjective for accuracy of interpretation to occur with consistency. This is because different cues have different meanings depending on where they were learned, who is interpreting them, and so on.

2   THE SCOPE OF NONVERBAL BEHAVIOR

Concept: Background, culture, physical conditions, communication ability, and many other factors influence whether and how well people use body cues.

In addition to verbal and written messages, you continually provide nonverbal cues that tell a lot about your personality, attitude, and willingness and ability to assist customers. Customers receive and interpret the messages you send, just as you receive and interpret their messages.

BODY LANGUAGE

By recognizing, understanding, and reacting appropriately to the body language of others, as well as using positive body language yourself, you will communicate with your customers more effectively. The key to "reading" **body language** is to realize that your interpretations should be used only as an indicator of the customer's true message meaning. This is because background, culture, physical condition, communication ability, and many other factors influence whether and how well people use body cues. Remember that not everyone uses nonverbal cues in the same manner that you do. Placing too much importance on nonverbal cues could lead to miscommunication and possibly a service breakdown. Some typical forms of body language are discussed in the following sections.

Eye Contact   It has been said that the eyes are "the windows to the soul." Eye contact is very powerful. This is why criminal investigators are often taught to observe eye movement in order to determine whether a suspect is being truthful or not. In most Western cultures, the typical period of time that is comfortable for holding eye contact is five to ten seconds; then an occasional glance away is normal. Looking away more often can send a message of disinterest, or dishonesty, or lack of confidence. If either the length or the frequency of eye contact differs from the "norm," many people might think that you are being rude or offensive. They might also interpret your behavior as an attempt to exert power or as flirting.

In any case, your customer might become uncomfortable and may react in an undesirable manner (for example, becoming upset or ending the conversation). Also, looking down before answering questions, glancing away continually as your customer talks, blinking excessively, and other such eye movements can create a negative impression.

The customer's eye contact can also send meaningful messages to you. A customer's lack of direct eye contact with you could send a variety of messages, such as lack of interest, confidence or trust, or honesty. For example, if you are watching a customer shop and notice a quick loss of eye contact, the customer might be nervous because he or she is shoplifting, or the customer simply might not want your attention and assistance.

Another aspect of nonverbal communication has to do with the size of the pupils. Much research has been done on the correlation between a person's interest in an item or object being viewed and the size of the person's pupils. Typically, when a customer is interested in an item, his or her pupils will *dilate* (grow larger). This fact can be parlayed into

CUSTOMER SERVICE SUCCESS TIP

To get a better understanding of nonverbal cues that you might be using excessively or inappropriately, ask a number of your friends (or customers with whom you have a good rapport) if there are nonverbal cues that you use that stand out in their mind or even irritate them.

body language
Nonverbal communication cues that send powerful messages through gestures, vocal qualities, manner of dress and grooming, and many other cues.

increased sales and customer satisfaction because an astute and experienced salesperson can watch for dilation as a customer looks over merchandise. For example, even if a customer displays only mild interest in an item after asking the price, and then moves on to another, the salesperson who has observed the customer's interest as revealed by dilation of the pupils might be able to influence the customer's buying decision. But as with all nonverbal communication, if you are using this technique, remember that there is room for misinterpreting a cue. To avoid this kind of mistake, listen carefully to tone of voice and observe other signals so that you do not appear to be pushy.

Nonverbal cues such as eye contact, proximity, smiling, and gesturing send powerful messages. *What cues do you regularly send that impact the way customers perceive you and your organization?*

posture
Refers to how one sits and stands in order to project various nonverbal messages.

Posture Basically, **posture** (or stance) involves the way you position your body. Various terms describe posture (for example, formal, rigid, relaxed, slouched, awkward, sensual, defensive). By sitting or standing in an erect manner, or leaning forward or away as you speak with customers, you can send a variety of messages. By standing or sitting with an erect posture, walking confidently, or assuming a relaxed, open posture, you might appear to be attentive, confident, assertive, and ready to assist your customer. On the other hand, slouching in your seat, standing with slumped shoulders, keeping your arms crossed while speaking to someone, shuffling or not picking up your feet when walking, or averting eye contact can possibly signal that you are unsure of yourself, are being deceitful, or just have a poor customer service attitude.

In addition, your behavior when listening to a customer speak can affect his or her feedback and reaction to you. For example, if you lean forward and smile as the customer speaks, you can signal that you are interested in what is being said and that you are listening intently. Leaning away could send the opposite message.

Facial Expressions The face is capable of making many expressions. Your face can signal excitement, happiness, sadness, boredom, concern, dismay, and dozens of other emotions. By being aware of the power of your expressions and using positive ones, such as smiling, you can initiate and sustain relationships with others. In fact, smiling seems to be one of the few nonverbal cues that has a universal meaning of friendship or acceptance. Smiling typically expresses a mood of friendship, cheerfulness, pleasure, relaxation, and comfort with a situation. On the other hand, some people smile to mask nervousness, embarrassment, or deceit.

In some situations, smiling (yours and a customer's) may even lead to problems. For example, suppose that you are a male receptionist working at a walk-in care clinic. A male patient from the Middle East and his wife step up to your desk. You smile and greet the husband, and then turn your attention to the wife and do likewise, possibly adding, "That's a very pretty dress you have on?" She smiles and giggles as she looks away in an embarrassed effort to avoid eye contact. At this point, you notice that the husband looks displeased. A cultural element may be involved. Although your intention was to express friendliness and openness, because of his cultural attitudes, the husband may interpret your words and smiling as flirtatious and insulting.

Don't think that this means you should ignore the wives of your customers. Rather, be cognizant of cultural and personal differences that people may have, and take your cue from the

Facial Expressions

TAKE A FEW MINUTES TO LOOK AT EACH OF THE FACES SHOWN BELOW.

Write the emotion that you believe each image portrays on the rules.

customer. As the world grows smaller, it is more crucial than ever that you expand your knowledge of different cultural attitudes and recognize that your ways are not the ways of everyone.

Nodding of the Head Nodding of the head is often used (and overused) by many people to signal agreement or to indicate that they are listening to a speaker during a conversation.

You must be careful when you are using this technique, and when you are watching others who are doing so, to occasionally pause to ask a question for clarification. Stop and ask for or provide feedback through a paraphrased message. A question such as, "So what do you think of what I just said?" will quickly tell you whether the other person is listening and understands your meaning. The answer will also make it clear if the other person is simply politely smiling and nodding—but not understanding.

If you are a woman, be careful not to overuse the nodding technique. Research has shown that women often nod and smile more than men during a conversation. Doing so excessively might damage your credibility or effectiveness, especially when you are speaking to a man. The interpretation may be that you agree or that you have no opinion, whether you do or not.

Although nodding your head generally signals agreement, if you nod without a verbal acknowledgment or **paralanguage** (a vocal effect such as "uh huh, I see, hmmm"), a

paralanguage
Consists of voice qualities (e.g., pitch, rate, tone, or other vocal qualities) or noises and vocalizations (e.g., "Hmmm" or "Ahhh") made as someone speaks, which let the speaker know that his or her message is being listened to and followed.

missed or misinterpreted cue could result. For example, suppose that you want to signal to a customer that you are listening to and understand her request. You may nod slowly, vocalize an occasional "I see" or "Uh-huh," and smile as she speaks. She might interpret this to mean that you are following her meaning and are nonverbally signaling acceptance of it. But if she is stating something contrary to your organization's policy or outside your level of authority, she might misinterpret your signals thinking that you *agree* with her, not that you are merely signaling *understanding*. Later, she might be upset, saying something like, "Well, earlier you nodded agreement when I said I wanted a replacement."

Gestures   The use of the head, hands, arms, and shoulders to accentuate verbal messages adds color, excitement, and enthusiasm to your communication. Using physical movements naturally during a conversation with a customer may help make a point or result in added credibility.

Typically, such movements are designed to gain and hold attention (for example, waving a hand to attract the attention of someone), clarify or describe further (for example, holding up one finger to indicate the number 1), or emphasize a point (for example, pointing a finger while angrily making a point verbally).

Open, flowing gestures encourage listening and help explain messages to customers (gesturing with arms, palms open and upward, out and away from the body). On the other hand, closed, restrained movements could send a message of coolness, insecurity, or disinterest (tightly crossed arms, clinched fists, hands in pockets, hands or fingers intertwined and held below waist level or behind the back).

vocal cues
Qualities of the voice that send powerful nonverbal messages. Examples are rate, pitch, volume, and tone.

The key is to make gestures seem natural. If you do not normally use gestures when communicating, you may want to practice in front of a mirror until you feel relaxed and the gestures complement your verbal messages without distracting. Figure 4.2 summarizes positive and negative communication behaviors discussed in this chapter.

inflection
The change in tone of the voice as one speaks. This quality is also called pitch and adds vocal variety and punctuation to verbal messages.

VOCAL CUES

pitch
Refers to the change in tone of the voice as one speaks. This quality is also called inflection and adds vocal variety and punctuation to verbal messages.

Vocal cues, that is, pitch, volume (loudness), rate, quality, and articulation and other attributes of verbal communication, can send nonverbal messages to customers.

Pitch   Changes in voice tone (either higher or lower) add vocal variety to messages and can dramatically affect interpretation of meaning. These changes are referred to as **inflection** or **pitch**

✦ **FIGURE 4.2**

Positive and Negative Nonverbal Communication Behaviors

Positive	Negative
Brief eye contact (3 to 5 seconds)	Yawning
Eyes wide open	Frowning or sneering
Smiling	Attending to matters other than the customer
Facing the customer	Manipulating items impatiently
Nodding affirmatively	Leaning away from customer as he or she speaks
Expressive hand gestures	Subdued or minimal hand gestures
Open body stance	Crossed arms
Listening actively	Staring blankly or coolly at customer
Remaining silent as customer speaks	Interrupting
Gesturing with open hand	Pointing finger or object at customer
Maintaining professional appearance	Casual unkempt appearance
Clean, organized work area	Disorganized, cluttered work space

of the voice or tone. Inflection is the "vocal punctuation" in oral message delivery. For example, a raised inflection occurs at the end of a question and indicates a vocal "question mark." Some people have a bad habit of raising inflection inappropriately at the end of a statement. This practice can confuse listeners for they hear the vocal question mark, but they realize that the words were actually a statement. To rectify this communication error, be sure that your inflection normally falls at the end of sentence statements. Another technique is to use a vocal "comma" in the form of a brief pause as you speak.

Volume   The range in which vocal messages are delivered is referred to as the degree of loudness or **volume.** Depending on surrounding noise or your customers' ability to hear properly, you may have to raise or lower your volume as you speak. Be careful to listen to customer comments, especially on the telephone. If the customer keeps asking you to speak up, check the position of the mouthpiece in relation to your mouth, adjust outgoing volume (if your equipment allows this), and try to eliminate background noise, or simply speak up. On the other hand, if he or she is saying, "You don't have to shout," adjust your voice volume or the positioning of the mouthpiece accordingly or lower your voice.

Also, be aware of the volume of your voice, for changes in volume can indicate emotion and may send a negative message to your customer. For example, if a communication exchange with a customer becomes emotionally charged, your voice may rise in volume, indicating that you are angry or upset. This may escalate emotions and possibly lead to a relationship breakdown.

Rate of Speech   **Rate of speech** varies for many people. This is often a result of the person's communication abilities, the region of the United States in which he or she was reared, or his or her country of origin. An average rate of speech for most adults in Western cultures is 125 to 150 words per minute (wpm). You should recognize this because, as we discussed in Chapter 3, speed of delivery can affect whether your message is received and interpreted correctly. Speech that is either too fast or too slow can be distracting and cause loss of message effectiveness.

Voice Quality   Message interpretation is often affected by the sound or quality of your voice.

The variations in your **voice quality** can help encourage customers to listen (if your voice sounds pleasant and is accompanied by a smile) or discourage them (if it is harsh-sounding), depending on their perception of how your voice sounds. Some terms that describe unpleasant voice quality are *raspy, nasal, hoarse,* and *gravelly.* Such qualities can be a problem because others are less likely to listen to or interact with you if your voice quality is irritating. If you have been told, or you recognize, that your voice exhibits one or more of these characteristics, you may want to meet with a speech coach who specializes in helping improve vocal presentation of messages. Most local colleges and universities that have speech programs can supply the name of an expert, possibly someone on their staff. By taking the initiative to improve your voice quality, you can enhance your customer service image.

Articulation   **Articulation, enunciation,** or **pronunciation** of words refers to the clarity of your word usage. If you tend to slur words ("Whadju say?" "I hafta go whitja") or cut off endings (goin', doin', gettin', bein'), you can distort meaning or frustrate listeners. This is especially true when communicating with customers who do not speak English well and with customers who view speech ability as indicative of educational achievement or

Simple nonverbal cues like smiling at a customer send powerful messages that a service provider is customer-focused. *How do you feel when a service provider smiles at you?*

volume
Refers to loudness or softness of the voice when speaking.

rate of speech
Refers to the number of words spoken per minute. Some research studies have found that the average rate of speech for adults in Western cultures is approximately 125–150 words per minute (wpm).

voice quality
Refers to the sound of one's voice. Terms often attributed to voice quality are raspy, nasal, hoarse, and gravelly.

articulation, enunciation, or pronunciation
Refers to the manner or clarity in which verbal messages are delivered.

93

Gesture Practice

To see what you look like when you gesture and communicate nonverbally, stand in front of a mirror or videotape yourself as you practice expressing nonverbal cues that demonstrate the following emotions:

1. Sadness
2. Frustration
3. Disgust
4. Happiness
5. Love
6. Fear
7. Anger
8. Excitement
9. Concern
10. Boredom
11. Skepticism
12. Complacency
13. Frustration
14. Optimism

pauses
A verbal technique of delaying response in order to allow time to process information received, think of a response, or gain attention.

interferences
Noises that can interfere with messages being effectively communicated between two people.

verbal fillers
Verbal sounds, words, or utterances that break silence but add little to a conversation. Examples are uh, um, ah, and you know.

silence
Technique used to gain attention when speaking, to allow thought, or to process information received.

semantics
The scientific study of relationships between signs, symbols, and words and their meaning. The way words are used or stressed often affects their perceived meaning.

your ability to assist them effectively. If you have a problem articulating well, practice by gripping a pencil horizontally between your teeth, reading sentences aloud, and forcing yourself to enunciate each word clearly. Over time, you will find that you slow down and form words more precisely.

Pauses **Pauses** in communication can be either positive or negative depending on how you use them. From a positive standpoint, they can be used to allow a customer to reflect on what you just said, to verbally punctuate a point made or a sentence (through intonation and inflection in the voice), or to indicate that you are waiting for a response. On the negative side, you can irritate someone through the use of too many vocal pauses or **interferences.** The latter can be audible sounds ("uh," "er," "um," "uh-huh") and are often used when you have doubts or are unsure of what you are saying, not being truthful, or nervous. They are sometimes called **verbal fillers.** Interferences can also be external noises that make hearing difficult.

Silence **Silence** is a form of tacit communication that can be used in a number of ways, some more productive than others. Many people have trouble dealing with silence in a conversation. This is unfortunate, because silence is a good way to show respect or show that you are listening to the customer while he or she speaks. It is also a simple way to indicate that the other person should say something or contribute some information after you have asked a question. You can also indicate agreement or comprehension by using body language and paralanguage, as discussed earlier. On the negative side, you can indicate defiance or indifference by coupling your silence with some of the nonverbal behaviors listed in Figure 4.2. Obviously, this can damage the customer-provider relationship.

Semantics **Semantics** has to do with choice of words. Although not nonverbal in nature, semantics is a crucial element of message delivery and interpretation. You can add to or detract from effective communication depending on the words you use and how you use them. Keep in mind what you read earlier about the Mehrabian study and the fact that 7 percent of message meaning comes from the words you choose to use.

If you use a lot of jargon (technical or industry-related terms) or complex words that customers may not understand because of their background, education, culture, or experience, you run the risk of irritating, frustrating, or dissatisfying them and thus damaging the customer-provider relationship.

WORK IT OUT 4.3

Adding Emphasis to Words

TO PRACTICE HOW CHANGES IN YOUR VOCAL QUALITY AFFECT THE MEANING OF YOUR MESSAGE, TRY THIS ACTIVITY. Pair up with someone. Take turns verbally delivering the following sentences one at a time. Each time, place the vocal emphasis on the word in boldface type. Following the delivery of each sentence, stop and discuss how you perceived the meaning based on your partner's enunciation and intonation of the key word in the sentence. Also, discuss the impact that you believe such emphasis could have on a customer interaction.

I said I'd do it.   I said I'd **do** it.

I **said** I'd do it.   I said I'd do **it.**

I said **I'd** do it.

APPEARANCE AND GROOMING

The way you look physically (hygiene and grooming) and your manner of dress send a message of either professionalism or indifference. Even though you provide attentive, quality service, the customer will typically form an opinion of you and your organization within 30 seconds based on your appearance and that of your work space. This opinion may make the difference in whether the customer will continue to patronize your organization or go to a competitor. For example, your clothing, grooming, and choice of jewelry or other accessories could send a negative message to some people. It is crucial to be able to distinguish between what is appropriate for the workplace and what is inappropriate for a business setting.

Through your **appearance and grooming** habits, you project an image of yourself and the organization. Good personal hygiene and attention to your appearance are crucial in a customer environment. Remember, customers do not have to return if they find you or your peers offensive in any manner. And without customers, you do not have a job.

Hygiene   Effective **hygiene** (regular washing and combing of hair, bathing, brushing teeth, use of mouthwash and deodorant, and washing hands and cleaning fingernails) is basic to successful customer service. This is true even when you work with tools and equipment, or in other skilled trades in which you get dirty easily. Most customers accept that some jobs are going to result in more dirt and grime than others. However, they often have a negative feeling about someone who does not take pride in his or her personal appearance and/or hygiene. Such people are often perceived as inconsiderate, lazy, or simply dirty. If you failed to wash your hair, bathe or shave prior to reporting to work, you could be offensive in appearance to customers and coworkers (you might even have an unpleasant odor). This could result in people avoiding you or complaining about you. Naturally, this would reduce your effectiveness on the job and lower customer satisfaction.

A number of grooming trends have been prompted by many Hollywood actors. One is for men to appear with a one- or two-day beard stubble. While this may look sexy in movies, it has little place in most professional work environments. Likewise, many studies show that prominent tattoos and visible piercings are becoming more commonplace. Still, in many instances they can not only raise some eyebrows, but also can cause a negative customer reaction based on stereotypes of people who have such things. In many cases, these reactions are from older customers, for example, older baby boomers. Since this group is one of the largest market forces, their views should be considered if you want to be a successful service provider.

Although good hygiene and grooming are important, going to an extreme through excessive use of makeup, cologne, or perfume can create a negative impression and may even cause people to avoid you. This is especially true of people who have allergies or

appearance and grooming
Nonverbal characteristics exhibited by service providers that can send a variety of messages that range from being a professional to having a negative attitude.

hygiene
The healthy maintenance of the body through such practices as regular bathing, washing of hair, brushing of teeth, cleaning of fingernails, and using commercial products to eliminate or mask odors.

Being aware of how people may react to violations of their space is necessary for those in customer service. Depending on circumstances, there might be misperceptions of intentions and harassment claims.

proxemics or spatial cues
Relates to the invisible barrier surrounding people in which they feel comfortable interacting with others. This zone varies depending on the level of relationship a person has with someone else.

spatial cues
Nonverbal messages sent on the basis of how close or far someone stands from another person.

environmental cues
Any aspect of the workplace with which a customer comes into contact. Such things as the general appearance of an area, clutter, unsightly or offensive items, or general disorganization contribute to the perception of an environment.

respiratory problems, or people with whom you work in confined spaces.

Clothing and Accessories For a number of years, casual dress, "dress-down days," and business casual have been buzz words in many organizations as management tried to adapt to the changing values of today's workforce. For example, many hi-tech and graphic work environments often have employees in jeans, t-shirts, and sandals. This trend toward being a bit too lax is now starting to reverse a bit in many companies because some employees have taken the concept of "casual" to an extreme. As a result, they have begun to negatively affect the workplace and the opinions that many customers have of some organizations.

Work clothing does not have to be expensive, but should be well-maintained and appropriate to your work setting. No matter what type of clothing is designated in your organization, clean and pressed clothing, as well as polished shoes (where appropriate), help to project a positive, professional image. Certain types of clothing and accessories are acceptable in the work environment, but others are inappropriate. If your organization does not have a policy outlining dress standards, always check with your supervisor before wearing something that might deviate from the standards observed by other employees or might create an unfavorable image to the public. For example, very high heels and miniskirts, or jeans, bare midriffs, T-shirts, pants with holes or tattered cuffs, or that hang low on the hips, and tennis shoes, might be appropriate for a date or social outing, but they may not be appropriate on the job. They could actually be distracting or cause customer disapproval and/or complaints and lost business to your organization.

If you are in doubt about appropriate attire, many publications and videos are available on the subject of selecting the right clothing, jewelry, eyeglasses, and accessories. Check with your company's human resources department, your local public library, or the Internet for more information.

SPATIAL CUES

Each culture (Figure 4.3) has its own **proxemics or spatial cues** (zones or distances in which interpersonal interactions take place) for various situations. When you violate this distance, the comfort level of other people is likely to decrease, and they may become visibly anxious, move away, and/or become defensive or offended. Suppose you have an intimate or friendly spatial relationship with a coworker or with someone who regularly comes into your place of business. Outside the workplace, you and this person typically engage in interactions from zero to four feet (joking around, touching, kissing, and holding hands). But if you exhibited similar behavior in the workplace, you could create a feeling of discomfort in others, especially customers or other people who do not know you. Even if they are aware of your relationship with this person, the workplace is not the appropriate place for such behavior. Any touching should be restricted to standard business practices. In fact, touching other than this can lead to claims of a hostile work environment and could lead to a lawsuit according to numerous federal and state laws.

ENVIRONMENTAL CUES

The **environmental cues** of the surroundings in which you work or service customers also send messages. For example, if your work area looks dirty or disorganized, with tools, pencils,

FIGURE 4.3

**Typical Spatial
Distances in Western
Cultures**

In the United States and many Western cultures, studies have resulted in definitions of approximate comfort zones. These may vary, for example, when someone has immigrated to a Western environment and still retains some of his or her own culture's practices related to space.

Intimate distance (0 to 18 inches). Typically this distance is reserved for your family and intimate relationships. Most people will feel uncomfortable when a service provider intrudes into this space uninvited.

Personal distance (18 inches to 4 feet). This distance is used when close friends or business colleagues, with whom you have established a level of comfort and trust, are together. It might also occur if you have established a long-term customer relationship that has blossomed into a semi-friendship. In such a situation, you and the customer may sometimes exchange personal information (vacation plans, children, and so forth) and feel comfortable standing or sitting closer to one another than would normally be the case.

Social and work distance (4 to 12 feet). This is usually the distance range in a customer service setting. It is also typically maintained at casual business events and during business transactions.

Public distance (12 or more feet). This distance range is likely to be maintained at large gatherings, activities, or presentations where most people do not know one another, or where the interactions are formal in nature.

files, and papers scattered about, outdated or inappropriate Information or items tacked to a bulletin board, or if there are stacks of boxes, papers stapled or taped to walls, and trash or clutter visible, customers may perceive that you and the organization have a lackadaisical attitude or approach to business. This perception may cause customers to question your ability and commitment to serve. Granted, in some professions keeping a work area clean all the time is difficult (service station, construction site office, manufacturing environment). However, that is no excuse for giving up on cleanliness and organization of your area. If each employee takes responsibility for cleaning his or her area, cleaning becomes a routine event during work hours and no one has to get stuck with the job of doing cleaning tasks at a specific time. Also, the chance that a customer may react negatively to the work area is reduced or eliminated.

To help reduce negative perceptions, organize and clean your area regularly, put things away and out of sight once you have used them (calculators, extra pencils, order forms, extra paper for the printer or copier, tools and equipment, supplies). Also, clean your equipment and desk area regularly (telephone mouthpiece, computer monitor and keyboard, cash register and/or calculator key surface, tools).

It is also important to remove any potentially offensive items (photos of or calendars displaying scantily clad men or women; cartoons that have ethnic, racial, sexual, or otherwise offensive messages or that target a particular group; literature, posters, or objects that support specific political or religious views; or any item that could be unpleasant or offensive to view). These items have no place in a professional setting. Failure to remove such material might result in legal liability for you and your organization and create a hostile work environment.

MISCELLANEOUS CUES

Other factors, such as the **miscellaneous cues** discussed in the following sections, can affect customer perception or feelings about you or your organization.

Personal Habits   If you have annoying or distracting habits, you could send negative messages to your customer. For example, eating, smoking, drinking, or chewing

miscellaneous cues
Refers to factors used to send messages that impact a customer's perception or feelings about a service provider or organization. Examples are personal habits, etiquette, and manners.

Spatial Perceptions

PAIR UP WITH SOMEONE AND STAND FACING HIM OR HER FROM ACROSS THE ROOM. Start a conversation about any topic (for example, how you feel about the concepts addressed in this chapter or how you feel about the activity in which you are participating) and slowly begin to move toward one another. As you do so, think about your feelings related to the distance at which you are communicating. Keep moving until you are approximately one inch from your partner. At that point, start slowly backing away, again thinking about your feelings. When you get back to your side of the room, have a seat and answer these questions:

1. How did you feel when you were communicating from the opposite side of the room (what were your thoughts)?
2. At what distance (moving forward or back) did you feel most comfortable? Why?
3. Did you feel uncomfortable at any point? Why or why not?
4. How can you use the information learned from this activity in the customer service environment?

---

time allocation
Amount of attention given to a person or project.

food or gum while servicing customers can lead to negative impressions about you and your organization. Any of the following habits can lead to relationship breakdowns:

> Touching the customer.
>
> Scratching or touching certain parts of your body typically viewed as personal.
>
> Using pet phrases or speech patterns excessively ("Cool," "You know," "Groovy," "Am I right?" "Awesome," "Solid").
>
> Talking endlessly without letting the customer speak.
>
> Talking about personal problems.
>
> Complaining about your job, employer, coworkers, or other customers.

Time Allocation and Attention Some organizations have standards for servicing customers within a specific time frame (for example, returning phone calls within four hours), but these **time allocations** should be targets because customer transactions cannot all be resolved in a specified period of time. The key is to be efficient and effective in your efforts. Continually reevaluate your work habits and patterns to see whether you can accomplish tasks in a more timely fashion. The amount of time you spend with customers often sends subliminal messages of how you perceive their importance.

Follow-Through Follow-through, or lack of it, sends a very powerful nonverbal message to customers. If you tell a customer you will do something, it is critical to your relationship that you do so. If you can't meet agreed-upon terms or time frames, get back to the customer and renegotiate. Otherwise, you may lose the customer's trust. For example, suppose you assure a customer that an item that is out of stock will arrive by Wednesday. On Tuesday, you find out that the shipment is delayed. If you fail to inform the customer, you may lose the sale and the customer.

Proper Etiquette and Manners People appreciate receiving appropriate respect and prefer dealing with others who have good **etiquette and manners.** Many books and seminars address the dos and don'ts of servicing and working with customers. From a nonverbal message standpoint, the polite things you do (saying "please" and "thank you," asking permission, or acknowledging contributions) go far in establishing and building relationships. Such language says, "I care" or "I respect you." In addition, behavior that affects your customer's perception of you can also affect your interaction

Ethical Dilemma 4.1

Suppose that you are a receptionist In a hospital emergency room waiting area and an older homeless male who is dirty, with cutoff jeans, sandals and a t-shirt with holes in it comes up to your desk. He has a dirty bloody rag wrapped around his hand and complains that he has cut himself with a rusty can lid. You greet him without a smile, hand him a clipboard with paperwork, and tell him to have a seat and complete the forms. At the same time that the Indigent patient arrived, a well-dressed older woman wearing a suit arrives with a small crying girl and states that the child fell out of a tree

Red	Stimulates and evokes excitement, passion, power, energy, anger, intensity. Can also indicate "stop," negativity, financial trouble, or shortage.
Yellow	Indicates caution, warmth, mellowness, positive meaning, optimism, and cheerfulness. Yellow can also stimulate thinking and visualizing.
Dark blue	Depending on shade, can relax, soothe, indicate maturity, and evoke trust and tranquility or peace.
Light blue	Projects a cool, youthful, or masculine image.
Purple	Projects assertiveness or boldness and youthfulness. Has a contemporary "feel." Often used as a sign of royalty, richness, spirituality, or power.
Orange	Can indicate high energy or enthusiasm. Is an emotional color and sometimes stimulates positive thinking.
Brown	An earth tone that creates a feeling of security, wholesomeness, strength, support, and lack of pretentiousness.
Green	Can bring to mind nature, productivity, positive image, moving forward or "go," comforting, growth, or financial success or prosperity. Also, can give a feeling of balance.
Gold and silver	prestige, status, wealth, elegance, or conservatism.
Pink	Signal Projects a youthful, feminine, or warm image.
White	Not really a color (actually, an absence of it). Typically used to indicate purity, cleanliness, honesty and wholesomeness. Is visually relaxing.
Black	Lack of color. Creates sense of independence, completeness, and solidarity. Often used to indicate financial success, death, or seriousness of situation.

FIGURE 4.4   The Emotional Messages of Color Emotion or Message

and ability to provide service (interrupting others as they speak, talking with food in your mouth, pointing with your finger or other items such as a fork while eating). Many good books are available on business manners and dining etiquette if you are unsure of yourself.

Color   Although color is not as important as some other factors related to nonverbal communication in the customer service environment, the way in which you use various colors in decorating a work space and in your clothing can have an emotional impact. You should at least consider the colors you choose when dressing for work. Much research has been done by marketing and communication experts to determine which colors evoke the most positive reactions from customers. In various studies involving the reaction people had to colors, some clear patterns evolved. Figure 4.4 lists various colors and the possible **emotional messages of color** they can send.

3   THE ROLE OF GENDER IN NONVERBAL COMMUNICATION

Concept: Research indicates that boys and girls and men and women behave differently. Young children are sometimes treated differently by their parents because of their gender preference (either male or female may be the preferred gender, no matter the gender of the parent).

etiquette and manners
Includes the acceptable rules, manners, and ceremonies for an organization, profession, or society.

emotional messages of color
Research-based use of color to send nonverbal messages through advertisements and other elements of the organization.

CUSTOMER SERVICE SUCCESS TIP

Professional image is an important part of service. Strive to create a work environment that sends a positive message and will not cause offense or negative perceptions in others.

Ethical Dilemma 4.1 (continued)

and hurt her shoulder. You greet her warmly with a smile and proceed to engage her in conversation and assist attentively. Meanwhile the injured homeless patient waits to have a question answered about his paperwork. This certainly could tell the man patient that he is not welcome or respected.

1. How do you think you would feel if you were the homeless patient? Why?

2. Why do you think the receptionist used different standards of service for the two patients?

3. What could the receptionist have done differently/better to improve the service delivery in this situation?

4. What Is the likely impact of the service delivery outlined in this situation?

Gender Communication

TO GET A BETTER IDEA OF HOW MALES AND FEMALES COMMUNICATE AND INTERACT DIFFERENTLY, GO TO A LIBRARY OR TO THE INTERNET AND GATHER INFORMATION ON THE TOPIC. Look specifically for information on the following topics:

Brain differences between men and women and the impact of these differences on communication and relationships.

Differences in nonverbal cues used by men and women.

Base for the communication differences in the workplace or business world between men and women.

gender communication
Term used to refer to communication between genders.

Much has been discovered and written about differences in **gender communication** and interactions with others. For example, some researchers have found that females are more comfortable being in close physical proximity with other females than males are being close to other males. Although similarities exist between the ways in which males and females relate to one another, there are distinct differences in behavior, beginning in childhood and carrying through into adulthood.

In the book *The Difference,* Judy Mann[3] hypothesizes that boys and girls are different in many ways, are acculturated to act and behave differently, and have some real biological differences that account for their actions (and inactions), which are examined from a number of perspectives. The book discusses various studies that have found that boys and girls typically learn to interact with each other, and with members of their own gender, in different ways. Girls tend to learn more nurturing and relationship skills early, whereas boys approach life from a more aggressive, competitive stance. Girls often search for more "relationship" messages during an interaction and strive to develop a collaborative approach; boys typically focus on competitiveness or "bottom-line" responses in which there is a distinct winner. Obviously, these differences in approaches to relationship building can have an impact in the customer service environment, where people of all walks of life come together.

CUSTOMER SERVICE SUCCESS TIP

Use knowledge of how males and females differ to improve your service by structuring your communication and approach to their preferences; however, remember that each person is unique so service customers individually.

The lessons learned early in life usually carry over into the workplace and affect customer interactions. If you fail to recognize the differences between the sexes and do not develop the skills necessary to interact with both men and women, you could experience some breakdowns in communication and ultimately in the customer-provider relationship.

The basis for gender differences is the fact that the brains of males and females develop at different rates and focus on different priorities throughout life. Women often tend to be more bilateral in the use of their brain (they can switch readily between the left and right brain hemispheres in various situations). Men, on the other hand, tend to be more lateral in their thinking. This means that they favor either the left hemisphere (analytical, logical, factual, facts-and-figures oriented) or the right hemisphere (emotional, creative, artistic, romantic, and expressive of feelings). This results in a difference in the way each gender communicates, relates to others, and deals with various situations. Figure 4.5 lists some basic behavioral differences between females and males. Keep in mind that behavioral preferences (discussed in Chapter 6) will influence how people communicate.

---

[3] Mann, J, *The Difference: Discovering the Hidden Ways We Silence Girls: Finding Alternatives that can give Them a Voice,* werner Roohr, New York, N.Y. (1996).

	Females	Males
BODY	Claim small areas of personal space (e.g., cross legs at knees or ankles).	Claim large areas of personal space (e.g., use figure-four leg cross, or armrests on airplanes).
	Cross arms and legs frequently.	Use relaxed arm and leg posture (e.g., over arm of a chair).
	Sit or stand close to same sex.	Sit or stand away from same sex but closer to females.
	Use subdued gestures.	Use dramatic gestures.
	Touch more (both sexes).	Touch males less, females more.
	Nods frequently to indicate receptiveness.	Nod occasionally to indicate agreement.
	Lean forward toward speaker.	Lean away from speaker.
	Glance casually at watch.	Glance dramatically at watch (e.g., with arm fully extended and retracted to raise sleeve).
	Hug and possibly kiss both sexes upon greeting.	Hug and possibly kiss females upon greeting.
VOCAL	Use high inflection at end of statements (sounds like a question).	Use subdued vocal inflection.
	Use high pitch.	Use low pitch.
	Speak at faster rate.	Speak at slower rate.
	Use paralanguage frequently.	Use paralanguage occasionally.
	Express more emotion.	Express less emotion.
	Use more polite "requesting" language (e.g., "Would you please?")	Use more "command" language (e.g., "Get me the . . .)
	Focus on relationship messages.	Focus on business messages.
	Use vocal variety.	Often use monotone.
	Interrupt less, more tolerant of interruptions.	Interrupt more, but tolerate interruptions less.
	Use more precise articulation.	Use less precision in word endings and enunciation (e.g., drop the "g" in -ing endings).
FACIAL	Maintain eye contact.	Glance away frequently.
	Smile frequently.	Smile infrequently (with strangers).
	Use expressive facial movements.	Show little variation in facial expression.
BEHAVIOR	Focus more on details.	Focus less on details.
	Are more emotional in problem solving.	Are analytical in problem solving, (e.g., try to find cause and fix problem).
	View verbal rejection as personal.	Do not dwell on verbal rejection.

(continued)

FIGURE 4.5

Men and women differ in their approach to relationships. Here are some general behavioral differences that are seen in many men and women.

FIGURE 4.5
(continued)

	Apologize after disagreements.	Apologize less after disagreements.
	Hold grudges longer.	Do not hold grudges.
ENVIRONMENTAL	Commonly display personal objects in the workplace.	Commonly display items symbolizing achievement in the workplace.
	Use bright colors in clothing and decorations.	Use more subdued colors in clothing and decorations.
	Use patterns in clothing and decoration.	Use few patterns in clothing.

4   THE IMPACT OF CULTURE ON NONVERBAL COMMUNICATION

Concept: To be successful in a global economy, you need to be familiar with the many cultures, habits, values, and beliefs of a wide variety of people.

impact of culture
Refers to the outcome of people from various countries or backgrounds coming into contact with one another and potentially experiencing misunderstandings or relationship breakdowns.

As you read in Chapter 1, and will again in Chapter 8, cultural diversity is having a significant impact on the customer service environment. The number of service providers and customers with varied backgrounds is growing at a rapid pace. This trend provides a tremendous opportunity for expanding your personal knowledge and interaction with people from cultures you might not otherwise encounter. However, with this opportunity comes challenge. If you are to understand and serve people who might be different from you, you must first become aware that they are also very similar to you. In addition, if you are to be successful in interacting with a wide variety of people, you will need to understand the **impact of culture** by learning about many cultures, habits, values, and beliefs from around the world. The Internet is a fertile source for such information. Take advantage of it, or visit your local library to check out books on different countries and their people. Join the National Geographic Society, and you will receive its monthly magazine, which highlights different cultures and people from around the globe.[4]

To become more skilled at dealing with people from other cultures, develop an action plan of things to learn and explore. At a minimum, familiarize yourself with common nonverbal cues that differ dramatically from one culture to another. Specifically, look for cues that might be perceived as negative in some cultures so that you can avoid them. Learn to recognize the different views and approaches to matters such as time, distance, touching, eye contact, and use of colors so that you will not inadvertently violate someone's personal space or cause offense.

5   UNPRODUCTIVE BEHAVIORS

Concept: You should be aware of habits or mannerisms that can send annoying or negative messages to customers.

Many people develop unproductive nonverbal behaviors without even realizing it. These may be nervous habits or mannerisms carried to excess (scratching, pulling an ear, or playing

---

[4] National Geographic Society, www.nationalgeographic.com.

with hair). In a customer environment, you should try to minimize such actions because they might send a negative or annoying message to your customers. An easy way to discover whether you have such behaviors is to ask people who know you well to observe you for a period of time and tell you about anything they observe that could be a problem. Following are some more common behaviors that can annoy people and cause relationship breakdowns or comments about you and your organization.

UNPROFESSIONAL HANDSHAKE

Hundreds of years ago, a handshake was used to determine whether a person was holding a weapon. Later, a firm handshake became a show of commitment, of one's word, or of "manhood." Today, in Western cultures and many others in which the Western way of doing business has been adopted, both men and women in the workplace are expected to convey greeting and/or commitment with a firm handshake. Failure to shake hands appropriately (palm-to-palm), with a couple of firm pumps up and down, can lead to an impression that you are weak or lack confidence. The grip should not be overly loose or overly firm. An overly firm handshake has its own problems. You may inadvertently injure a person who has specific medical issues (arthritis) with an overly powerful handshake. This type of handshake can be just as much a turn-off as a limp or clammy handshake.

FIDGETING

Using some mannerisms can indicate to a customer that you are anxious, annoyed, or distracted, and should therefore be avoided, if possible. Such signals can also indicate that you are nervous or lack confidence. Cues such as playing with or putting hair in your mouth, tugging at clothing, hand-wringing, throat-clearing, playing with items as you speak (pencil, pen, or other object), biting or licking your lips, or drumming your fingers or tapping a surface with a pencil or other object can all send a potentially annoying and/or negative message.

POINTING A FINGER OR OTHER OBJECT

This is a very accusatory mannerism and can lead to anger or violence on the part of your customer. If you must gesture toward a customer, do so with an open flat hand (palm up) in a casual manner. The result is a less threatening gesture that almost invites comment or feedback, because it looks as if you are offering the customer an opportunity to speak.

RAISING EYEBROW

This mannerism is sometimes called the *editorial eyebrow* because some television broadcasters raise their eyebrow. With the editorial eyebrow, only one eyebrow is arched, usually in response to something that the person has heard. This mannerism often signals skepticism or doubt about what you have heard. It can be viewed as questioning the customer's honesty.

PEERING OVER GLASSES

This gesture might be associated with a professor, teacher, or someone who is in a position of authority looking down on a student or subordinate. For that reason, a customer may not react positively if you peer over your glasses. Typical nonverbal messages that this cue might send are displeasure, condescension, scrutiny, or disbelief.

Our nonverbal cues tell others a great deal about us, particularly when we display unproductive behaviors. *What are some possible reasons for the behaviors being displayed in these photos?*

CROSSING ARMS OR PUTTING HANDS ON HIPS

Typically viewed as a closed or defiant posture, crossing your arms or putting your hands in your hips may send a negative message to your customer and cause a confrontation. People often view this gesture as demonstrating a closed mind, resistance, or opposition.

HOLDING HANDS NEAR MOUTH

By holding your hands near your mouth, you will muffle your voice or distort your message. If someone is hearing-impaired or speaks English as a second language and relies partly on reading your lips, this person will be unable to understand your message. Also, placing your hands over or in front of your mouth can send messages of doubt or uncertainty, or can suggest that you are hiding something.

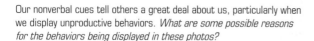

6   STRATEGIES FOR IMPROVING NONVERBAL COMMUNICATION

Concept: Nonverbal cues are all around us. Vocal and visual cues related to customers' feelings or needs are important and may mean the difference between a successful or unsuccessful customer service experience.

The four strategies discussed in this section will help improve your nonverbal communication skills if you practice them and try to understand the behavior of others.

SEEK OUT NONVERBAL CUES

Too often, service providers miss important vocal and visual clues related to customer feelings or needs because they are distracted doing other things or not being attentive. These missed opportunities can often mean the difference between successful and unsuccessful customer experiences. Train yourself to look for nonverbal cues by becoming a "student of human nature."

Nonverbal cues are all around you, if you simply open your eyes and mind to them. Start spending time watching people in public places (at supermarkets, malls, airports, bus stops, school, or wherever you have the chance). Watch the behavior of others you see, and the behavior of the people with whom they are interacting. Try to interpret the results of each behavior. However, keep in mind that human nature is not exact and that many factors affect the nonverbal cues used by yourself and others (culture, gender, environment, and many more). Be aware that you may be viewing through your own filters or biases, so evaluate carefully. Also, look at **clusters of nonverbal behavior,** and the language accompanying them instead of interpreting individual signals. These clusters might be positive (smiling, open body posture, friendly touching) or negative (crossed arms, looking away as someone talks, or angry facial expressions or gestures). Evaluating clusters can help you gain a more accurate view of what is going on in a communication exchange.

From your observations, objectively evaluate what works and what doesn't, and then modify your behavior accordingly to mimic the positive things you learn.

CONFIRM YOUR PERCEPTIONS

Let others know that you have received and interpreted their nonverbal cues. Ask for clarification by **perception checking** (see Chapter 6), if necessary. This involves stating the behavior observed, giving one or two possible interpretations, and then asking for clarification of message meaning.

For example, suppose that you are explaining the features of a piece of office equipment to a customer and he reacts with a quizzical look. You might respond with a statement such as, "You seem astonished by what I just said. I'm not sure whether you were surprised by something I said or whether I was unclear in my explanation. What questions do you have?" By doing this, you focus on his behavior and also provide an opportunity for him to gain additional necessary information.

SEEK CLARIFYING FEEDBACK

In many instances you need feedback in order to adjust your behavior. You may be sending cues you do not mean to send or to which others may react negatively. Assume that you are on a cross-functional work team with members of various departments in your organization and have been in a meeting to discuss ideas for creating a new work process. During a heated discussion of ideas, you excuse yourself briefly to get a drink of water in order to take a prescribed pill. Later, a teammate mentions that others commented about your frustration level and the fact that you bolted out of the room. To determine what behaviors led to the team's reaction, you might ask something like, "What did I do that made people perceive that I was upset?" If you find out why people viewed your behavior the way they did, you can offer an explanation in your next team meeting and avoid exhibiting similar behaviors in the future.

Another example might be to ask a coworker whether the clothing you have on seems too formal for a presentation you will give later in the day. Keep in mind, though, that some people will not give you honest, open feedback. Instead, they tell you what they think you want to hear or what they think will not hurt your feelings. It is usually best to elicit information from a variety of sources before making any behavioral changes, or deciding not to make them.

ANALYZE YOUR INTERPRETATIONS OF NONVERBAL CUES

One way to ensure that you are accurately evaluating nonverbal cues given by a variety of people is to analyze your own perceptions, stereotypes, and biases. The way you view certain situations or groups of people might negatively affect your ability to provide professional and

clusters of nonverbal behavior
Groupings of nonverbal behaviors that indicate a possible negative intent (e.g., crossed arms, closed body posturing, frowning, or turning away) while other behavior (e.g., smiling, open gestures with arms and hands, and friendly) touching indicate a positive message intent).

perception checking
The process of clarifying a nonverbal cue that was received by stating what behavior was observed, giving one or two possible interpretations, then asking the message sender for clarification.

effective customer service to all your customers. This is especially true of customers in the groups toward which you feel a bias. Without realizing it, you may send negative nonverbal cues that could cause a relationship breakdown and lead to a dissatisfied customer.

You will explore interactions with various groups and relationship-building strategies in more detail in Chapter 8.

7   CUSTOMER-FOCUSED BEHAVIOR

Concept: Being customer-focused in your behavior may help you solve a customer's problem or eliminate the opportunity for a problem to develop. The nonverbal cues discussed in this section can help you stay customer-focused.

The nonverbal behavior you exhibit in the presence of a customer can send powerful messages. You should constantly remind yourself of advice you may have heard often: "Be nice to people." One way you can indicate that you intend to be nice is to send customer-focused messages regularly and enthusiastically through your nonverbal cues. Figure 4.6 lists some important benefits of customer-focused behavior. Here are some simple ways to accomplish this when you are dealing with internal and external customers:

Stand Up, if Appropriate   If you are seated when a customer arrives or approaches you, stand up and greet him or her. This shows that you respect the person as an equal and are eager to assist her or him.

Act Promptly   The speed with which you recognize and assist customers, gather information, or respond to customers tells them what you think of their importance. If your service to the customer will take longer than planned or will be delayed, notify the customer, tell him or her the reason, and offer service alternatives if they are appropriate and available.

Guide Rather Than Direct   If customers must go to another person or area in the organization, or if they ask directions, personally guide them or have someone else do so, if possible. Do not simply point or direct. If you are on the telephone and you need to transfer a customer, give the extension of the person you're connecting to (in case of disconnection), transfer the call, and stay on the line to introduce the customer to the other service provider. Once the connection is made, excuse yourself and thank the customer for calling; then disconnect quietly.

Be Patient with Customers   Provide whatever assistance is necessary without appearing to push customers away. Patiently take the time to determine whether a customer has additional needs. It is fine to ask questions such as, "Will there be anything else I can assist you with?" to signal the end of your interaction with a customer. Just be sure that you do it with a smile and pleasant tone so that the customer does not feel "dumped" or abandoned.

Offer Assistance   Offer to assist with packages, especially if a customer is elderly, has a disability, has numerous packages, or appears to need help. Similarly, if someone needs assistance with a door or in getting from one place to another, offer to help. If the person says, "No, thank you," smile and go on your way. Do not assume that someone needs help, grab an arm to guide him or her, or push open a door. Such actions could surprise a person and throw him or her off balance. This is especially true of someone with a mobility or sight impairment who has learned to navigate using canes or other assistance. Upsetting a person's momentum or "system" could cause a fall or injury, which in turn could result in embarrassment and/or a liability situation for you or your organization.

Reduce Customer Wait Times   Nobody likes waiting, so keep waits to a minimum. If long delays are anticipated, inform the customer, offer alternatives, and work to reduce wait time.

Allow Customers to Go First   As a show of respect, encourage and allow customers to precede you through cafeteria lines, through doors, onto escalators or elevators, into vehicles, and so on. This projects an air of respect and courtesy. If he or she declines, do not make a scene and insist; simply go first yourself.

Offer Refreshments, if Appropriate   Take care of your "guests" the same way you would at home. Offer to get them something to drink if they come to your office or if they are attending lengthy meetings. You may also want to offer reading materials if they are in a waiting area. Be sure that reading materials are current and professional-looking. Discard old or worn materials.

CUSTOMER SERVICE SUCCESS TIP

Treat each customer professionally and in a manner that makes them feel welcome, important, and as if you really care about them and their needs and you will be successful.

Because of the competitive nature of business, organizations and customer service professionals should strive to pull ahead of the competition in any positive way possible. Simple courteous nonverbal behavior can be one way to beat the service quality levels of other companies. Why should you be courteous?

Image is Enhanced   First impressions are often lasting impressions. A more professional impression is created when you and the organizational culture are customer-focused. When your customers feel comfortable about you and the image projected, they are more likely to develop a higher level of trust and willingness to be more tolerant when things do go wrong occasionally.

Customer Loyalty Increases   People often return to organizations where they feel welcome, serviced properly, and respected. In Chapter 10, you will explore specific strategies for increasing customer loyalty.

Word-of-Mouth Advertising Increases   Sending regular positive nonverbal messages can help create a feeling of satisfaction and rapport. When customers are satisfied, and feel comfortable with you and your organization, they typically tell three to five other people. This increases your customer base while holding down formal advertising costs (newspapers and other publications, television, and radio).

Complaints are Reduced   When people are treated fairly and courteously, they are less likely to complain. If they do complain, their complaints are generally directed to a lower level (below supervisory level) and are generally expressed with low levels of anger. Simple things like smiling or attentive actions can help customers relax and feel appreciated.

Employee morale and esteem increase   If employees feel that they are doing a good job and get positive customer and management feedback, they will probably feel better about themselves. This increased level of self-esteem affects the quality of service delivered. Keep in mind your role in helping peers feel appreciated. They are often your internal customers and expect the same consideration and treatment as your external customers expect.

Financial Losses Decrease   When customers are satisfied, they are less likely to file lawsuits, steal, and be abusive toward employees (who might ultimately resign), and spread negative stories about employees and the organization. Building good rapport through communication can help in this area.

Employee-Customer Communication Improves   By treating customers in a professional, courteous manner, you encourage them to freely approach and talk to you. Needs, expectations, and satisfaction levels can then be more easily determined.

FIGURE 4.6   Courtesy Pays

Be Professional   Avoid smirking, making faces, or commenting to other customers after a customer leaves or turns his or her back. Such activity is unprofessional and will probably make the second customer wonder what you'll do when he or she leaves.

Once you become aware of the potential and scope of nonverbal communication, it can be one of the most important ways you have of sharing information and messages with customers. Limitless messages can be conveyed through a look, a gesture, a posture, or a vocal intonation. To be sure that the messages received are the ones you intended to send, be vigilant about what you say and do and how you communicate. Also, watch carefully the responses of your customers. Keep in mind that gender, culture, and a host of other factors affect the way you and your customers interpret received nonverbal cues.

To avoid distorting customer messages, or sending inappropriate messages yourself, keep these two points in mind: (1) Use a nonverbal cue you receive from others as an indicator and not as an absolute message. Analyze the cue in conjunction with the verbal message to more accurately assess the meaning of the message. (2) Continually seek to improve your understanding of nonverbal signals.

One final point: Remember that you are constantly sending nonverbal messages. Be certain that they complement your verbal communication and say to the customer, "I'm here to serve you."

KEY TERMS

appearance and grooming 95
articulation, enunciation, or pronunciation 93
body language 89
clusters of nonverbal behavior 105
emotional messages of color 99
environmental cues 96
etiquette and manners 99
gender communication 100
hygiene 95
impact of culture 102
inflection 92
interferences 94
miscellaneous cues 98
nonverbal messages 88
paralanguage 92

pauses 94
perception checking 105
pitch 92
posture 90
proxemics 96
rate of speech 93
semantics 94
silence 94
spatial cues 96
time allocation 98
verbal fillers 94
vocal cues 92
voice quality 93
volume 93

REVIEW QUESTIONS

1. What are six categories of nonverbal cues?
2. What are some of the voice qualities that can affect message meaning?
3. What are some examples of inappropriate workplace attire?
4. How can grooming affect your relationship with customers?
5. What are the four spatial distances observed in Western cultures, and for which people or situations are each typically reserved?
6. What are some of the miscellaneous nonverbal cues that can affect your effectiveness in a customer environment?
7. What are some ways in which men and women differ in their nonverbal communication?
8. What are some examples of unproductive communication?
9. List four strategies for improving nonverbal communication.
10. What are five examples of customer-focused behavior?

SEARCH IT OUT

Use the Internet to Further Your Knowledge of Nonverbal Communication

Now that you have learned some of the basics of nonverbal communication and the impact it can have on your customer relationships, use the Internet to explore the topic further.

Select two topics from the following list, check out as many reputable sites as you can find, and prepare a report of at least two pages in length to present to your peers.

Body language
Nonverbal cues

Dr. Albert Mehrabian
Gender communication
Spatial distances
The role of vocal cues in nonverbal communication
Professional appearance and grooming for the workplace
The impact of culture on nonverbal cues

COLLABORATIVE LEARNING ACTIVITY

Focus on Your Speech Patterns

Set up an audiocassette player. Then pair up with someone to discuss what you believe are the benefits of understanding and using nonverbal cues for building customer relations (spend at least 5 minutes presenting your ideas). Your partner should then present his or her views to you. Once both of you have presented your ideas, listen to the audiocassette with your partner and focus on your speech patterns.

1   Are you using appropriate verbal cues in your relationships with others? In what ways?

2   Do you use silence effectively? If so, how?

3   How did you sound in regard to the following?

Rate

Pitch

Volume

Articulation

4   Once you've identified positive and negative areas in your communication, set up an action plan for improvement by targeting the following:

Area(s) for improvement

Target improvement date

Resources needed to improve (assistance of others, training, training materials)

Support person(s)—who will coach or encourage you toward improvement?

FACE TO FACE

Handling Customer Complaints at Central Petroleum National Bank Background

Central Petroleum National Bank is one of the largest financial institutions in the Dallas–Fort Worth, Texas, area. With revenues of more than $200 million and investment holdings all over the world, the bank does business with many individuals and organizations in the region and other parts of Texas. The bank has 17 branch offices in addition to the home office in downtown Dallas.

Your Role

As one of the 125 employees of Central Petroleum's Western Branch Office, you provide customer service and establish new checking and savings accounts.

On Tuesday, a new customer, Mr. Gomez, came in to open an account. He stated that he was moving his money, over $200,000, from an account at a competing bank because of poor service. As you spoke with Mr. Gomez, one of your established patrons, Mrs. Wyatt, came into the office. As she signed in, you looked over, smiled, nodded, and held up one finger to indicate that you'd be with her momentarily. She smiled in return as she went to sit in the waiting area. As you were finishing the paperwork with Mr. Gomez, his teenage son came in and joined him. The son had been working at a summer job and had saved several hundred dollars. He also wished to establish a checking account. He placed his money on your desk and asked what he needed to do. He stated that he was on his lunch break and had only 20 more minutes to fill out the necessary forms. By then, you noticed that Mrs. Wyatt was looking at her watch and glancing frequently in your direction. Shortly thereafter, she left abruptly.

When you arrived at work the next day, the branch vice president called you into her office to tell you that she had received a complaint letter from Mrs. Wyatt concerning your lack of customer service and uncaring attitude.

Critical Thinking Questions

1   What did you do right in this situation?

2   What could you have done differently?

3   Do you believe that Mrs. Wyatt was justified in her perception of the situation? Explain.

4   Could Mrs. Wyatt have misinterpreted your nonverbal messages? Explain.

RETAIL—Starbucks Corporation

Go to www.starbucks.com and research the organization. Look at their annual report, values/mission, and other historical information about the organization on the website.

Think about what you read about Starbucks Corporation at the beginning of the chapter and answer the following questions. Your instructor may have you work together and share ideas in a group.

1   Have you been a customer of Starbucks or known anyone who has? What has been your experience or what have you heard about the company?

2   Do you believe Starbucks is truly customer-centric? Why or why not?

3   What do you believe are some of the driving forces behind the Starbucks success? Why?

4   If you were going to start a coffee-based business tomorrow, would you model after Starbucks Corporation? Why or why not?

Based on the content of this chapter, create a personal action plan focused on improving your nonverbal service to customers. Begin by taking an objective assessment of your current nonverbal skill strengths and areas for improvement. Once you have identified deficit areas, set goals for improvement.

Start your assessment by listing as many strengths and areas for improvement as you are aware of. Share your list with other people who know you well to see if they agree or can add additional items. Keep in mind that you will likely be more critical of yourself than other people will. Additionally, you may be sending nonverbal signals that you are not aware of.

For those reasons, keep an open mind when considering their comments.

Once you have a list, choose two or three items that you think need the most work and can add the most value when interacting with others. List these items on a sheet of paper along with specific courses of action you will take for improvement, the name of someone you will enlist to provide feedback on your behavior, and a specific date by which you want to see improvement. Related to the latter, keep in mind that it takes on average 21 to 30 days to see behavioral change; therefore, set a date that is at least in this range.

Nonverbal Communication Strengths	Areas for Improvement

Top Three Items	Who Will Help	Date for Change
1.		
2.		
3.		

1	F	5	T	9	T
2	F	6	T	10	F
3	T	7	F	11	T
4	T	8	T	12	T

. . . .

Ethical Dilemma 41. Possible Answers

1   How do you think you would feel if you were the homeless patient? Why?

He likely feels that there is a double standard, that the receptionist views him as less important because he has not assets or resources, and that the quality and degree of service that he will receive, if any, will be inferior to that of other patients. This is likely due to his financial standing and social status level and the perception that the receptionist might have of such people.

2   Why do you think the receptionist used different standards of service for the two patients?

He possibly has preconceived ideas about homeless people and negative stereotypes (e.g., they are lazy, drug/alcohol abusers, etc). Also, that the hospital will not recoup its costs for treatment from the homeless man.

3   What could the receptionist have done differently/better to improve the service delivery in this situation?

Attempt to avoid stereotypes about homeless people, treat the homeless man with more respect and as a customer who was not homeless, and use more positive nonverbal signals when dealing with all customers.

4   What Is the likely Impact of the service delivery outlined In this situation?

The homeless person will likely have a negative impression about the receptionist and medical facility, he may possibly have lowered self-esteem as a result of his treatment, stereotypes might be reinforced with other patients, and possible legal action might result, especially, if the homeless man has complications due to lack of or inferior treatment.

. . . .

Listening to the Customer

If there is any one secret of success, it lies in the ability to get the other person's point of view and see things from that person's angle as well as from your own.

—Henry Ford

After completing this chapter, you will be able to:

1   Describe why listening is important to customer service.

2   Define the four steps in the listening process.

3   List the characteristics of a good listener.

4   Recognize the causes of listening breakdown.

5   Develop strategies to improve your listening ability.

6   Use information-gathering techniques learned to better serve customers.

In the Real World Education—Jenks Public Schools

In an age where dropout levels are increasing, public school efficiency is dropping throughout the country, dropout rates are rising, and students are being labeled as inferior in many instances to those of other countries, Jenks Public Schools stands out as exemplary. In 2005, the school district won the coveted Baldrige Quality Award.

According to the school's website, "Jenks Public Schools is the 11th largest school district in Oklahoma, serving 9,400 students from pre-kindergarten through 12th grade. The district operates nine schools on five campuses, has an annual budget of $48 million and its own transportation, maintenance, print shop, warehouse, food service, and technology operations. There are over 1,200 employees.

"Continuous improvement is the watchword for this organization and leaders, teachers, staff, and parents are regularly trying to exceed previous achievements. In addition to continuous improvement, there are three other 'pillars' that serve as the model for the district: Strong Quality Leadership, Customer Focus, and Systems/Process Focus."

The following are some indicators of the district's success:

Jenks Public Schools are in the top 1 percent of schools in the state of Oklahoma;

Average student scores in all subject areas in all grades tested are significantly higher than state and national levels;

In the past seven years, the district produced 65 National Merit semifinals, 48 National Merit finalists, and two Presidential Scholars;

Southeast Elementary School was one of only four in Okalahoma to achieve an API perfect score (1,500 points); district students consistently outperform other students statewide and nationwide in the ACTA and SAT scores;

Eighty-five percent of the 2004 graduating class enrolled in colleges or universities;

Drop-out rates have decreased steadily from 6.9 percent in 1999 to 1.2 percent at the end of 2004;

Staff retention rate for teachers is 91 percent and 85 percent for nonteaching positions.

For more information about this organization, visit www.quality.nist.gov/PDF_files/Jenks_Public_Schools_Profile.pdf.

See activity based on this section on page 135.

Quick Preview

Before reviewing the chapter content, respond to the following questions by placing a "T" for true or an "F" for false on the rules. Use any questions you miss as a checklist of material to which you will pay particular attention as you read through the chapter. For those you get right, congratulate yourself, but review the sections they address in order to learn additional details about the topic.

_____ 1. Listening is a passive process similar to hearing.

_____ 2. Listening is a learned process.

_____ 3. During the comprehending stage of the listening process, messages received are compared and matched to memorized data in order to attach meaning to the messages.

_____ 4. The two categories of obstacles that contribute to listening breakdowns are personal and professional.

_____ 5. Biases sometimes get in the way of effective customer service.

_____ 6. A customer's inability to communicate ideas effectively can be an obstacle to effective listening.

_____ 7. A faulty assumption arises when you react to or make a decision about a customer's message on the basis of your past experiences or encounters.

_____ 8. A customer's refusal to deal with you, coupled with a request to be served by someone else, could indicate that you are viewed as a poor listener.

_____ 9. Many people can listen effectively to several people at one time.

_____ 10. By showing a willingness to listen and eliminate distractions, you can encourage meaningful customer dialogue.

_____ **11.** Two types of questions that are effective for gathering information are reflective and direct.

_____ **12.** Open-end questions elicit more information than closed-end questions do because they allow customers to provide what they feel is necessary to answer your question.

Answers to Quick Preview can be found at the end of the chapter.

1 WHY IS LISTENING SO IMPORTANT?

Concept: To be a better customer service professional, it is necessary to improve your listening skills.

Listening effectively is the primary means that many customer service professionals use to determine the needs of their customers. Many times, these needs are not communicated to you directly but through inferences, indirect comments, or nonverbal signals. A skilled listener will pick up on a customer's words and these cues and conduct follow-up questioning or probe deeper to determine the real need.

Most people take the listening skill for granted. They incorrectly assume that anyone can listen effectively. Unfortunately, this is untrue. Many people are complacent about listening and only go through the motions of listening. According to Andrew Wolvin and Carolyn Coakley in their book *Listening,* one survey found that three-fourths (74.3 percent) of 129 managers surveyed perceived themselves to be passive or detached listeners.

In a classic study on listening conducted by Dr. Ralph G. Nichols, who is sometimes called the *father of listening,* data revealed that the average white-collar worker in the United States typically has only about a 25 percent efficiency rate when listening. This means that 75 percent of the message is lost. Think about what such a loss in message reception could mean in an organization if the poor listening skills of customer service professionals led to a loss of 75 percent of customer opportunities. Figure 5.1 gives you some idea of the impact of this loss.

2 WHAT IS LISTENING?

Concept: Listening is a learned process, not a physical one.

Listening is your primary means of gathering information from a customer or any other person. True listening is an active learned process, as opposed to hearing, which is the physical

CUSTOMER SERVICE SUCCESS TIP

To help increase listening efficiency, stop doing other tasks and focus on what your customers are saying. Ask clarifying questions where appropriate.

listening
An active, learned process consisting of four phases—receiving/hearing the message, attending, comprehending/assigning meaning, and responding.

FIGURE 5.1

Missed Opportunities (Based on a 25 Percent Efficiency Rate)

Opportunities	Action Taken	Impact
100 customers a day, each with a $10 order	25 orders were filled successfully	Loss of $750 per day ($273,750 per year)
1,000 customers went to a store in one day	250 were serviced properly	750 were dissatisfied
1,000,000 members were eligible for membership renewal in an association	250,000 returned their application after receiving a reminder call	750,000 members were lost

Implied Messages

To help reinforce the concept that many customer messages are implied rather than actually spoken to service providers, form a group with two other students and role-play the following scenarios. Choose one in which you play the customer, one in which you play the service provider, and one in which you are the observer.

When you are the customer, simply state your issue or need in a way that does not ask the service provider to do something. Also, do not suggest a solution to the problem or issue. Let the person playing the provider role figure out your need and offer one or more solutions.

At the end of each scenario, you and your teammates should take time to answer the following questions:

1. What unspoken need was the customer sending to the service provider?
2. How well did the service provider do in identifying the customer's issue or need?
3. Specifically, what did the service provider do or say to address the customer's need or issue?
4. What could the service provider have done differently to improve service or satisfy the customer?

Possible answers to these scenarios can be found at www.mhhe.com/lucas09.

Scenario 1

A customer has a mortgage payment due on the first day of each month. In the past, payday was on the 10th and 25th; however, he/she started a new job and now gets paid on the 15th and 30th of each month.

Scenario 2

You work in a customer care center as a call center representative. A customer contacts you because he/she just placed an order on your company's website but forgot to enter a coupon code for free shipping that he/she received in the mail last week. His/her credit card had already been charged for the shipping when the order was sent.

Scenario 3

A customer moved into her/his newly built house in February and subsequently requested the cable company (your organization) to install cable service to the home. The installers came out with a backhoe, dug a trench, and installed the cable. It is now June and service has been fine until the customer turned on her/his lawn sprinkler system. The water pressure dropped immediately and upon investigation soggy ground was found where the cable company dug to install the cable months ago.

action of gathering sound waves through the ear canal. When you listen actively, you go through a process consisting of various phases—hearing or receiving the message, attending, comprehending or assigning meaning, and responding. Figure 5.2 illustrates the process.

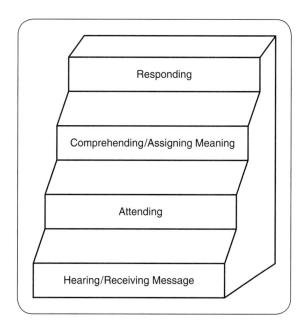

FIGURE 5.2

The Listening Process

Responding

Comprehending/Assigning Meaning

Attending

Hearing/Receiving Message

Personal Listening Experiences

THINK ABOUT EXPERIENCES YOU HAVE HAD AS A CUSTOMER IN WHICH THE PROVIDER DID NOT DO A GOOD JOB LISTENING TO YOU. Be prepared to share these in class.

How did you react to the behavior of the provider?
Did you take your business elsewhere?
What did you tell others about your experience?

Describe some of these experiences.

How did the behavior of the provider make you feel?

---

hearing
A passive physiological process of gathering sound waves and transmitting them to the brain for analysis. It is the first phase of the listening process.

attending
The phase of the listening process in which a listener focuses attention on a specific sound or message being received from the environment.

comprehending or assigning meaning
The phase of the listening process in which the brain attempts to match a received sound or message with other information stored in the brain in order to recognize or extract meaning from it.

memory
The ability to gain, store, retain and recall information in the brain for later application. Short-term memory stores small bits of information (7 items, plus or minus 2) for approximately 20 seconds while long-term memory can store much larger quantities of information for potentially unlimited duration.

recognition
A process that occurs in thinking when a previously experienced pattern, event, process, image, or object that is stored in memory is encountered again.

responding
Refers to sending back verbal and nonverbal messages to a message originator.

HEARING AND RECEIVING THE MESSAGE

Hearing is a passive physiological process of receiving sound waves and transmitting them to the brain, where they are analyzed. This is usually a simple process. Because of external noises and internal distracters (psychological and physical), however, a customer's message(s) may be lost or distorted. Using some of the strategies for improvement given in this chapter can help change your ability to listen more effectively.

ATTENDING

Once your ears pick up sound waves, your brain goes to work focusing on, or **attending** to, what was heard. In the process, it sorts out everything being heard. The effort involves deciding what's important so that you can focus attention on the proper sound. This becomes extremely difficult when you are receiving multiple messages or sounds. That is why it's important to eliminate as many distractions as possible. For example, during a meeting you could forward phone calls, or turn off your computer, or shut your door—or you could find a quiet place to meet.

COMPREHENDING OR ASSIGNING MEANING

Once you've decided to which message or customer you will listen, your brain begins a process of **comprehending or assigning meaning** to what you heard. Just like a computer, your brain has files of information—sounds, sights, shapes, images, experiences, knowledge on various topics in memory—which it sorts through. As it compares what was heard to what is stored, it tries to match the pieces. For example, when you hear a voice on the phone that sounds familiar, the brain goes to work trying to match the voice to a name or person you've dealt with before. This is called **memory** and **recognition.**

RESPONDING

The last phase of the listening process is **responding.** Selecting an appropriate response is crucial to the success of your customer interactions. The words you select, the way you deliver them, the timing and location, and the nonverbal signals you send all have meaning, and all affect the way others perceive and interpret your message. This is why you should be careful to consciously select the appropriate response and method of delivery when dealing with customers. A wrong choice could mean lost business or worse (the customer could get angry or violent).

Figure 5.3 gives some suggested questions you might ask yourself to check on your listening skills. Figure 5.4 provides questions for a self-assessment of your skills.

In analyzing your customer's message(s), ask yourself the following questions:

- Am I practicing active listening skills?
- What message is the customer trying to get across?
- What does the customer want or need me to do in response to his or her message?
- Should I take notes or remember key points being made?
- Am I forming premature conclusions, or do I need to listen further?
- Are there biases or distractions I need to avoid?
- Is the customer failing to provide information needed to make a sound decision?
- What other feedback clues are being provided in addition to words? Are they important to message meaning?
- What questions do I need to ask as a follow-up to the customer's message?

FIGURE 5.3

Questions for the Listener

To prepare yourself for effective customer interactions and to quickly assess how good your listening skills are, take a few moments to take the following assessment. Depending on your responses, you may need to develop a listening improvement plan using some of the strategies in this chapter and available from other sources.

Place a check mark in the appropriate column.

	Always	**Sometimes**	**Never**
1. When someone speaks to me, I stop what I am doing to focus on what they are saying.			
2. I listen to people even if I disagree with what they are saying.			
3. When I am unsure of someone's meaning, I ask for clarification.			
4. I avoid daydreaming when listening to others.			
5. I focus on main ideas, not details, when someone speaks to me.			
6. While listening, I am also conscious of nonverbal cues sent by the speaker.			
7. I consciously block out noise when someone speaks to me.			
8. I paraphrase the messages I receive in order to ensure I understood the speaker's meaning.			
9. I wait until I have received a person's entire message before forming my response.			
10. When receiving negative feedback (e.g., a customer complaint), I listen with an open mind.			

Rating key: Always = 5   **Sometimes** = 3   **Never** = 0
Add your total score. If you rated:

40–50	Your listening is excellent
26–39	Your listening is above average
15–25	Your listening likely falls into the range identified by Dr. Nichols' study (included in this chapter)
Below 14	You have a serious listening problem and should seek additional training or resources to improve.

FIGURE 5.4

Listening Self-Assessment

3 CHARACTERISTICS OF A GOOD LISTENER

Concept: Listening will improve as you "learn" in the customer's shoes.

Successful listening is essential to service excellence. Like any other skill, listening is a learned behavior that some people learn better than others. Some common characteristics possessed by most effective listeners are discussed in the following sections. The characteristics of effective and ineffective listeners are summarized in Figure 5.5.

Empathy. By putting yourself in the customer's place and trying to relate to the customer's needs, wants, and concerns, you can often reduce the risk of poor service. Some customer service professionals neglect the customer's need for compassion, especially when the customer is dissatisfied. Such negligence tends to magnify or compound the effect of the initial poor service the customer received.

Understanding. The ability to listen as customers verbalize their needs, and to ensure that you understand them, is essential in properly servicing the customer. Too often, you hear people say, "I understand what you mean," when it is obvious that they have no clue as to the level of emotion being felt. When this happens while a customer is upset or angry, the results could be flared tempers, loss of business, bad publicity, and at the far end of the continuum, acts of violence. Some techniques for demonstrating understanding will be covered later in this chapter.

Patience. Patience is especially important when a language barrier or speech disability is part of the situation. Your job is to take extra care to determine the customer's needs and then respond appropriately. In some cases, you may have to resort to the use of an interpreter or written communication in order to determine the customer's needs.

Attentiveness. By focusing your attention on the customer, you can better interpret his or her message and satisfy his or her needs. Attentiveness is often displayed through nonverbal cues (nodding or cocking of the head to one side or the other,

FIGURE 5.5

Characteristics of Effective and Ineffective Listeners

Many factors can indicate an effective or ineffective listener. Over the years, researchers have assigned the following characteristics to effective and ineffective listeners:

Effective Listeners	Ineffective Listeners
Focused	Inattentive
Responsive	Uncaring
Alert	Distracted
Understanding	Unconcerned
Caring	Insensitive
Empathetic	Complacent
Unemotional	Emotionally involved
Interested	Self-centered
Patient	Judgmental
Cautious	Haphazard
Open	Defensive

smiling, or using paralanguage), which were discussed in detail in Chapter 4. When you are reading, talking on the phone to someone while servicing your customer, or doing some other task while "listening" to your customer, you are not really focusing. In fact your absorption rate will fall into the 25 percent category discussed earlier.

Objectivity. In dealings with customers, try to avoid subjective opinions or judgments. If you have a preconceived idea about customers, their concerns or questions, the environment, or anything related to the customers, you could mishandle the situation. Listen openly and avoid making assumptions. Allow customers to describe their needs, wants, or concerns, and then analyze them fairly before taking appropriate action.

Active listening involves complete attention, a readiness and willingness to take action, and an open mind to evaluate customers and determine their needs. *What should customer service professionals do to achieve these goals of active listening?*

4   CAUSES OF LISTENING BREAKDOWN

Concept: Poor customer service may result from a breakdown of the listening process.

Many factors contribute to ineffective listening. Some are internal, but others are external and you cannot control them. The key is to recognize actual and potential factors that can cause ineffective listening and strive to eliminate them. The factors discussed in the following sections are some of the most common.

PERSONAL OBSTACLES

As a listener, you may have individual characteristics or qualities that get in the way of listening effectively to the customer. Some of these **personal obstacles** are discussed in the following sections.

Biases   Your opinions or beliefs about a specific person, group, situation, or issue can sometimes cloud your ability to listen objectively to what is being said. These **biases** may result in preconceived and sometimes incorrect assumptions. They can also lead to service breakdown, complaints, and angry or lost customers.

Psychological Distracters   Your psychological state can impede effective listening. **Psychological distracters,** such as being angry or upset, or simply not wanting to deal with a particular person or situation, may negatively affect your listening. Think about a time when you had a negative call or encounter with a customer or someone else and you became frustrated or angry. Did your mood, and possibly your voice tone, change as a result? Did that emotion then carry over and affect another person later?

Often when people become upset, time is needed to cool off before they deal with someone else. If you do not cool off, the chance that you will raise your voice or become frustrated with the next person you encounter is increased greatly. And, if this second encounter escalates because of the person's reaction to a negative tone or atti-

personal obstacles
Factors that can limit performance or success in life. Examples are disabilities, lack of education, or biases.

biases
Beliefs or opinions that a person has about an individual or group. Often based on unreasonable distortions or prejudice.

psychological distracters
Refers to mental factors that can cause a shift in focus in interacting with others. Examples are state of health and personal issues.

When a customer service professional gets angry, his or her tone and mood may likely carry over to a customer. *How do you feel when a customer service professional is angry and raises his or her voice?*

circadian rhythm
The physiological 24-hour cycle associated with the earth's rotation that affects metabolic and sleep patterns in humans as day replaces night.

tude, you might respond inappropriately. Thus, a vicious cycle is started. You get angry at a person, your tone carries over to a second, who in turn gets upset with your tone, your emotions escalate, and you carry that mood to a third person, and so on. All of this lessens your ability to listen and serve customers effectively.

Physical Condition   Another internal factor that can contribute to or detract from effective listening is your state of wellness and fitness. When you are ill, fatigued, in poor physical condition, or just not feeling well, listening can suffer. According to a study by the National Sleep Foundation, one-third of respondents say they experience daytime sleepiness and over 80 percent of American adults link inadequate sleep with impaired daytime performance and behavior. On average, American adults get about 6.9 hours of sleep a night.[1]

We often hear that a good diet and exercise are essential to good health. They are also crucial for effective listening. Try not to skip meals when you are working, stay away from foods high in sugar content, and get some form of regular exercise. These all affect physical condition. Try something as simple as using the stairs rather than the elevator or escalator. Another option is a brisk walk at lunchtime. All of these can help you maintain your "edge" so that you will be better prepared for a variety of customer encounters.

Circadian Rhythm   All people have a natural 24-hour biological pattern (**circadian rhythm**) by which they function. This "clock" often establishes the body's peak performance periods. Some people are said to be morning people; their best performance typically occurs early in the day. They often wake early, "hit the ground running," and continue until after lunch, when the natural rhythm or energy level in their body begins to slow down. For such people afternoons are often a struggle. They may not do their best thinking or perform physically at peak during that point in the day.

Evening people often have just the opposite pattern of energy. They struggle to get up or perform in the morning; however, during the afternoon and in the evening they are just hitting their stride. They often stay awake and work or engage in other activities until the early hours of the next day, when the morning people have been sound asleep for hours. From a listening standpoint, you should recognize your own natural body pattern so that you can deal with the most important listening and other activities during your peak period if possible. For example, if you are a morning person, you may want to ask your boss to assign you to customer contact or to handling problem situations early in the day. At that time, you are likely to be most alert and productive, less stressed, and less apt to become frustrated or irritated by abusive or offensive behavior by others.

Preoccupation   When you have personal or other matters on your mind (related to financial matters, school, marriage, family, or personal or work projects), it sometimes

---

[1]2005 Sleep in America Poll, The National Sleep Foundation, www.sleepfoundation.org.

WORK IT OUT 5.3

Personal Habits

TAKE A FEW MINUTES TO THINK ABOUT YOUR PERSONAL NUTRITIONAL AND EXERCISE HABITS SINCE THESE CAN AFFECT ATTENTION SPAN AND YOUR ABILITY TO LISTEN EFFECTIVELY; THEN CREATE A LIST OF THE ONES THAT ARE POSITIVE AND NEGATIVE.

becomes difficult to focus on the needs and expectations of the customer. This can frustrate both you and the customer. It is difficult to turn off personal problems, but you should try to resolve them before going to work, even if you must take time off to deal with them. Many companies offer programs to assist employees in dealing with their personal and performance issues. Through **employee assistance programs (EAPs)**, many organizations are offering counseling in such areas as finance, mental hygiene (health), substance abuse, marital and family issues, and workplace performance problems. Check with your supervisor to identify such resources in your organization, or ask about these services during the interview process when you apply for a position.

Hearing Loss   Many people suffer from hearing loss caused by physiological (physical) problems or extended exposure to loud noises. Sometimes they are not aware that their hearing is impaired. Often, out of vanity or embarrassment, people take no action to remedy the loss. If you find yourself regularly straining to hear someone, having to turn one ear or the other toward the speaker, or having to ask people to repeat what they said because you didn't get the entire message, you may have a hearing loss. If you suspect that you have hearing loss, go to your physician or an audiologist (hearing specialist) quickly to avoid complications or further loss of hearing.

Listening Skill Level   People communicate on different levels, depending on their knowledge and experiences in the area of communication. Adults are influenced by the experiences they had as children; that is, they are likely to repeat behavior they learned during childhood. For example, if you grew up in an environment where the people around you practiced positive skills related to listening, providing feedback and using nonverbal communication (covered in Chapter 4), and effective interpersonal skills for dealing with others, you will likely use similar techniques as an adult (Figure 5.6 shows some indicators of poor listening skills). On the other hand, if your childhood experiences were negative and you did not have good communication role models, the chances are that you struggle in dealing with others effectively.

As you read earlier, listening is the primary skill most people have for gathering information. Unfortunately, in the United States, listening as a skill is not routinely taught in most public school systems. People learn the proper techniques involved in the skill only if they read, listen to audiotapes, watch videos, and attend seminars or college courses on listening. Too often, even though an adult's intentions might be well meant, techniques used to teach listening to children are often ineffective.

Thought Speed   Your brain is capable of comprehending messages delivered at rates of as much as four to six times faster (**thought speed**) than the speed at which the average adult in the United States speaks (approximately 125 to 150 words per minute, or wpm). The difference between the two rates can be referred to as a **lag time or listening gap** during

employee assistance programs (EAPs)
Benefit package offered to employees by many organizations that provide services to help employees deal with personal problems that might adversely impact their work performance (e.g. legal, financial, behavioral and mental counseling services).

thought speed
The rate at which the human brain processes information.

lag time
The term applied to the difference in the rate at which the human brain can receive and process information and at which most adults speak.

listening gap
The difference in the speed at which the brain can comprehend communication and the speed at which the average adult speaks in the United States.

FIGURE 5.6

Indicators of Poor Listening

You cannot afford the luxury of failing to listen to your customer. Periodically, you should do a self-check on your listening style to see whether you need to improve. If any of the following events occur, you may need to refocus.

Customers specifically ask to speak to or be served by someone else.

You find yourself missing key details of conversations.

You regularly have to ask people to repeat information.

You end phone calls or personal encounters not knowing for sure what action is required of you.

Customers often make statements such as, "Did you hear what I said?" "Are you listening to me?" or "You're not listening."

You find yourself daydreaming or distracted as a customer is speaking.

You miss nonverbal cues sent by the customer as the two of you communicate.

You answer a question incorrectly because you didn't actually hear it.

Ethical Dilemma 5.1

A customer comes into your office at the Department of Water and Sewer on a Tuesday following a three-day holiday weekend. She has a toddler and a five-year-old daughter with her and is very upset. She is cursing and screaming that she was promised that her water, which was turned off due to nonpayment of her bill for two months, was supposed to be turned back on Friday afternoon, but was not. She states that she and her two infant children had no water or bathroom to use all weekend.

You know that no turn-offs are scheduled on Fridays since maintenance staffs have in-service training every Friday afternoon.

In checking your database, you find that she had promised to come in last Wednesday to give a money order for the delinquent bills but never showed up. You also see that she has a history of nonpayment.

1. What would you say to this customer? Explain.
2. What actions would you take to remedy the situation and get her water back on so that she and her children would have access to services?

faulty assumptions
Service provider projections made about underlying customer message meanings based on past experiences.

which the mind is actually idle. The result is that your brain does other things to occupy itself (for example, daydreaming). To prevent or reduce such distraction, you must consciously focus on your customer's message, look for key points, ask pertinent questions, and respond appropriately. If the customer has a complaint or suggestion, you may even want to take notes. This not only helps you focus on and recall information but also can demonstrate to the customer that you are truly interested in the ideas or subject of the conversation.

Faulty Assumptions   Because of past experiences or encounters with others, you may be tempted to make **faulty assumptions** about your customer's message(s). Don't. Each customer and each situation is different and should be regarded as such. Because you had a certain experience with one customer does not mean that you will have a similar experience with another. Suppose, for example, that you are a college registrar. You see lots of students and hear lots of stories when they try to change from one class to another or drop a course. One day a student comes into your office and asks to cancel her registration in one class in order to register for another even though the designated time for such a change has passed. Your immediate inclination might be to quote policy since you've "heard this one before." Your response might sound like, "I'm sorry, Ms. Molina, the period for adds or drops has passed." Don't respond so quickly; instead, hear the customer out. She may provide information (verbally or nonverbally) that will change your view. For example, Ms. Molina (crying) might say, "I've got to get out of that class. I need one more course to graduate, but I can't stay in this class."

If you are proactive in this situation and practicing active listening, you will pick up on the emotions and ask some questions in order to find out her real need or issue. For example, you might say, "Ms. Molina, you seem very upset, is anything wrong?" She might respond, "Yes. I need to graduate this semester and return to my country to help support my family. But I can't stay in Mr. Broward's class. He's . . . he's always leering at me and making lewd remarks. And, in a previous class, he would regularly massage my shoulders and that of other girls during class." Obviously, the rules don't apply in this case. If you didn't listen, you'd never know, and there would be a dissatisfied and distraught customer as a result. Also, you might be setting up the institution for a harassment lawsuit by forcing Ms. Molina to stay in the class or to seek other solutions (lawsuit, violence, or going to the media to expose the teacher).

EXTERNAL OBSTACLES

You cannot remove all barriers to effective listening, but you should still try to reduce them when dealing with customers. Some typical examples of **external obstacles** include the following.

Information Overload Each day you are bombarded with information from many sources. You get information in meetings, from the radio and television, from customers, and in a variety of public places. In many instances, you spend as much as 5 to 6 hours a day listening to customers, coworkers, family members, friends, and strangers. Such **information overload** can result in stress, inadequate time to deal with individual situations, and reduced levels of customer service.

Employees rarely have control over external distractions in the workplace. *What are some strategies to help cope with a noisy work environment?*

Other People Talking It is not possible for you to give your full attention to two speakers simultaneously. In order to serve customers effectively, deal with only one person at a time. If someone else approaches, smile, acknowledge him or her, and say, "I'll be with you in just a moment" or at least signal that message by holding up your index finger to indicate "1 minute" while you smile.

Ringing Phones Ringing telephones can be annoying, but you shouldn't stop helping one customer to get into a discussion with or try to serve another customer over the phone. This creates a dilemma, for you cannot ignore customers or others who depend on you to serve their needs over the telephone.

Several options are available. You might arrange with your supervisor or coworkers to have someone else take the calls. Those people can either provide service or take messages (as we'll explore in Chapter 9), depending on the business your organization conducts. Another option is the use of a voice mail system, answering service, or pager for message collection. Still another possibility would be to ask the person to whom you are speaking face-to-face to excuse you, professionally answer the phone, and either ask the caller to remain on hold or take a number for a callback.

No one solution is best. You can only try to provide the best service possible, depending on your situation. Before such situations develop, it is a good idea to speak with your supervisor or team leader and peers to determine the policy and procedures for handling customers in these instances.

Speakerphones These devices allow for hands-free telephone conversations. They are great because you can continue your conversation while searching for something the customer has requested. Unfortunately, many people put callers on the loudspeaker while continuing to do work not related to the caller. This not only is rude but it results in ineffective communication. Because the speakerphone picks up background noise, it is often difficult to hear the caller, especially if you are moving around the room and are not next to the phone. Many people dislike speakerphones. Be aware that improper use of the speakerphone could cause customers to stop calling. An additional issue with the speakerphone is confidentiality. Since others can hear the caller's conversation, the caller may be reluctant to provide certain information (credit card and

external obstacles
Factors outside an organization or the sphere of one's influence that can cause challenges in delivering service.

information overload
Refers to having too many messages coming together and causing confusion, frustration, or an inability to act.

Dealing with Interruptions

social security numbers, medical information, or personal data). Whenever you use a speakerphone, inform the caller if someone else is in the room with you and/or close your office door, if possible.

Office and Maintenance Equipment   Noisy printers, computers, photocopying machines, electric staplers, vacuum cleaners, and other devices can also be distractions. When servicing customers, eliminate or minimize the use of these types of items. If others are using noisy equipment, try to position yourself or them as far away from the customer service area as possible.

Physical Barriers   Desks, counters, furniture, or other items separating you from your customer can stifle communication. Depending on your job function, you might be able to eliminate barriers. If possible, do so. These obstacles can distance you physically from your customer or depersonalize your service. Be conscious of how you arrange your office or work space. Side-by-side (facing the customer at an angle) seating next to a table is preferable to sitting across from a customer in most situations. An exception to this approach would be appropriate if you provide service to customers who might become agitated or violent. Some examples: city or state clerks who deal with people who have been charged with traffic or other violations of the law; public utility employees who deal with people who are complaining about service problems; employees in motor vehicle offices where people may have frustrating problems with drivers' licenses or vehicle registration.

AN ADDITIONAL OBSTACLE

In addition to the issues already addressed, customers themselves can negatively affect communication—through their inability to convey a message.

Although it is not specifically a listening issue, if customers are unable to deliver their message effectively, you will be unable to receive and properly analyze their meaning. No amount of dedication and effort on your part will make up for a language barrier, a disability (speech, physical) that limits speech and nonverbal body language, or poor communication skills. In these situations, it is often necessary to seek out others to help (translators, signers) or to use alternative means of communication [gestures, written, symbols, or a text telephone (TTY/TDD)] to discover the customers' meaning and satisfy their needs.

By recognizing these limiting factors, you can improve your chances of communicating more effectively. Use Worksheet 5-4 (see www.mhhe.com/lucas09) to evaluate listening distractions in your environment.

Inattentive Listening Behavior

To HELP YOU IMPROVE YOUR LISTENING SKILLS AND OFFER BETTER SERVICE TO YOUR CUSTOMERS, COMPLETE THE FOLLOWING ACTIVITY. Think of a time when you were trying to verbally communicate ideas to someone but you realized (from verbal and nonverbal responses) that this person was not listening to you.

1. What led you to believe that this person was not paying attention to your message(s)? How was your ability to get your message across affected? How did you feel?

Next, think of times when you were involved in conversations but were not really focused and listening to the other person.

2. What was going on that prevented you from listening effectively? What reaction did your listener have to your distraction or lack of focus?

Use your responses to these questions to improve your listening skills.

5 STRATEGIES FOR IMPROVED LISTENING

Concept: You can improve your listening skills in several different ways. One important way is to listen more than you talk.

Numerous techniques can be used to become a more effective listener. The following tips can be used as a basis for improvement.

STOP TALKING!

You cannot talk and actively listen at the same time. When the customer starts talking, stop talking and listen carefully. One common mistake that many people make is to ask a question, hesitate, and if no answer is immediately offered, ask a second question or "clarify" the meaning by providing additional information. A habit like this is not only confusing to the listener, but rude.

Some people like to reflect on what they have heard and then formulate just the right answer before responding. People who speak another language, or who have a disability, may either be translating the information received into their own language or trying to assimilate your message before making an appropriate response. If you interrupt with additional information or questions, you may interfere with their thought patterns and cause them to become frustrated. The end result is that the listener may not speak or respond at all because he or she believes that you aren't really listening or interested in the response anyhow, or because he or she is embarrassed or confused. To avoid such a scenario, plan what you want to say, ask the question, and then stop speaking. You might ask, "Mr. Swanson, how do you think we might resolve this issue?" Once you have asked the question, stop talking and wait for a response. If a response does not come in a minute or so, try asking the question another way (paraphrase), possibly offering some guidance to a response and concluding with an open-end question (one that encourages the listener to give opinions or longer responses). You might say, "Mr. Swanson, I'd really like to help resolve this issue. Perhaps we could try _____ or _____. How do you think that would work?"

PREPARE YOURSELF

Before you can listen effectively to someone, you must be ready to receive what this person has to say. Stop reading, writing, talking to others, thinking about other things, working on

Correcting Common Listening Problems

HERE ARE SOME COMMON LISTENING PROBLEMS. Try to think of one or two means for reducing or eliminating them in your customer service.

Listening to words, not concepts, ideas, or emotions.

Pretending interest in a customer's problem, question, suggestion, or concern.

Planning your next remarks while the customer is talking.

Being distracted by external factors.

Listening only for what you perceive is the real issue or point.

Reacting emotionally to what the customer is saying.

---

your computer, answering phones, and dealing with other matters that distract you. For example, if a customer approaches while you're using a calculator to add up a row of figures, smile and say, "I'll be with you in just a moment" or smile and hold up your index finger to indicate "1 minute." As quickly as possible, complete your task, apologize for the delay, and then ask, "How may I assist you?"

LISTEN ACTIVELY

Use the basics of sound communication when a customer is speaking. The following strategies are typically helpful in sending an "I care" message when done naturally and with sincerity:

SMILE!

Do not interrupt to interject your ideas or make comments unless they are designed to clarify a point made by the customer.

Sit or stand up straight and make eye contact with the customer.

Lean forward or turn an ear toward the customer, if appropriate and necessary.

Paraphrase their statements occasionally.

Nod and offer affirmative paralanguage statements ("I see," "Uh-huh," "Really," "Yes") to show that you're following the conversation.

Do not finish a customer's sentence. Let the customer talk.

In addition, focus on complete messages. A complete message consists of the words, nonverbal messages, and emotions of the customer. If a customer says that she's satisfied with a product but is sending nonverbal signals that contradict her statement, you should investigate further. Suppose that the supply of blue bowls being given away as gifts to people who stop by your trade show exhibit is gone. The customer might say, "Oh, that's okay. I guess a green one will do." Her tone and facial expression may, however, indicate disappointment. You could counter with, "I'm sorry we're out of the blue bowls, Mrs. Zagowski. If you'd like one, I can give you a certificate that will allow you to pick one up when you visit our store, or I can take your address and ship one to you when I get back to the store. Would you prefer one of those options?" By being "tuned in" to your customer and taking this extra initiative, you have gone beyond the ordinary and moved into the realm of exceptional customer service. Mrs. Zagowski will probably appreciate your gesture and tell others about the wonderful, customer-focused person she met at the trade show exhibit.

Active Listening Strategies

THINK ABOUT STRATEGIES USED BY PEOPLE WHOM YOU BELIEVE ARE LISTENING TO YOU.   List some of the behaviors and techniques they use.

SHOW A WILLINGNESS TO LISTEN

By eliminating distractions, sending positive verbal and nonverbal responses, and actively focusing on what is being said, you can help the customer relax and have a more meaningful dialogue. For example, when dealing with customers, you should make sure that you take some of the positive approaches to listening outlined earlier (turning off noisy equipment, facing the person, making eye contact, and smiling while responding in a positive manner). These small efforts can pay big dividends in the form of higher satisfaction, lower frustration, and a sense of being cared for on the customer's part.

SHOW EMPATHY

Put yourself in the customer's place by empathizing, especially when the customer is complaining about what he or she perceives to be poor service or inferior products. This is sometimes referred to as "walking a mile in your customer's shoes." For example, if a customer complains that she was expecting a specific service by a certain date but didn't get it, you might respond as follows: "Mrs. Ellis, I apologize that we were unable to complete _____ on the tenth as promised. We dispatched a truck, but the driver was involved in an accident. Can we make it up to you by _____? (Offer a gift, suggest an alternative such as hand delivery, and so on.) This technique, known as service recovery, is a crucial step in delivering quality service and remaining competitive into the twenty-first century.

LISTEN FOR CONCEPTS

Instead of focusing on one or two details, listen to the entire message before analyzing it and responding. For example, instead of trying to respond to one portion of a message, wait for the customer to provide all the details. Then ask any questions necessary to get the information you need to respond appropriately. For example, "Mr. Chi, if I understand you correctly, you'd like us to build a new prototype part to replace the one currently being used in the assembly. You're looking for a total cost for development and manufacture not to exceed $10,000. Is that correct?"

BE PATIENT

Not everyone communicates in the same manner. Keep in mind that it is your job to serve the customer. Do your best to listen well so that you can get at the customer's meaning or need. Don't rush a customer who seems to be processing information and forming opinions or making a decision. This is especially important after you have presented product

Note taking can help focus listening and later aid recall of what was discussed. *What system do you use to take notes while talking on the phone or to follow-up on customer issues?*

congruence
In communication, this relates to ensuring that verbal messages sent match or are in agreement with the nonverbal cues used.

information and have asked for a buying decision. Answer questions, provide additional information requested, but don't push. Doing so could frustrate, anger, and ultimately alienate the customer. You could end up with a complaint or lost customer.

LISTEN OPENLY

Avoid the biases discussed earlier. Remember that you don't have to like everyone you encounter, but you do have to respect and treat customers fairly and impartially if you want to maintain a business relationship. For example, whenever you encounter a person who is rude or is the type of person for whom you have a personal dislike, try to maintain your professionalism. You represent your organization and you are paid by your employer to serve the customer (whoever he or she is). If a situation arises that you feel you cannot or prefer not to handle, call in a coworker or supervisor. However, be careful in taking this action because you will likely reveal a personal preference or bias that could later be held against you when you apply for other positions in your organization or positions in other companies. Try to work through your differences or biases rather than letting them hinder your ability to deal with others. Your ability to serve each customer fairly and competently is important to your job success.

SEND POSITIVE NONVERBAL CUES

Be conscious of the nonverbal messages you are sending. Even when you are verbally agreeing or saying yes, you may be unconsciously sending negative nonverbal messages. When sending a message, you should make sure that your verbal cues (words) and nonverbal cues (gestures, facial expressions) are in **congruence.** For example, if you say, "Good morning. How may I help you?" in a gruff tone, with no smile, and while looking away from the customer, that customer is not going to feel welcome or believe that you are sincere in your offer to assist. (Nonverbal cues were covered in detail in Chapter 4.)

DON'T ARGUE

Remember the "Did not," "Did too" quarrels you had when you were a child? Such verbal exchanges got heated, voices rose and tempers escalated, and someone might have started hitting or pushing. Who won? No one. You should avoid similar childish behaviors in dealing with others—especially your customers or potential customers.

When you argue, you become part of the problem and cannot be part of the solution. Learn to phrase responses or questions positively (as discussed in Chapter 3). Even when you go out of your way to properly serve customers, some of them will respond negatively. Some people seem to enjoy conflict. In such situations, maintain your composure (count to 10 silently before responding), listen, and attempt to satisfy their needs. If necessary, refer such customers to your supervisor or a peer for service.

TAKE NOTES, IF NECESSARY

If information is complicated, or if names, dates, numbers, or numerous details are involved in a customer encounter, you may want to take notes for future reference. Notes can help prevent your forgetting or confusing information. Once you have made your notes, verify your understanding of the facts with your customer before proceeding. For example, in an important client or customer meeting, you may want to jot down key issues, points, follow-up actions, or questions. Doing so shows that you are committed to getting it right or taking action.

ASK QUESTIONS

Use questions to determine customer needs and to verify and clarify information received. This will ensure that you thoroughly understand the customer's message prior to taking action or responding. For example, when you first encounter a customer, you must discover his or her needs or what is wanted. Through a series of open-end questions (typically they start with words such as *when, what, how,* or *why,* and seek substantial amounts of information) and closed-end questions (they often start with words such as *do, did, are,* and *will,* and elicit one-syllable or single-word responses), you can gain useful information.

6   INFORMATION-GATHERING TECHNIQUES

Concept: Use questions to sort out facts from fiction.

Your purpose in listening to your customers is to gather information about their needs on which you can base decisions on how to best satisfy them. Sometimes, you will need to prompt your customers to provide additional or different types of information. To generate and gather information, you can use a variety of questions. Most questions are either open-end or closed-end.

OPEN-END QUESTIONS

This type of questioning follows the time-tested approach of the five W's and one H used by journalists who ask questions that help determine who, what, when, where, why, and how. Basically, **open-end questions** establish a number of facts. They:

Identify Customer Needs   By asking questions, you can help determine **customer needs,** what he or she wants or expects. This is a crucial task because some customers are either unsure of what they need or want or do not adequately express their needs or wants.

> *Examples:*
> "Ms. Deloach, what type of car are you looking for?"
> "Mr. Petell, why is an extended warranty important to you?"

Gather a Lot of Information   Open-end questions are helpful when you're just beginning a customer relationship and aren't sure what the customer has in mind or what's important. By uncovering more details, you can better serve your customer.

> *Example:*
> "Mr. and Mrs. Milton, to help me better serve you, could you please describe what your ideal house would look like if you could build it?"

open-end questions
Typically start with words like who, when, what, how, and why and are used to engage others in conversation or to gain input and ideas.

customer needs
Motivators or drivers that cause customers to seek out specific types of products or services. These may be marketing-driven based on advertising they have seen or may tie directly to Dr. Abraham Maslow's Hierarchy of Needs Theory.

Uncover Background Data   When a customer calls to complain about a problem, often he or she has already taken unsuccessful steps to solve it. In such cases, it is important to find out the background information about the customer or situation. By asking open-end questions, you allow customers to tell you as much information as they feel is necessary to answer your question. This is why open-end questions are generally more effective for gathering data than are closed-end questions. If you feel you need more information after your customer responds to an open-end question, you can always ask further questions.

Example:

"Mrs. Chan, will you please tell me the history behind this problem, including all of your previous contacts with this office?"

Uncover Objections during a Sale   If you are in sales or cross-selling or upselling products or services (getting a customer to buy a higher quality or different brand of product or extend or enhance existing service agreements) to current customers as a service representative, you will likely encounter **objections.** The reasons for a customer not wanting or needing your product and/or service can be identified through the use of open-end questions.

objections

Reasons given by customers for not wanting to purchase a product or service during an interaction with a salesperson or service provider (e.g., I don't need one," "I can't afford it," or "I already have one").

Such questions can be used to determine whether your customer has questions or objections. Many times, people are not rejecting what you are offering outright; they simply do not see an immediate need for the product or cannot think of appropriate questions to ask. In these cases, you can help them focus their thinking or guide their decision through the use of open-end questions. Be careful to listen to your customer's words and tone when he or she offers objections. If the customer seems adamant, such as, "I really don't want it," don't go any further with your questions. The customer will probably become angry because he or she will feel that you are not listening. A fine line exists between helping and pushing, and if you cross it, you could end up with a confrontation on your hands. Often active listening and experience will help you determine what course of action to take.

Example:

"Ms. Williams, from what you told me, all the features of the new RD10 model that we talked about will definitely ease some of your workload, so let me get the paperwork started so you can take it home with you. What do you think?"

Give the Customer an Opportunity to Speak   Although it is important to control the conversation in order to save time and thus allow you to serve more customers, sometimes you may want to give the customer an opportunity to talk. This is crucial if the customer is upset or dissatisfied about something. By allowing a customer to "vent" as you listen actively, you can sometimes reduce the level of tension and help solve the problem.

Examples of Open-End Questions

"What suggestions for improving our complaint-handling process should I present to my boss?"

"Why is this feature so important to you?"

"How has the printer been malfunctioning, Jim?"

"What is the main use of this product?

"What are some of the common symptoms that you have been experiencing?"

"When would you most likely need to have us come out each month?"

"Where have you seen our product or similar ones being used?"

"Why do you feel that this product is better than others you've tried?"

"How do you normally use the product?"

"How has the new hearing aid been performing for you?"

"Mr. O'Connell, I can see you're unhappy. What can I do to help solve this problem?"

CLOSED-END QUESTIONS

Open-end questions are designed to draw out a lot of information. Traditionally, **closed-end questions** elicit short, one-syllable responses and gain little new information. Many closed-end questions can be answered yes or no or with a specific answer, such as a number or a date. Closed-end questions can be used for:

closed-end questions Inquiries that typically start with a verb and solicit short one-syllable answers (e.g., yes, no, one word, or a number) and can be used for such purposes as clarifying, verifying information already given, controlling conversation, or affirming something.

Verifying Information   Closed-end questions are a quick way to check what was already said or agreed on. Using them reinforces that you're listening and also helps prevent you from making mistakes because you misinterpreted or misunderstood information.

> *Example:*
>
> "Mr. Christopherson, earlier I believe you said you saw Doctor Naglapadi before about this problem. Is that correct?"

Closing an Order   Once you've discovered needs and presented the benefits and features of your product and service, you need to ask for a buying decision. This brings closure to your discussion. Asking for a decision also signals the customer that it is his or her turn to speak. If the customer offers an objection, you can use the open-end questioning format discussed earlier.

> *Example:*
>
> "Mr. Jones, this tie will go nicely with your new suit. May I wrap it for you?"

Gaining Agreement   When there has been ongoing dialogue and closure or commitment is needed, closed-end questions can often bring about that result.

> *Example:*
>
> "Veronica, with everything we've accomplished today, I'd really like to be able to conclude this project before we leave. Can we work for one more hour?"

Clarifying Information   Closed-end questions can also help ensure that you have the details correct and thus help prevent future misunderstandings or mistakes. Closed-end questions also help save time and reduce the number of complaints and/or product returns you or someone else will have to deal with.

> *Example:*
>
> "Ms. Jovanovick, if I heard you correctly, you said that the problem occurs when you increase power to the engine. Is that as soon as you turn the ignition key or after you've been driving the car for a while?"

Examples of Closed-End Questions

"Do you agree that we should begin right away?" (obtaining agreement)

"Mrs. Leonard, did you say this was your first visit to our restaurant?" (verifying understanding)

"Mr. Morris, did you say you normally travel three or four times a month and have been doing so for the past 10 years?" (verifying facts)

"Is the pain in your tooth constant or just periodic?" (obtaining information)

"How many employees do you have, Mr. Carroll?" (obtaining information)

7 ADDITIONAL QUESTION GUIDELINES

Concept: Use questions to further your feedback.

In order to generate meaningful responses from customers, keep the following points in mind.

AVOID CRITICISM

Be careful not to seem to be critical in the way you ask questions. For example, a question like, "You really aren't going to need two of the same item, are you?" sounds as if you are challenging the customer's decision making. And the bottom line is that what customers choose should not be your concern. Your job is to help them by providing excellent service. Also, as you read in Chapter 4, nonverbal messages delivered via tone or body language can suggest criticism, even if your spoken words do not.

ASK ONLY POSITIVELY PHRASED QUESTIONS

You can ask for the same information in different ways, some more positive than others. As you interact with your customers, it is crucial to send messages in an open, pleasant manner. This is done by tone of voice and proper word selection. In the examples, you can see how a negative or positive word choice affects meaning.

Examples:

"You really don't want that color do you, Mrs. Handly?" (potentially negative or directive)

"We offer a wide selection of colors. Would you consider another color as an alternative, Mrs. Handly?" (positive or suggestive)

ASK DIRECT QUESTIONS

You generally get what you ask for. Therefore, being very specific with your questions can often result in your receiving useful information. Being specific can also save time and effort. This should not be construed to mean that you should be abrupt or curt in your communication with customers or anyone else.

Example:

If you want to know what style of furniture the customer prefers, but you know that only three styles are available, don't ask a general open-end question, such as "Mrs. Harris, what style of furniture were you looking for?" Instead, try a more structured closed-end question, such as "Mrs. Harris, we stock colonial, French provincial, and Victorian styles. Do any of those meet your needs?"

This approach prevents you from having to respond, "I'm sorry, we don't stock that style," when Mrs. Harris answers your open-end question by telling you that she's looking for art deco style furniture.

ASK CUSTOMERS HOW YOU CAN BETTER SERVE

You will find no better or easier way to determine what customers want and expect than to ask them. They'll appreciate it, and you'll do a better job serving them. *Note:* If appropriate, a good follow-up question to gain additional information after a customer has responded to a question is "That's interesting, will you please explain to me why you feel that way or believe that's true?"

No matter what your current level of listening skill is, there is usually room for improvement. Customers expect and should receive your undivided attention in any encounter they have with you. You should continually reevaluate your own listening style, decide which areas need development, and strive for improvement. In addition, you should keep in mind that active listening involves more than just focusing on spoken words. Remember that there are many obstacles that can impede listening. To overcome them, you need to develop the characteristics of an effective listener and strive to minimize negative habits. Through the use of the active listening process and positive questioning, you can better determine and satisfy customer needs.

attending 116
biases 119
circadian rhythm 120
closed-end questions 131
comprehending or assigning meaning 116
congruence 128
customer needs 129
employee assistance programs (EAPs) 121
external obstacles 123
faulty assumptions 122
hearing 116
information overload 123

lag time 121
listening 114
listening gap 121
memory 116
objections 130
open-end questions 129
personal obstacles 119
psychological distracters 119
recognition 116
responding 116
thought speed 121

1   What phases make up the active listening process?

2   How does hearing differ from listening?

3   According to studies, what is the average rate of listening efficiency for most adults in the United States? Why is this significant in a customer service environment?

4   List 14 characteristics of effective listeners.

5   What is an important reason for practicing good listening skills in a customer service?

6   Of the characteristics common to good listeners, which do you consider the most important in a customer service organization? Explain.

7   What obstacles to effective listening have you experienced, either as a customer service professional or as a customer?

8   How can you determine when someone is not listening to what you say?

9   What techniques or strategies can be used to improve your listening skills?

10   How is the outcome of customer service encounters improved by using a variety of questions?

Search the Internet for Items on Listening Skills

To find out more about the listening process and how you can improve your listening skills, log on to the Internet and type in Listening or any of the other topic headings or subheadings in this chapter. Search for the following items:

Listening activities
Quotations about listening

Books and articles on listening (create a bibliographic list) or interpersonal communication
Research data on listening
Any other topic covered in this chapter (open-end or closed-end questions, handling sales objections)
Bring your findings to class and be prepared to discuss them with your group.

Developing Team Listening Skills

To give you some practical experience in using the techniques described in this chapter, you will now have an opportunity to interact with others in your group. The activity will be done in groups of three or four members. One person will be the listener, one the speaker, and one or two will be observers. Each person will have an opportunity to play the different roles. For example, if there are four people in the group, there will be four rounds of activity. In the first round one member of the group will be the listener, one will be the speaker, and the other two will be observers. The roles will change in each of the next three rounds so that everyone will have had a turn at each role.

The speaker will spend about five to seven minutes sharing a customer service experience he or she has had in the past few weeks (it can be positive or negative). The experience should have been one that lasted for several minutes so that there will be enough detail to share with the other members of the group. The speaker should describe the type of organization, why he or she was there, how he or she was greeted, the behavior of the customer service provider, how the provider dealt with concerns and questions, and any other important point the speaker can recall. As the speaker talks, the listener should pay attention and use as many of the positive listening skills discussed in this chapter as possible. The observers should watch and take notes on what they see. Specifically, they should look for use of the positive listening skills and any other behaviors exhibited (positive or negative). After each speaker has finished his or her story, the listener, then the speaker, and finally the observers (in that order) should answer the following questions about the listener's behavior:

What was done well from a listening standpoint?
What needed improvement?
What comments or suggestions came to mind?

Handling an Irate Customer at Regal Florists

Background

Regal Florists is a small, third-generation family-owned flower shop in Willow Grove, Pennsylvania. Most customers are local residents, but Regal has a website and an FTD delivery arrangement so that it serves customers throughout the United States. Mr. and Mrs. Raymond Boyle have been doing business with Regal for more than 20 years and know the owners well. Quite often they order centerpiece arrangements for holidays and dinner parties, which they host frequently because of Mr. Boyle's position with a public relations firm. They also occasionally send flowers to their six children and four grandchildren living in various parts of the United States and overseas. Regal's owners and employees are usually especially cheerful, helpful, and efficient. That's one of the reasons the Boyles are loyal customers even though Regal's prices have risen above the industry average in recent years.

Your Role

During the past four years you have worked part-time at Regal's, at first delivering arrangements and for the past year creating arrangements and managing the shop. Mr. Boyle stopped by first thing this morning, just as you were opening the store. He was irate, demanding to know what happened with the arrangement delivered yesterday to his assistant for Secretary's Day, and swearing he'd never patronize Regal's again. Apparently, he had phoned in the order last week. The order was taken by a 16-year-old part-time employee who has since resigned. According to Mr. Boyle, he'd ordered a small arrangement with carnations and various other bright spring flowers for his assistant. Instead, his assistant received a dozen red roses along with a card, on the outside of which was a border of little hearts and the statement "Thinking of you." Inside the card was a message intended for his wife: "I don't know what I'd do without you." Unfortunately, Mrs. Boyle had dropped by Mr. Boyle's office and was near the assistant's desk when the flowers arrived, saw the card and flowers, and was quite upset. Rumor has it that Mr. and Mrs. Boyle are having marital problems. You were the only person in the shop when Mr. Boyle came in. Answer these questions.

Critical Thinking Questions

1   Do you think that Mr. Boyle should take Regal's past performance record into consideration? Why or why not?

2   What listening skills addressed in this chapter should you use in this situation? Why?

3   What can you possibly do or say that might resolve this situation positively?

4   Based on information provided, how would you have reacted in this situation if you were Mr. Boyle? Why?

5   If you were Mr. Boyle, what could be done or said to convince you to continue to do business with Regal?

EDUCATION—Jenks Public Schools

Think about what you read related to Jenks Public Schools at the beginning of the chapter and answer the following questions. Your instructor may have you work together and share ideas in a group.

1   With public schools across the nation struggling to improve and meet state and national standards, why do you think Jenks Public Schools might be succeeding?

2   From what you read at the beginning of the chapter and what you found on the Jenks website, what role do you think customer service might play in the success of this school district? Explain.

3   How do you think the emphasis on quality improvement has affected the success of this school district and what effect might that have on customer service (to students, parents, and employees)?

Using the content of this chapter, create a personal action plan focused on improving your listening skills when providing service to your customers. Begin by taking an objective assessment of your current listening strengths and areas for improvement. Once you have identified deficit areas, set goals for improvement.

Start your assessment by listing as many strengths and areas for improvement as you are aware of. Share your list with other people who know you well to see if they agree or can add additional items. Keep in mind that you will likely be more critical of yourself than other people will. Additionally, you may be sending nonverbal signals related to listening that

you are not aware of. For those reasons, keep an open mind when considering their comments.

Once you have a list, choose two or three items that you think need the most work and can add the most value when you are interacting with others. List these items on a sheet of paper along with specific courses of action you will take for improvement, the name of someone you will enlist to provide feedback on your behavior, and a specific date by which you want to see improvement. Related to the latter, keep in mind that research shows that it takes on average 21 to 30 days to see behavioral change; therefore, set a date that is at least in this range.

Listening	Areas for Improvement

Top Three Items	Who Will Help	Date for Change

1.
2.
3.

1	F	5	T	9	F
2	T	6	T	10	T
3	T	7	T	11	F
4	F	8	T	12	T

Ethical Dilemma 5.1 Possible answers

1. What would you say to this customer? Explain.

   There are a couple of issues in this scenario. First, there is the fact that she is cursing and screaming, which is not conducive to effective conflict resolution. She also has her children with her and they are being exposed to not only their mother's attitude and demeanor but also whatever you decide to do. This could leave a negative impression on them related to public utility workers in the future. Finally, there is the fact that she is providing potentially untrue information.

   Before you can even begin to deal with the water issue, you should address her use of profanity and her emotion. Try using the emotion reducing model that you read about in Chapter 3. Explain in an assertive manner that her tone and language are interfering with your ability to help her and that if she wants to get this issue resolved, she needs to calm down, and treat you in a more civil manner. Should she be unwilling to do so, excuse yourself and get a supervisor to intervene.

2. What actions would you take to remedy the situation and get her water back on so that she and her children would have access to services?

   To deal with this situation, you should keep in mind some of the strategies for effective listening and apply some of the information-gathering techniques described in this chapter. Specifically, be careful of faulty assumptions (e.g., that what she is telling you is untrue). Spend a bit of time asking open-end questions, such as "Who did you speak with that promised to turn on your water on Friday" and " I see that you were to come in last Wednesday with a money order. When did you make payment on the account?" (this affords her the benefit of the doubt that she did make payment and no one updated your system).

   Once you have ascertained whether payment was or was not made and that your department either did not fail to deliver service as promised or failed to follow though as promised, proceed as you normally would to collect payment and /or schedule to have services reinstated.

Building and Maintaining Relationships

CUSTOMER SERVICE INTERVIEW   Nick Daher

1 What are the personal qualities that you believe are essential for anyone working with customers in service environment? (Please be specific and explain why you believe this.)

When I'm playing the role of an academic advisor, regardless of whether the service is being provided face to face, online, or over the telephone, my main objective is to put the student (my customer) at ease, and then focus on delivering what the customer is trying to achieve. In order to accomplish that, you have to possess these characteristics:

Nick Daher, Academic Advisor at Webster University

- Communication skills, including written and oral techniques.

- The ability to establish an emotional connection with the customer.

- The aptitude to understand and decipher the customer's body language and nonverbal cues, which most of the time tells the truth, and nothing but the truth.

- The required sensitivity to customer diversity and its specific needs, including the various needs and idiosyncrasies of the baby boomers and the X and the Y generations.

- The skills to see things from different angles, especially from the customer's perspective.

- The capacity for patience and follow-through.

- The talent to be a good listener, and to ask open-end questions for the customer to realize that there is a customer "due process" that allows them to express themself and to be heard. This is especially true when you are trying to manage or resolve unavoidable conflicts in customer service.

138

- The know-how to educate the customer about the product or service at hand, as needed, instead of just giving the customers what they think they want.
- The gift to tailor the service to fit the need of the specific individual, instead of providing a standard "cookie cutter" service that fits the masses. Quality of product is a given, good service is a given, but pushing the envelope to customize the service to each individual is a competitive advantage.
- The ability to cultivate good relationships with your internal customers, who will assist and support the way you cater to your external customers.
- The commitment to operate ethically, and with integrity.
- The ability to *smile big always.*
- The capability to remain cognizant of the fact that you represent your entire organization or your institution.

2 What do you see as the most rewarding part of working with customers? Why?

As an academic advisor, I assist students in selecting their majors, and help them focus on their passion and what motivates them, aside from maximizing their income as the market conditions may dictate. Once they make an honest choice to select a major, and once they stop living up to other people's expectations, then everything falls into place in their lives.

My rewards are the phone calls I receive regularly from students and alumni who took the time from their busy and hectic lives to thank me for helping them put their lives on the right track and support their personal and professional success planning. This always reassures me that my values and beliefs are congruent with those of the institution or the organization that I choose to be a part of. It also reconfirms my place in society, the role I play in my community, and the positive contribution that influences people's lives.

3 What do you believe the biggest challenges are in working with customers?

There are a number of issues in my mind:
- Everyone can offer quality products or services, but only a few are able to tailor and customize the service to fit the specific needs of each individual customer.
- The multitasking approach that organizations adopt seems to take away from the quality of customer

service, as it increases the stress level and compromises the personable service.
- Work overload will also shortcut the process and will prevent you from delivering charming and inviting customer service.
- Continuing education is crucial to maintaining the skills needed to educating the customers and to restoring their confidence level.

4 What role does technology play in your job when working with customers and how have you seen this change since you started in the workplace?

We live in a fast-moving, technology-driven economy and efficiency has always been the focus. As we cater to more X and Y generation customers, who are computer and technology savvy, we seem to transition from a brick-and-mortar operation to a Web-based online environment, offering Internet applications, which provide tremendous efficiency to our younger students. The baby boomer generation however, remains more comfortable with the old-fashioned face-to-face concept, and the personal touch of customer service.

5 What future issues do you see evolving related to dealing with customers in your profession and why do you think these are important?

- Generational differences will remain a critical issue in terms of catering to, and distinguishing among, their specific needs and idiosyncrasies.
- Our target market now has the ability to bank online, shop online, and chat online, as well as go to school online. This will tremendously affect how we deal with customer service in the future. Offering courses online or hybrid courses that meet on campus as well as on the Web will require future automated customer service approaches via various technological innovations. Welcome to the world of your faceless, nameless, but friendly virtual academic advisor.

6 What advice related to customer service do you have for anyone seeking a career in a customer service environment?

Anyone seeking a career in a customer service environment should, in my opinion, examine the list of personal characteristics and traits I reflected on in answering question number 1. He or she should also pursue the required training to acquire and to master these essentials.

Customer Service and Behavior

To be successful, you have to be able to relate to people; they have to be satisfied with your personality to be able to do business with you and to build a relationship with mutual trust.

—George Ross

. . . .

After completing this chapter, you will be able to:

1 Explain what behavioral styles are and why you should be concerned with them.

2 Identify four key behavioral styles and the roles they play in customer service.

3 Develop strategies for communicating effectively with each behavioral style.

4 Respond to customer problems effectively while building relationships.

5 Use knowledge of behavioral styles to help manage perceptions of others.

. . . .

In the Real World   Hospitality-Ritz-Carlton Hotel Company

When asked what they think is the finest luxury hotel, many people would name the Ritz-Carlton, even though most have likely never stayed there or known anyone who has. Yet, the reputation of this top-of-the-line travel venue often sets the bar for competitors to reach. As an indication of its success, the Ritz-Carlton Hotel Company earned some of the highest rankings and awards from some of the premier service evaluation organizations (AAA Five-Diamond, Mobile Five-Star, *Forbes* magazine, *Consumer Reports*, Condé Nast, and *Travel and Leisure* magazine). In addition, the Ritz-Carlton has received the highest ranking in the luxury segment of the J. D. Power and Associates America Hotel Guest Satisfaction Index Study.

To determine the award winner, J. D. Power surveyed over 13,000 business and leisure guests who stayed at major hotel chains in the United States during a 12-month period. The Ritz- Carlton was awarded the highest scores in not only overall "Guest Satisfaction" but in every factor in the luxury segment, including prearrival, guest room, food and beverage, hotel services, and departure. In addition to the Power's ranking, the Ritz-Carlton is the first and only to have twice won the prestigious Malcolm Baldridge National Quality Award given by the U.S. Chamber of Commerce.

The fact that the Ritz-Carlton has received these highly coveted awards is a telling accomplishment since the hotel has only 63 properties in 21 countries around the world with 18,475 guest rooms. It employs over 32,000 employees worldwide to deliver exemplary service.

So, what does this hotel chain, founded in 1983, do that sets it apart from the competition? In a word—*service*. Not just ordinary service but the type that legends are made of. Nothing is left to chance in a Ritz hotel. Minute details that include such amenities as lighter fabrics in the guest rooms to allow for more thorough washing; white tie and apron uniforms for the wait staff, and black tie for the maitre d' and morning suits for all other staff; use of extensive fresh flower arrangements throughout the public areas; á la carte dining providing choices for diners; and an atmosphere conducive to a formal, professional appearance all combine to create the "Ritz experience" that continues to garner rave reviews from customers.

The Ritz-Carlton motto of "We are ladies and gentlemen serving ladies and gentlemen," coupled with its credo (below), help set the standards by which every employee functions. Each employee is taught to honor the following service values:

Service Values: I Am Proud to Be Ritz-Carlton

1. I build strong relationships and create Ritz-Carlton guests for life.

2. I am always responsive to the expressed and unexpressed wishes and needs of our guests.

3. I am empowered to create unique, memorable, and personal experiences for our guests.

4. I understand my role in achieving the Key Success Factors and creating the Ritz-Carlton mystique.

5. I continuously seek opportunities to innovate and improve the Ritz-Carlton experience.

6. I own and immediately resolve guest problems.

7. I create a work environment of teamwork and lateral service so that the needs of our guests and each other are met.

8. I have the opportunity to continuously learn and grow.

9. I am involved in the planning of the work that affects me.

10. I am proud of my professional appearance, language, and behavior.

11. I protect the privacy and security of our guests, my fellow employees, and the company's confidential information and assets.

12. I am responsible for uncompromising levels of cleanliness and creating a safe and accident-free environment.

In addition to their values, each employee is taught to follow the Three Steps of Service:

1. A warm and sincere greeting. Use the guest's name.

2. Anticipation and fulfillment of each guest's needs.

3. Fond farewell. Give a warm good-bye and use the guest's name.

The Ritz-Carlton Credo

"The Ritz-Carlton is a place where the genuine care and comfort of our guests is our highest mission.

We pledge to provide the finest personal service and facilities for our guests who will always enjoy a warm, relaxed yet refined ambience.

The Ritz-Carlton experience enlivens the senses, instills well-being, and fulfills even the unexpressed wishes and needs of our guests."

For additional information about this organization, visit www.ritzcarlton.com on the Internet.

See activity based on this section on page 162.

Quick Preview

Before reviewing the chapter content, respond to the following questions by placing a "T" for true or an "F" for false on the rules. Use any questions you miss as a checklist of material to which you will pay particular attention as you read through the chapter. For those you get right, congratulate yourself, but review the sections they address in order to learn additional details about the topic.

_____ **1.** Understanding behavioral styles can aid in establishing and maintaining positive customer relationships.

_____ **2.** You should treat others as individuals, not as members of a category.

_____ **3.** People whose primary behavioral style category is "E" focus their energy on working with people.

_____ **4.** People whose primary behavioral style category is "D" focus their energy on tasks or getting the job done.

_____ **5.** Some behavioral styles are better than others.

_____ **6.** People who exhibit the "D" style often tend to move slowly and speak in a low-key manner.

_____ **7.** People who exhibit the "E" style often tend to be highly animated in using gestures and speaking.

_____ **8.** People who exhibit the "R" style often tend to be very impatient.

_____ **9.** People who exhibit the "I" style often tend to express their emotions easily.

_____ **10.** You should attempt to determine a customer's behavioral style and then tailor your communication accordingly.

_____ **11.** To deliver total customer satisfaction, you need to make your customers feel special.

_____ **12.** When you say no to a customer, it is important to let him or her know what you cannot do and why.

_____ **13.** Service to your customers should be seamless; customers should not have to see or deal with problems or process breakdowns.

_____ **14.** Perceptions are based on education, experiences, events, and interpersonal contacts, as well as a person's intelligence level.

_____ **15.** Once you've made a perception, you should evaluate its accuracy.

Answers to Quick Preview can be found at the end of the chapter.

. . . .

1 WHAT ARE BEHAVIORAL STYLES?

Concept: Behavioral styles are actions exhibited when you and others deal with tasks or people. As a customer service professional, you need to be aware that everyone is not the same.

Behavioral styles are observable tendencies (actions that you can see or experience) that you and other people exhibit when dealing with tasks or people. As you grow from infancy, your personality forms, based on your experiences and your environment.

For thousands of years, people have devised systems in an attempt to better understand why people do what they do and how they accomplish what they do—and to categorize behavioral styles. Many of these systems are still in use today. For example, early astrologers grouped 12 astrological signs into the four categories Earth, Air, Fire, and Water. Hippocrates and other ancient physicians and philosophers observed and categorized people (for example, sanguine, phlegmatic, melancholy, and choleric). Modern researchers have examined behavior from a variety of perspectives.

Have you ever come into contact with someone with whom you simply did not feel comfortable or someone with whom you felt an immediate bond? If so, you were possibly experiencing and reacting to the effect of behavioral style. As a customer service professional, you need to be aware that everyone is different. Not everyone behaves as you do. For this reason, you should strive to provide service in a manner that addresses others' needs and desires, not the ones you prefer.

As a customer service professional, you need to understand human behavioral style characteristics. The more proficient you become at identifying your own behavioral characteristics and those of others, the better you will be at establishing and maintaining positive relationships with customers. Self-knowledge is the starting point. To help in this effort, we will examine some common behavior that you exhibit and that you may observe in various other people.

When dealing with your customers, you should recognize that someone else doing something or acting differently from the way you do doesn't mean that that person is wrong. It simply means that they approach situations differently. Relationships are built on accepting the characteristics of others. In customer service, adaptability is crucial, for many people do not always act the way you want them to. As you will read later in this chapter, there are many strategies that can be used to help modify and adapt your behavior so that it does not clash with that of your customers. This does not mean that you must make all the concessions when behaviors do not mesh. It simply means that, although you do not have control over the behavior of others, you do have control over your own behavior. Use this control to deal more effectively with your customers.

behavioral styles
Descriptive term that identifies categories of human behavior identified by behavioral researchers. Many of the models used to group behaviors date back to those identified by Carl Jung.

CUSTOMER SERVICE SUCCESS TIP

A key to successfully dealing with others is recognizing your own style. Too often we try to impose our beliefs, values, attitudes, and needs on others. This type of action from a service provider may cause a customer to become angry, withdrawn, or even disruptive. You will be better informed about yourself if you learn your own behavior preferences.

2 IDENTIFYING BEHAVIORAL STYLES

Concept: Each contact in a customer service environment has the potential for contributing to your success. Each person should be valued for his or her strengths and not belittled for what you perceive as shortcomings.

Through an assessment questionnaire you can discover your own behavioral tendencies in a variety of situations. An awareness of your own style preferences can then lead you to a better understanding of customers, since they also possess style preferences. By understanding these characteristics, you can improve communication, build stronger relationships, and offer better service to the customer.

Many self-assessment questionnaires and much research related to behavioral styles are based on the work begun by psychiatrist Carl Jung and others in the earlier part of the twentieth century. Jung explored human personality and behavior. He divided behavior into two "attitudes" (introvert and extrovert) and four "functions" (thinking, feeling, sensing, and intuitive). These attitudes and functions can intermingle to form eight psychological types; knowledge of these types is useful in defining and describing human behavioral characteristics.

From Jung's complex research (and that of others) have come many variations, additional studies, and a variety of behavioral style self-assessment questionnaires and models for explaining personal behavior. Examples of these questionnaires are the Myers-Briggs Type Indicator (MBTI) and the Personal Profile System (DiSC). Several organizations allow you to complete free surveys online. You can find these by searching the Internet for the topics and websites listed in "Search It Out" at the end of this chapter.

primary behavior pattern
Refers to a person's preferred style of dealing with others.

Although everyone typically has a **primary behavior pattern** (the way a person acts or reacts under certain circumstances) to which he/she reverts in stressful situations, people also have other characteristics in common and regularly demonstrate similar behavioral patterns. Identifying your own style preferences helps *you* identify similar ones in others.

To informally identify some of your own behavioral styles preferences, complete Work It Out 6.1. This is not a validated behavioral survey but will give a strong indication of your behavioral preferences in dealing with others.

Note: Keep in mind that this is only a quick indicator. A more thorough assessment, using a formal instrument (questionnaire), will be better at predicting your style preferences. For more information or to obtain written or computer-based surveys and reports, write the author at the address shown in the author information section of this book.

Because of the complexities of human behavior, you should not try to use behavioral characteristics and cues as absolute indicators of the type of person you are dealing with. (This is similar to the situation with nonverbal cues.) You and others have some of the characteristics listed for all four style categories shown in this chapter; you simply have learned through years of experience which behavior you are most comfortable with and when adaptation is helpful or necessary. Generally, most people are adaptable and can shift style categories or exhibit different characteristics depending on the situation. For example, a person who is normally very personable and amiable can revert to more directive behavior, if necessary, to manage an activity or process for which he or she will be held accountable. Similarly, a person who normally exhibits controlling or task-oriented behavior can socialize and react positively in "people" situations.

An important point to remember is that there is no "best" or "worst" style. Each person should be valued for his or her strengths and not belittled because of what you perceive as shortcomings. In a customer environment, each contact has the potential for contributing to your success and that of your organization. By appreciating the behavioral characteristics of people with whom you interact, you can avoid bias or prejudice and better serve your customers.

Describing Your Behavior

To determine your behavioral style preference, make a copy of this page and then complete the following survey.

Step 1. Read the following list of words and phrases and rate yourself by placing a number (from 1 to 5) next to each item. A 5 means that the word is an accurate description of yourself in most situations, a 3 indicates a balanced agreement about the word's application, and a 1 means that you do not feel that the word describes your behavior well. Before you begin, refer to the sample assessment in Figure 6.1.

Relaxed

Logical

Decisive

Talkative

Consistent

Nonaggressive (avoids conflict)

Calculating

Fun-loving

Loyal

Quality-focused

Competitive

Enthusiastic

Sincere

Accurate

Pragmatic (practical)

Popular

Patient

Detail-oriented

Objective

Optimistic

TOTAL R =   I =   D =   E =

Step 2. Once you have rated each word or phrase, start with the first word, *Relaxed,* and put the letter "R" to the right of it. Place an "I" to the right of the second word, a "D" to the right of the third word, and an "E" to the right of the fourth word. Then start over with the fifth word and repeat the "RIDE" pattern until all words have a letter at their right.

Step 3. Next, go through the list and count point values for all words that have an "R" beside them. Put the total at the bottom of the grid next to "R = ." Do the same for the other letters. Once you have finished, one letter will probably have the highest total score. This is your natural style tendency.

For example, if "R" has the highest score, your primary style is rational. If "I" has the highest score, you exhibit more Inquisitive behavior. "D" indicates decisive, and "E" is an expressive style preference.

If two or more of your scores have the same high totals, you probably generally put forth similar amounts of effort in both these style areas.

Most people have a primary and secondary style (one they revert to frequently).

How can a person who demonstrates one of the four styles be described? How might this person act, react, or interact? Some generalizations about behavior are listed in this section. Keep in mind that even though people have a primary style, they demonstrate other style behaviors too. By becoming familiar with these style characteristics, recognizing them in yourself, and observing how others display them, you can begin to learn how to better adapt to various behaviors. When interacting with others, remember to monitor their overall actions and behavior in order to get a better perception of their style preferences rather than react to one or two actions. Remember that these characteristics are generalitier and not absolutes when dealing with others. People can and do adapt and change behavior depending on a variety of circumstances.

R: RATIONAL

People who have a preference for the **rational style** may tend to:

* Be very patient.
* Wait or stand in one place for periods of time without complaining, although they may be internally irritated about a breakdown in the system or lack of organization.

rational style
One of four behavioral groups characterized by being quiet, reflective, task-focused, and systematic.

FIGURE 6.1

Sample Completed Self-Assessment

5	Relaxed	R
3	Logical	I
1	Decisive	D
4	Talkative	E
5	Consistent	R
3	Nonaggressive (avoids conflict)	I
5	Calculating	D
3	Fun-loving	E
5	Loyal	R
1	Quality-focused	I
3	Competitive	D
2	Enthusiastic	E
5	Sincere	R
1	Accurate	I
3	Pragmatic (practical)	D
1	Popular	E
5	Patient	R
2	Detail-oriented	I
1	Objective	D
2	Optimistic	E
TOTAL	R = 25 I = 10 D = 13	E = 12

- Exhibit congenial eye contact and facial expressions.
- Prefer one-on-one or small-group interactions over solitary or large-group ones.
- Seek specific or complete explanations to questions (e.g., "That's our policy" does not work well with an "R" customer).
- Dislike calling attention to themselves or a situation.
- Avoid conflict and anger.
- Often wear subdued colors and informal, conservative, or conventional clothing styles and accessories.
- Ask questions rather than state their opinion.
- Listen and observe more than they talk (especially in groups).
- Communicate more in writing and like the use of notes, birthday, or thank-you cards just to stay in touch.
- Like to be on a first-name basis with others.
- Have intermittent eye contact with a brief, businesslike handshake.
- Have informal, comfortable office spaces, possibly with pictures of family in view.
- Like leisure activities that involve people (often family).

I: INQUISITIVE

inquisitive style
One of four behavioral groups characterized by being introverted, task-focused, and detail-oriented.

People who have a preference for the **inquisitive style** may tend to:

- Rarely volunteer feelings freely.
- Ask specific, pertinent questions rather than make statements of their feelings.
- Rely heavily on facts, times, dates, and practical information to make their point.
- Prefer to interact in writing rather than in person or on the phone.
- Prefer formality and distance in interactions. They often lean back when talking, even when emphasizing key points.

- Use formal titles and last names as opposed to first names. They may also stress the use of full names, not nicknames (e.g., Cynthia instead of Cindy or Charles instead of Chuck).
- Use cool, brief handshakes, often without a smile. If they do smile, it may appear forced.
- Wear conservative clothing although their accessories are matched well.
- Be impeccable in their grooming but may differ in their choice of styles from those around them (e.g., hair and makeup).
- Be very punctual and time-conscious.
- Carry on lengthy conversations, especially when trying to get answers to questions.
- Be diplomatic with others.
- Prefer solitary leisure activities (e.g., reading or listening to relaxing music).
- Keep their personal life separate from business.

ethical dilemma 6.1 You have a supervisor who typically demonstrates high decisive-type behavior and very rarely asks for your opinion. When she does take the time to get your input, and that of other employees, it seems that she really does not listen to what you have to say and usually does not take your advice or suggestions. Should you address your perceptions with her? Why or why not?

D: DECISIVE

People who have a preference for the **decisive style** may tend to:

- Move quickly.
- Seek immediate gratification of needs or results.
- Work proactively toward a solution to a problem.
- Be forceful and assertive in their approach (sometimes overly so).
- Project a competitive nature.
- Display a confident, possibly arrogant demeanor.
- Ask specific, direct questions and give short, straight answers.
- Discuss rather than write about something (e.g., call or come in rather than write about a complaint).
- Talk and interrupt more than listen.
- Display symbols of power to demonstrate their own importance (e.g., expensive jewelry, clothes, cars, power colors in business attire such as navy blue or charcoal gray).
- Be solemn and use closed, nonverbal body cues.
- Have firm handshakes and strong, direct eye contact.
- Have functionally decorated offices (all items have a purpose and are not there to make the environment more attractive).
- Prefer active, competitive leisure activities.

decisive style
One of four behavior style groupings characterized by a direct, no-nonsense approach to people and situations.

E: EXPRESSIVE

People who have a preference for the **expressive style** may tend to:

- Look for opportunities to socialize or talk with others (e.g., checkout lines at stores, bus stops, waiting areas).
- Project a friendly, positive attitude.
- Be enthusiastic, even animated when talking, using wide, free-flowing gestures.
- Use direct eye contact and enthusiastic, warm (often two-handed) handshake.
- Smile and use open body language.
- Get close or touch when speaking to someone.
- Talk rather than write about something (e.g., call or come in with a complaint rather than writing to complain).

expressive style
One of four behavior groups characterized as people-oriented, fun-loving, upbeat, and extroverted.

- Initiate projects.
- Wear bright, modern, or unusual clothes and jewelry because it gets them noticed or fits their mood.
- Dislike routine.
- Share feelings and express opinions or ideas easily and readily.
- Get distracted in conversations and start discussing other issues.
- Prefer informal use of names and like first-name communication.
- Not be time-conscious and may often be late for appointments.
- Speak loudly and expressively with a wide range of inflection.
- Like action-oriented, people-centered leisure activities.

3   COMMUNICATING WITH EACH STYLE

Concept: Each behavior style features various indicators of this style in practice. Remember, these cues are indicators, not absolutes, as you begin to use them to interact appropriately with others.

Once you recognize people's style tendencies, you can improve your relationships and chances of success by tailoring your communication strategies. As you examine Figure 6.2, think about how you can use these strategies with people you know in each style category. Keep in mind that these and other characteristics outlined in this chapter are only general in nature. Everyone is a mixture of all four styles and can change to a different style to address a variety of situations. Use these examples as indicators of style and not as absolutes. Also, be careful *not* to label a person as being one style (for example, Toni is a high "R"), since people use all four styles.

FIGURE 6.2

Communicating with Different Personality Styles

Style	Behaviors	Strategy	Customer Relationship Strategies
RATIONAL	*Nonverbal Cues* Gentle handshake, flowing, nondramatic gestures. Fleeting eye contact.	Return firm, brief handshake; avoid aggressive gestures. Make intermittent (3 to 5 seconds) eye contact.	• Often want to maintain peace and group stability. • Focus on their need for security and amiable relationships. • Show a sincere interest in them and their views.
	Verbal Cues Steady, even delivery. Subdued volume. Slower rate of speech.	Mirror their style somewhat. Relax your message delivery. Slow your rate if necessary; be patient.	• Organize your information in a logical sequence and provide background data, if necessary. • Take a slow, low-key approach in recommending products or services.
	Keeps communication brief.	Ask open-ended questions to draw out information.	• Use open-ended questions to obtain information.
	Communication follows a logical pattern (e.g., step 1, step 2).	Use structured approach in communications.	• Explain how your product or service can help simplify and support their relationships and systems.

Additional Cues

Avoids confrontation.

Attempt to solve problems without creating a situation in which they feel challenged or obliged to defend themselves.

- Stress low risk and benefits to them.
- Encourage them to verify facts, and so on, with others whose opinions they value.
- When change occurs, explain the need for the change and allow time for them to adjust.
- Provide information on available warranties, guarantees, and support systems.

INQUISITIVE

Nonverbal Cues

Deliberate body movements. Use little physical contact.

Correspondence is formal and includes many details.

Use careful, restrained body cues. Avoid touching. Respond similarly.

- Often desire quality, efficiency, and precision.
- Focus on their need for accuracy and efficiency by methodically outlining steps, processes, or details related to a product or service.

Verbal Cues

Quiet, slow-paced speech (especially in groups). Minimal vocal variety.

Mirror rate and pattern. Use subdued tone and volume.

- Tie communication into facts, not feelings.
- Prepare information in advance and be thoroughly familiar with it.
- Approach encounters in a direct, businesslike, low-key manner.

Additional Cues

Value concise communication. Use details to make points.

Use brief, accurate statements. Provide background information and data.

- Avoid small talk and speaking about yourself.
- Ask specific open-ended questions about their background or experiences related to the product or service.

Prefer confirmation and backup in writing.

Respond in writing and provide adequate background information.

- Present solutions in a sequential fashion, stressing advantages, value, quality, reliability, and price. Also, be prepared to point out and discuss disadvantages.

Uses formal names instead of nicknames.

Address them by title and last name unless told otherwise.

Additional Cues

Sharing of personal information is minimal.

Communicate on business level unless they initiate personal conversation.

- Have documentation available to substantiate your claims.
- Don't pressure their decisions.
- Follow through on promises.

Focus on task at hand.

Organize thoughts before responding.

DECISIVE

Nonverbal Cues

Steady, direct eye contact.

Return eye contact (3 to 5 seconds) and smile.

- Often want to save time and money.

(*continued*)

FIGURE 6.2

Communicating with Different Personality Styles (*continued*)

Style	Behaviors	Strategy	Customer Relationship Strategies
	Writing tends to be short and specific.	Respond in similar fashion; minimize small talk and details.	• Focus on their need for control by finding out what they wish to do, what they want or need, or what motivates them.
	Gestures tend to be autocratic (e.g., pointing fingers or hands on hips).	Stand your ground without antagonizing. Maintain a professional demeanor.	• Provide direct, concise, and factual answers to their questions.
	Verbal Cues		• Keep explanations brief and provide solutions, not excuses.
	Forceful tone.	Don't react defensively or in a retaliatory manner.	• Avoid trying to "get to know them." They often perceive this as a waste of time, and they may distrust your motives.
	Speak in statements.	Use facts and logic and avoid unnecessary details.	• Be conscious of time, by making your point and then concluding the interaction appropriately.
	Direct and challenging (short, abrupt).	Listen rather than defend.	• Provide opportunities for the customer to talk by alternately providing small bits of information and asking specific questions aimed at solving the problem and serving the customer.
	Fast rate of speech.	Match rate somewhat.	
	Additional Cues		
	Short attention span when listening.	Keep sentences and communication brief.	
	Very direct and decisive.	Support opinions, ideas, and vision.	• Be prepared with information, necessary forms, details, warranties, and so on, before they arrive.
			• When appropriate, provide options supported by evidence and focus on how the solution will affect their time, effort, and money.
			• Focus on new, innovative products or services, emphasizing especially those that are environmentally sensitive or responsive.
EXPRESSIVE	*Nonverbal Cues*		• Typically people-oriented and want to be around people.
	Enthusiasm and inflection in voice.	Listen and respond enthusiastically.	
	Active body language.	Use open, positive body language and smile easily.	• Focus on their need to be liked and accepted by appealing to their emotions.
	Enthusiastic, possibly two-hand shake.	Return firm, professional one shake.	• Give positive feedback, acknowledging their ideas.
	Use touch to emphasize points.	Acknowledge but use caution in returning touch (this action could be misinterpreted by them or others).	• Listen to their stories and share humorous ones about yourself.
			• Use an open-ended, friendly approach.

Very intense, dramatic.	Show interest and ask pertinent questions.	• Ask questions such as "What attracted you to this product or service?"
Writing tends to be flowery and includes many details.	When writing, use a friendly reader-focused style.	• Keep product details to a minimum unless they ask for them.

Verbal Cues

Excessive details when describing something.	Ask specific open-ended questions to help them refocus.
Fast rate of speech.	Mirror or match their rate and excitement where appropriate.
Emphasize storytelling and fun.	Relax, listen, and respond appropriately.

• Describe how your product or service can help them get closer to their goals or to fulfilling their needs.

• Explain solutions or suggestions in terms of the impact on them and their relationships with others.

• If appropriate, provide incentives to encourage a decision.

Additional Cues

Inattentive to details in tasks.	Ask questions to involve them.
Share personal information and virtually anything else freely.	Reciprocate if you are comfortable doing so; however, stay focused on task at hand.

problem solving
The system of identifying issues, determining alternatives for dealing with them, then selecting and monitoring a strategy for resolution.

People send verbal and nonverbal clues to their behavioral style preference. Observe your customers' eye contact, level of directness or evasiveness, how quickly or slowly they speak, and their level of warmth versus formality. Once you can read these clues, you'll be better able to individualize the customer service you provide. *Can you think of a person in your life who exhibits clues to his or her behavioral style?*

4   BUILDING STRONGER RELATIONSHIPS

Concept: Sometimes building stronger customer relationships means that you discover customer needs, seek opportunities for service, and respond appropriately to customers' behavioral styles. Occasionally you will need to deemphasize a no and say it as positively as you can.

Recognizing and relating to customers' behavioral styles is just the first step in providing better service. To deliver total customer satisfaction, you will need to make the customer feel special, which often requires skills such as relationship building (through the effective communication discussed in earlier chapters) and **problem solving.** Whether a situation involves simply answering a question, guiding someone to a desired product or location, or performing a service, customers should leave the interac-

Monitoring Behavior

TO PRACTICE MATCHING BEHAVIOR WITH STYLES, TRY THIS ACTIVITY. Make four or five copies of Worksheet 6.1 (see www.mhhe.com/lucas09). Select four or five friends or coworkers whom you see and interact with regularly. Write one of their names at the top of each worksheet copy. Covertly (without their knowledge) observe these people for a week or so and make notes about their behavior under each category listed on the worksheet. Focus specifically on the following areas:

Writing pattern or style

Interpersonal communication style (e.g., direct, indirect, specific or nonspecific questions, good or poor listener)

Body movements and other nonverbal gestures

Dress style (e.g., flashy, conservative, formal, informal)

Surroundings (e.g., office decorations or organization, car, home)

Personality (e.g., activities and interactions preferred—solitary, group, active, passive)

At the end of the week, decide which primary and/or secondary style of behavior each person exhibits most often. Then ask these people to assist you in an experiment that will involve them completing the quick style assessment that you did earlier (Figure 6.1).

After they have rated themselves, explain that you have been observing them for the past week.

Compare their ratings to the characteristics described in this chapter, and to your own assessment. Were you able to predict their primary or, at least, their secondary style?

---

win-win situation
An outcome to a disagreement in which both parties walk away feeling that they got much of what they wanted or needed.

tion feeling good about what they experienced. Providing this feeling is not only good business sense on your part but also helps guarantee the customers return or favorable word-of-mouth advertising. There are many ways of partnering with either internal or external customers to solve problems and produce a **win-win situation** (one in which the customer and you and your organization succeed). Whatever you do to achieve this result, your customers should realize that you are their advocate and are acting in their best interests to solve their problems (see problem-solving process on pages 181–183. Some suggestions for building stronger customer relationships follow.

DISCOVER CUSTOMER NEEDS

Using the communication skills addressed in earlier chapters, engage customers in a dialogue that allows them to identify what they really want or need. If you can determine a customer's behavioral style, you can tailor your communication strategy to that style. Keep in mind that some customer needs may not be expressed aloud. In these instances, you should attempt to validate your impressions or suspicions by asking questions or requesting feedback. Gather information about a customer from observing vocal qualities, phrasing, nonverbal expressions and movements, and emotional state. For example, while providing service to Mr. Delgado, you told him that the product he was ordering would not arrive for three weeks. You noticed that he grimaced and made a concerned sound of "Um." At this point, a perception check would have been appropriate. You could have said, "Mr. Delgado, you looked concerned or disappointed when I mentioned the delivery date. Is that a problem for you?" You might have discovered that he needed the item sooner but resigned himself to the delay and didn't ask about other options. In effect, he was exhibiting "I" or possibly "R" behavior (silence and low-key reaction). Rather than have a confrontation, he accepted the situation without voicing disappointment or concern. He might then have gone to a competitor. By reacting positively to his nonverbal signals, you could identify and address a concern and thus prevent a dissatisfied and/or lost customer.

SAY "YES"

If you must decline a request or cannot provide a product or service, do so in a positive manner. Deemphasizing what you cannot do and providing an alternative puts the customer in a power position. That is, even though she may not get her first request, she is once again in control because she can say yes or no to the alternative you have offered, or she can decide on the next step. For example, when a customer requests a brand or product not stocked by your organization, you could offer alternatives. You might counter with, "Mrs. Hanslik, although we don't stock that brand, we do have a comparable product which has been rated higher by *Consumer's Report* than the one you requested. May I show you?" This approach not only serves the customer but also (sometimes) results in a sale.

Figure 6.3 provides some strategies to use when responding to customer complaints and solving problems involving people who demonstrate the four behavioral styles you have learned about. By tailoring customer service strategies to individual style preferences, you address the customer's specific needs. Active listening is a key skill in any service situation. As you review these strategies, think of other things you might do to better serve each behavioral type.

FIGURE 6.3

Strategies for Responding to Customer Problems

Style	Behaviors	Strategies
RATIONAL	Seeks systematic resolution to the situation.	Stress resolution and security of the issue.
	Avoids conflict or disagreement.	Smile, when appropriate.
	Strives for acceptance of ideas.	Provide references or resources.
	Intermittent eye contact.	Listen actively; make eye contact.
	Uses hand and subdued body movements and speech to emphasize key points.	Focus on personal movements to convey your feelings about the incident (e.g., "How do you feel we can best resolve this problem?").
INQUISITIVE	Listens to explanations.	Focus on the problem, not the person.
	Demands specifics.	Have details and facts available.
	Mild demeanor.	Approach in nonthreatening manner.
	Intermittent eye contact.	Listen actively, make eye contact, and focus on the situation.
	Gives list of issues, in chronological order.	Be specific in outlining actions to be taken by everyone.
	Exhibits patience.	Follow through on commitments.
	Seeks reassurance.	Offer guarantees of resolution if possible.
	Focuses on facts.	Give facts and pros and cons of suggestions.
DECISIVE	Seeks to avoid conflict; just wants resolution.	Use low-pitched, unemotional speech; be patient; listen.
	Loud voice.	Be patient; listen empathetically.
	Finger pointing or aggressive body gestures.	Don't internalize; they are angry with the product or service, not necessarily you.
	Firm, active handshake.	Return a firm businesslike handshake.
Style	Directly places blame on service provider.	Be brief; tell them what you can do; offer solutions.

[continued]

FIGURE 6.3

Strategies for Responding to Customer Problems (continued)

	Behaviors	Strategies
	Direct eye contact.	Be formal, businesslike.
	Sarcasm.	Don't take a happy-go-lucky or flippant approach.
	Impatient.	Be time-conscious; time is money to a "D."
	Demanding verbiage (e.g., "You'd better fix this"; "I want to see the manager *now*!").	Project competence; find the best person to solve problem.
	Irrational assertions (e.g., "You people *never* or *always* . . .")	Ask questions that focus on what they need or want (e.g., "What do you think is a reasonable solution?").
EXPRESSIVE	Threats (e.g., "If you can't help, I'll go to a company that can.")	Reassure; say what you can do.
	Intermittent smiling along with verbalizing dissatisfaction.	Be supportive; tell them what you *can* do for them.
	Uses nonaggressive language (e.g., "I'd like to talk with someone about . . .")	Allow them to vent frustrations or verbalize thoughts.
	Steady eye contact.	Smile, if appropriate; return eye contact while conversing.
	Elicits your assistance and follow-up (e.g., "I really don't want to run all over town searching. Will you please call . . .").	Take the time to offer assistance and comply with their requests, if possible.
	Shows sincere interest.	Focus on feelings through empathy (e.g., "I feel that . . .").
	Enthusiastic active handshake.	Return a firm businesslike handshake.
	Enthusiastically explains a situation.	Patiently provide active listening; offer ideas and suggestions for resolution.

SEEK OPPORTUNITIES FOR SERVICE

View complaints as a chance to create a favorable impression by solving a problem. Watch the behavioral characteristics being exhibited by your customer. Using what you see and hear, take appropriate action to adapt to the customer's personality needs and solve the problem professionally. For example, Mrs. Minga complained loudly to you that the service woman who installed her new washing machine tracked oil onto the dining room carpet. As she is speaking, Mrs. Minga is pointing her finger at you, raising her voice, and threatening to go to the manager if you do not handle this situation immediately. You can take the opportunity to solve the problem and strengthen the relationship at the same time. You might try the following. Make direct eye contact (no staring), smile, and empathize by saying, "Mrs. Minga, I'm terribly sorry about your carpet. I know that it must be very upsetting. If you'll allow me to, I'll arrange to have your dining room carpet cleaned, and for your inconvenience, while they're at it we'll have them clean the carpets in adjoining rooms at no cost to you. How does that sound?" In reacting this way, you have professionally and assertively taken control of the situation. This is important because Mrs. Minga is exhibiting high "D" behavior. Responding in a less decisive manner might result in an escalation of her emotions and a demand to see someone in authority.

The process just described, which involves an attempt at righting a wrong and compensating for inconvenience, is called *service recovery*. The concept will be addressed in detail in Chapter 7.

FOCUS ON PROCESS IMPROVEMENT

Customers generally do not like being kept waiting when your system is not functioning properly. They rightfully view their time as valuable. To expect them to patiently wait while a new cashier tries to figure out the register codes, someone gets a price check because the product was coded incorrectly, you have to call the office for information or approvals, and so on, is unfair and unreasonable. Defects or delays should be handled when the customer is not present. You should strive to provide **seamless service** to customers. This means that they should get great service and never have to worry about your problems or breakdowns. When breakdowns do occur, they should be fixed quickly, and the customer relationship smoothed over. In addition, it is important to recognize that customers with different behavioral styles will react differently to such breakdowns. "R" style customers are likely to complain in an inoffensive manner and may even smile but may also seek out a supervisor. Those with "I" style may seem to be patient and not say anything or cause a confrontation but will possibly request directions to the supervisor's office and/or later send a detailed letter of complaint. Someone who exhibits "D" behavior may get loud, aggressive, and vocal and demand a supervisor after only a brief delay. The "E" types may get upset but will often make the best of their time complaining to other customers and comparing notes on similar past experiences. No matter what style the customer exhibits, you should strive to reduce or eliminate customer inconvenience and distress.

In all cases, after a delay you may want to compensate the customer for the inconvenience. At the least, such a situation warrants a sincere apology. Such an occurrence might be handled in the following manner: "Mr. Westgate, I am sorry for the delay. We've been experiencing computer problems all day. I'd like to make up for your inconvenience by giving you a 10 percent discount off your meal check. Would that be acceptable?" Although this is not a significant offering, your intention is to show remorse and to placate the customer so that he or she will continue to use your products and/or services. You will read more about this technique in Chapter 7.

After you have dealt with the situation, your next concern should be to personally fix the process that caused the breakdown or make a recommendation to your supervisor or other appropriate person. Quality and **process improvement** are the responsibility of all employees.

MAKE CUSTOMERS FEEL SPECIAL

When customers feel good about themselves as a result of something you did or said, they are likely to better appreciate what you and your organization can offer them. For example, as appreciation for long-term patronage, you may want to recognize a customer as follows: "Mr. and Mrs. Hoffmeister, we really appreciate your loyalty. Our records indicate that you've been a patient in our office for over 20 years. In recognition, on behalf of Dr. Naglapadi here is a complimentary dinner certificate for $25 dollars. Please accept it with our compliments." Such a reward would likely surprise and amaze most patients since many doctor's office have a reputation of not valuing patient's time or business. This type of strategy goes a long way in guaranteeing customer loyalty.

seamless service
Service which is done in a manner that seems effortless and natural to the customer. Processes and systems are fully functional, effective, and efficient, service representatives are well-trained and proficient in delivering service, and there is no inconvenience to the customer.

process improvement
Refers to the process of continually evaluating products and services to ensure that maximum effectiveness, efficiency, and potential are being obtained from them.

CUSTOMER SERVICE SUCCESS TIP

No matter which style tendencies a customer has, everyone likes to feel appreciated. By taking the time to recognize customers' value and by communicating effectively, you can bolster their self-esteem.

BE CULTURALLY AWARE

The reality of a multicultural customer service environment further challenges your ability to deal with behaviors. This is because in today's multicultural business environment, it is likely that you will come into contact with someone of a different background, belief system, or culture. Many problems that develop in these encounters are a result of diversity ignorance. Even after you master the concepts of behavioral styles, you must remember that because values and beliefs vary from one culture to another, behavior is also likely to vary. For example, in many countries or cultures, the nonverbal gestures that North Americans use have completely different meanings. Also, the reactions to such gestures will differ based on the recipient's personality style. Variations of symbols such as joining the thumb and index finger to form an O, signaling "Okay," have sexual connotations in parts of several countries (e.g., Germany, Sardinia, Malta, Greece, Turkey, Russia, the Middle East, and parts of South America). Likewise, variations of the V symbolizing "victory" or "peace" to many people in Western cultures have negative connotations in some parts of the world (e. g., British Isles and parts of Malta).[1] Symbols and gestures, therefore, might anger or offend some customers. Also, seemingly innocent behaviors such as crossing your legs so that the sole of your shoe points toward someone or patting a small child on the top of his or her head may cause offense. The sole of the foot is the lowest part of the body and touches the ground. In some parts of the world, pointing the sole of the foot toward a person implies that the person is lowly. Males from a Western culture, and specifically males who have "D," "I," and "R" styles and tend to adopt a formal posture when seated, should be aware of the effect of crossing their legs might have on certain customers. ("E" style people tend to be more relaxed and sprawling in their posture.) As for the head, many countries (e.g., in the Far East, especially Thailand)[2] view it as a sacred part of the body. Patting a child on the head is sometimes considered to invite evil spirits or bad omens. This action might easily be taken by people who have high "E" behavioral tendencies, for they tend to be touchy-feely.

Some books listed in the Bibliography address these kinds of issues. Also, we will explore other culturally related subjects in Chapter 8.

To help send a positive message to customers from other cultures, you can do simple things that might have major effects. For example, if you work in a restaurant and want to show appreciation for the large numbers of customers from another country who patronize the restaurant, you might recommend to your boss that a special dish from that area of the world be added to the menu. This offering could be promoted through flyers or advertisements. Such a strategy shows appreciation of the customers and their culture while encouraging them to eat at your establishment. However, be sure that the special dish is correctly prepared and uses the correct ingredients. Otherwise, you might offend rather than please the customer.

All these strategies, combined with a heightened knowledge of behavioral styles, can better prepare you to serve a wide variety of customers.

KNOW YOUR PRODUCTS AND SERVICES

Customers expect that you will be able to identify and describe the products and services offered by your company. Depending on the behavioral style of the customer, the type of questions will vary. For example, an "R" personality may want to know who uses your services and products and ask to see the instructions; an "I" may ask many questions

CUSTOMER SERVICE SUCCESS TIP

To better prepare yourself for serving others, read whatever you can get your hands on related to customer service and take classes on how to interact and communicate with a variety of different types of people. Courses in psychology, sociology, and interpersonal communication are invaluable for providing a basis of understanding why people act as they do. Focus on issues of differences and similarities between men and women, cultural diversity, behavioral styles, and any other topic that will expand and round out your knowledge of people.

Of course, each person is unique, but the more you know about human behavior in general, the more successful you will be in dealing with the individuals you serve.

---

[1] Desmond Morris, *Bodytalk: The Meaning of Human Gestures,* Crown Trade Paperbacks, New York, 1994, pp. 118–119; 130–131.

[2] Ibid., p. 142.

Determining Styles

READ THE FOLLOWING DESCRIPTIONS AND THEN DETER-MINE WHICH BEHAVIORAL STYLE YOU ARE DEALING WITH. Keep in mind that each person can switch behavioral styles depending on the situation. To help you determine styles, refer to the style tendencies described in previous sections of this chapter. Suggested answers are given below the situation.

Situation 1

You are a salesperson at a jewelry counter and observe a professionally dressed female customer waiting in line for several minutes. She is checking her watch frequently, anxiously looking around, and sighing often. When she arrives at the counter, she makes direct eye contact with you and without smiling states, "I want to buy a 16-inch 14-karat gold twisted-link necklace like the one advertised in today's paper. I also want a small gold heart pendant and would like these to cost no more than $125. Can you help me? Oh yes, I almost forgot. Wrap that in birthday paper. This gift is for my daughter's birthday."

Suggested answers: Behavioral style D; telltale indicators are impatience, directive "D" language, direct eye contact, and no indication of smiling.

Situation 2

You stop by the office of a director of a department that provides data you use to prepare your end-of-month reports. As you look around, you see a photograph of his family. Your coworker smiles weakly and asks you to have a seat. As you begin to state your purpose by saying, "Thanks for taking the time to see me, Mr. Cohen," he interrupts and says, "Call me Lenny, please."

Suggested answers: Behavioral style R; telltale indicators are low-key, friendly approach to communicating; smiling; offering a seat; suggesting that the less formal name *Lenny* be used; family photos present.

Situation 3

As a customer service representative for an automobile dealer, you return a phone message from Cynthia McGregor. When the phone is answered, you say, "Good morning, may I speak with Cindy McGregor?" The curt response is, "This is *Cynthia* McGregor. How may I help you?" During the conversation, Ms. McGregor asks a variety of very specific questions about an automotive recall. Even though it seems obvious that the recall does not apply to her car, she asks very detailed follow-up questions such as why the recall was necessary, who was affected, and what was being done. Throughout the conversation, she is very focused on facts, times, dates, and technical aspects of the recall.

Suggested answers: Behavioral style I; telltale indicators are insistence on formal name *Cynthia* as opposed to more informal *Cindy*; direct, to the point, specific questions; detail-focused approach to gathering information.

Situation 4

You are a teller in a bank. Mrs. Vittelli, one of the customers, comes into your branch several times a week. You know that she has just become a grandmother because she has brought along photos of her grandson. She has shared them, and all the details of her daughter's pregnancy, in a loud, exuberant manner with several of your coworkers. As she speaks, you have noticed that she has a beautiful smile, and that throughout conversations she is very animated, using gestures and often reaching over to lightly touch others as they speak.

Suggested answers: Behavioral style E; telltale indicators are freely sharing personal information about her family with strangers, outgoing demeanor, smiling, gesturing, and communicating in a loud, animated voice.

related to options, testing, rebates, and similar detailed technical information; a person with a strong "D" behavioral tendency may want to know the "bottom line" of using your service or product; and an "E" may want to talk about uses, colors, and sizes. If you cannot answer their questions, frustration, complaints, and/or loss of a customer may result.

Service providers need to know the products they are offering so that they can provide the best customer service possible. For example, when a new product line is introduced, orientation classes for employees can be arranged. In the classes, the features, benefits, and operation of the new items can be explained and demonstrated. Taking this approach increases knowledge of products and helps ensure better customer service.

PREPARE YOURSELF

Before you come into contact with customers, take a minute to review your appearance. Ask yourself, "What image do I project?" Think about how well your appearance is in tune with that of your typical customer. Evaluate your knowledge of your job and of the products and services offered by your organization. Are you ready and able to describe them to people regardless of their style preference? If not, start getting ready by learning as much as you can and practicing your message delivery by reviewing and implementing some of the strategies related to each style preference discussed earlier in this chapter.

5   DEALING WITH PERCEPTIONS

perceptions
How someone views an item, situation, or others.

Concept: Often there are many different perceptions of an event. Our perceptions are often influenced by many factors such as physical qualities, social roles and behaviors, psychological qualities, and group affiliations.

Everyone has **perceptions** about the people and events he or she encounters (see Figure 6.4). A person's behavioral style as well as background, based on education, experiences, events, and interpersonal contacts, can influence how he or she views the world. In effect, there are sometimes as many different perceptions of an event as there are people involved.

stereotype
Generalization made about an Individual or group and not based on reality. Similar people are often lumped together for ease In categorizing them.

PERCEPTIONS AND STEREOTYPES

People's perceptions of events vary greatly, as do their perceptions of each other. As a customer service provider, you should be aware of how you perceive your customers and, in turn, how they perceive you.

In some cases, you may **stereotype** people and, in doing so, adversely affect delivery of services. For example, your perception of older customers may be that they are all slow, hard of hearing, cranky, and politically conservative. This perception may be based on past experiences or from what you've heard or seen on television. This view might cause you to treat most older people in the same way, rather than treating each person as unique. However, you are basing your behavior on a stereotype, not on reality. Think about it—aren't

ethical dilemma 6.2

You often hear one of your coworkers making improper comments about customers from other cultures (e.g., the way they dress, their accent, and so on).

What should you do about the situation, if anything?

How are our perceptions shaped within a customer service framework? In essence, there are five categories that form the basis of many perceptions. We tend to base our perceptions of others and categorize people by thinking about the following:

- *Physical qualities.* What does a person look like? What gender? What body shape? Color of skin? Physical characteristics (hair color or type, facial features, height or weight)?
- *Social roles.* What is a person's position in society? Job title? Honors received? Involvement in social or volunteer organizations?
- *Social behaviors.* How does this person act, in terms of the behavioral style characteristics? What social skills does he or she exhibit in social and business settings? How well does he or she interact with people (peers, customers, seniors, subordinates, and people of other races, gender, or backgrounds)?
- *Psychological qualities.* How does he or she process information mentally? Is this person confident? Stressed out? Insecure? Curious? Paranoid?
- *Group affiliations.* Does this person belong to a recognizable religious, ethnic, or political group? What kinds of qualities are associated with each group? Does he or she assume leadership roles and demonstrate competence in such roles?

FIGURE 6.4   **Factors Affecting Perceptions**

Discovering Common Characteristics

REFER TO WORK IT OUT 6.1 (DESCRIBING YOUR BEHAVIOR). Select four to eight friends or coworkers and ask them to rate themselves using Work It Out 6.1. Next, ask each person to answer the following questions:

What do I look for when I shop?

What is my main reason for shopping?

What do I do when I need to buy or replace something?

What is the most important thing to me when I'm looking to replace something?

Once everyone has finished, gather in a group to compare and discuss answers. Focus on the fact that each person and each style is unique but that we all have common characteristics and needs. Discuss how this knowledge of common needs or drives can be used to provide customer service more effectively.

there many older people who don't have these characteristics? Thus, you need to be very careful that your perceptions are not influenced by stereotypes, because this clearly works against treating each customer as an individual.

Stereotyping people affects our relationships with customers. For this reason, you should consciously guard against stereotyping when you interact with others. If you pigeonhole people right away because of preconceptions, you may negatively affect future interactions. For example, suppose you use your new knowledge about behavioral styles to walk up to a coworker and say something like, "I figured out what your problem is when dealing with people. You're a 'D.'" Could this create a confrontational situation? Might this person react negatively? What impact might your behavior have on your relationship with

Many preconceived ideas about an individual or group can lead to disparate treatment and poor service. *What preconceived ideas might affect how one group of diners is treated versus the other group?*

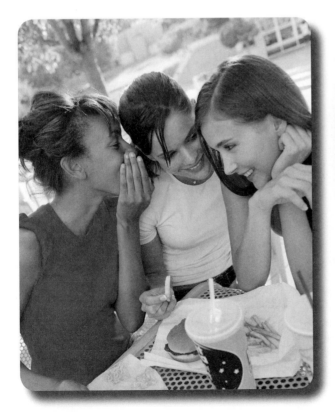

your coworker (and possibly others)? Based on what you have read regarding communication in earlier chapters, several things are wrong with such an approach. First of all, no one is always a "D." Although a person might exhibit this behavior a lot, he or she draws from all four styles, just as you do. Second, exhibiting any particular style is not a "problem." As you have seen in this chapter, "D" behavior can provide some valuable input to any situation. And finally, although a behavioral style may contribute to a person's actions, many other factors come into play (communication ability, timing, location, situation, etc.).

To avoid categorizing people, spend time observing them, listen to them objectively, and respond according to each situation and person. Doing this can lead to better relationships and improved customer service.

SUMMARY

Everything a customer experiences from the time he or she makes contact with an organization, in person, on the phone, or through other means, affects that customer's perception of the organization and its employees. To positively influence the customer's opinion, customer service professionals must be constantly alert for opportunities to provide excellent service. Making a little extra effort can often mean the difference between total customer satisfaction and service breakdown.

As you have seen in this chapter, people are varied and have different behavioral styles. Recognizing the differences and dealing with customers on a case-by-case basis is the foundation of solid customer service. By examining individual behavioral tendencies, actions, communication styles, and needs, you can better determine a course of action for each customer. The test of your effectiveness is whether your customers return and what they tell their friends about you and your organization.

KEY TERMS

behavioral styles 143
decisive style 147
expressive style 147
inquisitive style 147
perceptions 146
primary behavior pattern 144

problem solving 151
process improvement 155
rational style 145
seamless service 155
stereotype 158
win-win situation 152

REVIEW QUESTIONS

1 What are behavioral styles?

2 What are the four behavioral style categories discussed in this chapter?

3 What are some of the characteristics that can help you identify a person who has the following style preferences: R, I, D, E?

4 When communicating with someone who has an "R" preference, what can you do to improve your effectiveness?

5 When communicating with someone who has an "I" preference, what can you do to improve your effectiveness?

6 When communicating with someone who has a "D" preference, what can you do to improve your effectiveness?

7 When communicating with someone who has an "E" preference, what can you do to improve your effectiveness?

8 What are some strategies for eliminating service barriers by using your knowledge of behavioral styles?

9 What are perceptions?

10 How can perceptions affect customer relations?

Search for Behavioral Styles on the Internet

Log onto the Internet and look for information and research data on behavioral styles and other types of personal surveys. Specifically look for the various theories and surveys that describe and categorize behavior. Also try to find information about some of the people who have done research on behavior:

Sigmund Freud
Carl Jung
Alfred Adler
Abraham Maslow

William Moulton Marston
Ivan Pavlov
B. F. Skinner
Behavioral style surveys
Personality surveys
www.myersbriggs.org
www.inscapepublishing.com
www.tickle.com
www.tracomcorp.com
www.personalitypathways.com

Be prepared to present some of your findings at the next scheduled class.

Observing and Analyzing Behavioral Styles

With a partner or team, go to a public place (park, mall, airport, train or bus station, or restaurant) to observe three different people. Using the Worksheet 6.1 on the McGraw-Hill website www.mhhe.com/lucas09, note the specific behaviors each person exhibits. After you have finished this part of the activity, take a guess at each person's behavioral style preference based on behaviors you saw. Compare notes with your teammates and discuss similarities and differences among findings. Also, discuss how this information can be helpful in your workplace to deliver better customer service.

Working through Technology and People Problems at Child's Play Toy Company

Background

Since opening its newest store in Princeton, New Jersey, Child's Play Toy Company of Minneapolis, Minnesota, has been getting mixed customer reviews. Designed to be state of the art, open, and customer-friendly, the store includes an attended activity area where small children can play while parents shop. In addition, an innovative system makes it possible for local customers to order products from catalogs or from the company's website and then go to a drive-up window to pick up their purchases without leaving their cars. Another creative feature involves interactive television monitors in the store—where customers can see a customer service representative at the same time the representative sees them. To reduce staffing costs, the customer service representatives are actually at a Philadelphia, Pennsylvania, location and are remotely connected via satellite and computer to all new stores. This system is used for special ordering, billing questions, and complaint resolution. Customers can also use a computer keyboard to enter data or search for product information online through the company's website while in the store.

In recent months, the number of customer complaints has been rising. Many people complain about not getting the product that they ordered over the system, some are uncomfortable using the computer keyboard, while others dislike the impersonal touch and the fact that they have to answer a series of standard questions asked by a "talking head" on the screen, they have encountered system or computer breakdowns, and they cannot get timely service or resolution of problems.

Your Role

As a customer service representative and cashier at the store, you are responsible for operating a cash register in the store at Child's Play when all lines are operational and more than two customers are waiting in each line. You are also responsible for supervising other cashiers on your shift and dealing with customer questions, complaints, or problems. You report directly to the assistant store manager, Meg Giarnelli. Prior to coming to this store, you worked in two other New Jersey store branches during the five preceding years.

This afternoon, Mrs. Sakuro, a regular customer, came to you. She was obviously frustrated and pointed her finger at you as she shouted, "You people are stupid!" She also demanded to speak with the manager and threatened that, "If you people do not want my business, I will go to another store!" Apparently, a doll that Mrs. Sakuro had ordered two weeks ago over the in-store system had not arrived. The doll was to be for her daughter's birthday, which is in two days. Although Mrs. Sakuro has a heavy accent, you understood that she had been directed by a

cashier to check with a customer service representative via the monitor to determine the status of the order. When she did this, she was informed that there was a problem with the order. The representative who took the original order apparently wrote down the credit card number incorrectly, and the order was not processed. When Mrs. Sakuro asked the customer service representative why someone hadn't called her, the representative said that the customer service department was in another state and that long-distance calls were not allowed by front-line employees. She was told that the local store where she was picking up is responsible for verifying order status, contacting the customer via telephone, and handling problems. There was no valid explanation given when Ms. Sakuro asked why someone in New Jersey had not just e-mailed her, since they had her e-mail address. Mrs. Sakuro's behavior and attitude are upsetting to you.

Critical Thinking Questions

1 From the behavioral style information in this chapter and other subjects discussed in this book, what do you think is causing the complaints being made?

2 What system changes would you suggest for Child's Play? Why?

3 What can you do at this point to solve the problem?

4 What primary behavioral style is Mrs. Sakuro exhibiting? What specific strategies should you use to address her behavior?

HOSPITALITY-Ritz-Carlton Hotel Company

In order to ensure that you are prepared to provide premium service to your customers, take some time to think about typical customer situations in which you were personally involved or that you have witnessed. Answer the following questions on the basis of situations recalled.

1. What types of behaviors do the average customer exhibit?

2. Based on what you learned about behavioral styles in general, and your preferred style, what service strategies could you use if you were involved with the behaviors identified in Question 1?

3. In difficult or emotional service situations, what behaviors often manifest themselves?

4. What strategies might help you in dealing with such customer behaviors?

Go to www.ritzcarlton.com and research the organization. Look at their annual report, values/mission, and other historical information about the organization on their website.

1 Have you been a customer of Ritz Carlton or known anyone who has? What has been your experience or what have you heard about the company?

2 Do you believe that the Ritz Carlton Hotel is truly customer-centric? Why or why not?

3 What do you believe are some of the driving forces behind the Ritz Carlton success? Why?

4 If you could stay in a luxury hotel, would you choose the Ritz Carlton? Why or why not?

1	T		6	F		11	T
2	T		7	T		12	F
3	T		8	F		13	T
4	T		9	F		14	F
5	F		10	T		15	T

Ethical Dilemma 6.1 Possible Answers

High "D" behavior can be frustrating and cause relationship breakdowns with others. Many times, people exhibiting such behavior are not aware that they are doing so and the effect it is potentially having on those around them. In a service environment, this can be a real issue.

As with any other workplace issue, if someone's behavior (including the boss) is causing a problem, you should diplomatically, and nonemotionally, bring the issue up to the person. In doing so, be careful not to accuse or blame so that you do not provoke a defensive or emotional reaction. Instead be prepared to provide specific examples of when the person has used such behavior and explain the effect on you (and others). Make sure this conversation takes place in a private place where others do not overhear it so that you do not put the supervisor in a situation of having to "stand his/her" ground because of having to maintain an image of being in control (remember they do have a high "D" type of personality preference). Also, remember the old adage of "The boss may not always be right, but he/she *is* always the boss."

Ethical Dilemma 6.2 Possible Answers

Comments about factors that someone cannot change (e.g., culture or physical characteristics) are often a sign of more underlying prejudices against a group or type of people. They can lead to bias and discrimination as well as to provoking emotional confrontations with others.

In the workplace, you sometimes have to walk a fine line between doing what is right and potentially offending your coworkers. In this case, if you have a good rapport with the coworker, you might consider approaching the person in a nonthreatening, rational manner and using unemotional language (see Chapter 3). If you do not know the person well, perhaps you can get one of their friends to take action to correct the situation.

If you do decide to speak to your coworker, point out that such language is offensive and can actually get him/her into trouble with the customer and the organization. It can also be viewed as discriminatory and can lead to possible legal action against the employee and the organization. This is often best done through a question format (e.g., When you say things like that about people from other countries, do you really dislike them or are you just trying to be funny?). Depending on their answer, you may want to try to get them to see that others might perceive them as being prejudiced because of such comments. In some cases, depending on the remarks, attitude of the coworker, and situation, it may even be appropriate to point out the comments to a supervisor. The bottom line, is to try to share your views in a manner that helps the other person see that their actions may not be appropriate and to help them curtail future such language without damaging your work relationship or creating more serious situations.

Service Breakdowns and Service Recovery

Customers don't expect you to be perfect. They expect you to fix things when they go wrong.

—Donald Porter, V.P., British Airways

After completing this chapter, you will be able to:

1 Define what a service breakdown is.

2 Apply knowledge of behavioral styles in difficult customer situations.

3 Recognize different types of difficult customers and effectively deal with them.

4 Use the emotion-reducing model to help keep difficult situations from escalating.

5 Explain why customers defect.

6 Develop effective strategies for working with internal customers.

7 Identify strategies for preventing customer dissatisfaction and problem solving.

8 Explain the six steps of the problem-solving model.

9 Implement a front-line service recovery strategy, and spot roadblocks to service recovery.

In the Real World   Service—Southwest Airlines

When Rollin King and Herb Kelleher got together to start Southwest Airlines, they wanted to be different from their competition. According to their website, "They began with one simple notion: If you get your passengers to their destinations when they want to get there, on time, at the lowest possible fares, and make darn sure they have a good time doing it, people will fly your airline."

Founded In 1971 as a less expensive alternative to air travel, with only three planes, "the mission of Southwest Airlines is dedication to the highest quality of Customer Service delivered with a sense of warmth, friendliness, individual price, and Company Spirit." The company mission statement says a lot about the Southwest culture. As a result, after three-plus decades of passenger service, the airline is the fourth largest in the United States, flying more than 83 million passengers a year to 64 cities.

The approach to business and customers is what makes Southwest a popular airline with passengers. The airline has won the coveted industry Triple Crown—Best On-Time Record, Best Baggage Handling, and Fewest Customer Complaints six times between 1988 and 1996. It was the first airline to accomplish this feat. They have since spearheaded other customer-focused initiatives by being the first airline to award frequent flyer points for number of trips flown with them instead of based on miles. According to Department of Transportation reports, Southwest consistently had highest customer satisfaction and best on-time performance of all major airlines during 2006. To help maintain a competitive edge, Southwest has pioneered senior discounts, Fun Fares, Fun Packs, a same-day air freight delivery service, ticketless travel, and many other unique programs. The airline's emphasis is not just on travel, but on making the journey fun.

Much of the way that Southwest does business is founded in their focus on their employees (internal customers). Their mission statement includes the following: "We are committed to provide our Employees a stable work environment with equal opportunity for learning and personal growth. Creativity and innovation are encouraged for improving the effectiveness of Southwest Airlines. Above all, Employees will be provided the same concern, respect, and caring attitude within the organization that they are expected to share externally with every Southwest Customer."

The result of doing business that is attuned to customer needs and preferences has been a growth to over 33,000 employees, 500 aircraft, and net income of over $499 million in 2006. Also in 2006, Southwest was named as one of the world's top 25 most innovative companies by *BusinessWeek* magazine and as one of America's most admired companies by *Forbes* magazine.

For additional information about this organization, visit www.southwest.com.

See activity based on this section on page 190.

Quick Preview

Before reviewing the chapter content, respond to the following questions by placing a "T" for true or an "F" for false on the rules. Use any questions you miss as a checklist of material to which you will pay particular attention as you read through the chapter. For those you get right, congratulate yourself, but review the sections they address in order to learn additional details about the topic.

_____ 1. Service breakdowns often occur because customer needs and wants are not met.
_____ 2. Customer expectations do not affect how service is delivered.
_____ 3. Behavioral style preferences do not affect customer needs or satisfaction levels.
_____ 4. An upset customer is usually annoyed with a specific person rather than the organization or system.
_____ 5. When you cannot comply with the demands of an angry customer, you should try to negotiate an alternative solution.
_____ 6. Competency in communicating can eliminate the need for service recovery.

_____ **7.** Demanding customers often act in a domineering manner because they are very self-confident. This is a function of behavioral style.

_____ **8.** Service recovery occurs when a provider is able to make restitution, solve a problem, or regain customer trust after service breakdown.

_____ **9.** One key strategy for preventing dissatisfaction is to learn to think like a customer.

_____ **10.** Adopting a "good neighbor policy" can help in dealings with internal customers.

_____ **11.** As part of trying to help solve a customer problem, you should assess its seriousness.

_____ **12.** When something does not go as the customer needs or expects, service recovery becomes a vital step in maintaining the relationship.

Answers to Quick Preview can be found at the end of the chapter.

service breakdowns
Situations when customers have expectations of a certain type or level of service that are not met by a service provider.

wants
Things that customers typically desire but do not necessarily need.

needs
Motivators or drivers that cause customers to seek out specific types of products or services. These may be marketing-driven, based on advertising they have seen, or may tie directly to Abraham Maslow's hierarchy of needs theory.

customer expectations
The perceptions that customers have when they contact an organization or service provider about the kind and level and quality of products and services they should receive.

1 WHAT IS A SERVICE BREAKDOWN?

Concept: Service breakdowns occur whenever any product or service fails to meet the customer's expectations.

Service breakdowns occur daily in all types of organizations. They happen whenever the product or service delivered fails to meet customer expectations (see Figure 7.1). In some cases the product or service delivered may function exactly as it was designed, but if the customer perceived that it should work another way, a breakdown occurs. Additionally, when a product or service fails to meet what the customer **wants** or **needs**, dissatisfaction and frustration can result.

In addition, **customer expectations** can affect how service is delivered and perceived. Today's customers are more discerning, better educated, have access to more up-to-date and accurate information, and are often more demanding than in the past. They have certain expectations about your products and services, and the way that you will provide them. Figure 7.2 shows some common expectations customers might have of a service organization. Failure to fulfill some or all of these expectations can lead to dissatisfaction and in some cases confrontation and/or loss of business.

2 THE ROLE OF BEHAVIORAL STYLE

Concept: Behavioral preferences have a major effect on the interactions of people. The more you know about style tendencies, the better you will understand your customers.

CUSTOMER SERVICE SUCCESS TIP

Go out of your way to identify and satisfy customer needs and expectations by being prepared and conscientious and thinking like a customer.

As you read in Chapter 6, behavioral style preferences play a major part in how people interact. Styles also affect the types of things people want and value. For example, those with high expressive tendencies will probably buy more colorful and people-oriented items than will those who have high decisive tendencies.

The more you know about style tendencies, the easier it becomes to deal with people in a variety of situations and to help match their needs with the products and services you and your organization can provide. The suggested strategies found in Chapter 6 can assist you in dealing with customers who exhibit a specific behavioral style preference and are

Service Breakdown Examples

WHAT EXAMPLES OF SERVICE BREAKDOWN HAVE YOU EX-PERIENCED OR CAN YOU RECALL FROM SOMEONE ELSE'S STORY? List and then discuss them with classmates.

After discussing your lists, brainstorm ways that the organization did or could have recovered.

upset, irrational, or confrontational. Keep in mind that everyone possesses all four behavioral styles discussed in Chapter 6 and can display various types of behavior from time to time. Therefore, carefully observe your customer's behavior and use the information you learned about each style as an indicator of the type of person with whom you are dealing. Do not use such information as the definitive answer for resolving the situation. Human beings are complex and react to stimuli in various ways—so adapt your approach as necessary. In addition, learn to deal with your emotions so that you can prevent or resolve heated emotional situations.

FIGURE 7.1

Examples of Service Breakdowns

Here are some examples of service breakdowns:

- A waiter serves a meal containing an ingredient not expected by the customer, or one that the customer specified should not be added. A note of caution: If you are in food service, be vigilant in monitoring orders when customers ask that certain ingredients not be used. Check food and drinks before you deliver them to your customer to be sure that the cook staff did not forget the special request. Also, do not simply remove a food item if it was placed on a plate inadvertently. Some people have severe allergies to certain foods that could cause serious illness and even death—and a huge liability for you and your organization.
- A hotel room is not available when the customer arrives. (In some cases a stated check-in time may exist and the customer may be early. Make every effort to accommodate the customer if this happens.)
- According to the customer, room service food was cold when delivered (e.g., not at the degree of warmth desired or expected).
- An optometrist provides glasses or contact lenses that do not adequately correct a patient's vision.
- A volunteer at a silent auction for charity misplaces an item won by a donor.
- A coworker expects your assistance in providing information needed for a monthly report, but you failed to get it to her on time or as agreed.
- A manufacturer does not receive a parts delivery as you promised, and an assembly line has to be shut down.
- A garment you needed for a meeting returns from the laundry with broken buttons and cannot be worn.

In any of the situations described, customers may have not received what they were promised, or at least they perceived that they did not. When such incidents occur, there is a breakdown and they often lead to emotional or difficult situations. In many instances service providers are uncomfortable and unprepared to deal with such events.

FIGURE 7.2

Typical Customer Expectations

Customers come to you expecting that certain things will occur in regard to the products and services they obtain. Customers typically expect the following:

Expectations Related to People

Friendly, knowledgeable service providers

Respect (they want to be treated as if they are intelligent)

Empathy (they want their feelings and emotions to be recognized)

Courtesy (they want to be recognized as "the customer" and as someone who is important to you and your organization)

Equitable treatment (they do not want to feel that one individual or group gets preferential benefits or treatment over another)

Expectations Related to Products and Services

Easily accessible and available products and services (no lengthy delays)

Reasonable and competitive pricing

Products and services that adequately address needs

Quality (appropriate value for money and time invested)

Ease of use

Safe (warranty available and product free of defects that might cause physical injury)

State-of-the-art products and service delivery

Easy-to-understand instructions (and follow-up assistance availability)

Ease of return or exchange (flexible policies that provide alternatives depending on the situation)

Appropriate and expedient problem resolution

3   DIFFICULT CUSTOMERS

Concept: Successful service will ultimately be delivered through effective communication skills, positive attitude, patience, and a willingness to help the customer.

difficult customers
People who challenge a service provider's ability to deliver service and who require special skills and patience.

You may think of **difficult customer** contacts as those in which you have to deal with negative, angry, demanding or aggressive people. These are just a few of the types of potentially difficult interactions. From time to time, you will also be called upon to help customers who can be described in one or more of the following ways:

Dissatisfied with your service or products.

Indecisive or lacking knowledge about your product, service, or policies.

Rude or inconsiderate of others.

Talkative.

Internal customers with special requests.

Speak English as a second language (discussed in Chapter 8).

Elderly and need extra assistance (discussed In Chapter 8).

Have a disability (discussed In Chapter 8).

Each of the above categories can be difficult to handle, depending on your knowledge, experience, and abilities. A key to successfully serving all type of customers is to treat each person as an individual. If you stereotype people, you will likely damage the customer-provider relationship. Avoid labeling people according to their behavior. Do not mentally categorize people (put them into groups) according to the way they speak or act or look—and then treat everyone in a "group" the same way.

Ultimately, you will deliver successful service through your effective communication skills, positive attitude, patience, and willingness to help the customer. Your ability to focus on the situation or problem and

Handling difficult customers will be one of your biggest challenges so be prepared. *How would you deal with an unhappy customer?*

not on the person will be a very important factor in your success. Making the distinction between the person and the problem is especially important when you are faced with difficult situations in the service environment. Although you may not understand or approve of a person's behavior, he or she is still your customer. Try to make the interaction a positive one, and if necessary ask for assistance from a coworker or refer the problem to an appropriate level in your operational chain of command.

Many difficult situations you will deal with as a service provider will be caused by your customer's needs, wants, and expectations. You will read about service challenges in this chapter, along with their causes and some strategies for effectively dealing with them.

DEMANDING OR DOMINEERING CUSTOMERS

Customers can be **demanding or domineering** for a number of reasons. Many times, domineering behavior is part of a personality style or simply behavior that they have learned, as discussed in Chapter 6. In other instances, it could be a reaction to past customer service encounters. A demanding customer may feel a need to be or stay in control, especially if he or she has felt out of control in the past. Often, such people are insecure. Some strategies for effectively handling demanding customers are discussed in the following sections:

demanding or domineering customers
Customers who have definite ideas about what they want and are unwilling to compromise or accept alternatives.

- *Be professional.* Don't raise your voice or retaliate verbally. Children engage in name-calling, which often escalates into shoving matches. Unfortunately, some adults "regress" to childish behavior. Your customer may revert to negative behavior learned in the past. Both you and the customer lose when this happens.
- *Respect the customer.* Showing respect does not mean that you must accommodate your customer's every wish. It means that you should make positive eye contact (but not glare), remain calm, use the customer's name, apologize when appropriate and/or necessary, and let the customer know that he or she is important to you and your organization. Work positively toward a resolution of the problem.
- *Be firm and fair and focus on the customer's needs.* As you read in Chapter 3, assertive behavior is an appropriate response to a domineering or demanding person; aggression is not. Also, remember the importance of treating each customer as an individual.
- *Tell the customer what you can do.* Don't focus on negatives or what can't be done when dealing with your customers. Stick with what is possible and what you are willing to do. Be flexible and willing to listen to requests. If something suggested is possible and will help solve the problem, compliment the person on his or her idea (e.g., "Mr. Hollister, that's a good suggestion, and one that I think will work"), and then try to make it happen. Doing this will show that you are receptive to new ideas, are truly

Helping an Indecisive Customer

THINK ABOUT A RECENT TIME WHEN YOU WERE INDECISIVE ABOUT PURCHASING A PRODUCT OR SERVICE, AND THEN RESPOND TO THE FOLLOWING QUESTIONS:

1. What caused your indecisiveness?

2. What ultimately helped you to make a decision?

3. How can you use your own strategies to help satisfy an indecisive customer?

working to meet the customer's needs and expectations, and value the customer's opinion. Also, remember that if you can psychologically partner with a customer, he or she is less likely to attack. You do need to make sure that your willingness to assist and comply is not seen as giving in or backing down. If it is, the customer may make additional demands or return in the future with similar demands. To avoid this, you could add to the earlier statement by saying something like, "Mr. Hollister, that's a good suggestion, and although we cannot do this in every instance, I think that your suggestion is one that will work at this time." This puts the customer on alert that although he or she may get his or her way this time, it will not necessarily happen in the future. Another strategy is to make a counteroffer.

If you are thoroughly familiar with your organization's policies and procedures and your limits of authority, you will be prepared to negotiate with demanding customers. If they want something you cannot provide, you might offer an alternative that will satisfy them. Remember that your goal is complete customer satisfaction, but not at the expense of excessive loss to your organization.

INDECISIVE CUSTOMERS

indecisive customers
People who have difficulty making a decision or making a selection when given choices of products or services.

You will encounter people who cannot or will not make a decision. They sometimes spend hours vacillating. In some cases, **indecisive customers** truly do not know what they want or need, as when they are looking for a gift for a special occasion. Sometimes such customers are afraid that they will choose incorrectly. In these situations, use all your communication skills. Otherwise, indecisive customers will occupy large amounts of your time and detract from your ability to do your job effectively or to assist other customers.

Be aware, however, that some people really *are* just looking as they check out sales, kill time between appointments, or relax, or they may be lonely and want to be around others. Strategies for dealing with an indecisive person are:

- *Be patient.*   Keep in mind that, although indecisive people can be frustrating (especially if you have a high D behavioral style preference), they are still customers.
- *Ask open-ended questions.*   Just as you would do with a dissatisfied customer, try to get as much background information as possible. The more data you can gather, the better you can evaluate the situation, determine needs, and assist in the solution of any problems.
- *Listen actively.*   Focus on verbal and nonverbal messages for clues to determine emotions, concerns, and interests.
- *Suggest other options.*   Offer alternatives that will help in decision making and reduce the customer's anxiety. Suggesting a warranty or exchange possibility may make the customer more secure in the decision-making process.

WORK IT OUT 7.3

Handling the Demanding Customer

SURVEY CUSTOMER SERVICE PROFESSIONALS IN VARIOUS PROFESSIONS TO SEE HOW THEY HANDLE DEMANDING OR DOMINEERING CUSTOMERS. Make a list for future reference and role-play a variety of scenarios involving demanding customers with a peer.

• *Guide decision making.* By assertively, not aggressively, offering suggestions or ideas and providing product and/or service Information, you can help customers make a decision. Note that you are helping them, not making the decision for them. If you push your preferences on them, they may be dissatisfied and return the item. Then you, or someone else, will have to deal with an unhappy customer.

DISSATISFIED AND ANGRY CUSTOMERS

Occasionally, you will encounter **dissatisfied customers** or angry ones. Possibly they have been improperly served by you or one of your peers, or by a competitor in the past. Even if you were not personally involved in their previous experience, you represent the organization or you may be considered "just like that last service employee." Unfair as this may be, you have to try to make these customers happy. To do so, try the following strategies:

• *Listen.*
• *Remain positive and flexible.*
• *Smile, give your name, and offer assistance.*
• *Be compassionate and don't make excuses.*
• *Ask open-ended questions and verify information.*
• *Take appropriate action.*

Remember: if you get defensive, you become part of the problem and not part of the solution. Keep in mind what you read about the power of positive wording in Chapter 3. Figure 7.3 shows some examples of negative wording and some possible alternatives.

Dealing with angry people requires a certain amount of caution. For you to effectively serve an **angry customer,** you must move beyond the emotions to discover the reason for his or her anger. *Note:* Before dealing with customers, check with your supervisor to find out what your policies are and what level of authority you have in making decisions. This relates to empowerment discussed earlier in the book. By having this information before a customer encounter, you will have the tools

dissatisfied customers
Someone who does not (or perceives that he or she does not) receive promised products or services.

angry customers
Customers who become emotional because either their needs are not met or they are dissatisfied with the services or products purchased from an organization.

Indecisive people can be frustrating as you try to serve their needs. *What steps would you take to help a customer made a decision?*

Dealing with Angry Customers

WORK WITH A PARTNER. Discuss situations in which you had to deal with an angry person. Think about what made the person angry and what seemed to reduce tension. Make a list of these factors and be prepared to share your list with the class. Use the results of this discussion to develop strategies to help calm angry people in the future.

FIGURE 7.3

Positive Wording

When faced with a customer encounter that isn't going well, remain positive in language. This will help you avoid escalating the situation.

Negative Words or Phrases	Positive Alternatives
Problem	Situation, issue, concern, challenge
No	What I (or) we can do is . . .
Cannot	What I (or) we can do is . . .
It's not my job (or my fault)	Although I do not normally handle that, I'm happy to assist you.
You'll have to (or you must . . .)	Would you mind . . . ? Would you please . . . ?
Our policy says . . .	While I'm unable to . . . What I can do is . . .

CUSTOMER SERVICE SUCCESS TIP

*Do whatever it takes to rectify a situation in which a customer is dissatisfied with your product or service, it (within your authority) to ensure customer satisfaction. As a rule of thumb, **underpromise and overdeliver**. In other words, strive to do the unexpected and provide quality service to create a memorable customer experience.*

underpromise and overdeliver
A service strategy in which service providers strive for excellent customer service and satisfaction by doing more than they say they will for the customer or exceeding customer expectations.

and knowledge necessary to handle your customers effectively and professionally. Here are some possible tactics:

- *Be positive.*   Tell the customer what you can do rather than what you cannot do.
- *Acknowledge the customer's feelings or anger.*   By taking this approach, you've acknowledged the customer's feelings, demonstrated a willingness to assist, and asked the customer to participate in solving the problem.
- *Reassure.*   Indicate that you understand why he or she is angry and that you will work to solve the problems.
- *Remain objective.*   Remember, angry customers are usually angry at the organization, product, or service that you represent, not at *you.*
- *Listen actively; determine the cause.*   Whether the customer is "right" or "wrong" makes no difference in situations like these. Actively listening and trying to discover the problem will assure the customer that you are trying to take care of it for him or her.
- *Reduce frustrations.*   Don't say or do anything that will create further tension. Do your best to handle the situation with this customer before serving another.
- *Negotiate a solution and conduct a follow-up.*   Elicit ideas or negotiate an alternative with the customer. Follow-up as soon as you can. Don't assume that the organization's system will work as designed.

RUDE OR INCONSIDERATE CUSTOMERS

Some people seem to go out of their way to be offensive or to get attention. Although they seem confident and self-assured outwardly, they are often insecure and defensive. Some behaviors they might exhibit are raising the voice, demanding to speak to a supervisor,

Responding to Rudeness

WORKING WITH A PARTNER, DEVELOP A LIST OF RUDE COMMENTS THAT A CUSTOMER MIGHT MAKE TO YOU (e.g., "If you're not too busy, I'd like some assistance") along with responses you might give (e.g., "If you could please wait, I'll be happy to assist you as soon as I finish, sir (or madam). I want to be able to give you my full attention and don't want to be distracted.").

using profanity, cutting in front of someone else in a line, being verbally abrupt (snapping back at you) even though you're trying to assist, calling you by your last name, which they see on your name tag (e.g., "Listen, Smith"), ignoring what you say, or otherwise going out of the way to be offensive or in control. Try the following strategies for dealing with **rude or inconsiderate customers:**

- *Remain professional.*   Just because the customer is exhibiting inappropriate behavior does not justify your reacting in kind. Remain calm, assertive, and in control of the situation. For example, if you are waiting on a customer and a rude person barges in or cuts off your conversation, pause, make direct eye contact, smile, and firmly say, "I'll be with you as soon as I finish with this customer, sir (or madam)." If he or she insists, repeat your comment and let the person know that the faster you serve the current customer, the faster you can get to the person waiting. Also, maintaining decorum may help win over the person or at least keep him or her in check.
- *Don't resort to retaliation.*   Retaliation will only infuriate this type of customer, especially if you have embarrassed him or her in the presence of others. Remember that such people are still customers, and if they or someone else perceives your actions as inappropriate, you could lose more than just the battle at hand.

rude or inconsiderate customers
People who seem to take pleasure in being obstinate and contrary when dealing with service providers and who seem to have their own agenda without concern for the feelings of others.

talkative customers
Customers exhibiting extroverted behavior who are very people-oriented.

Before you can deal with a customer's business needs, you must first address the customer's emotional issues and try to calm him or her. *What would you do to calm such customers?*

TALKATIVE CUSTOMERS

Some people phone or approach you and then spend excessive amounts of time discussing irrelevant matters such as personal experiences, family, friends, schooling, accomplishments, other customer service situations, and the weather. The following tips might help when dealing with **talkative customers:**

- *Remain warm and cordial, but focused.*   Recognize that this person's personality style is probably mainly Expressive and that his or her natural inclination is to connect with others. You can smile, acknowledge comments, and carry on a brief conversation as you are serving this customer. For example, if

the person comments that your last name is spelled exactly like his or her great aunt's and then asks where your family is from, you could respond with "That's interesting. My family is from . . . but I don't believe we have any relatives outside that area." You have responded but possibly cut off the next question. Anything less would probably be viewed as rude by the customer. Anything more could invite additional discussion. Your next statement should then be business-related (e.g., "Is there anything else I can assist you with today?").

- *Ask specific open-ended questions.* These types of questions can assist in determining needs and addressing customer concerns.
- *Use closed-end questions to control.* Once you have determined the customer's needs, switch to closed-end (discussed in Chapter 3) questions to better control the situation and limit the opportunity for the customer to continue talking.
- *Manage the conversation.* Keep in mind that if you spend a lot of time with one customer, other customers may be neglected. You can manage a customer encounter through questioning and through statements that let the customer know your objective is to serve customers. You might say, "I know you said you have a lot of shopping to do, so I won't keep you any longer. Thanks for coming in. Please let me know if I can assist in the future." Imply that you are ending the interaction to benefit the customer.

4 HANDLING EMOTIONS WITH THE EMOTION-REDUCING MODEL

Concept: Using the emotion-reducing model helps to calm the customer so that you can then solve the problem.

It is important to remember when dealing with people who are behaving emotionally (e.g., irritated, angry, upset, crying, or raising their voice) that they are typically upset with the structure, process, organization, or other factors over which you and/or they have no control. They are usually not upset with you (unless you have provoked them by exhibiting poor customer service skills or attitude). Remain rational and do not react to them emotionally.

Before you can get your customer to calm down, listen, and address the situation, you must first deal with her or his emotional state. Once you do this, you can proceed to use problem-solving strategies (discussed later in this chapter) to assist in solving the problem. Until you reduce the customer's emotional level, he or she will probably not listen to you or be receptive to what you are saying or your attempts to assist. In some cases, she or he may even become irritated because you seem uncaring.

To help calm the customer down, you must send customer-focused verbal and nonverbal messages. You need to demonstrate patience and use all the positive communication

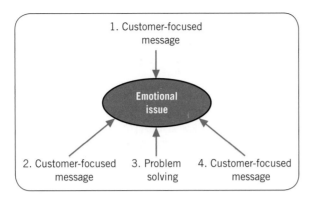

FIGURE 7.4   **Emotion-Reducing Model**

skills you read about in Chapters 3 to 5. Most important among those skills are the ability and the willingness to listen calmly to what the customer has to say without interrupting or interjecting your views. This lesson is taught to many law enforcement officers to help them deal with crisis situations such as domestic disturbances. If your customer perceives that you are not attuned to his or her emotional needs or thinks that you are not working in his or her best interest, you become part of the problem, rather than part of the solution.

Keep in mind that a customer generally wants to be respected and *acknowledged* as an individual and as being important. As you interact with the customer, you can soften the situation and reduce emotion by providing customer-focused responses. Simple customer-focused messages can put you on a friendly (human) level while at the same time helping to calm the emotion.

The key to helping resolve any service breakdowns is to frame your problem resolution with customer-focused messages through use of the emotion-reducing model (Figure 7.4). Here's how the **emotion-reducing model** works: Assume a customer has a problem. As the customer approaches (or when you answer the telephone), greet him or her with "Good morning (or afternoon)," a smile, and open body language and gesturing (1. customer-focused message). Then, as the customer explains the issue (emotional issue), you can offer statements such as, "I see," "I can appreciate your concern (or frustration, or anger)," or "I understand how that can feel" (2. customer- focused). Such statements can help you connect psychologically with the customer. Continue to use positive reinforcement and communication throughout your interaction. Once the problem has been defined and resolved (3. problem solving), take one more opportunity at the end of your interaction to send a customer-focused message by smiling and thanking the customer for allowing you to assist. Also, one last apology may be appropriate for inconvenience, frustration, mistreatment, and so on (4. customer-focused).

emotion-reducing model
Process for reducing customer emotion in situations when frustration or anger exists.

5 REASONS FOR CUSTOMER DEFECTION

Concept: Failing to meet the customer's needs, handling problems inefficiently, treating the customer unfairly, and using inadequate systems are reasons for the customer to leave you and go elsewhere.

Following a service breakdown, there is often a possibility that you may never see the customer again. This is potentially disastrous to your organization, because it costs five to six times as much to win a new customer as it costs to retain a current one. And, as we saw

FIGURE 7.5

Reasons for Customer Defection

Poor service and complacency. If customers perceive that you and/or your organization do not sincerely care about them or about solving their problems, they may go elsewhere. If a concern is important enough for the customer to verbalize (formally or informally) or to write down, it is important enough for you to take seriously. You should immediately address the problem by listening, gathering information, and taking appropriate action. Customer comments might be casual, for example, "You know, I sure wish you folks stocked a wider variety of rose bush colors. I love shopping here, but your selection is so limited." In this instance, you might write down the customer's name, phone number, and address and then follow up with your manager or buyers about it. Also, practice your questioning skills by asking, "What color did you have in mind?" or "What is your favorite color?" If the customer has a specific request, you could pass that along. You or someone else should try to obtain the item and then contact the customer to discuss your efforts and findings. Sometimes the obvious solutions are the ones that are overlooked, so be perceptive when dealing with customers and look for little clues such as these. It could mean the difference in continued business and word-of-mouth advertising by your customer.

Inappropriate complaint resolution. The key thing to remember about complaint resolution is that it is the *customer's* perception of the situation, not yours, that counts. If customers believe that they were not treated fairly, honestly, in a timely manner, and in an appropriate fashion, or if they are still dissatisfied, your efforts failed. Remember that only a small percentage of your customers complain. Second attempts at resolution by customers are almost unheard of.

Unmet needs. Customers have very specific needs to which you must attend. When these needs are not addressed or are unsatisfactorily met, the customer is likely to seek an alternative source of fulfillment.

customer defection
Customers often take their business to competitors when they feel that their needs or wants are not met or if they encounter breakdown in customer service or poor quality products.

earlier in this chapter, a dissatisfied customer is also likely to tell other people about the bad experience. Thus, you and others in your organization must be especially careful to identify reasons for **customer defection** (Figure 7.5) and remedy potential and actual problems before they negatively affect customers.

So often, service providers make the mistake of trying to project their personal needs onto others. Their feeling is that "I like it, so everybody should like it." However, as you will read in Chapter 8, today's diverse world requires you to be more knowledgeable and accepting of the ideas, values, beliefs, and needs of others. Failure to be sensitive to diversity may set you, your organization, and your customers on a collision course. Remember what you have read about trust and how quickly it can be destroyed in relationships.

6 WORKING WITH INTERNAL CUSTOMERS (COWORKERS)

Concept: Relationships with your internal customers are important. You should meet your commitments and build a professional reputation.

As we discussed in earlier chapters, you have to deal with internal as well as external customers. Although your interactions with internal customers may not be difficult, they can often be more sensitive than your dealings with outsiders.

After all, you see peers and coworkers regularly, and because of your job, office politics, and protocol, your interactions with them are ongoing. Therefore, extend all the same courtesies to internal customers that you do to external ones—in some cases, more so. Some suggestions that might help you enhance your interactions with internal customers are given below.

STAY CONNECTED

Since relationships within the organization are so important, go out of your way to make contact with internal customers periodically. You can do this by dropping by their work area to say hello, sending an e-mail, or leaving a voice mail message. This helps keep the door to communication open so that if service does break down someday, you will have a better chance of hearing about it and solving the problem amiably. You might describe your co-workers as your "normal" internal customers, but do not forget the importance of your relationships with other employees, such as the cleaning crew (they service your office and work area), security force (they protect you, your organization, and your vehicle), support staff (who provide services like purchasing, payroll, travel, and logistical assistance), and the information technology people (they maintain computer equipment). All these groups and many others within the organization add value and can be a big help to you at some point.

MEET ALL COMMITMENTS

Too often, service providers forget the importance of internal customers. Because of familiarity, they sometimes become lax and tend to not give the attention to internal customers that they would give to external customers. This can be a big mistake. For example, if you depend on someone else to obtain or send products or services to external customers, that relationship is as crucial as the ones you have with external customers. Don't forget that if you depend on internal suppliers for materials, products, or information, these people can negatively affect your ability to serve external customers by delaying or withholding the items you need. Such actions might be unintentional or intentional, depending on your relationship.

To prevent, or at least reduce, the possibility of such breakdowns, honor all commitments you make to internal customers. If you promise to do something, do your best to deliver, and in the agreed-upon time. If you can't do something, say so when your internal customer asks. If something comes up that prevents you from fulfilling your commitment, let the customer know of the change in a timely manner.

Remember, it is better to exceed customer expectations than not meet them. If you beat a deadline, they will probably be pleasantly surprised and appreciative.

DON'T SIT ON YOUR EMOTIONS

Some people hold on to anger, frustration, and other negative emotions rather than get their feelings out into the open and dealing with them. Not only is this potentially damaging to health, for it might cause stress-related illnesses, but it can also destroy working relationships. Whenever something goes wrong or you are troubled by something, go to the person and, using the feedback skills you learned in Chapter 3, talk about the situation. Failure to do so can result in disgruntled internal customers, damage to the customer-supplier relationship, and damage to your reputation. Don't forget that you will continue to rely on your customer in the future, so you cannot afford a relationship problem.

BUILD A PROFESSIONAL REPUTATION

Through your words and actions, go out of your way to let your customer and your boss know that you have a positive, can-do, customer-focused attitude. Let them know that you will do whatever it takes to create an environment in which internal and external customers

ethical dilemma 7.1

A coworker promised to help you complete a project where you were to compile information and mail it to customers on Tuesday even though it was not her job. You have helped her in similar situations In the past. It is now Thursday and the coworker still has not come to your aid and you are now behind schedule.
1. How would you handle this situation? Why?
2. Would you report the situation to your supervisor? Why or why not?
3. What effect might her behavior have on your relationship? Why?

are important. Also, regularly demonstrate your commitment to *proactive* service. This means gathering information, products, and other tools before coming into contact with a customer so that you are prepared to deal with a variety of situations and people. It also means doing the unexpected for customers and providing service that makes them excited about doing business with you and your organization.

ADOPT A GOOD-NEIGHBOR POLICY

Take a proactive approach to building internal relationships so that you can head off negative situations. If your internal customers are in your department, act in a manner that preserves sound working relationships. You can accomplish this in part by avoiding the following negative work habits:

- *Avoid gatherings of friends and loud conversation in your work space.* This can be especially annoying if the office setup consists of cubicles, as sound travels easily. Respect your coworkers' right to work in a professional environment. If you must hold meetings or gatherings, go to the cafeteria or some other place away from the work area.
- *Maintain good grooming and hygiene habits.* Demonstrate professionalism in your dress and grooming. Avoid excessive amounts of colognes and perfumes.
- *Don't overdo call forwarding.* Sometimes you must be away from your work space. Company policy may require that you forward your calls. Do not overdo forwarding your calls. Your coworkers may be inconvenienced and resentful if you do.
- *Avoid unloading personal problems.* Everyone has personal problems now and then. Do not bring personal problems to the workplace and burden coworkers with them. If you have personal problems and need assistance, go to your supervisor or team leader or human resources department and ask for some suggestions. If you get a reputation for often having personal problems—and bringing them to the workplace—your career could suffer.
- *Avoid office politics and gossip.* Your purpose in the workplace is to serve the customer and do your job. If you have extra time to spread gossip and network often with others, you should approach your supervisor or team leader about job opportunities in which you can learn new skills or take on additional responsibilities. This can increase your effectiveness and marketability in the workplace.
- *Pitch in to help.* If you have spare time and your coworkers need assistance with a project, volunteer to help out. They may do the same at some point in the future when you are feeling overwhelmed with a project or assignment.
- *Be truthful.* One of the fastest ways for you to suffer a damaged relationship, or lose the trust and confidence of your coworkers and customers, is to be caught in a lie. Regard your word as your bond.

7 STRATEGIES FOR PREVENTING DISSATISFACTION AND PROBLEM SOLVING

strategies for preventing dissatisfaction
Techniques used to prevent a breakdown in needs fulfillment when you are dealing with customers.

Concept: Focusing on the customers' needs and seeking ways to satisfy their needs quickly while exceeding customer expectations are ways to prevent dissatisfaction.

The best way to deal with a service breakdown is to prevent it from occurring. Here are some specific **strategies for preventing dissatisfaction.**

THINK LIKE THE CUSTOMER

Learn to use the interactive communication techniques described in this book. Once you've mastered them, set out to discover what customers want by observing nonverbal behavior, asking specific questions, and listening to their comments and responses. Learn to listen for their unspoken as well as verbalized needs, concerns, and questions. Think about how you would like to be served under the conditions you are dealing with and act accordingly.

PAMPER THE CUSTOMER

Make customers feel special and important. Treat them as if they are the center of your attention and that you are there for no other purpose than to serve them. Do the unexpected, and take any extra effort necessary to meet and exceed their needs. Even if you can't satisfy all their wishes, if you are positive, enthusiastic, and show initiative, customers can walk away feeling good about the encounter.

RESPECT THE CUSTOMER

Before you begin focusing on customers' problems, take time to listen and show that you support them and their viewpoint. By using a people-centered approach to problem analysis and problem solving, you can win the customer over. With both of you working together, you can define the problem and jointly reach an acceptable solution.

FOCUS ON THE CUSTOMER

When a customer takes the time to share a concern, complaint, or question, take the following actions:

React to remarks or actions.   Let customers know that you heard what they said or received their written message. If the information is given in person, remember to use the verbal, nonverbal, and listening skills discussed earlier in this book. Smile and acknowledge their presence and comments. If you can't deal with them at that moment because you are serving another customer, let them know when you will be available. If customer comments are in writing, respond quickly. If a phone number is available, try calling to speed up the response and then follow up in writing.

Empathize.   Let customers know that you are concerned, that you do appreciate their views, feelings, or concerns, and that you'll do your best to serve them. Really try to "feel their pain" and act as if you were resolving a personal issue of your own. Chances are you will then put more effort into it and appear more sincere.

Take action.   Once you've gathered enough information to determine an appropriate response, get agreement from your customer and then act. The faster you act, the more important the customer will feel.

Reassure or reaffirm.   Take measures to let customers know that you and the organization have their best interests at heart. Stress their value to you and your commitment to resolving their complaints. Part of this is providing your name and phone number, and telling them what actions you will take; for example, "Mrs. Lupe, I appreciate your concern about not receiving the package on time. My name is Bob Lucas, my number is 407 555 6134, and I will research the problem. Once I've

Focusing on the Customer

THINK ABOUT THE TECHNIQUES DESCRIBED IN THIS BOOK
FOR FOCUSING ON THE CUSTOMER.   What additional strategies can you think of?

discovered what happened, I'll call you back. If it looks as though it will take more than a day, I'll call you by 4 P.M. tomorrow to update you. Is that acceptable?"

Follow up.   Once a customer transaction is completed, make sure that any necessary follow-up actions are begun. For example, if appropriate, make an additional phone call to customers to be sure that they received their orders, that they are satisfied with your actions, or simply to reassure them and provide an opportunity for questions. If you promised to take some action, do so and coordinate with others who need to be involved.

EXCEED EXPECTATIONS

Go the extra mile by giving your customers exemplary service. Strive to get the highest rating possible on the relationship-rating point scale (see Chapter 10). To do so, work hard to understand what the customer wants and expects. Observe customers, monitor trends, and talk to customers. Constantly look for ways to go beyond the expected or what the competition provides. Provide it faster, better, and more efficiently than others, and exceed customer expectations. Do things for your customer that set your service attitude apart from that of other providers. Some things cost little or nothing and return your "investment" many times over through goodwill and positive word-of-mouth publicity. To raise your rating and please your customers, try some of these simple strategies:

Auto repair technician: "After I rotated and balanced your tires, I checked and filled all your fluids, free of charge."

Clothing salesperson: "While you try on that outfit, I'll go pick out a couple of other blouses that would suit you perfectly."

Bank customer service representative: "While you are waiting for a loan officer, can I get you a cup of coffee?"

Hotel operator: "Along with your wake-up call, I'll have some coffee or tea brought up. Which would you prefer?"

Restaurant host: "The wait for a table is approximately 30 minutes. Can I get you a complimentary glass of wine or soft drink from the bar?"

Travel agent: "Since this is your honeymoon cruise, I've arranged for a complimentary bottle of champagne to be delivered to your room along with a book of discount coupons for onboard services."

Call center representative: "Because you were on hold so long to place your order, I'm taking 10 percent off your order."

Dentist: "For referring your friend to us, I've told my receptionist to take $25 off your next cleaning fee."

Plumber: "While I was fixing your toilet stopper, I noticed that the lift arm was almost rusted through, so I changed it too, at no charge."

8   THE PROBLEM-SOLVING PROCESS

Concept: Helping customers find a solution to a problem through use of the six-step Problem-Solving Model to strengthen customer provider relationships.

To solve a problem, you need to first identify the problem and determine if the problem is one that should be solved. Once you decide to solve the problem, follow the six proven steps to problem solving. Figure 7.6 shows a concise six-step **Problem-Solving Model**.

Before you begin to solve a customer's problem, consider the fact that he or she may not really want you to "solve the problem." In some cases, a person simply wants to vent frustration or be heard. This is where the empathetic listening you have read about will come in handy. In many cases, your customer will often have a solution in mind when he or she calls or comes in. Your role may be to simply listen and offer to facilitate the implementation of the suggested solution. In some situations, you may have to "plant a seed" by asking an open-ended question that suggests a solution. If the customer picks up on your "seed" and nourishes it, you end up with an outcome for which he or she feels ownership. For example, assume that a customer wants a product that you do not have in stock. Instead of saying, "I'm sorry, that item is out of stock," you could ask a question such as "How do you think _____ would work as an alternative?" You have now subtly made a suggestion without saying, "You could use _____ instead. It does the same thing."

If you jointly solve a problem, the customer feels ownership—that he or she has made the decision. This customer is likely to be a satisfied customer. The following six steps describe some key actions involved in this process.

1. Identify the Problem   Before you can decide on a course of action, you must first know the nature and scope of the issue you are facing. Often, the customer may not know how to explain his or her problem well, especially if he or she speaks English as a second language or has a communication-related disability. In such cases, it is up to you to do a little detective work and ask questions or review available information.

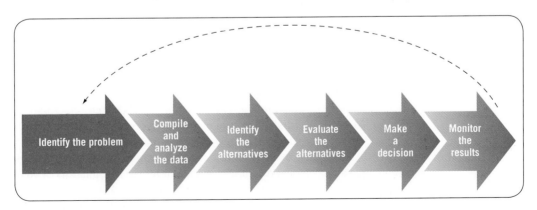

FIGURE 7.6   **The Problem Solving Model**

Begin your journey into problem solving by apologizing for any inconvenience you or your organization has caused. The customer likely wants someone to be responsible. A simple, "I'm sorry you were inconvenienced, how may I assist you?," coupled with some of the other techniques listed in this book can go a long way to mending the relationship. Take responsibility for the problem or concern, even if you didn't actually cause it. Remember that you represent the organization to the customer. Since you are representing the company, you are "chosen" to be responsible. Don't point fingers at other employees, policies, procedures, or other factors. It is also important to let the customer know that you are sincerely remorseful and will do whatever possible to quickly and effectively resolve the issue.

To learn as much about the issue as you can, start by speaking directly to the customer, when possible. Collect any documentation or other background information available.

Ask questions of your customers similar to the following:

What model is it?

What, exactly, is wrong?

Does it have an antenna attached?

Is there a remote control?

Have you checked to see that the power cord is firmly attached?

Have you tried using a different electrical outlet?

Have you checked to make sure that the power strip is turned on?

When did you first notice the issue?

2. Compile and Analyze the Data   To be able to effectively determine a course of action, you need as much information as possible and a thorough understanding of what you are dealing with. To get that data requires the use of active listening and a little investigative work. You may need to collect information from a variety of sources, such as sales receipts, correspondence, the customer, public records, the manufacturer, and organizational files.

In gathering data, you should also do a quick assessment of how serious the problem is. You may be hearing about one incident of a defective product or inefficient service. In fact, there may be many unspoken complaints. Also, look for patterns or trends in complaints.

Once you have collected information through questioning and from other sources, spend some time looking over what you have found. If time permits and you think it necessary or helpful (e.g., the customer is not standing in front of you or on the telephone), ask for the opinions of others (e.g., coworkers, team leader/supervisor, technical experts). Ultimately, what you are trying to do is determine alternatives available to you that will help satisfy the customer and resolve the issue.

3. Identify Alternatives   Let the customers know you are willing to work with them to find an acceptable resolution to the issue. Tell them what you can do, gain agreement, then set about taking action.

Since you are just being brought into the situation when a customer notifies you of a problem or his or her dissatisfaction, you can offer an objective, outside perspective. Use this perspective to offer suggestions or viewpoints that the customer may not see or has overlooked. Additionally, make sure you consider various possibilities and alternatives when thinking about potential resolutions. Look out for the best interests of your customer and your organization. To do this, be willing to listen to the customer's suggestions and to "think outside of the box" for ideas other than the ones that you and your organization typically use. Don't opt for convenience at the risk of customer satisfaction. If necessary, seek any necessary approval from higher authority to access other options (e.g., to make a special purchase of an alternative item from a manufacturer for the customer, or to give a refund even though the time frame for refunds has expired according to organizational policy).

4. Evaluate Alternatives   Once all the facts have been collected, look at your alternatives or possible options. Be careful not to let cost be the deciding factor. A little extra time and money spent to resolve an issue could save a customer and prevent recurring problems later. Consider the following factors in this evaluation process:

What is the most efficient way to solve this problem?

Which are the most effective options for solving this problem?

Which options are the most cost-effective?

Will the options being considered solve the problem and satisfy the customer?

Will the selected alternative create new issues?

5. Make a Decision   On the basis of the questions in step 4, and any others you wish to use in evaluation, make a decision on what your course of action will be. To do this, ask the customer "Which option would you prefer?"

This simple question now puts the customer into the decision-making position and he or she feels empowered. It now becomes his or her choice, and recurring problems may be avoided. If the customer's request is reasonable and possible, proceed and resolve the issue. If not, negotiate a different alternative.

6. Monitor the Results   Once you have made a decision, monitor the effect or results. Do not assume that your customer is satisfied, especially if any negotiation occurred between the two of you.

You can monitor the situation with a follow-up call, by asking if the customer needs anything else when you next see or speak to him or her, or by sending a written follow-up (e.g., a thank-you letter with a query concerning satisfaction, or service survey, or e-mail).

If you determine that your customer is not satisfied or additional needs are present, go back to step 1 and start over.

9   IMPLEMENTING A SERVICE RECOVERY STRATEGY

Concept: The job of a service provider is to return the customer to a satisfied state. Not listening, poor communication, and lack of respect are roadblocks to service recovery.

Humans make mistakes. As a service provider, mistakes often appear glaring to customers, who can be very demanding and unforgiving at times. The best you can hope for when something goes wrong is that you can identify the cause and remedy it quickly to your customer's satisfaction. The primary purpose of any good service recovery program should be to return the customer-provider relationship to its normal state. When this is done well, a disgruntled customer can become one who is very loyal and who acts as a publicist for the organization.

Some typical reasons that necessitate service recovery action are:

A product or service did not deliver as expected.

A promise was not kept (such as failure to follow up).

A deadline was missed.

Customer service was not adequately provided (the customer had to wait excessively or was ignored).

A service provider lacked adequate knowledge or skills to handle a situation.

Actions taken by you or the organization inconvenienced the customer (e.g., a lab technician took blood during a patient's visit and the sample was mishandled, requiring the patient to have to return for a retest).

A customer request or order was not handled properly (e.g., wrong product or service delivered).

Attempts to return or exchange an item were hampered by policy or an uncooperative employee.

A customer was given the "runaround" being transferred to various employees or departments and being required to explain the situation to each individual.

The customer was treated (or perceived he or she was) unprofessionally or in a rude manner.

Corrective action was taken for any of the above reasons and the customer is still not satisfied.

Actually, there are numerous factors in the service process that can lead to a failure to meet customer expectations. Ultimately, they can all influence service recovery.

According to a consumer survey reported in 2004 by the internationally known training company Achieve Global of Tampa, Florida, customers—regardless of industry, geography, or product/service—want the service they receive to be:

- *Seamless.*   The company is able to manage behind-the-scenes service factors so that they remain invisible to the customer.
- *Trustworthy.*   The company provides what is promised, dependably and with quality.
- *Attentive.*   The company provides caring, personalized attention to customers, recognizing both their human and business needs.
- *Resourceful.*   The company efficiently provides flexible and creative solutions.

Typically, there are five phases to the service recovery process (see Figure 7.7):

1. *Apologize, apologize, and apologize again.*   Showing sincere remorse throughout the recovery cycle is crucial. *Listen* carefully. Empathize with the customer as he or she explains and *do not* make excuses, interrupt, or otherwise indicate (verbally or nonverbally) that you do not have time for the customer. You want to retain the customer and have an opportunity for recovery. You must demonstrate that you care for the customer and that he or she is *very* important to you and your organization. Interestingly, many service providers do not accept responsibility and/or apologize when customers become dissatisfied. Such an apology should come immediately after the discovery of the customer's dissatisfaction and should be delivered in person, if possible. The phone is a second option. Written apologies are the last choice.

service options
Alternatives offered by service providers when an original request by a customer cannot be honored because of such restrictions as governmental statutory regulations, nonavailability of products, or inability to perform as requested.

prohibitions
Local, state, or federal regulations that prevent a service provider from satisfying a customer's request even though the provider would normally do so.

2. *Take immediate action.*   As soon as your customer has identified a problem, you must set about positively resolving it. As you proceed, it is crucial that you keep the customer informed of actions, barriers encountered, or successful efforts. Even if you are unable to make a quick resolution, the customer may be satisfied if he or she perceives your efforts as sincere and ongoing. You must convince customers through your actions and words that you are doing your best to solve the problem in a timely manner. Also, do not forget what you read earlier in the book about avoiding having to say no without offering **service options.** Remember that your customers want to hear what you *can* do for them, not what you cannot.

Certainly, there may be times when, even though you want to give customers exactly what they want, you will not be able to do so because of regulations or **prohibitions**

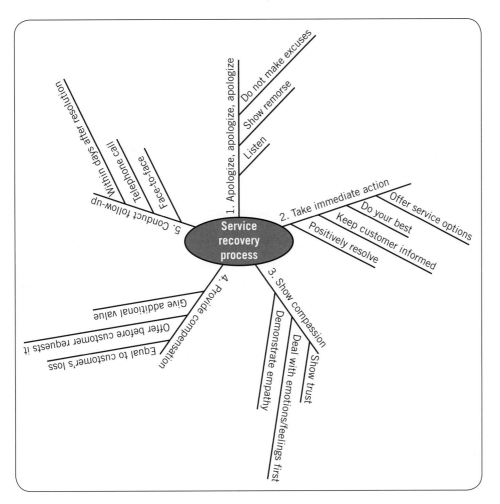

FIGURE 7.7   **Service Recovery Process**

(e.g., local, state, or federal laws or regulations). In such cases, it is important to use all the interpersonal skills discussed throughout this book (e.g., active listening, empathizing, and providing feedback) to let customers know that you are prohibited from fulfilling their needs. It is also important to explain the "why" in such situations rather than just saying, "I'm sorry, the law won't let me do that." This type of response sounds as if you are not being truthful, do not want to assist, and are hiding behind an invisible barrier.

An example of a prohibition would be when the sister of a patient goes to a doctor's office to get a copy of her brother's medical records. Without specific permission, this would be against the law, because of a patient's right to privacy and confidentiality between patient and doctor. If you were the receptionist in a doctor's office and someone made such a request, your response might be: "Ms. Ramsey, I apologize for your inconvenience in coming in for nothing. I know it's frustrating. However, although I would love to assist you, I cannot because of state and federal regulations that protect a patient's privacy and confidentiality. If you can get me a signed medical release from your brother, I would be happy to copy his file for you. Can you do that? And, so you won't have to make another trip in here, if you have a fax number, I can get them to you that way." In this instance, you have empathized with the customer, stated what you cannot do, explained why, and offered a way to resolve the problem along with a recovery strategy (e.g., fax).

In another situation, you may want to help a customer but cannot because your abilities, time constraints, resources, or the customer's timing of a request prevent fulfillment. Here are some examples of such situations, along with possible responses to your customer:

Your abilities.   You work in a pet supply store, you are the only person in the store, and you have a severe back injury that prevents you from lifting anything over 25 pounds. A customer comes in and buys 50 bags of chicken feed, each weighing 100 pounds. She asks that you help her load the bags onto her truck.

YOUR RESPONSE: "Ms. Saunders, we appreciate your business. I know your time is valuable and I'd love to help you. However, I have a back injury and the doctor told me not to lift anything over 25 pounds. I'm the only person working here during the lunch hour. If you can come back in half an hour, I'll have two guys who will load bags for you in no time. Would that be possible? For your inconvenience, I'll even take $10 off your order total."

Time constraints.   You work in a bakery and a distraught customer comes in at 3 P.M. Apparently he had forgotten that he was supposed to stop by on the way to work this morning to order a chocolate cake for his daughter's first birthday party, which is at 5 P.M. He wants you to make him a two-layer chocolate cake.

YOUR RESPONSE: "Mr. Simon, that first birthday party sounds exciting, and I want to help you make it a success. However, realistically, it just cannot be done. We sold our last chocolate cake half an hour ago, and if I bake a new one, it will still have to cool before I can decorate it. You will never make it by five o'clock. I know it's frustrating not to get exactly what you want. However, since your daughter is only one year old and won't know the difference in the type of cake, can I suggest an alternative? We have virtually any other kind of cake you could want, and I can put on chocolate icing and decorate it for you in less than 15 minutes. Would that work?"

Available resources.   You are in North Carolina, near the coastline. A customer comes into your lumberyard in search of plywood to board up his house a day before a major hurricane is predicted to hit the area. Since the impending hurricane was announced on the news, you have been overwhelmed with purchases of plywood and sold out two hours ago.

YOUR RESPONSE: "Mr. Rasheed, I can appreciate the urgency of your need. Unfortunately, as you know, everyone in town is buying plywood and we sold out two hours ago. However, I do have a couple of options for you. I can call our store in Jacksonville to find out whether any plywood is left. If there is some, I can have it held if you want to drive over there. The other option is that we have a shipment on the way that should arrive sometime around 3 A.M. I'll be here and can hold some for you if you want to come back at that time. Would either of those options work for you?"

Timing.   It is April 13 and you are an accountant. With the federal tax filing deadline two days away, you and the entire staff of your firm have been working 12- to 14-hour days for weeks. A regular customer calls and wants to come in the next couple of days to discuss incorporating her business and to get some information on the tax advantages for doing so.

YOUR RESPONSE: "Ruth, it's great that you are ready to move forward with the incorporation. I think you will find that it will be very beneficial for you. However, with tax deadlines two days away, we are swamped and there is just no way I can take on anything else. Since your incorporation is not under a deadline, can we set up our meeting some time around the first of next week? That will give me time to wrap up taxes, take a breather, and then give you the full attention you deserve."

In all of these instances, you show a willingness to assist and meet the customers' requests even though you are prevented from doing so. You also partner with them and offer alternatives for consideration. This is important, since you do not want to close the door on customer opportunities. Doing so will surely send customers to a competitor.

There might be other occasions when you or your organization do not meet a customer's request even though it is possible to do so. In such cases, company restrictions keep you from fulfilling the customers' request. In this type of situation, you sometimes hear service providers hide behind a phrase such as "Policy says . . . " The reality is that someone in the organization has decided for business reasons that certain actions cannot or should not be taken. If you encounter such "policies" that prohibit you from delivering service to customers, bring them to the attention of your team leader or management for discussion. These restrictions will most likely cost your organization some customers and result in bad word-of-mouth publicity. An example of such a situation, along with a possible response, is described below:

> *Situation.*   You work in a gas station in a major tourist area that has a policy that prohibits accepting out-of-town checks. A tourist from another state has her family with her and fills her car with gas. She then comes to you to pay for her purchase. She tells you that she has only personal checks and $2 in cash with her. She is leaving town to return home at this time.
>
> YOUR RESPONSE: "I know that this is an inconvenience, and I apologize. However, because of problems we've had in the past, we do not accept checks from banks out of this area. We will gladly accept major credit cards, travelers' checks, or cash. Does anyone else in your car have a credit card or cash? We also have an ATM machine where you can use a bank debit card to get cash."

3. *Show compassion.*   To help the customer see that your remorse and desire to solve a problem are genuine, you must demonstrate empathy. Expressions such as "I can appreciate your trust," "I understand how we have inconvenienced you," or "I can imagine how you must feel" can go a long way in soothing and winning the customer over. Before you can truly address the customers' problem, however, you must deal with their emotions or feelings. If you disregard their feelings, customers may not give you a chance to help resolve the breakdown. Also, keep in mind what you read about trust in an earlier chapter: you must give it to receive it.

4. *Provide compensation.*   Prove to customers that they are valuable and that you are trying to make up for their inconvenience or loss. This penance or symbolic self punishment should be significant enough that the customer feels that you and your organization have suffered an equal loss. The value or degree of your atonement should equal the customer's loss in time, money, energy, or frustration. For example, if a customer's meal was cooked improperly and the customer and others in the party had to wait, you might give the customer a free meal. If you forgot a vegetable that was ordered and it came much later, a free dessert might suffice. The key is to make the offer without the customer having to suggest or demand it.

   Not only must the recovery compensate original loss, it should give additional value. For example, if a customer had an oil change done on his or her car and oil was spilled on the carpet, an appropriate gesture might be to give the oil change free and have the carpet cleaned at your company's expense. This solution compensates for inconvenience and lost time while providing added value (saving the cost of the oil change).

5. *Conduct follow-up.*   The only way to find out whether you were successful in your recovery efforts or whether the customer is truly satisfied is to follow up. The preferable methods are face-to-face questioning or a phone call. This contact should come

within a few days after the complaint was resolved. It could take the form of a few simple statements or questions (e.g., "I am following up in case you had any additional questions" or "I'm calling to make sure that _____ is now working as it should be. Is there anything else we can do to assist you?").

This last step in the recovery process can be the deciding factor in whether the customer returns to you or your organization. It is the phase that reemphasizes the message "We truly care."

SUMMARY

Dealing with various types of people can be frustrating, but it can also be very satisfying. Many times, you will have to deal with a variety of external and internal customers, including those who are angry, indecisive, dissatisfied, demanding, domineering, rude, or talkative. Your goal in all your efforts should be to work harmoniously with all customers. Whenever you can address customer needs in a variety of situations and find acceptable solutions, you, the customer, and the organization win. To assist customers effectively doesn't take magic; all it takes is a positive attitude, preparation, and a sincere desire to help others. If you use the techniques outlined in this chapter, and others in this book, you're on your way to providing stellar customer service and satisfying customer needs. Whenever a customer experiences an actual or perceived breakdown in service, prompt, appropriate recovery efforts may be your only hope of retaining the customer. In a profession that has seen major strides in quality and technology as well as increased domestic and global competition, service is often the deciding factor. Customers often expect and demand their rights. When they are disappointed, they simply go elsewhere. Your role in the process is to remain vigilant, recognize customer needs, and provide service levels that will keep them coming back.

KEY TERMS

angry customers 171
customer defection 176
customer expectations 166
demanding or domineering customers 169
difficult customers 168
dissatisfied customers 171
emotion-reducing model 175
indecisive customers 170
needs 166

problem-solving model 181
prohibitions 184
rude or inconsiderate customers 173
service breakdowns 166
service options 184
strategies for preventing dissatisfaction 178
talkative customers 173
underpromise and overdeliver 172
wants 166

REVIEW QUESTIONS

1 What is meant by the term *service breakdown*? Define.
2 What causes customers to become dissatisfied?
3 What tactics can you use to deal with angry customers?
4 What can you do to assist indecisive people in coming to a decision?
5 Why might some customers feel they have to demand things from others?
6 How can you effectively deal with rude or inconsiderate customers?
7 What are some strategies for refocusing a talkative customer?
8 What are some strategies for preventing customer dissatisfaction? List them.
9 How does the emotion-reducing model work?
10 Why do customers defect?
11 What strategies can you use to build strong relationships with coworkers?
12 List the strategies for effective problem solving.
13 What is service recovery and when do you need to implement it?

Search the Internet for Information on Problem Solving

Log onto the Internet and locate information on providing customer service to irate customers. Also look for information on the following topics:

Conflict resolution
Problem solving

Handling stressful situations
Service breakdown
Service recovery

Be prepared to share what you find with your classmates at the next scheduled class.

Role-Playing Difficult Customer Situations

Work with a partner and role-play one or more of the following scenarios. Each of you should choose at least one scenario in which you will play the service provider role. The other person will play the customer. In each instance, discuss what type of difficult customer you are dealing with and how such an encounter might go. At the end of each role-play, both persons should answer the following questions and discuss ideas for improvement:

Scenario 1: Terry Welch entered your shoe store over 30 minutes ago and seems to be having trouble deciding the style and color of shoes he wants.

Scenario 2: Chris Dulaney is back in your lawn mower repair shop. This is the third time in less than two weeks that she has been in for repairs on a riding mower. Chris is getting upset because the problem stems from a defective carburetor that has been repaired on each previous visit. She is beginning to raise her voice, and her frustration is becoming evident.

Scenario 3: You are a telephone service representative for a large retail catalog distribution center. You've been at work for about an hour when you receive a call from Pat Mason, who immediately starts making demands (e.g., "I've only got a few minutes for you to tell me how to order." "Look, I've read all the articles about the scams telemarketers pull. I'll tell you what I want, and you tell me how much it will cost."

"Listen, what I want you to do is take my order and get me the products within the next two days. I need them for a conference.")

Scenario 4: You are a cashier in the express lane at a supermarket. As you are ringing up a customer's order, a second customer approaches, squeezes past several people in line and says, "I'm in a hurry. All I have is a quart of milk. Can you just tell me how much it costs, and I'll leave the money right here on the register."

Scenario 5: You are a very busy switchboard operator for ComTech, a large corporation. A vendor whom you recognize from previous encounters has just called to speak with your purchasing manager. As in previous calls, the vendor starts a friendly conversation about the weather, how things are going, and other topics not related to business.

Questions

1   How well was service provided?

2   Were any negative or unclear messages, verbal or nonverbal, communicated? If so, discuss.

3   How can you incorporate the improvements you have identified into a real customer service encounter?

4   What open-ended questions were used to discover customer needs? What others could have been used?

Handling Service Breakdowns at AAA Landscaping

Background

You are the owner of AAA Landscaping, a small company in Orlando, Florida, that specializes in resodding and maintenance of lawns. Much of your business is through word-of-mouth advertising. Once a contract is negotiated, portions of it are subcontracted out to other companies (e.g., sprinkler system repair and pesticide services). Recently, you went to the

home of Stu Murphy to bid on resodding Stu's lawn. Several other bids were obtained, but yours was the lowest. You arranged for work to begin to remove old grass and replace it with St. Augustine grass sod.

As part of the contract, Stu had asked that some basic maintenance be done (e.g., hedge and tree trimming, hauling away of old decorative wooden logs from around flower beds, and general sprucing up of the front area of the house). Also, fertilizer and pesticide were to be applied within two weeks. The contract was signed on Wednesday, and the work was to be completed by Saturday, when Stu had planned a party.

Your Role

You were pleased to get the contract worth over $1,200. This is actually the third or fourth contract in the same subdivision because of word-of-mouth advertising. The initial sod removal and replacement, weeding, and pruning were completed on Saturday, and you received full payment on Monday.

Later in the week you received a call from Stu stating that several trees were not trimmed to his satisfaction, debris covering decorative rocks along hedges was not removed as agreed, and bags of clippings had been left behind. Because of other commitments, it was several days before you sent someone out to finish the job. A day later, Stu left another message on your answering machine stating that there was still an untrimmed tree, the debris remained, and the clippings were still in the garage. You didn't get around to returning his call. Over a week later Stu called again, repeating the message he'd left before and reminding you that the contract called for pesticide and fertilizer to be applied to the lawn. You called back and said that someone would be out later in the week. Again, other commitments kept you from following through. Stu called on Saturday and left a fourth message on your answering machine. He said that he was getting irritated at not getting callbacks and action on his needs. Without returning Stu's call, you responded by sending someone out on Tuesday to take care of the outstanding work.

It's been several days since the work was completed, and you assume that Stu is now satisfied since you have heard nothing else from him.

Critical Thinking Questions

1 Based on information in this chapter, how have you done on providing service to Stu? Explain.

2 What were Stu's needs in this case?

3 Could you have done anything differently?

4 Are you sure that Stu will give a good recommendation to neighbors or friends in the future? Why or why not?

SERVICE-Southwest Airlines

1 From what you read in this chapter and on their website, do you think the company has accomplished Rollin King's and Herb Kelleher's vision of "getting their passengers to their destinations when they want to get there, on time, at the lowest possible fares, and make darn sure they have a good time doing it?" Why or why not?

2 Have you ever flown on Southwest Airlines? If so what was your experience like? If you have not, would you want to? Why or why not?

3 How do Southwest's accomplishments stack up to other airlines with which you are familiar? Why?

4 From a customer perspective, do you think Southwest does a good job meeting passenger needs? Explain.

Go to www.southwest.com and research the organization. Look at their annual report, values/mission, and other historical information about the organization on their website.

To help better prepare yourself to deal with difficult customer service situations and to help you to prevent service breakdown or to aid in service recovery, respond to the following statements. On the basis of your responses, seek out resources (e.g., materials, training programs, and people) that can help broaden your knowledge on these topics. Try to discuss these questions—and your answers—with your coworkers or classmates. This can ultimately help improve your own skills, employee morale, and service to customers.

1	I approach what I believe to be a difficult customer with a positive attitude and believe that I can turn the situation around.	Yes	No
2	In dealing with customers, I seek to determine their true needs before offering a service solution.	Yes	No
3	What actions or circumstances have you noticed lead to service breakdowns in organizations where you were either a customer or service provider?		
4	When you were a customer and service broke down, what recovery strategies were effectively used to help "make you whole"?		
5	I consciously monitor my language, and elicit feedback from peers on it to ensure that I typically use positive words and phrases when communicating.	Yes	No
6	When dealing with the types of difficult customers described in this chapter, I maintain my professionalism and actively listen in order to better serve their needs.	Yes	No

7   When working with coworkers, I afford the same courtesies and professionalism that is required   Yes   No
    for external customers.

8   When you were a customer and service broke down, what ineffective recovery strategies did
    you experience?

1	T	5	T	9	T
2	F	6	T	10	T
3	F	7	T	11	T
4	F	8	T	12	T

Ethical Dilemma 7.1 Possible Answers

1   How would you handle this situation? Why?

This is a touchy situation in which you basically asked the coworker to do you a favor and she agreed to do so. Rather than jump to conclusions, it is probably best to approach the coworker in a friendly and nonthreatening manner, using some strategies you read about in Chapters 3 and 4. Ask why she failed to assist as she agreed and listen to her response rationally. Depending on what she tells you, let her know that you are disappointed that she failed to either help or come to you before now to explain that she could not do so. Also, let her know how you feel about her failure to come forward. The latter is important because people often do not realize the effect their behavior has on others and how it might impact relationships.

2   Would you report the situation to your supervisor? Why or why not?

Since this was not a task assigned to both of you, it is probably best not to go to your supervisor or to point fingers and blame your coworker for your missing the deadline. After all, it is your job and not hers.

3   What effect might her behavior have on your relationship? Why?

Because relationships are built on trust, your coworker's behavior could certainly negatively affect your relationship in the future, depending on her reason for failing to assist you. Even if she has a good reason, the fact that she did not at least let you know of the obstacle could influence how you feel toward her and your ability to trust and work with her effectively in the future.

Customer Service in a Diverse World

The winner is the chef who takes the same ingredients as everyone else and produces the best results.

— Edward de Bono

After completing this chapter, you will be able to:

1. Recognize that diversity is not a bad thing.

2. Describe some of the characteristics that make people unique.

3. Embrace the need to treat customers as individuals.

4. Determine actions for dealing with various types of people.

5. Identify a variety of factors that make people diverse and that help to better serve them.

6. Communicate effectively with a diverse customer population.

In the Real World   Retail-Nordstrom

Nordstrom was started by a 16-year old immigrant, John W. Nordstrom, who could not speak English and arrived in New York with only $5 in his pocket. After spending time in mining and logging camps in Washington and California, he moved to Alaska and made enough money in a gold mine stake to return to Seattle, Washington. There, he partnered with a friend from Alaska and opened a shoe store, which would grow to be the largest independent shoe chain in the country.

Nordstrom retired in 1928 and turned the company over to his sons. By the 1960s they had expanded throughout several Western states and added clothing apparel to their stores and in 1968 turned the company over to their children and other relatives.

In 1971, the company went public, changed its name to Nordstrom Inc., was recognized as the largest-volume West Coast fashion specialty store and surpassed the $100 million dollar sales mark.

In the late 1980s, Nordstrom had opened its first Nordstrom's Rack (clearance center), expanded to the East Coast, and focused on catering to customers' needs, individually. As stated on their website, "Instead of categorizing departments by merchandise, Nordstrom created fashion departments that fit individuals' lifestyles."

In recent years, Nordstrom has analyzed customer needs and has added online shopping capabilities to allow customers more options for accessing products. The result has been continued growth. In 2006, Nordstrom reported record sales of $8.6 billion dollars to its investors.

Throughout Nordstrom's history, the founder's guiding principle, "offering the customer the best possible service, selection, quality and value," has led to national reputation as a truly service-focused organization that caters to the wants and needs of its customers. The result of their efforts has paid off. According to their website, "In 2007, Nordstrom was named for the tenth time by *Fortune* magazine as one of the 100 best places to work and for the second year in a row as the number-one most admired company in its industry category. Last year, Nordstrom also was named one of the 100 best corporate citizens by *Business Ethics;* named one of the top employers for minorities by *Fortune* magazine; and honored as retailer of the year by the American Apparel and Footwear Association."

For more information about this organization, visit http://about.nordstrom.com/aboutus/.

See activity related to this section on page 215.

Quick Preview

Before reviewing the chapter content, respond to the following questions by placing a "T" for true or an "F" for false on the rules. Use any questions you miss as a checklist of material to which you will pay particular attention as you read through the chapter. For those you get right, congratulate yourself, but review the sections they address in order to learn additional details about the topic.

_____ 1. Diversity is an important aspect of everyone's life that presents many negative challenges.

_____ 2. Many people associate the term *diversity* with the word *cultural,* which describes the differences between groups of people from various countries and with differing beliefs.

_____ 3. The diverse nature of your customer population requires you to be aware of the various ways people from different cultures interact in the business setting.

_____ 4. Values are the "rules" that people use to evaluate situations, make decisions, interact with others, and deal with conflict.

_____ 5. In some cultures, direct eye contact is often discouraged, for it suggests disrespect.

_____ 6. Today, many cultures use less formality in the business environment and do not stress the importance of using titles and family names as often as they did in the past.

_____ 7. When encountering someone who speaks English as a second language, you should avoid jokes, words, or acronyms that are uniquely North American or tied to sports, historical events, or specific aspects of North American culture.

_____ 8. In serving customers from other cultures, it is important to avoid the use of the word *no* because this word may cause the customer to become embarrassed or experience a "loss of face."

_____ 9. According to the U.S. Census Bureau, approximately 54 billion Americans have some level of disability.

_____ 10. When a customer has a disability, the disability should be deemphasized by thinking of the person first and the disability second.

_____ 11. When dealing with an elderly customer, you should always be respectful.

_____ 12. Young customers are as valuable as those in any other group and should be professionally served.

Answers to Quick Preview can be found at the end of the chapter.

. . . .

1   THE IMPACT OF DIVERSITY

Concept: Diversity is an important aspect of everyone's life. Encounters with others give us an opportunity to expand our knowledge of others.

diversity
The different characteristics, values, beliefs, and factors that make people different, yet similar.

As the world grows smaller economically and otherwise (e.g., in world trade, international travel, outsourcing of jobs, and technologically transmitted information exchange), the likelihood that you will have contact on the job with people from other cultures, or who are different from you in other ways, increases. This likelihood also carries over into your personal life. **Diversity** is encountered everywhere (over the telephone, in supermarkets, religious organizations, public transportation) and so is an important aspect of everyone's life. Although it presents challenges in making us think of differences and similarities, it also enriches our lives—each encounter we have with another person gives us an opportunity to expand our knowledge of others and build relationships, while growing personally.

2   DEFINING DIVERSITY

Concept: Diversity is not a simple matter; it is not difficult to deal with if you are fair to people and keep an open mind.

cultural diversity
Refers to the differences and similarities attributed to various groups of people within a culture.

The word *diversity* encompasses a broad range of differences. Many people associate the term diversity with **cultural diversity,** which has to do with the differences between groups of people, depending on their country of origin and their beliefs. They fail to recognize that diversity is not just cultural. Certainly, diversity occurs within each cultural group; however, many other characteristics are involved. For example, within a group of Japanese people are subgroups such as males, females, children, the elderly, athletes, thin people, gay or lesbian people, Buddhists, Christians, married people, and single people, to mention just a few of the possible characteristics, beliefs, and values.

Diversity is not a simple matter, yet it is not difficult to deal with, if you are fair to people and keep an open mind when interacting with them. In fact, when you look more closely at, and think about, diversity, it provides wonderful opportunities because people from varying groups and geographic locations bring with them special knowledge, experience, and value. This is because even though people may have differences, they also have many traits in common. Their similarities form a solid basis for successful interpersonal relationships if you are knowledgeable and think of people as unique individuals; you can

Encountering Diversity

TAKE A FEW MINUTES TO THINK ABOUT DIVERSITY AND WHAT IT MEANS TO YOU. Write your own definition of diversity.

During the past week, in what situations have you encountered someone from a different culture (someone whose values or beliefs differed from yours or who looked or dressed differently from you or your group)? Make a list of the diversity and the situations encountered.

Once you have created your responses, form a group with two to three other students, share your responses, and discuss the implications of providing quality service to customers.

then capitalize on this uniqueness. If you cannot think of the person instead of the group, you may stereotype people—lump them together and treat them all the same. The is a recipe for interpersonal disaster and service breakdown.

The basic customer service techniques related to communication found in this book can be applied to many situations in which you encounter customers from various groups. Coupled with specific strategies for adapting to special customer needs, these techniques provide the tools you need to provide excellent customer service.

Some factors that make people different are innate and they are born with them, such as height, weight, hair color, gender, skin color, physical and mental condition, and sibling birth order. All these factors contribute to our uniqueness and help or inhibit us throughout our lives, depending on the perceptions we and others have. Other factors that make us unique are learned or gained through our environment and our life experiences. Examples of these factors include religion, **values, beliefs,** economic level, lifestyle choices, profession, marital status, education, and political affiliation. These factors are often used to assign people to categories. Caution must be used when considering any of these characteristics, since grouping people can lead to stereotyping and possible discrimination.

The bottom line is that all of these factors affect each customer encounter. Your awareness of differences and of your own preferences is crucial in determining the success you will have in each instance.

3   CUSTOMER AWARENESS

Concept: Applying your own cultural practices and beliefs to a situation involving someone from another culture can result in frustration, anger, poor service, and lost business.

Aren't all customers alike? Emphatically, no! No two people are alike, no two generations are alike, and no two cultures are alike. In addition, as we discussed in Chapter 7, each customer has needs based on his or her own perceptions and situation.

In our highly mobile, technologically connected world, it is not unusual to encounter a wide variety of people with differing backgrounds, experiences, religions, modes of dress, values, and beliefs within the course of a single day. All these factors affect customer needs and create situations in which you must be alert to the verbal and nonverbal messages that indicate those needs. Moreover, the diverse nature of your customer population requires you to be aware of the various ways people from different cultures interact in the business setting. Applying your own cultural practices and beliefs to a situation involving someone from another culture can result in frustration, anger, poor service, and lost business.

[1]Tony Alessandra and Michael J. O'Connor, *The Platinum Rule,* Warner Books, 1996.

CUSTOMER SERVICE SUCCESS TIP

A key point to remember is that the concept of treating others as you would like to be treated (a value common in many religions) can lead to service breakdowns. This is because your customers are unique and may not value what you do. To better ensure service success, find out what customers want and treat them as they want to be treated. This concept has been termed the Platinum Rule.[1]

Platinum Rule
Term coined by speaker and author Tony Alessandra related to going beyond the step of treating customers the way you want to be treated, to the next level of treating them the way they would like to be treated.

values
Long-term appraisals of the worth of an idea, person, place, thing, or practice held by individuals, groups, or cultures. They affect attitudes and behavior.

beliefs
Perceptions or assumptions that individuals or cultures maintain. These perceptions are based on past experiences, memories, and interpretations and influence how people act and interact with certain individuals or groups.

● 4 THE IMPACT OF CULTURAL VALUES

Concept: Values often dictate which behaviors and practices are acceptable or unacceptable. These values may or may not have a direct bearing on serving the customer.

Although many cultures have similar values and beliefs, specific cultural values are often taught to members of particular groups starting at a very young age. This does not mean that a particular group's values and beliefs are better or worse than those of any other culture; they are simply important to that particular group. These values often dictate which behaviors and practices are acceptable or unacceptable. These values may or may not have a direct bearing on serving the customer, but they can have a very powerful influence on what the customer wants, needs, thinks is important, and is willing to seek or accept. Values can also influence your perceptions and actions toward others. Being conscious of differences can lead to a better understanding of customers and potentially reduce conflict or misunderstandings in dealing with them.

Many service providers take values for granted. This is a mistake. Values are the "rules" that people use to evaluate issues or situations, make decisions, interact with others, and deal with conflict. As a whole, a person's value system often guides thinking and helps him or her determine right from wrong or good from bad. From a customer service perspective, values often strongly drive customer needs and influence the buying decision. Values also

The mobility of modern-day society may put you in regular contact with customers from a variety of cultures. The more informed you are about similarities and differences, the greater the likelihood that you will provide quality service. *How should you provide customer service to someone of another culture?*

differ from one culture to another, depending on its views on ethics, morals, religion, and many other factors. For example, if customers perceive clothing as either too sexy or too conservative, they may not purchase the items, depending on what need they are trying to meet. Or they may not buy a house because it's in the "wrong" neighborhood.

Values are based on the deeply held beliefs of a culture or subculture. These beliefs might be founded in religion, politics, or group mores. They drive thinking and actions and are so powerful that they have served as the basis for arguments, conflicts, and wars.

To be effective in dealing with others, service providers should not ignore the power of values and beliefs, nor should they think that their value system is better than that of someone else's. The key to success is to be open-minded and accept that someone else has a different belief system that determines his or her needs. With this in mind, you as a service provider should strive to use all the positive communication and needs identification you have read about thus far in order to satisfy the customer.

Cultural values can be openly expressed or subtly demonstrated through behavior. They can affect your interactions with your customers in a variety of ways. In the next few pages, consider the connection of values with behavior, and how you can adjust your customer service to ensure a satisfactory experience for diverse customers. Keep in mind that the degree to which customers have been acculturated to prominent cultural standards will determine how they act.

The goal is to provide service to the customer. In order to achieve success in accomplishing this goal, service providers must be sensitive to, tolerant of, and empathetic toward customers. You do not need to adopt the beliefs of others, but you should adapt to them to the extent that you provide the best service possible to all of your customers. As mentioned earlier, apply the Platinum Rule of service when dealing with customers.

modesty
Refers to the way that cultures view propriety of dress and conduct.

MODESTY

Modesty is exhibited in many ways. In some cultures (e.g., Muslim and Quaker) conservative dress by women is one manifestation of modesty. For example, in some cultures women demonstrate modesty and a dedication to traditional beliefs by wearing a veil or head dress. Such practices are tied to religious and cultural beliefs that originated hundreds of years ago. In other cultures, nonverbal communication cues send messages. For example, direct eye contact is viewed as an effective communication approach in the many Western cultures, and lack of eye contact could suggest dishonesty or lack of confidence to a Westerner. In some cultures (India, Iran, Iraq and Japan), direct eye contact is often discouraged, in particular between men and women or between people who are of different social or business status, for it is considered disrespectful. Often a sense of modesty is instilled into people at an early age (more so in females). Modesty may be demonstrated by covering the mouth or part of the face with an open hand when laughing or speaking, or through avoiding direct eye contact in certain situations.

Another way that you might offend someone's modesty is through your environment. For example, if you have a waiting room that has magazines which show advertisements with scantily clad models or a television or radio station broadcasting for customers that contains sexual situations (e.g., soap operas) or racy talk show hosts, you may want to rethink the situation.

Impact on Service   When encountering examples of modest behavior, evaluate the situation for the true message being delivered. The person may really be exhibiting suspicious behavior. However, instead of assuming that the customer is being evasive or dishonest, consider the possible impact of culture. Don't force the issue or draw undue attention to a customer's nonverbal behavior, cultural dress, or beliefs being demonstrated. Instead, continue to verbally probe for customer needs and address them. In addition, provide the same quality of friendly service as you would to others who display behavior or cultural characteristics that do not differ from your own.

EXPECTATIONS OF PRIVACY

Based on your personality and prior life experiences, you may be more or less likely to disclose personal information, especially to people you do not know well. You should be aware that disclosing personal information about oneself is often a cultural factor and that **expectations of privacy** vary. Many people who are British, German, Australian, Korean, or Japanese display a tendency to disclose less about themselves than Americans do.

Impact on Service   If you tend to be gregarious and speak freely about virtually any topic, you should curtail this tendency in the customer service environment. Failure to do so could make some customers feel uneasy and uncomfortable. This is true in part because often, in Western cultures, when someone asks a question or shares information, there is an expectation that the other party will reciprocate. Reluctance to do so is sometimes perceived as being unfriendly or even rude. A good rule of thumb is to stay focused on the business of serving your customer in an expeditious and professional manner. Keeping your conversations centered on satisfying the customers' needs can accomplish this.

ethical dilemma 8.1

In a post-9/11 world, there is ongoing scrutiny and reevaluation of handling different situations because of security concerns worldwide. Airports limit what can be carried onto planes, people are checked by security personnel and devices (e.g., metal detectors and scanners), and organizational policies and procedures related to service and various situations have been modified (e.g., entrance into buildings, background checks for current and new employees, and access to certain types of data and equipment).

Assume that you are an employee of a store in a local shopping mall and a customer or client comes in carrying a paper bag that appears to have some sort of greasy stain in the bottom corner. When you approach him to offer assistance he appears nervous and states that he is "just killing time while his wife has her hair done." You know that there is not a hair stylist in the mall. You observe him leave your store, wander into several others and then return a second time.

1. What action should you take, if any?
2. If you decide to take some action, why would you do so?
3. What are possible repercussions if you either act or decide not to act?

expectations of privacy
The belief that personal information provided to an organization will be safeguarded against inappropriate or unauthorized use or dissemination.

This should not be construed to mean that you should totally avoid "small talk," just keep it under control and watch customer reactions closely.

FORMS OF ADDRESS

Although many North Americans often pride themselves on their informality, people from other countries see informality as rudeness, arrogance, or overfamiliarity. Many cultures stress formality in the business environment and place importance on the use of titles and family names when addressing others (e.g., Argentina, European countries, China).

form of address
Title used to address people. Examples are Mister, Miss, and Doctor.

Hispanic cultures
Refers to people who were born in Mexico, Puerto Rico, Cuba, or Central or South America.

Latino cultures
Refers to people of Hispanic descent.

Chicano cultures
Refers primarily to people with a heritage based in Mexico.

To further confuse the issue of how to address a customer, some cultures have differing rules on how family names are listed and used. For example, in China, each person is given a family name, a generational name (for the period during which they are born), and a personal name at birth. The generational and personal names might be separated by a hyphen or space (a female might be named Li Teng Jiang or Li Teng-Jiang). Women typically do not take their husband's surnames. When addressing someone from the Chinese culture, use an appropriate title such as *Mr.* or *Mrs.* followed by the family name (Mrs. Li) unless you are asked to use a different **form of address.** Many people adopt a Western first name (e.g., Amanda or Richard) when they immigrate to or work with people from the United States to make It easier for their customers and coworkers to pronounce their names. In Argentina (and most **Hispanic, Chicano, or Latino cultures**), people have two surnames: one from their father (listed first) and one from their mother (Jose Ricardo Gutierrez Martinez). Usually, when addressing the person, use a title only with the father's surname (Mr. or Mrs. Gutierrez).

Impact on Service   A customer's preference for a particular name or form of address has an impact upon your ability to effectively deal with him or her. If you start a conversation with someone and immediately alienate the person by incorrectly using his or her name, you may not be able to recover. Moreover, informality or improper use of family names could send a message of lack of knowledge or concern for the customer as an individual or as being important to you.

**CUSTOMER SERVICE
SUCCESS TIP**

It is always best to ask your customer his or her preference for being addressed rather than to assume familiarity and make the choice yourself. The latter can lead to a service relationship breakdown.

RESPECT FOR ELDERS

In most cultures, some level of respect is paid to older people. Often this **respect for elders** is focused more on males (when older men are viewed as revered, as among Chinese). This arises from a belief that with age come knowledge, experience, wisdom, authority, and often, higher status. Thus, respect for or deference to elders is normal. Also, in many cultures age brings with it unique privileges and rights (such as the right to rule or to be the leader). This is true in many Native American cultures.[2]

respect for elders
A value held by people of many cultures.

Impact on Service   You must be careful to pay appropriate respect when speaking to older customers. Further, you should be sensitive to the fact that if the customer demands to speak to a senior person or to the manager or owner, he or she may be simply exhibiting a customary expectation for his or her culture or generation.

If you can assist without creating conflict, do so; if not, honor the request when possible.

---

[2] American Indian Policy Center, www.airpi.org/research/tdlead.html.

FIGURE 8.1

Relationship-Focused Countries (Partial Listing)

Bangladesh	Iran	Pakistan	Singapore
Brazil	Iraq	Philippines	South Korea
China	Japan	Poland	Thailand
Egypt	Kuwait	Qatar	Turkey
Greece	Malaysia	Romania	Vietnam
India	Mexico	Russia	
Indonesia	Myanmar	Saudi Arabia	

IMPORTANCE OF RELATIONSHIPS

In many Asian, Latin American, and Middle Eastern cultures, the building of a strong **interpersonal relationship** is extremely important before business is conducted. For example, in Malaysia, Indonesia, Myanmar (Burma), Korea, and Japan it is not unusual to have a number of meetings with people in an organization before coming to an agreement. Lunch, dinner, and office meetings often occur for weeks before an agreement is reached. Also, unless you reach the right level of management in the organization for these meetings, all your efforts may be wasted. Figure 8.1 shows a partial listing of some of the world's more relationship-focused countries.

interpersonal relationship
Focuses on the need for service providers to build strong bonds with customers.

Impact on Service   Failure to establish support or an environment of trust could lead to a breakdown in service and/or lost customers. This does not mean that you should not assume a quicker familiarity with customers from such cultures. This could also alienate them. Instead, when you will be having ongoing contact or be doing repeat business, follow the customers' lead. Get to know them and share information about your organization and yourself that can lead to mutual respect and trust. You may find that you have to take time at the beginning of each encounter with your established customer to reestablish the relationship. This may involve spending time in conversations related to nonbusiness topics (sports, hobbies, pets, or other topics in which the customer is interested).

Relationship building may also involve presenting gifts to persuade various people in the organization that you are a friend and have their interests at heart. Only then can you proceed to determine needs and provide service.

GENDER ROLES

Culturally and individually, people view the role of men and women differently. Although **gender roles** are continually evolving throughout the world, decision making and authority are often clearly established as male prerogatives within a culture, subculture, or family. For example, in many Middle Eastern, Asian, South American, and European countries, women have not gained the respect or credibility in the business environment that they have achieved in many parts of North America. In some countries it is not unusual for women to be expected to take a "seen and not heard" role or to remain out of business transactions. In Korea and other Pacific Rim countries, it is rare for women to participate in business. Men still have higher social status than females. You don't have to agree with this behavior, but you will need to take it into consideration when facing it in customer encounters. People leave a country, but they take their culture and values with them. Failure to consider alternative ways of dealing with people in certain instances might cause you to react negatively to a situation and nonverbally communicate your bias.

gender roles
Behaviors attributed to or assigned by societal norms.

Impact on Service If you are a female dealing with a male whose cultural background is like one of those just described, he may reject your assistance and ask for a male service provider. If you are a male dealing with a male and female from such a culture, don't be surprised if your conversation involves only the male. Attempts to draw a woman into such a transaction may embarrass, offend, or even anger customers and/or their family members who are present.

ATTITUDE TOWARD CONFLICT

Conflict is possible when two people come together in a customer environment, but it does not have to happen. By recognizing your biases and preferences, and being familiar with other cultures, you can reduce the potential for disagreement. Certainly, there will be times when a customer initiates conflict. In this case all you can do is to use the positive communication techniques described throughout this book.

Many times, **attitudes** toward conflict are rooted in the individual's culture or subculture and based on behavioral style preference (discussed in Chapter 6). Some cultures are **individualistic cultures** (emphasis is placed on individuals' goals, as in Western countries), and some are **collective cultures** (individuals are viewed as part of a group, as in Japan or in Native American cultures). Members of individualistic cultures are likely to take a direct approach to conflict, whereas people whose culture is collective may address conflict indirectly, using an informal mediator in an effort to prevent loss of face or embarrassment for those involved. Even within subcultures of a society, there are often differing styles of communication and dealing with conflict. Of course, regardless of culture or group, people choose different forms of **conflict resolution styles** on the basis of personality style preferences.

Impact on Service Depending on the individuals you encounter and their cultural background, you and your customers may deal differently with conflict. If you use the wrong strategy, emotions could escalate and customer dissatisfaction could follow. The key is to listen and remain calm, especially if the customer becomes agitated.

THE CONCEPT OF TIME

In relation to time, people and societies are often referred to as being either **monochronic** or **polychronic.** People from monochronic societies tend to do one thing at a time, take time commitments seriously, are often focused on short-term projects or relationships, and adhere closely to plans. On the other hand, polychronic people are used to distractions, juggle multiple things (e.g., conversations) without feeling stressed, consider time as a guide and flexible commodity, work toward long-term deadlines, and base promptness on relationships.

People from the United States are typically very time-conscious (monochronic). You often hear such phrases as "time is money," "faster than a New York minute," and "time is of the essence," which stress their impatience and need to maximize time usage. Similarly, in Germany, punctuality is almost a religion, and being late is viewed as very unprofessional and rude. In most business settings in the United States, anyone over 5 minutes late for a meeting is often chastised. In many colleges and universities, etiquette dictates that students wait no longer than 15 to 20 minutes when an instructor (depending on whether he or she is a full or associate professor) is late. Americans tend to expect people from other cultures to be as time-conscious as they are. This is not the case, however. For example, it is not unusual for people from Arab countries (polychronic) to be a half hour or more late for an appointment or for a person from Hispanic and some Asian cultures to be an hour late. A phrase used by some Asian Indians sums up the concept and justifies the lateness:

attitudes
Emotional responses to people, ideas, and objects. They are based on values, differ between individuals and cultures, and affect the way people deal with various issues and situations.

individualistic cultures
Groups in which members value themselves as individuals who are separate from their group and are responsible for their own destiny.

collective cultures
Members of a group sharing common interests and values. They see themselves as an interdependent unit and conform and cooperate for the good of the group.

conflict resolution style
The manner in which a person handles conflict. People typically use one of five approaches to resolving conflict—avoidance, compromise, competition, accommodation, or collaboration.

monochronic
Refers to the perception of time as being a central focus with deadlines being a crucial element of societal norms.

polychronic
Refers to the perception of time as a fluid commodity that does not interfere with relationships and elements of happiness.

FIGURE 8.2

**Monochronic and
Polychronic Countries**

Most cultures can be described as either monochronic or polychronic. Some are both in that people exhibit one focus in the workplace and another with relationships. In some countries, a monochronic approach is prevalent in major urban areas, whereas a polychronic view is taken elsewhere. The following is a sampling of countries and their perspective on time.

Monochronic	Polychronic		Both
Australia	Africa	Latvia	Brazil
England	Bahrain	Lebanon	France
Canada	Bangladesh	Mexico	Japan
Czech Republic	Cambodia	Myanmar	Spain
Germany	China	Native American tribes	
Hungary	Croatia	Pakistan	
New Zealand	Ethiopia	Philippines	
Norway	Estonia	Portugal	
The Netherlands	Greece	Romania	
Poland	India	Russia	
Slovakia	Indonesia	Saudi Arabia	
Sweden	Ireland	Serbia	
Switzerland	Italy	South Korea	
United States	Java	Thailand	
	Jordan	Turkey	
	Kuwait	Ukraine	
	Laos	Vietnam	

"Indian standard time." Such tardiness is not viewed as disrespect for the time of others or rudeness; it is simply indicative of a cultural value or way of life. Figure 8.2 lists countries according to their **concept of time.**

concept of time
Term used to describe how certain societies view time as either polychronic or monochronic.

Impact on Service   In Western and other monochronic cultures you are expected to be punctual. This is a crucial factor in delivering effective service. Although others may not have the same beliefs and may be late for meetings, you must observe time rules in order to project an appropriate image and to satisfy the needs of your customers and organization.

OWNERSHIP OF PROPERTY

In many cultures (e.g., Buddhist, certain African tribes, and the Chickasaw Indian Nation) **ownership of property,** or accumulation of worldly goods or wealth, is frowned upon. In the case of the Chickasaw Indians and other tribes, such things as the earth, nature, natural resources, possessions, and individual skills are shared among the tribal group. They are not to be owned or kept from others, for the Creator gave them.[3] Many devout Buddhists believe that giving away personal belongings to others can help them reach a higher spiritual state. Thus the amassing of material things is not at all important to them.

ownership of property
Refers to how people of a given culture view property.

**CUSTOMER SERVICE
SUCCESS TIP**

When dealing with customers or clients from other cultures, you can reduce your own stress level by being aware of the time values that you and your customers have and proceeding accordingly.

Impact on Service   People have differing levels of needs. Ask customers what their needs are and listen to their responses. Don't persist in upgrading a customer's request to a higher level or more expensive product if he or she declines your suggestion. You may offend and lose a customer. Of course, if you are in sales, you must make a judgment on whether an objection is one that you should attempt to overcome or whether it is culturally based and means no.

[3] Chickasaw Nation home page, //www.chickasaw.net/site06/heritage/250_965.htm.

5   PROVIDING QUALITY SERVICE TO DIVERSE CUSTOMER GROUPS

Concept: As a service provider, you should become proficient in working with customers with language differences and disabilities; you also need to work with young and elderly customers.

Given the potential diversity of your customer base, it may be impossible to establish a service strategy for each group. However, you should think of what you might do to address the needs of some of the larger categories of customers with whom you will probably come into contact. The next few sections provide some strategies for dealing effectively with people from four diverse groups: customers with language differences, those with disabilities, elderly customers, and young customers.

CUSTOMERS WITH LANGUAGE DIFFERENCES

One major obstacle for service providers in the United States is that many adult Americans believe that just over half (52 percent) of the world's population speaks English. According to findings from the National Foreign Language Center in Washington, D.C., cited by Harris Interactive,[4] the number is closer to 20 percent.

foreign-born people
Refers to people not born in a given country.

According to U.S. Census Bureau figures, over 34 million **foreign-born people** live in the United States. Figure 8.3 gives an idea of how these numbers break down by country or origin. The key to effectively serving people from different cultures is flexibility. Since you are likely to encounter customers from virtually any country in the world, you need to be prepared. You need to have a way to use alternative methods or strategies for providing service. For example, you might identify people in your organization who speak languages other than English so that you can call upon them, if necessary. Or, you can do research on the Internet and at the library to learn about different cultures or countries. You might subscribe to publications that focus on cultural issues and a variety of countries, such as *National Geographic.*[5] If a customer speaks a little English or has a heavy accent, try the strategies described in the following sections.

CUSTOMER SERVICE SUCCESS TIP

Keep in mind when dealing with someone from another cultural background that their reaction to your language and actions depends on how "Westernized" (familiar with Western culture and language) they are.

Let Your Customer Guide the Conversation   When possible, let your customer take the lead in guiding the service interaction. Some customers may want to spend time getting to know you, others may take a rigid or formal approach and get right down to business by taking the lead, and still others may choose to have someone else act as a mediator or an intermediary. Learn to recognize the cues and follow along when you can.

FIGURE 8.3

Foreign-Born Population by Sex, Age, and World Region of Birth: 2004 (Numbers in Thousands)

Sex	Foreign Born	Latin America	Europe	Asia	Other areas
Total male and female	34,244	18,314	4,661	8,685	2,584
Total male	17,221	9,650	2,109	4,108	1,354
Total female	17,023	8,663	2,552	4,577	1,230

Source: U.S. Census Bureau, Foreign-Born Population by Sex, Age, and World Region of Birth, 2004. www.census.gov/population/socdemo/foreign/ppl-176/tab03-1.csv.

[4] www.harrisinteractive.com/harris_poll/index.asp?PID=146.
[5] National Geographic Society, Washington, D.C., http://nationalgeographic.com.

Be Flexible   Communicating with people from other cultures who do not speak English fluently can be frustrating and complicated. Even if you do not understand their culture or language, using the positive listening, nonverbal, and verbal techniques you read about in Chapters 3 to 6 can help. If you are having difficulties, try some of the specific ideas included in this section of the book. Part of being flexible is recognizing that your views are not the way of the world. Making the mistake of believing that everyone has the same experiences and sees things the way you do can lead to communication and relationship breakdown. It is probably wise to assume that people from other cultures with whom you come into contact do not have the same knowledge and experience that you have. You can then proceed to share information with each other openly and freely. Listen for points of agreement or commonality.

Listen Patiently   You may be frustrated, but so is the other person. Focus on what he or she is saying and try to understand the meaning of the message and the needs being communicated by your customer.

Speak Clearly and Slowly   Depending on what survey results you view, most adults in the United States speak at a rate of about 125 to 150 words a minute. Speak at a rate slow enough that allows your customers to understand you without being insulting.

Speak at a Normal Volume and Tone   Yelling or changing tone does nothing to enhance understanding. A customer who is unable to speak English is not necessarily deaf. You may naturally raise your voice if a customer cannot speak English, but if you do, the customer may become offended or think that you are hard of hearing and raise his or her voice also. This is not an effective way to communicate or provide effective customer service.

Use Open-End Questions   Open-end questions encourage customers to share information. On the other hand, closed-end questions do not allow you to accurately gauge a customer's viewpoint or understanding. Either because of embarrassment or to avoid saying no, some customers from other cultures may not admit that they do not agree, have an answer, or want to do something if you used a closed-end question. This reluctance can lead to misunderstandings and possibly resentment if you do not recognize a customer's nonverbal signals.

Pause Frequently   Pausing allows your customer to translate what you have said into her or his language, comprehend, and then respond in English or ask questions.

Use Standard English   Avoid technical terms, contractions (e.g., *don't, can't*), slang (e.g., *like, you know, whoopee, rubberneck*), or broken English (e.g., sentences that fail to follow standard rules of grammar or syntax). Some people, when encountering non-English-speaking customers, revert to an insulting singsong, almost childish, form of English. This does nothing to aid communication, for it is offensive and any English the customer understands gets lost in translation. Remember, some people understand English though they may not be able to speak it well. Also, some people do not speak English because they are self-conscious about their ability or choose not to. Many cultures value and use silence as an important aspect to communication, something that people of Western cultures find difficult to understand. Many Westerners often believe that silence means that a person does not understand.

A scene in the first *Rush Hour* movie, with Chris Tucker and Jackie Chan, is a perfect example of how some people make assumptions about people from other cultures and end up communicating ineffectively. Tucker (playing a Los Angeles police officer) is sent to the airport to pick up a Chinese police officer (Chan). Tucker immediately makes assumptions about Chan's ability to communicate in English:

> Tucker [upon meeting Chan]: "Please tell me you speak English."
>
> Chan [gives no response; just looks at a Chinese airline pilot standing next to him]
>
> Tucker [raises his voice]: "I'm Detective Carter. You speaka any English?"
>
> Chan [again looks at others and says nothing]
>
> Tucker [in a loud, exaggerated voice and gesturing toward his mouth]: "Do you understand the words coming out of my mouth?"
>
> Chan [smiles and says nothing]

Later in the movie, as the two are riding in Tucker's car, Chan finally speaks in English.

> Tucker: "All of a sudden, you're speaking English now."
>
> Chan: "A little."
>
> Tucker: "You lied to me."
>
> Chan: "I didn't say I didn't speak English. You assumed I didn't. Not being able to speak is not the same as not speaking."

Use Globally Understood References To reduce the risk of misunderstandings by people who speak English as a second language, stick with basic verbiage. Avoid jokes, words, or acronyms that are uniquely North American or tied to sports, historical events, or North American culture. For example, avoid these types of statements:

- "I'll need your John Hancock on this form" (referring to Hancock signing the Declaration of Independence).
- "If plan A fails, we'll drop back and punt" (referring to American football).
- "We scored a base hit with that proposal yesterday" (referring to baseball).

These phrases might be understood by someone acculturated to North American society but will likely make no sense to others.

Be Conscious of Nonverbal Cues Continually monitor nonverbal reactions as you converse with a customer. If you sense confusion or lack of comprehension, stop and try to reestablish a bond. Also, be aware of the cues you send and make sure that they are in line with your verbal message.

Paraphrase the Customer's Message After focusing on what you think is the customer's message, you may convey your understanding to the customer in your own words. When you think that you don't understand, either paraphrase the part of the customer's message up to the point at which you did understand or ask clarifying questions. For example, "Mr. Rasheed, I understand your complaint, but I'm not sure I understand what you expect us to do. How can I help make this better for you?"

Try Writing Your Message Some people understand written English better than they speak it. If a customer seems to be having trouble understanding what you are saying, try printing your message (legibly) to see if he or she can understand your meaning. You might even try using recognizable symbols, if appropriate (e.g., a stop sign when you are giving directions or a picture of an object if you are describing something).

Try Another Language If you speak a second language, try using it. Your non-English-speaking customers may understand, since many countries require students to learn multiple languages in school. At the very least, they will appreciate your efforts to communicate with them.

Avoid Humor and Sarcasm   Humor and sarcasm do not work well with customers whose first language is not English. They could lead to customer confusion and embarrassment. Differing cultural values and beliefs result in different points of view about what is socially acceptable. Also, jokes and other types of humor are typically based on incidents or people connected to a specific culture. They do not "travel well" and may not be understood by someone not of that culture.

Look for Positive Options   Many North Americans are often very direct. Many tend to use an abrupt *no* in response to a request they cannot fulfill. This behavior is viewed as rude, arrogant, and closed-minded in many cultures. Some countries do not even have a literal word in their language for *no* (e.g., Burmese). In many cases (e.g., parts of Asia) the response *no* in a conversation may cause a person embarrassment or loss of **face** (the esteem of others). Many people try to avoid such embarrassment at all costs. In some instances, people from certain parts of Asia may say yes to your proposal and then not follow through on your suggestion rather than tell you no. Such behavior is acceptable in some cultures.

face
Refers to the concept of esteem in many Asian cultures. In such cultures one tries not to cause embarrassment or otherwise create a situation in which someone looks bad in the eyes of others.

If you are dealing with customers who might react to your saying no in these ways—and you must decline—smile, apologize, and then try something like, "I am not sure we can do this" or "That will be difficult to do." Then, offer an alternative.

Use Questions Carefully   As mentioned earlier, phrase questions simply and avoid the use of closed-end questions that require a yes or no. Watch your customer's nonverbal responses so that you will be able to gauge his or her reactions to your questions.

In some cultures, people believe that questioning someone is intrusive, and they therefore avoid it. This is especially true if the questions are personal (e.g., "How is your family?").

Use a Step-by-Step Approach   When explaining something, outline exactly what you will do or what will be expected of the customer. Write this information down for the customer's future reference in order to prevent misunderstandings. If the customer cannot read it, and does not want to admit this out of embarrassment, he or she now has something to take to someone else for translation.

Keep Your Message Brief   Avoid lengthy explanations or details that might frustrate or confuse your customer. Use simple one-syllable words and short sentences. But also avoid being too brisk. Make sure you allow time for interpretation of, translation of, and response to your message.

Check Frequently for Understanding   In addition to using short words and sentences, pause often to verify the customer's understanding of your message before continuing. Avoid questions such as "Do you understand?" Not only can this be answered with a "yes" or "no" as you read earlier, but it can also offend someone who speaks and understands English reasonably well. The nonverbal message is that the person may not be smart enough to get your meaning. Instead, try tie-in questions such as "How do you think you will use this?" or others that will give you an indication of whether the customer understands the information you have provided. These types of questions help you and the customer visualize how the information will be put to use. They also give you a chance to find out if the person has misunderstood what you explained.

Keep Smiling   Smiling is a universal language. Speak it fluently!

CUSTOMER SERVICE SUCCESS TIP

If a customer makes a mistake (e.g., improperly fills out a form or uses the wrong word), do not point out the mistake. Instead, take responsibility for correcting the error or clearing up the misunderstanding (e.g., "I am sorry that these forms are so confusing. I have trouble with them too."). This strategy helps them avoid embarrassment (save face) and sends a nonjudgmental message that you are there to assist them.

CUSTOMERS WITH DISABILITIES

According to the U.S. Census Bureau, approximately 51 million (18.1 percent) of Americans over the age of five and noninstitutionalized have some level of disability. As of 2003,

2.5 million veterans have some form of disability. It is also estimated that about 32.5 million (11.5 percent) of Americans have what are defined as severe disabilities.[6] These numbers are projected to continue to grow as the population ages.

From a customer service perspective, it is certain that you will encounter someone who has a disability that requires your assistance in serving him or her. Some customer service professionals are uncomfortable working with **customers with disabilities** because they have had little prior exposure to people who have disabilities, they are uninformed about various disabilities, or they have unfounded fear or anxiety. Even though you may be unfamiliar with how people with disabilities adapt to life experiences, you should provide excellent service to them. In most cases, customers who have disabilities do not want to be treated differently; they want to be treated equally.

In addition to all the factors you have read about previously, to be effective in dealing with customers, you must be aware of the **Americans with Disabilities Act of 1990** (ADA) and other legislation passed by Congress to protect individuals and groups. You should also understand the court interpretations of these laws that require businesses to provide certain services to customers with disabilities and to make certain premises accessible to them. The laws also prohibit any form of discrimination or harassment.

Since the passage of the ADA, much has been published about the rights of and accommodations for people with disabilities. Figure 8.4 provides general strategies for working with customers and others with disabilities and complying with the ADA. In addition, the following sections discuss specific approaches you can take to work well with people with certain disabilities.

Customers with Hearing Disabilities Customers who have **hearing disabilities** have special needs, but they also have certain abilities. Do not assume that

customers with disabilities
Descriptive phrase that refers to anyone with a physical or mental disability.

Americans with Disabilities Act of 1990
A United States federal act signed into law in July of 1990 guaranteeing people with disabilities equal access to workplace and public opportunities.

hearing disabilities
Conditions in which the ability to hear is diminished below established auditory standards.

FIGURE 8.4

General Strategies for Servicing Customers With Disabilities

In addition to the suggestions offered in this chapter for serving customers with specific disabilities, here are some general guidelines for success:

Be prepared and informed. You can find a lot of literature and information about disabilities. Do some reading to learn about the capabilities and needs of customers with disabilities.

Be careful not to patronize. Refrain from talking "down" to customers with disabilities. Just because they have a physical or mental disability does not mean that they should be valued less as a customer or person.

Treat them equally, not differently. Just as you would other customers, work to discover their needs and then set about satisfying them.

Refer to the person, not the disability. Instead of referring to the *blind man, refer to the man wearing the red shirt* or *man who is standing by the. . . . ,* or better yet, *the man who needs. . . .*

Offer assistance, but do not rush to help without asking. Just as you would ask someone without a disability whether you might hold a door or carry a package, do the same for a person with a disability. Unsolicited assistance can be offensive and might even be dangerous, if it is unexpected and causes the person to lose his or her balance, for example.

Be respectful. The amount of respect you show to all customers should be at a consistently high level. This includes tone of voice (showing patience), gestures, eye contact, and all the other communication techniques you have learned about.

[6] Americans with Disabilities 2002, U.S. Census Bureau, www.census.gov/prod/2006pubs/p70-107.pdf.

people who are hearing impaired are helpless. In interactions with such customers, you can do a variety of things to provide effective service:

- Provide written information and instructions where appropriate and possible.
- Use pictures, objects, diagrams, or other such items to communicate more clearly.
- To get the person's attention, use nonverbal cues such as gesturing.
- Use facial expressions and gestures to emphasize key words or express thoughts.
- Face the person directly.
- Enunciate your words and speak slowly so that the customer can see your mouth form words.
- Use short sentences and words.
- Check for understanding frequently by using open-end questions to which the customer must provide descriptive answers.
- Communicate in a well-lighted room when possible.
- Watch backlighting (light coming from behind you that can cast a shadow on your face), which may reduce the ability to see your mouth.
- Reduce background noise, if possible.

Customers with Vision Disabilities   According to the U.S. Census Bureau, approximately 9.7 million people have difficulty seeing or are unable to see. This means that you are likely to encounter someone with a vision impairment. Like people who have hearing impairments, customers with **vision disabilities** may need special assistance but are not helpless. Depending on your organization's product and service focus, you can do things to assist visually impaired customers. Be aware that, depending on the type of impairment, a person may have limited vision that can be used to advantage. Here are some strategies to use:

vision disabilities
Condition resulting from reduced or lost visual acuity or ability.

- Talk to a visually impaired person the same way you would talk to anyone else.
- You do not have to raise your voice; the person is visually impaired.
- Do not feel embarrassed or change your vocabulary. It is okay to say things like "Do you see my point?" or "Do you get the picture?"
- Speak directly to the customer.
- If the customer uses a guide dog, do not pet, feed, or otherwise distract the animal without the owner's permission. A guide dog is especially trained to perform specific functions. If you interfere, the dog might become confused. The owner could possibly be injured as a result.
- Speak to the person as he or she enters the room or approach the person so that he or she knows where you are. Also, introduce others who are present, or at least inform the customer of their presence.
- If appropriate, ask how much sight he or she has and how you can best assist.
- Give very specific information and directions (e.g., "A chair is approximately ten feet ahead on your left").
- If you are seating the person, face him or her away from bright lights that might interfere with any limited vision he or she may have.
- When walking with someone who is blind, offer your arm. Do not take the person's arm without permission; this could startle him or her. Let the person take your elbow and walk slightly behind you.
- When helping a blind person to a chair, guide his or her hand to the back of the chair. Also, inform the person if a chair has arms to prevent him or her from overturning the chair by leaning or sitting on an arm.
- Leave doors either completely closed or open. Partially open doors pose a danger to visually impaired people.

Customers with mobility impairment have typically learned to overcome or compensate for their disability. Offer assistance without interfering. *In what ways would you offer assistance to someone with a mobility impairment?*

mobility or motion impairments
Physical limitations that some people have, requiring accommodation or special consideration to allow access to products or services.

baby boomer
A term applied to anyone born between 1946 and 1964. People in this age group are often called "boomers."

Customers with Mobility or Motion Impairments   There are approximately 11.9 millions Americans with mobility impairments.[7] Customers who have **mobility or motion impairments** often use specially designed equipment and have had extensive training in how to best use assistive devices to compensate for the loss of the use of some part of their body. You can best assist them by offering to help and then following their lead or instructions. Do not make the assumption that they need your assistance and then set about giving it. You can cause injury if you upset their balance or routine. Here are some strategies for better serving these customers:

Prior to a situation in which you may have to accommodate someone who uses a walker, wheelchair, crutches, or other device, do an environmental survey of your workplace. Note areas where space is inadequate to permit mobility (a minimum of 36 inches is needed for a standard wheelchair) or where hazards exist. If you can correct the situation, do so. For example, move or bring in a different table or chair or rearrange furniture for better access. Otherwise, make suggestions for improvements to the proper people in your organization. Remind them that the ADA and state regulations require an organization to accommodate customers with such disabilities.

Do not assume that someone who has such an impairment cannot perform certain tasks. As mentioned earlier, people who have disabilities are often given extensive training. They have learned how to overcome obstacles and perform various tasks in different ways.

Make sure that you place information or materials at a level that makes it possible for the person to see without undue strain (e.g., eye level for someone in a wheelchair so that he or she does not have to look up).

Stand or sit so that you can make direct eye contact with a person in a wheelchair without forcing the person to look up at an uncomfortable angle for extended periods.

Do not push or lean on someone's wheelchair without his or her permission.

ELDERLY CUSTOMERS

Being elderly does not make a person or a customer less valuable. In fact, many older customers are in excellent physical and mental shape, are still employed, and have more time to be active now than when they were younger. Studies show that senior citizens have more disposable income now than at any other time in history. And, as the **baby boomer** population (people born between 1946 and 1964) ages, there are more senior citizens than ever (35.9 million in 2003).[8] Moreover, as the population ages, there will be a greater need for services—and service providers—to care for people and allow them to enjoy a good quality of life. Figure 8.5 shows the U.S. population aged 65 and older between 2000 and 2050. Consider the following strategies when you are interacting with an **elderly customer.**

---

[7]www.census.gov/prod/2006pubs/p70-107.pdf.
[8]65+ in the United States: 2005, U.S. Census Bureau,www.census.gov/prod/2006pubs/p23-209.pdf.

Identifying Resources

CHECK WITH LOCAL ADVOCACY GROUPS OR ON THE INTERNET FOR INFORMATION ON THE TYPES OF ACCOMMODATIONS YOU MIGHT MAKE FOR PEOPLE WITH VARIOUS DISABILITIES AND HOW BEST TO INTERACT WITH PEOPLE WHO HAVE SPECIFIC DISABILITIES (E.G., SIGHT, MOBILITY, HEARING IMPAIRMENT). Collect and read literature on the subject. Share the information with other students and/or coworkers (if you currently work in a customer service environment).

What to look for:

Definitions of various disabilities.

Strategies for better communication.

Accommodations necessary to allow customer access to products and services.

Resources available (e.g., tools, equipment, training, or organizations).

Bibliographic information on disabilities (e.g., books or articles).

Be Respectful As you would with any customer, be respectful. Even if the customer seems a bit arrogant, disoriented, or disrespectful, don't lose your professionalism. Recognize that sometimes these behaviors are a response to perceptions based on your cues. When this happens, quickly evaluate your behavior and make adjustments, if necessary. If an older customer seems abrupt in his or her response, think about whether you might have nonverbally signaled impatience because of your perception that he or she was slow in acting or responding.

Be Patient Allow older customers the time to look around, respond, react, or ask questions. Value their decisions. Also, keep in mind that as some people age, their ability to process information lessens and their attention span becomes shorter. Do not assume that this is true of all older customers, but be patient when it does occur.

Answer Questions Providing information to customers is crucial in order to help them make reasoned decisions. Even though you may have just explained something, listen to the customer's questions, respond, and restate. If it appears that the customer has misunderstood, try repeating the information, possibly using slightly different words.

Try Not to Sound Patronizing If you appear to talk down to older customers, problems could arise and you could lose a customer. Customers who are elderly should not be treated as if they are senile! A condescending attitude will often cause any customer, elderly or otherwise, to take his or her business elsewhere.

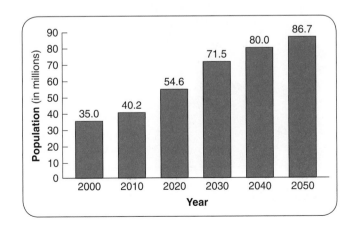

FIGURE 8.5

Population Aged 65 and Older: 2000 to 2050 (in Millions)

Note: The reference population is the resident population.

Sources: 2000, U.S. Census Bureau, 2001, Table PCT 12; 2010 to 2050. U.S. Census Bureau, 2004.

younger customers
Subjective term referring to anyone younger than the service provider. Sometimes used to describe members of generation X (born to baby boomers) or later.

Remain Professional   Addressing senior citizens accompanied by their children or grandchildren with "Good morning, Grandma" because one of their family members used that language is inappropriate, disrespectful, and rude.

Guard against Biases   Be careful not to let biases about older people interfere with good service. Don't ignore or offend older customers by making statements such as "Hang on, old timer. I'll be with you in a minute." Such a statement might be in jest, but is nonetheless potentially offensive to the person, and to others who might hear it.

YOUNGER CUSTOMERS

You have heard the various terms describing the "younger generation"—generation Y, nexters, MTV generation, millennial generation, cyberkids. Whatever the term, this group follows generation X (born 1964–1977) and is now entering the workplace as employees and as consumers in great numbers. Financially, the group accounts for billions of dollars in business revenue for products such as clothes, music, videos, and electronic entertainment equipment. Generation Y is a spending force to be reckoned with, and marketers are going after them with a vengeance. If you don't believe this, pick up a magazine and look at the faces of the models, look at the products being sold, and watch the shows being added to television lineups each year. All of this affects the way you will provide service to this generation of customers. Depending on your own age, your attitude toward them will vary. If you are of gen Y, you may make the mistake of being overly familiar with your age group in delivering service. If you are a baby boomer or older, you may feel paternalistic or maternalistic or might believe some of the stereotypical rhetoric about this group (e.g., low moral values, fragmented in focus, overprotected by legislation and programs). Although some of these descriptions may be accurate, it is dangerous to pigeonhole any group or individual as you have read. This is especially true when providing service, since service is based on satisfying personal needs and wants.

Remember when you were young and felt that adults didn't understand or care about your wants or needs? Well, your **younger customers** probably feel the same way and will remember how you treat them. Their memories could prompt them to take their business elsewhere if their experience with you is negative. If you are older, you may be tempted to talk down to them or be flippant. Don't give in to the temptation. Keep in mind that they are customers. If they feel unwelcome, they will take their business and money elsewhere, and they will tell their friends of the poor treatment they received. Just as with older customers, avoid demeaning language and condescending forms of address (*kid, sonny, sweetie, sugar or young woman/man*).

Additional points to remember when dealing with younger customers is that they may not have the product knowledge and sophistication in communicating that older

Younger customers can often have a completely different set of needs. *What are some effective strategies for handling customers of a younger generation?*

Serving a Variety of Customers

PAIR UP WITH A PEER AND USE THE FOLLOWING SCENARIOS AS THE BASIS OF ROLE-PLAYS TO GIVE YOU PRACTICE AND FEEDBACK IN DEALING WITH VARIOUS CATEGORIES OF CUSTOMERS. Before beginning, discuss how you might deal with each customer in a real-life situation. After the role-plays, both persons should answer the following questions and discuss any ideas for improvement.

Questions

1. How well do you feel that service was provided?
2. Were any negative or unclear messages, verbal or nonverbal, communicated? If yes, discuss.
3. What open-ended questions were used to discover customer needs? What others could have been used?
4. How can identified areas for improvement be incorporated into a real customer service encounter?

Scenario 1. You are a shuttle driver for the airport and just received a call from your dispatcher to proceed to 8172 Dealy Lane to pick up Cassandra Fenton. You were told that Ms. Fenton is blind and will need assistance getting her bags from the house to the bus. Upon arrival, you find Ms. Fenton waiting on her front porch with her bags.

Scenario 2. Mrs. Zagowski is 62 years old and is in the library where you are working at the circulation desk. As you observe her, you notice that she seems a bit frustrated and confused. You saw her browse through several aisles of books, then talk briefly with the reference librarian, and finally go to the computer containing the publication listings and their locations. You are going to try to assist her. Upon meeting her, you realize that she has a hearing deficit and has difficulty hearing what you are saying.

Scenario 3. You are the owner of a small hobby shop that specializes in coins, stamps, comics, and sports memorabilia. Tommy Chin, whom you recognize as a regular "browser," has come in while you are particularly busy. After looking through numerous racks of comic books and trading cards, he is now focused on autographed baseballs in a display case. You believe that he cannot afford them, although he is asking about prices and for other information.

---

customers do. You can decrease confusion and increase communication effectiveness by using words that are appropriate for their age group and by taking the time to explain and/or demonstrate technical points. Keep it simple without being patronizing.

6 COMMUNICATING WITH DIVERSE CUSTOMERS

Concept: Many considerations need to be taken into account when you are delivering service to a diverse customer base. Appropriate language usage is a meaningful tool that you should master for good customer service.

Given all this diversity, you must be wondering how to provide service that is acceptable to all of these customer groups. As you've seen, there are many considerations in delivering service to a diverse customer base. Therefore, consider the following basic guidelines for communicating; these tips are appropriate for dealing with all types of customers.

Be Careful with Your Remarks and Jokes Comments that focus on any aspect of diversity (religion, sexual preference, weight, hair color, age) can be offensive and should not be made. Also, humor does not cross cultural boundaries well. Each culture has a different interpretation of what is humorous and socially acceptable.

Make Sure That Your Language Is "Inclusive" When speaking, address or refer to the people from various groups that are present. If you are addressing a group of two men and one woman, using the term *guys* or *fellows* excludes the woman and thus is not **inclusive.**

Respect Personal Preferences When Addressing People As you read earlier, don't assume familiarity when addressing others. (Don't call someone by her or his first name unless he or she gives permission.) Don't use *Ms.* if a female customer

CUSTOMER SERVICE SUCCESS TIP

Members of generations X and Y are very technically savvy. If you plan to effectively provide service to these customers, learn as much technology as you can (e.g., cell phones, iPods, computer hardware and software, Internet options and services, and service delivery technology (e.g., Wiki, blogs, podcasts).

inclusive
The concept of ensuring that people of all races, genders, and religious and ethnic backgrounds, as well as a multitude of other diverse factors, are included in communications and activities in the workplace.

211

FIGURE 8.6

Nonverbal Cue Meanings

The following are symbols and gestures that are commonly used in the United States but have different—and negative or offensive—meanings in other parts of the world:

American Gesture or Symbol	Meaning in Other Cultures	Country
Beckoning by curling and uncurling index finger*†	Used for calling animals or ladies of the evening	Hong Kong, Australia, Indonesia, Yugoslavia, Malaysia
V for victory sign (with palm facing you)*†	Rude gesture	England
Sole of foot pointed toward a person*‡	You are lowly (the sole is lowest part of the body and contacts the ground).	Thailand, Saudi Arabia, Singapore, Egypt
"Halt" gesture with palm and extended fingers thrust toward someone*†‡	Rude epithet	Greece
Thumb up (fingers curled) indicating *okay, good going,* or *everything is fine**‡	The number 5 Rude gesture	Japan, Nigeria, Australia
Thumb and forefinger forming an O, meaning okay*‡	Zero or worthless Money Rude gesture	France Japan Brazil, Malta, Greece, Tunisia, Turkey, Italy, Paraguay, Russia
Waving good-bye with fingers extended, palm down, and moving the fingers up and down toward yourself*‡	Come here	Parts of Europe, Myanmar, Colombia, Peru
Patting the head of a child	Insult, inviting evil spirits	Parts of the Far East
Using red ink for documents	Death; offensive	Parts of Korea, Mexico, and China
Passing things with left hand (especially food)	Socially unacceptable	India, Pakistan

*R. Axtell, *Gestures: The Do's and Taboos of Body Language Around the World,* John Wiley and Sons, New York, 1991.

†A. Wolfgang, *Everybody's Guide to People Watching,* International Press, Yarmouth, Mass., 1995.

‡D. Morris, *Bodytalk, The Meaning of Human Gestures,* Crown Trade Paperback, New York, 1994.

Wiki
A form of server software that allows nontechnical personnel to create and edit website pages using any web browser and without complex programming knowledge.

blogs
Online journals or diaries that allow people to add content. Many organizational websites use them to post "What's new" sections and to receive feedback (good and bad) from customers and website visitors.

podcasts
A word that is a derivative of Apple® computers IPod® media player and the term *broadcasting.* Specifically it means Portable On Demand broadCAST. Through podcasts, web sites can offer direct download or streaming of their content (e.g., music or video files) to customers or website visitors.

prefers another form of address. Also, avoid derogatory or demeaning terms such as *honey, sugar,* and *sweetheart* or other overly familiar language.

Use General Terms   Instead of singling a customer out or focusing on exceptions in a group, describe people in general terms. That is, instead of referring to someone as a *female supervisor, black salesperson,* or *disabled administrative assistant,* say *supervisor, salesperson,* or *administrative assistant.*

Recognize the Impact of Words   Keep in mind that certain words have a negative connotation and could insult or offend. Even if you do not intend to offend, the customer's perception is the deciding factor of your actions. For example, using the terms *handicapped* or *crippled, boy, girl, homo,* or *idiot* may conjure up a negative image to some groups or individuals. Using such terminology can also reflect negatively upon you and your organization and should never be used.

Use Care with Nonverbal Cues   The nonverbal cues that you are familiar with may carry different meanings in other cultures. Be careful when you use symbols or gestures if you are not certain how your customer will receive them. Figure 8.6 lists some cues that are common in Western cultures but have negative meanings in other cultures.

Opportunities to deal with a diverse customer base will increase as the global economy expands. With continuing immigrations, an aging world population, changes in values, and increased ease of mobility, the only thing certain is that the next customer you speak with will be different from you. Remember, however, that he or she will also be similar to you in many ways and that both of you will have a basis for discussion.

The success you have in the area of dealing with others is totally dependent on your preparation and attitude toward providing quality service. Learn as much as you can about various groups of people in order to effectively evaluate situations, determine needs, and serve all customers on an equal basis.

Americans with Disabilities Act of 1990 206
attitudes 200
baby boomer 208
beliefs 195
blogs 211
Chicano cultures 198
collective cultures 200
concept of time 201
conflict resolution style 200
cultural diversity 194
customers with disabilities 206
diversity 194
expectations of privacy 198
face 205
foreign-born people 202
form of address 198
gender roles 199
hearing disabilities 206

Hispanic cultures 198
inclusive 212
individualistic cultures 200
interpersonal relationship 199
Latino cultures 198
mobility or motion impairments 208
modesty 197
monochronic 200
ownership of property 201
Platinum Rule 195
podcasts 211
polychronic 200
respect for elders 198
values 197
vision disabilities 207
wiki 211
younger customers 210

1 What are some innate qualities or characteristics that make people unique?
2 What external or societal factors affect the way members of a group are seen or perceived?
3 What are values?
4 Do beliefs differ from values? Explain.
5 Why would some people be reluctant to make eye contact with you?
6 When dealing with customers with a disability, how can you best help them?
7 How can recognition of the cultural value of "importance of family" be helpful in customer service?
8 What are some considerations for improving communication in a diverse environment?
9 How can you effectively communicate with someone who has difficulty with the English language?
10 What are some techniques for effectively providing service to older customers?

Search the Internet for Diversity Information

Log on to the Internet to locate information and articles related to topics covered in this chapter. Be prepared to share what you found at your next scheduled class or session. The following are some key words you might use in your search:

Any country name (e.g., Australia, Canada, Sri Lanka)
Baby boomers
Beliefs
Any religion (e.g., Muslim, Hindu, Buddhist, Christian)
Cultural diversity

Cultural values
Disabilities
Disability advocacy
Diversity
Elderly
Generation X
Generation Y
Intercultural communication
Intercultural dynamics
Population projections

Awareness of Diversity

To help raise your awareness of diversity in the customer service environment, try the following activities:

1   Pair up with someone to role-play scenarios in which you are a service provider and have customers from the following groups:

An elderly person who has a hearing loss and wants directions on how to use some equipment (you choose the equipment and provide instruction).

Someone who speaks English as a second language (with a heavy accent) and needs to fill out a credit card application or some other form.

Someone with a sight impairment who wants to "see" several blouses or shirts or needs directions to another part of your store.

A 10-year-old who wants a new computer and has questions about various types, components, and how they work.

2   Interview a variety of people: from different cultures, from various age groups, with disabilities, male or female (opposite of your sex), or gay or lesbian. Find out whether they have preferences in the type of customer service they receive or in the kind of language used to refer to their group. Also, ask about ways you can better communicate with and understand them and people from their group.

3   Suggest to your supervisor, team leader, or work group peers that employees meet as a group to discuss situations in which all of you have encountered people from different cultures or groups. Exchange ideas on how to better serve such people in the future. Report the results of your efforts to your class members at the next scheduled meeting.

4   Working in teams assigned by your instructor, set up an appointment to visit a local advocacy group for the disabled or aging, or contact a national group (e.g., the National Society to Prevent Blindness, assisted-living facilities, World Federation of the Deaf, National Information Center on Deafness, National Eye Institute, National Institute on Aging). Focus on gathering information that will help you understand various disabilities and develop strategies for effectively communicating with and serving people who have disabilities. Write a brief summary of your experience and report back to your peers.

Dealing with Difficult People on the Phone at MedMobile

Background

MedMobile is a medical supply business located in Los Angeles employing 62 full-time and 11 part-time workers. The company specializes in equipment designed to improve patient mobility (walkers, motorized carts, wheelchairs, mechanized beds and chairs). Average yearly sales are in the area of $1.5 million.

The primary client base for the company is insurance companies that pay for rehabilitation after worker accidents or injuries. Medical professionals who conduct the patient medical case file reviews and recommend treatment programs are in regular contact with the account representatives for MedMobile.

Your Role

As an account representative with MedMobile, you have been with the company for about 18 months. Your main job is to help clients determine and obtain the correct equipment needed to assist their patients. To do this, you spend hours on the phone daily and often know clients by voice. In the past month you have become extremely frustrated, almost to the point of anger. A new claims adjuster works for one of your primary account companies, TrueCare Insurance Company. His name is Abeyola Pepukayi, and he has been with TrueCare eight weeks. He has been an adjuster for a little over a year.

You just got off the phone after a lengthy conversation with Abeyola and you are agitated. For over half an hour you tried unsuccessfully to explain why you felt the equipment being ordered by Abeyola was not the best for the patient's injury, as he described it to you.

Because this isn't the first time such an encounter has taken place, you are now in your supervisor's office venting. While discussing the situation with your boss, you note the following about Abeyola:

He doesn't listen. No matter what you say, he asks totally irrelevant questions about other equipment.

He usually has no idea what you're talking about.

He is rude and interrupts, often making statements such as "One moment, please. That makes no sense."

You have spent hours discussing equipment design and function because he doesn't know anything about it.

He spends endless amounts of time getting offtrack and trying to discuss other issues or topics.

After your conversation, your boss called a friend at True Care to see what he knew of the situation. The friend, David

Helmstedter, supervises Abeyola. Apparently, Abeyola has been venting to David about you. From what David has been told:

> You are rude and abrupt and aren't very friendly. Abeyola has tried to establish a relationship, but you have ignored his efforts.
>
> Abeyola is trying hard to learn the terminology and equipment but you are unwilling to help.
>
> You speak rapidly, using a lot of technical language that you don't explain.

Critical Thinking Questions

1 What seems to be happening here? Does Abeyola have any legitimate complaints? If so, what are they?
2 What steps or process can you use to clarify understanding?
3 What cultural differences might be involved in this scenario?

Identifying Your Biases

We sometimes have biases that interfere with our interactions with others. Typically, these biases are learned behavior (something we have personally experienced or have been taught by others). By thinking of your biases and bringing them to a conscious level, you can better control or eliminate them in dealing with your customers and others.

Think about the qualities of other people or groups that you do not like or prefer to avoid. List them, along with the basis (why you believe them to be true) for each.

RETAIL-Nordstrom

1 From what you know or read about the Nordstrom organization, how well do you feel they address the needs of their customers? Explain.
2 After visiting www.nordstrom.com, what do you feel are the organization's strength's related to customer service? Weaknesses (if any)?
3 What do you think of John W. Nordstrom's "guiding principle" and the impact it has had on the organization? Explain.

1	F	5	T	9	F
2	T	6	F	10	T
3	T	7	T	11	T
4	T	8	T	12	T

PLANNING TO SERVE · IN THE REAL WORLD · QUICK PREVIEW ANSWERS

Ethical Dilemma 8.1 Possible Answers

1   What action should you take, if any?

As an employee of any type of organization (retail or otherwise) you should take ownership of your environment. After all, your employer pays you to be professional and alert on the job. In this situation, the customer seems to be acting in an unusual and possibly suspicious manner. Certainly, security is a concern for anyone these days. You would be correct and prudent to monitor the man's actions and to notify your supervisor, a coworker, and/or security of the situation just in case the person is up to some unlawful or otherwise inappropriate activity. Because of potential risk, you should not confront such a person yourself, and certainly not alone without others watching the situation.

2   If you decide to take some action, why would you do so?

Any action you take would likely be precautionary to prevent loss (financial or physical) to your organization yourself and others. Also, in the event that the person is really up to illegal activity, you would likely be doing it out of concern for safety (yours and others).

3   What are possible repercussions if you either act or decide not to act?

If you fail to act and the person is engaged in some unlawful or mischievous activity, you, others, and the organization could sustain loss, damage, and possible injury. If you do act, and the man is not doing anything more than "killing time," the person's perception could be that you are targeting him and potentially could become upset or even claim some sort of discrimination. You could also lose his business and that of anyone to whom he relates his experience.

Customer Service via Technology

In the world of Internet Customer Service, it's important to remember that a competitor is only one mouse click away.

—Doug Warner

After completing this chapter, you will be able to:

1 Recognize the extent to which customer service is facilitated by the effective use of technology.

2 Use technology to enhance service delivery capabilities.

3 Communicate effectively via e-mail, the Internet, and fax.

4 Deliver quality service through effective telephone techniques.

In the Real World   Technology-eBay Inc.

Founded in 1995 by Pierre Omidyar (chairman of the board) and headquartered in San Jose, California, eBay Inc. has grown to be a household name through a series of continued growth and acquisitions. According to its website, eBay's net revenues the second quarter of 2007 were over $1.83 billion. On any given day, there are millions of items available through auction-style and fixed-price trading to millions of buyers worldwide. The consumer research firm Scarborough Research found in 2007 that, in the United States, "Nationally, almost one-third (31 percent) of Internet users are eBay visitors."[1] EBay has localized sites in Europe, Asia-Pacific, and North America and a presence in Latin America.

From a beginning as a small Web-based auction company to the megagiant of today and one of history's fastest growing companies, eBay continues to set milestones for others to follow. All has not been glory for eBay, however, according to Meg Whitman (CEO) in a 2005 *USAToday* interview.[2] According to Whitman, a date that stands out in her memory is June 10, 1999, when eBay's site crashed for 22 hours. She says, "It humbled the company." Changes in item listing fees and a policy that would limit the number of products that someone could list on auction set up a scenario for disaster. Sellers frantically went onto the site to list as many products as possible before new changes took effect and that overloaded the system. To counter potential user outrage, Whitman had all 400 of eBay's employees take a portion of their user list and start calling to personally apologize to them for the technical breakdown. This initiative won accolades from users and the business world and helped cement eBay's place in business history as a way to turn a negative event into a positive opportunity.

Some of eBay's holdings include the following companies:

PayPal (acquired in 2002), which allows individuals or businesses with an e-mail address to securely, easily, and quickly send and receive payments online.

Skype (acquired in 2005) is the world's fastest-growing Internet communication offering, allowing people everywhere to make unlimited voice and video communication for free between the users of Skype software. Skype is available in 27 languages.

Shopping.com (acquired in 2005) allows online comparison shopping and is one of the fastest-growing shopping destinations on the Internet.

Rent.com (acquired in 2005) is the most visited apartment listing in the United States and has more than 20,000 properties listed across the country.

Online Classifieds where people can meet, share ideas, and trade on a local level. eBay's online sites include Kijiji, Gumtree.com, LoQUo.com, Intoko, Netherlands-based Marktplaats.nl, and German automotive classifieds site mobile.de. In addition, eBay owns a minority investment in craigslist.

For additional information about this organization, visit http://pages.ebay.com/aboutebay.html.

See activity related to this section on page 244.

Quick Preview

Before reviewing the chapter content, respond to the following questions by placing a "T" for true or an "F" for false on the rules. Use any questions you miss as a checklist of material to which you will pay particular attention as you read through the chapter. For those you get right, congratulate yourself, but review the sections they address in order to learn additional details about the topic.

_____ **1.** According to the Cellular Telecommunications Industry Association, over 233 million people In the United States subscribe to a wireless telephone service.

_____ **2.** *E-commerce* is a term that means that the commerce of the United States is in excellent condition.

[1]The South Reins for EBay Visitors, July 31, 2007. www.scarborough.com/press_releases/eBay%20Final%20731%2007.pdf

[2]Maney, K., 10 years ago, eBay changed the world, *USAToday,* www.usatoday.com/tech/news/2005-03-21-ebay-cover_x.htm

_____ **3.** A customer service representative might also have one of the following job titles: associate, sales representative, consumer affairs counselor, consultant, technical service representative, operator, account executive, attendant, or engineer.

_____ **4.** The acronym TTY is used by call center staff members to indicate that something is to be done today.

_____ **5.** Many organizations think of technology as a way to reduce staff and save money.

_____ **6.** One way to improve your image over the telephone is to continually evaluate your speech.

_____ **7.** Jargon, slang, and colloquialisms can distort message meaning.

_____ **8.** Adjusting your rate of speech to mirror a customer's rate can aid comprehension.

_____ **9.** Quoting policy is one way to ensure that customers understand why you can't give them what they want.

_____ **10.** To ensure that accurate communication has taken place, you should summarize key points at the end of a telephone conversation.

_____ **11.** Blind transfers are effective if you don't take too much time explaining who is calling.

_____ **12.** Chewing food and gum, drinking, or talking to others while on the telephone can be distracting and should be avoided.

_____ **13.** Using voice mail to answer calls is an effective way to avoid interruptions while you are speaking to a customer.

_____ **14.** Planning calls and the information you will leave is an effective way to avoid telephone tag.

Answers to Quick Preview can be found at the end of the chapter.

. . . .

1 THE INCREASING ROLE OF TECHNOLOGY IN CUSTOMER SERVICE

Concept: Customer service is a 24/7 responsibility, and technology can assist in making it effective.

To say that technology has permeated almost every aspect of life in most developed countries would be an understatement. Of the estimated $916.9 billion dollars in retail sales In the first quarter of 2005, $19.8 billion was from e-commerce sales.[3] As of June 2006, 93 percent of residential end-users had access to cable modems while 79 percent had access to high-speed cable or DSL services.[4]

Computers and other forms of technology are continually becoming smaller, more complex, and powerful; we have only started to see the impact that technology will have on shaping the future. Most businesses in the United States are technologically dependent in some form. Calculators, cash registers, maintenance equipment, telephones, radios, cellular phones, pagers, computer systems, and handheld personal planners are typical examples of technology that we rely upon. We have become a 24/7 society (we access technology 24 hours a day, 7 days a week) and can communicate at any time and in virtually any place. According to the Cellular Telecommunications Industry Association, over 233 million

[3]Quarterly Retail E-Commerce Sales. 1st Quarter 2005. U.S. Census Bureau. www.census.gov/mrts/www/data/html/05Q1.html

[4]Trends in Telephone Usage, February 2007: Percentage of Residential End-User Premises with Access to High-Speed Services as of June 30,2006. http://hraunfoss.fcc.gov/edocs_public/attachmatch/DOC-270407A1.pdf

FIGURE 9.1

Using Technology to Better Serve

Many organizations are striving to find new ways to apply technology to enhance service.

Organization	Application
American Automobile Association www.aaa.com	AAA mobile services are being provided via GPS-enabled wireless telephones. Members can access directions and restaurant and hotel information, and in case of a need for roadside assistance, their vehicle's location can be determined in order to dispatch help.
Travelocity, Expedia, and Priceline	All three services and others like them act as www.travelocity.com online discount brokers for hotels, car rental www.expedia.com companies, airlines, and other travel related www.priceline.com services. These organizations have pulled together a huge system of discounted travel services that consumers can access and through which they can make reservations for a fee.
Meriwether Lewis Elementary School www.lewiselementary.org/	This school uses blogs as an organization as well as providing a location for educators to create their own blogs related to their classes and extracurricular activities. Parents, staff, students, and other interested parties can access important information 24/7 via the Internet, even when the school is closed.

people In the United States subscribe to wireless telephone service.[5] This is in addition to almost 94 percent of U.S. households that had telephones in 2005.[6] A result is that more people are accessing telephone-related customer service and the economies of many countries are being significantly influenced by technology-based customer services.

One study of 3,000 **customer contact center** operations estimated that in New England alone, 1 in 6 jobs is in a contact center. The study also predicts that by 2010 the U.S. call center industry will shrink by 2.8 percent in terms of call centers and by 2.0 percent in terms of jobs by 2010. This is due to **offshoring or outsourcing** call center functions to other countries and the rise in self-service Web or speech recognition technologies that allow customers to place their own orders and access information without contacting a customer care representative.[7]

All of this means that companies that are not prepared to meet the future will lose business as customers migrate to providers that are better prepared. With access to products and services at almost any time through telephones, wireless telephones,e-mail, facsimile machines, and the Internet, customers are in a power position as never before. They will likely use alternative resources, considering that the United States has enjoyed the lowest unemployment rate in almost two decades during the first half of the new millenium. Thus, fewer service providers are available to fill jobs. That translates to longer wait times and increased frustration that many customers will simply not accept. To help counter this, many organizations are looking for new service applications for available technology. Figure 9.1

customer contact center
A central point within an organization from which all customer service contacts are managed via various forms of technology.

offshoring
Refers to the relocation of business services from one country to another (e.g. services, production, and manufacturing).

[5] Annualized Wireless Industry Survey Results–December 1985 to December 2006. http://files.ctia.org/pdf/CTIA_Survey_Year_End_2006_Graphics.pdf

[6] Trends in Telephone Usage, February 2007: Telephone Penetration By State (Annual Average Percentage of Households with telephone Service). Federal Communication Commission. http://hraunfoss.fcc.gov/edocs_public/attachmatch/DOC-270407A1.pdf

[7] North American Contact Centers in 2006: The State of the Industry. www.callcentermagazine.com/shared/article/showArticle.jhtml?articleId=191000328

Illustrates how some organizations are embracing technology to better serve their customers.

2   THE CUSTOMER CONTACT/CALL CENTER OR HELP DESK

Concept: Electronic commerce is a new and powerful way to employ technology to conduct business.

Because of the expansion of technology used by customer support staff in many organizations, customer contact or customer care centers (called call centers and by other names by some organizations) providing technology-based service are on the rise. The growing trend to reduce staff and costs, while maintaining or increasing service effectiveness, necessitates employing technology in addition to people. Most organizations now have free 800 or 888 numbers that people can use to call the organization to get information, place orders, or receive service and for a variety of other functions. Organizations are also employing **fee-based 900 numbers** through which customer and others can call for information and service (e.g., computer technical support). Such numbers are pay-as-you go with the caller incurring a per-minute charge for service from the telephone company and/or a flat fee from the organization for services rendered.

> **fee-based 900 numbers**
> A premium telephone number provided by organizations and individuals that, when called, can provide information and services that are billed back to the caller's local telephone bill.

In the past, operations that used technology were seen as labor-intensive (because of the need to maintain and operate equipment) and behind-the-scenes or "back-office" functions. They typically supplemented the front-line service providers and were not viewed as a strategic initiative related to the overall operation of the organization. With the availability of technology-literate and computer-trained employees, and a shift in expectations of customers who are more capable of accessing products and services through technology, customer support through customer contact centers is now an integral part of many organizations. Corporate and organizational officers and stake holders in all types of organizations now recognize the potential of such operations and are pumping billions of dollars into the development, maintenance, and improvement of customer contact center operations. Customer contact centers, or **help desks,** are more powerful and complicated than ever before. They also provide more functions than their rather ineffectual predecessors.

> **help desk**
> Term used to describe a service provider trained and assigned to assist customers with questions, problems, or suggestions.

The influence is so significant in terms of dollars that the way that organizations do business using technology has been labeled electronic commerce (e-commerce).

Even with all the technological advances, one thing remains clear: customers still appreciate old-fashioned personalized customer service. Successful service organizations realize that each customer is unique. Some people are *high touch* (preferring assistance) while others are *low touch;* (preferring to serve themselves) therefore, offering a variety of service delivery systems is smart business. Whether service is delivered face to face or via technology, there is often no substitute for a dedicated, knowledgeable, and well-trained employee. You and your peers are the lifeline of your organization.

TYPES OF TECHNOLOGY

Technology is advancing at such a rapid rate that the typical organization and its employees are unable to cope with the changes. Previously, when a customer had a question or needed assistance, he or she would call an 800 or 888 number. When the call arrived at the call center, a customer service representative would answer, and after obtaining information, might be able to handle the customer's situation.

Technology has drastically changed customer service expectations with regard to response time and accessibility of information. *What are some innovations that have contributed to this trend?*

Today, customer service representatives have a vast amount of technology at their disposal. Some of the typical systems found in customer care centers follow. Figure 9.2 also shows additional technologies being used to better serve customers:

Automated Attendant   **Automated attendants** provide callers with a menu of options from which they can select by pressing a key on their telephone keypad. These systems can also be used to provide prerecorded responses to frequently asked questions (FAQs) and to route callers to specific representatives or other employees and departments.

Automatic Call Distribution (ACD) System   An **automatic call distribution (ACD) system** routes incoming calls to the next available agent based on number called, time of day, caller ID, or caller-selected codes. When agents are busy or lines are full, an ACD automatically places callers on hold and plays a prerecorded announcement. Many companies use the announcement to make callers aware of other products and services offered by the organization.

Automatic Number Identification (ANI)   **Automatic number identification (ANI) system** (pronounced "Annie") is a form of caller ID similar to that on many home telephones. The system allows customers to be identified and their calls directed appropriately before an agent talks to them. For example, a customer could be routed to a special agent who is multilingual or who has specialized product or service knowledge. This saves time for the agent, as the customer's telephone number does not have to be keyed in and the agent can identify the customer's geographic location before speaking with him or her. The agent might also be able to access information on a computer screen about the customer's history with the organization. Also, calls can be routed to the same agent who most recently handled a specific caller. Finally, with ANI, calls can be routed to the service center closest to the customer's home.

Computer Telephony Integration (CTI)   **Computer telephony integration (CTI)** systems integrate a representative's computer and phone to facilitate the automatic retrieval of customer records and other information needed to satisfy a customer's needs and requests.

automated attendants
Provide callers with a menu of options from which they can select by pressing a key on their telephone keypad.

automatic call distribution (ACD) system
Telecommunications system used by many companies in their call centers and customer care facilities to capture incoming calls and route them to available service providers.

automatic number identification (ANI) system
A form of caller identification system similar to home telephone caller-ID systems. ANI allows incoming customers to be identified on a computer screen with background information so that they can be routed to an appropriate service representative for assistance.

computer telephony integration (CIT)
A system that integrates a representative's computer and phone to facilitate the automatic retrieval of customer records and other information needed to satisfy a customer's needs and requests.

Technology and its applications continue to multiply and expand on a daily basis, and so do ways in which businesses are learning to harness their power. Everything from delivery of information and new products to communicating and helping satisfy customer needs is evolving rapidly.

The following are some ways that organizations are tapping into today's technology to better serve potential, new and existing customers:

Text Messaging. Travel agencies, entertainment companies, and others that deal with scheduling, events, and changing information for customers use this format to send short updates or information related to products and events to customers' cellular phones.

On-call personnel, such as maintenance, engineering, and medical staff can be notified when an issue or emergency needing their attention arises.

Service organizations, such as auto repair, hair salon, and dentists' and doctors' offices can remind customers and patients of upcoming appointments.

Retail and other organizations can send confirmations of bill payments.

Schools can notify students and/or parents of upcoming events, reminders of tasks that need to be handled, school closings, or class cancellations.

Podcasts (Portable on-Demand Broadcasts). This form of media can share information (e.g., advertisements, product information, training program content, entertainment, or information updates) with potential and current customers or the community. Organizations can transmit scheduled material to customers as a free service or as a subscription or per-event/item purchase. Consultants often use this vehicle to conduct client meetings or to train employees. Other organizations tap into the technology to save money on travel by providing information to remote clients or employees.

Cell Phone. Cell phones are becoming more sophisticated every day and have traditionally functioned as a way to share voice and text information with customers. With the Introduction of the **iPod** telephone In 2007 from Apple® Computer, new opportunities opened to organizations wishing to get Information and services to mobile phone customers. For the first time, the iPod phone integrated the functions of a mobile phone, a widescreen iPod (media player), and an Internet connection device into one small, lightweight, handheld device. It allows users to make phone calls, send e-mail and text messages, access computer applications (software programs), and connect to the Internet on a large multitouch screen. The potential for helping customers is huge and all in their hands on a mobile basis wherever they travel.

Wikis. Many employers and organizations are using websites (Wikis) to allow a form of social networking among their internal customers (employees). These sites provide a means of collecting and exchanging information and to brainstorm ideas related to a project. This exchange of knowledge and ideas can facilitate harmony as well as enhance productivity if used effectively. They are the "water coolers" of today's technically savvy employees who might prefer to fire off thoughts via their keypad rather than gather at a bar after work. Wikis allow users to add and edit content at any time by simply logging on.

Wikis are also being used by some employers to provide information that would normally be delivered in a training session, thus saving time and money. For example, if an organization uses a lot of acronyms or jargon, a Wiki could be used as a place to define terms so that employees can determine the meaning of a term they come across in the workplace without having to go to the supervisor or someone else.

Blogs. A relatively new tool being created and used by individuals and organizations is weblogs (blogs). These chronological "diaries" are a creative way for organizations to provide updates and information to internal and external customers (e.g., product recalls, updates, procedures, processes, policy changes, and so on). Many blogs contain only text; however, they can have images and other media in them as well as links to helpful websites. Typically, readers are able to ask questions or leave comments in the blog. A key component of a successful blog is to have a webmaster or editor who monitors comments to prevent someone from posting obscenities or other embarrassing or damaging Information.

iPod
A brand of portable media player that has been manufactured and marketed by Apple® computer since 2001. It can play digital audio files and videos and can also function as an external data storage unit.

Electronic Mail (e-mail)   This form of technology provides an inexpensive, rapid way of communicating with customers in writing worldwide. **Electronic mail (e-mail)** allows customers to access information via telephone and then, through prompting (and using the telephone keypad), have the information delivered to them via e-mail. A big advantage of e-mail is that you can write a single message and have it delivered to hundreds of people worldwide in a matter of minutes at little or no cost. The downside of using this vehicle from a customer standpoint is that **spamming** by unscrupulous people and organizations has given e-mail advertisers in general a bad reputation.

Facsimile (Fax) Machine   A **facsimile (fax) machine** allows graphics and text messages to be transported as electronic signals via telephone lines or from a personal computer equipped with a modem. Information can be sent anywhere in the world in minutes, or a customer can make a call, key in a code number, and have information delivered to his or her fax machine or computer without ever speaking to a person (**fax-on-demand** system).

Internet Callback   An **Internet callback** system allows someone browsing the Internet to click on words or phrases (e.g., *Call me*), enter his or her phone number, and continue browsing. This triggers a predictive dialing system (discussed later in this chapter) and assigns an agent to handle the call when it rings at the customer's end.

Internet Telephony   **Internet telephony** allows users to have voice communications over the Internet. Although widely discussed in the industry, call center Internet telephony is in its infancy, lacks standards, and is not currently embraced by consumers. Power outages, quality issues with transmissions and other technical glitches have prevented this medium from becoming widely used by most organizations.

Interactive Voice Response (IVR) or Voice Response Unit (VRU)   An **interactive voice response (IVR) system** or a **voice response unit (VRU)** allows customers to call in 24 hours a day, 7 days a week, even when customer service representatives are not available. By keying in a series of numbers on the phone, customers can get information or answers to questions. Such systems perform a text-to-speech conversion to present database information audibly to a caller. They also ensure consistency of information. Banks and credit card companies use such systems to allow customers to access account information.

Media Blending   **Media blending** allows agents to communicate with a customer over a telephone line at the same time information is displayed over the Internet to the customer. As with Internet telephony, this technology has not yet been taken to its full potential.

Online Information Fulfillment System   An **online information fulfillment system** allows customers to go to the World Wide Web, access an organization's website, and click on desired information. This is one of the fastest-growing customer service technologies. Every competitive business will eventually use this system so that customers can get information and place orders.

Predictive Dialing System   A **predictive dialing system** automatically places outgoing calls and delivers incoming calls to the next available agent. This system is often used in outbound (telemarketing/call center) operations. Because of numerous abuses, the government is continually restricting its use.

Screen Pop-Ups   **Screen pop-ups** are used in conjunction with ANI and IVR systems to identify callers. As a call is received and dispatched to an agent, the system provides information about the caller that "pops" onto the agent's screen before he or she

---

electronic mail (e-mail)
System used to transmit messages around the Internet.

spamming or spam
An abusive use of various electronic messaging systems and technology to send unsolicited and indiscriminant bulk messages to people (also used with instant messaging, Web search engines, blogs, and other formats).

facsimile (fax) machine
Equipment that converts printed words and graphics into electronic signals and allows them to be transmitted across telephone lines then reassembled into a facsimile of the words and graphics on the receiving end.

fax on demand
Technology that allows information, such as a form, stored in a computer to be requested electronically via a telephone and transmitted to a customer.

Internet callback
Technology that allows someone browsing the Internet to key a prompt on a website and have a service representative call a phone number provided.

Internet telephony
Technology that allows people to talk to one another anywhere in the world via the Internet as if they were on a regular telephone and often at no cost.

interactive voice response (IVR) system
Technology that allows customers to call an organization 24 hours a day, 7 days a week to get information from recorded messages or a computer by keying a series of numbers on the telephone keypad in response to questions or prompts.

voice response unit (VRU)
System that allows customers to call 24 hours a day, 7 days a week by keying a series of numbers on the telephone keypad in order to get information or answers to questions.

media blending
Technology that allows a service provider to communicate with a customer via telephone while at the same time displaying information to the customer over the computer.

online information fulfillment system
Technology that allows a customer to access an organization's website and click on desired information without having to interact with a service provider.

predictive dialing system
Technology that automatically places outgoing calls and delivers incoming calls to the next available service representative in a call center.

screen pop-ups
Small screen images that are programmed to appear on someone's computer monitor when a website is accessed.

teletype systems (TTY)
A typewriter-type device used by people with hearing disabilities for typing messages back and forth via telephone lines. Also known as telephone device for the disabled (TDD).

answers the telephone (e.g., order information, membership data, service history, contact history).

Speech Recognition   Speech recognition programs allow a system to recognize keywords or phrases from a caller. These systems can be for routing callers to a representative and for retrieving information from a database. This technology is incorporated into a customer contact center's voice response system. It is typically used by individuals to dictate data directly into a computer, which then converts the spoken words into text. There are a variety of potential applications for voice-recognition systems for all contact centers. Some companies are recording customers' voices (passwords and phrases) as a means of identification so that customers can gain access to their accounts. With other applications, agents speak into a computer, instead of typing data, and people who have disabilities can obtain data from their accounts by speaking into the computer.

Teletype Systems (TTY)   Partly because of the passage of the 1990 Americans with Disabilities Act, which required that telecommunication services be available to people with disabilities, organizations now have the technology to assist customers who have hearing and speech impairments. By using a **teletype system (TTY)**—a typewriter-type device for sending messages back and forth over telephone lines—a person who has a hearing or speech impairment can contact someone who is using a standard telephone. The sender and the receiver type their messages using the TTY. To do this, the sender or receiver can go through an operator-assisted relay service provided by local and long-distance telephone companies to reach companies and individuals who do not have TTY receiving technology, or the user can get in touch directly with companies that have TTYs. The service is free of charge. Operators can help first-time hearing users understand the rules in using TTY. Also, local speech and hearing centers can often provide training on the use of TTY in a call center environment.

The federal government has a similar service (Federal Information Relay Service, or FIRS) for individuals who wish to conduct business with any branch of the federal government nationwide.

Video   For customers and customer contact centers equipped with video camera–computer hookups, this evolving technology allows customers and agents to interact via the computer. Like the interactive video kiosks discussed earlier in this book, this technology allows customers and agents to see one another during their interactions. Because of privacy concerns or preference, some software allows customers to block their image, yet they still see the agent to whom they are speaking.

ADVANTAGES AND DISADVANTAGES OF TECHNOLOGY

Like anything else related to customer service, technology offers advantages and disadvantages. The following sections briefly review some of the issues resulting from the use of technology.

Organizational Issues   Distinct advantages accrue to organizations that use technology. Through the use of computers, software, and various telecommunication devices, a company can extend its presence without physically establishing a business site and without adding staff. Simply by setting up a website, organizations can become known and develop a worldwide customer base while helping to equalize the playing field with larger competitors. This is because, on the Internet, visitors do not know how many employees or buildings and how much money an organization has when they view a website. Information and services can be provided on demand to customers. Often, many customers can be served simultaneously through the telephone, fax, and so on.

The challenge for organizations is to have well-maintained, state-of-the-art equipment and qualified, competent people to operate it. In a low-unemployment period, this can be a challenge and can possibly result in disgruntled customers who have to wait on hold for service until an agent is available to help them.

Staying on top of competition with technology is an expensive venture. New and upgraded software and hardware appear almost every day. If a company is using systems that are six months old, these systems are on their way to becoming obsolete. Also, new technology typically brings with it a need to train or retrain staff. The end result is that employees have to be taken away from their jobs for training.

Employee Issues   Technology brings many benefits to employees. The greatest benefit is that it frees them from mundane tasks such as taking information and mailing out forms, information, or other materials. These tasks can be done by using fax-on-demand, IVR, or online fulfillment systems. Technology also allows employees to serve more people in a shorter period of time—and to do it better.

The downside for employees is that many organizations see technology as a way to reduce staff costs and overhead related to employees, and they therefore eliminate positions. Moreover, as mentioned before, new technology requires new training and skills. Some people have difficulty using technology and are not able to master it. This in turn can lead to reassignment or dismissal. To avoid such negative outcomes, you and your peers should continually work to stay abreast of technology trends by checking the Internet or taking refresher courses through your organization's training department or local community resources.

Another problem created is an increase in stress levels of both employee and customer. This arises from the increased pace of business and daily life, from the need for employees to keep up to date with technology, and so on. Stress accounts for some of the high turnover rate in call center staff and for customer defection. But it doesn't necessarily have to be that way. For more information on dealing with stress and time more effectively in a service environment, visit www.mhhe.com/lucas09.

Customer Issues   From a customer standpoint, technology can be a blessing. From the comfort and convenience of a home, office, car, or anywhere a customer may have a telephone or laptop computer, he or she can access products and services. More people than ever have access to the Internet and computers. Some research estimates that almost 233 million people in North America and 1,173,109,925 people throughout the world use the Internet.[8] Technologies allow a customer to get information, order products, have questions about billing or other matters answered, and access virtually anything she or he wants on the World Wide Web.

However, this convenience comes with a cost to customers, just as it does for organizations. To have the latest gadgets is costly in terms of time and money. For example, when a customer calls an 800 or 888 support number, or must pay for a call to a support center, it is not unusual for the customer to wait on hold for the next available agent. Also, technology does not always work as it is designed to. For example, a website might not provide clear instructions about how to enter an account number or how to get a password. Even if a customer follows the instructions exactly, he or she might repeatedly get a frustrating error message instructing him or her to reenter the data. At some point, the customer will simply give up and go to another website. Another example would be to get caught in "voice mail jail." In this situation the customer follows the instructions, pressing the appropriate phone keys to get to a representative, only to find that the representative has forwarded his or her calls to another voice mailbox. Eventually the instructions lead the customer back to the first message or the customer is disconnected.

> **CUSTOMER SERVICE SUCCESS TIP**
>
> *Technology can aid service efficiency and reduce your stress levels if you learn to master and use it effectively. Take the time to read equipment manuals and clarify operational issues and questions before customers contact you.*

---

[8] World Internet Usage and Population Statistics (2007), Miniwatts Marketing Group, www.internetworldstats.com/stats.htm

Another major consumer issue related to telephone usage is that many organizations conduct direct marketing (telemarketing) and/or collections activities via the telephone. Unfortunately, many unscrupulous telemarketers pressure call recipients, illegally take advantage of them, and/or violate personal privacy. As a result many states and the federal government have passed laws dictating how business via the telephone can be done. If you are involved in this type of outbound calling, it is crucial that you and your organization adhere to laws prohibiting when you may call someone and how business can be conducted. Consumers can now apply to be on a national do-not-call list. Organizations and representatives who continue to call phone numbers that appear on this list, if they have not been given permission to do so by the consumer, can face stiff legal penalties.

Additional Issues   Just as with any system, there are people who will take advantage of it. Technology, especially the Internet, has spawned a new era of fraud and manipulation. This is a major concern for consumers and can create many challenges for you and your peers when you work in a call center. One of the biggest problems you must deal with is customers' fear of fraud and violation of privacy.

Informed customers go to great lengths to protect credit card, merchant account, and social security numbers, addresses, and personal data (e.g., arrest records, medical history, and family data). Many news stories have warned of criminal activity associated with technology. The result is that customers, especially those who are technically naive, have a level of distrust and paranoia related to giving information via the Internet. This is why many websites involved in e-commerce offer the option of calling an 800 number instead of entering credit card and other personal information into an Internet order form. If you, as a customer service provider, encounter a lot of this type of reluctance, notify your supervisor. Some systemic issues may be adding to your customers' fears. Helping identify these issues and dealing with them can make life easier for you and your customers while helping the organization improve the quality of service delivered.

One thing to remember is that a customer's reluctance to provide you with information is not necessarily a reflection on you or your service-providing peers; it is based more on a distrust in the system. Figure 9.3 lists some strategies you can use to help reduce customer fears related to communicating via technology.

3 TECHNOLOGY ETIQUETTE AND STRATEGIES

Concept: Using technology ethically and with correct etiquette is important.

As with any other interaction with people, you should be aware of some basic dos and don'ts related to using technology to interact with and serve your customers. Failure to observe some commonsense rules can cause loss of a customer.

E-MAIL

The e-mail system was designed as an inexpensive, quick way of communicating via the World Wide Web. E-mail was not originally intended to replace formal written correspondence, although many organizations now use it to send things like attached correspondence and receipts and to notify customers of order status, to gather additional information needed to serve a customer, and for other business-related issues. No matter what the function, e-mail has its own set of guidelines for effective usage to ensure that you do not

FIGURE 9.3

**Reducing Customer
Fears about Technology**

Avoiding customer concerns is often as simple as communicating effectively. Try some of the following approaches to help reassure your customers about the security of technology:

- Emphasize the organization's policy on security and service. If customers voice concerns about providing a credit card number over the phone, you might respond with "This is not a problem. You can either fax or mail the information to us."
- Stress participation in consumer watchdog or community organizations (e.g., Better Business Bureau or Chamber of Commerce).
- Ask for only pertinent information.
- Answer questions quickly and openly (e.g., if a customer asks why you need certain information, respond in terms of customer service, such as "We need that information to ensure that we credit the right account.").
- Inform customers of security devices that are in place to protect information (e.g., website software that encrypt personal information).
- Avoid asking for personal and account information when possible.
- Offer other options for data submission, if they are available.
- When using the telephone, smile and sound approachable in order to establish rapport (customers can "hear" a smile over the telephone).
- Listen carefully for voice tones that indicate hesitancy or uncertainty and respond appropriately (e.g., "You sound a bit hesitant about giving that information, Mr. Hopkins. Let me assure you that nothing will be processed until we have actually shipped your order.").
- Communicate in short, clear, and concise terms and sentences. Also, avoid technical or "legal" language that might confuse or frustrate the customer.
- Explain how personal information will be used or stored.

offend or otherwise create problems when dealing with customers via e-mail. Here are some e-mail tips to remember, as well as some etiquette for effective usage.

- *Use abbreviations and initials.* Since e-mail is an informal means of communicating, using acronyms and other short forms or abbreviations (e.g., USA versus United States of America) works fine in some cases. Just be sure that your receiver knows what the letters stand for; otherwise miscommunication could occur. Figure 9.4 lists some common abbreviations employed by e-mail users who typically know and e-mail one another frequently (e.g., internal customers, friends, and family members). When communicating with external customers, you may want to use abbreviations sparingly or avoid them altogether in order to prevent confusion, communication breakdown, and the perception that you are unprofessional.

- *Proofread and spell-check before sending a message.* Checking your message before sending an e-mail may help prevent damage to your

A recipient cannot always decipher your intended tone when reading an e-mail. *What are some things to keep in mind when composing professional e-mails to avoid unnecessary conflict and/or frustration?*

FIGURE 9.4

Common Abbreviations

LOL	Laugh out loud	ROTFL	Rolling on the floor laughing
BCNU	Be seeing you	TTFN	Ta ta for now
FYI	For your information	TTYL	Talk to you later
IMHO	In my humble opinion	BTW	By the way
FWIW	For what it's worth	ASAP	As soon as possible

professional image. This is especially true when writing customers, because you are representing your organization. Poor grammar, syntax, spelling, and usage can paint a poor picture of your abilities and professionalism and can leave a bad impression about your organization and its employees.

- *Think before writing.* This is especially important if you are answering an e-mail when you are upset or emotional. Take time to cool off before responding to a negative message (an insulting or provocative e-mail message is called a *flame*) or when you are angry. Remember that once you send an e-mail, you cannot take back your words. Your relationship with your receiver is at stake and the recipient can easily share your message with others (think about all the e-mailed messages you get regularly that have been forwarded to many other people and whose names appear in the text section of the e-mail). The latter is why you should never forward jokes, articles, or other materials that could be viewed as discriminatory or racist, or could cast a negative light on you and your organization. It is also why most companies do not allow personal use of their e-mail systems.

- *Use short, concise sentences.* The average person will not read lengthy messages sent by e-mail. Scrolling up and down pages of text is time-consuming and frustrating. Therefore, put your question or key idea in the first sentence or paragraph. Keep your sentences short and use new paragraphs often, for easier reading. A good rule of thumb is that if the entire message does not fit on a single viewing screen, consider whether another means of communication is more appropriate. An option would be to use the attachment feature so that lengthy documents can be printed out.

- *Use both upper- and lowercase letters.* With e-mail, writing a sentence or message in all-capital letters is like shouting at a person and could offend or cause relationship problems. In addition, reading a message written in all-capital letters is difficult and is likely to annoy your customer, whether or not he or she perceives it as "shouting."

- *Be careful with punctuation.* As with all-capital letters, you should use caution with punctuation marks, especially exclamation points, which can cause offense because, like all-capital letters, they indicate strong emotion.

- *Use e-mail only for informal correspondence.* Do not use e-mail when a more formal format is appropriate (see the additional information on Business Writers' Workshop at www.mhhe.com/lucas09). For example, it would be inappropriate to send a cancellation notice via e-mail. The receiver might think that the matter is not significant enough to warrant your organization's buying a stamp to mail a letter. However, this caution does not mean that you should not attach letters or other documents to an e-mail. Just consider the effect on the recipient. Another important thing to remember about e-mail is that it is sometimes unreliable. Many people do not check their e-mail regularly especially if they use free e-mail accounts offered by yahoo.com, google.com and other companies, computer systems fail, and individuals often change service providers without notifying you. If your message is critical and delivery is time-sensitive, choose another method (e.g., a telephone call or express mail).

  In some cases, e-mail that is not delivered is not returned to the sender, so you may not know why the recipient did not respond. If your computer system allows, you can also request a return receipt notification showing the time and date that a message was opened. The downside of that is that your receivers can cancel the return notification on their end and you will still not know if the message ever arrived.

- *Use organization e-mail for business only.* Many companies have policies prohibiting sending personal e-mail via their system. Some companies have started to actively monitor outgoing messages and many now can use unauthorized use of the e-mail as grounds for dismissal. Avoid violating your company's policy on this. Remember, too, that while you are sending personal messages, you are wasting productive time and your customers may be waiting.

Unless you have security software that will decode and mask the information, hackers or others who do not have a right or need to know such information can gain access to it. A good rule of thumb is to never send anything by e-mail that you would not want to see in tomorrow's newspaper.

- *Use blind courtesy copies sparingly.* Most e-mail systems allow you to send a copy to someone without the original addressee knowing it (a blind courtesy copy, or bcc). If the recipient becomes aware of the bcc, your actions might be viewed as suspicious, and your motives brought into question. A customer might view your actions as an attempt to hide something from him or her. Thus, a relationship breakdown could occur if the original recipient discovers the existence of the bcc or if the recipient of the bcc misuses the information.
- *Copy only necessary people.* Nowadays, most people are overloaded with work and do not have the time to read every e-mail. If someone does not need to see a message, do not send them a copy with the "reply to all" function available in e-mail programs.
- *Get permission to send advertisements or promotional materials.* As mentioned earlier, people have little time or patience to read lengthy e-mail messages, especially from someone trying to promote or sell them something. This is viewed the same way you probably think of unsolicited junk mail or telemarketing calls at home. Companies should routinely have an "opt-out" check box available when they are soliciting e-mail information from their customers. If your company does not have this option, it might be well for management to consider such an option as a service to their customers and potential customers.
- *Be cautious in using emoticons.* **Emoticons (emotional icons)** are the faces created through the use of computer keyboard characters. Many people believe that their use in business correspondence is inappropriate and too informal. Also, since humor is a matter of personal point of view, these symbols might be misinterpreted and confusing. This is especially true when you are corresponding with someone from a different culture. Figure 9.5 shows examples of emoticons.
- *Fill in your address line last.* This is a safety mechanism to ensure that you take the time to read and think about your message before you send the e-mail. The message cannot be transmitted until you address it. You will have one last chance to think about the effect of the message on the recipient.

emoticons (emotional icons)
Humorous characters that send visual messages such as smiling or frowning. They are created with various strokes of the computer keyboard characters and symbols.

FIGURE 9.5

Some Emoticons

:-)	Happy	:-}	Embarrassment or sarcasm
:-(	Sad	:-D	Big grin or laugh
;-)	Flirting or wink	<:-)	Stupid question (dunce cap)
0__ /\	Defiant or determined	0:-)	Angel or saint
:-O	Yelling or surprise	>:-)	Devil
:-x	Lips are sealed	:~/	Really confused

FACSIMILE

As with any other form of communication, there are certain dos and don'ts to abide by when you use a fax machine to transmit messages. Failing to adhere to these simple guidelines can cause frustration, anger, and a breakdown in the relationships between you and your customers or others to whom you send messages.

- *Be considerate of your receiver.* If you plan to send a multipage document to your customer, telephone in advance to make sure that it is OK and a good time to send it. This is especially true if you will be using a business number during the workday or if there is only one line for the telephone and fax machine. It is frustrating and irritating to customers when a fax is tied up because large documents are being transmitted. If you must send a large document, try to do so before or after working hours (i.e., before 9 A.M. or after 5 P.M.). Also, keep in mind geographic time differences. Following these tips can also help maintain good relationships with coworkers who may depend on the fax machine to conduct business with their customers.
- *Limit graphics.* Graphic images that are not needed to clarify written text waste the receiver's printer cartridge ink, tie up the machine unduly, and can irritate your receiver. Therefore, delete any unnecessary graphics (or solid colored areas) including your corporate logo on a cover sheet if it is heavily colored and requires a lot of ink to print. (If appropriate, create a special outline image of your logo for your fax cover sheets.)
- *Limit correspondence recipients.* As with e-mail and memorandums, limit the recipients of your messages. If they do not have a need to know, do not send them messages. Check your broadcast mailing list (a list of people who will receive all messages, often programmed into a computer) to ensure that it is limited to people who "have a need to know." This is also important from the standpoint of confidentiality. If the information you are sending is proprietary or sensitive in any way, think about who will receive it. Do not forget that unless the document is going directly to someone's computer fax modem, it may be lying in a stack of other incoming messages and accessible by people other than your intended recipient.

4   THE TELEPHONE IN CUSTOMER SERVICE

Concept: The telephone is the second most important link in customer service.

Not all service via technology, and specifically the telephone, is delivered from a customer contact center. Although many small- and medium-size organizations may have dedicated customer service professionals to staff their telephones, others do not. In the latter cases, the responsibility for answering the telephone and providing service falls on anyone who is available and hears the telephone ring (e.g., administrative assistant, salesperson, driver, nurse, partner, owner, CEO).

Modern businesses rely heavily on the use of telephones to conduct day-to-day operations and communicate with internal as well as external customers. Effective use of the telephone saves employee time and effort. Employees no longer have to take time to physically travel to another location to interact with customers and vendors. By simply dialing a telephone number or typing in a text message on a cell phone, you are almost instantaneously transported anywhere in the world. And with the use of the fax and computer modem, documents and information can also be sent in minutes to someone thousands of miles away—even during nonbusiness hours. Figure 9.6 lists some advantages of telephone customer service.

FIGURE 9.6

Advantages of Telephone Customer Service

Even though there are some disadvantages to telephone communication (for example, lack of face-to-face contact with the customer), there are many advantages. Some of the advantages are discussed in the following sections.

- *Convenience.* Sales, information exchange, money collection, customer satisfaction surveys, and complaint handling are only a few of the many tasks that can be effectively handled by using the telephone and related equipment. If a quick answer is needed, the telephone can provide it without the need to travel and meet with someone face to face or to endure the delays caused by the mail.
- *Ease of communication.* Although some countries have more advanced telephone systems and capabilities than others, you can call someone in nearly any country in the world. And, with advances in cellular phone technology, even mobile phones have international communication capability.
- *Economy.* Face-to-face visits or sales calls are expensive and can be reduced or eliminated by making contacts over the telephone as opposed to traveling to a customer's location. With competitive rates offered by many telephone companies since the deregulation of the telecommunication industry years ago, companies and customers have many options for calling plans. For example, customers can purchase a calling card and use it from any telephone. All of this makes accessing customer services a simple and relatively inexpensive task, especially when combined with the other technology discussed in this chapter.
- *Efficiency.* You and your customer can interact without being delayed by writing and responding. Telephone usage is so simple that it is taught to kindergarten and grade school children.

With these tools, more businesses are setting up inbound (e.g., order taking, customer service, information sources) and outbound (e.g., telemarketing sales, customer service, customer surveys) telephone staffs. Through these groups of trained specialists, companies can expand their customer contact and be more likely to accomplish total customer satisfaction.

COMMUNICATION SKILLS FOR SUCCESS

In Chapters 3 to 5, you read about the skills you need in face-to-face customer service. The same skills apply to providing effective customer service over the telephone, especially the use of vocal quality and listening skills. Your customer cannot communicate with or understand you if she or he doesn't accurately receive your message. To reduce the chances of message failure, think about the communication techniques discussed below.

- *Speak clearly.* By pronouncing words clearly and correctly, you increase the chances that your customer will accurately receive your intended message. Failure to use good diction could decrease a customer's comprehension of your message and be interpreted as a sign that you are lazy, unprofessional, or lack intelligence and/or education. If you are unsure how to improve your diction, review Chapter 3.
- *Limit jargon, slang, and colloquialisms.* Technical jargon (terms related to technology, an industry, a specific organization, or a job), slang (informal words used to make a message more colorful; e.g., *whoopee, blooper, groovy*), and colloquialisms (regional phrases or words such as, "fair to middling," "if the good Lord's willing and the creek don't rise," or "faster than a New York minute") can distort your message and detract from your ability to communicate effectively. This is especially true

Never underestimate the importance of smiling when you speak to customers. They really can hear it in your voice!

when your recipient speaks English as a second language (see Chapter 8 for more information on this topic). By using words or phrases unfamiliar to the customer, you draw the customer's attention away from listening to your message. This is because, when people encounter a word or phrase that is unfamiliar, they tend to stop and reflect on that word or phrase. When this occurs, the next part of the message is missed while the mind tries to focus on and decipher the unfamiliar element it encountered. You must then repeat the missed portion or end up with a miscommunication.

- *Adjust your volume.* As your conversation progresses, it may become apparent that you need to speak more loudly or more softly to your customer. Obvious cues are statements from the customer, such as, "You don't have to yell" or "Could you speak up?" Or if your customer is speaking really loudly, he or she may have a hearing impairment. To find out if this is the case, you could say, "I'm sorry, Mrs. Reynolds, are you able to hear me clearly? I'm having trouble with loud volume on my end."

- *Speak at a rate that allows comprehension.* Depending on the person to whom you are speaking, you may find yourself having to adjust your rate of speech (covered in Chapter 3) by either speeding up or slowing down. A good rule of thumb is to mirror or match the other person's rate of speech to some extent, since he or she is probably comfortable with it. Otherwise you risk boring the customer by speaking too slowly, or confusing the customer by speaking too rapidly. Be careful not to be too obvious or unnatural when doing this; otherwise, some customers may think that you're making fun of them.

- *Use voice inflection.* By using inflection and avoiding a tendency to speak in a monotone, you can help communicate your message in an interesting manner that will hold your customer's attention. The result might be saved time, since your message may be received correctly the first time and you will not have to repeat it.

- *Use correct grammar.* Just as important as enunciation, good grammar helps project a positive, competent image. When you fail to use good grammar in your communication, you may be perceived as lazy or uneducated. Keep in mind that your customer forms an image of you and the company you represent simply by listening to you and the way you speak. (Grammar is covered in more detail under Business Writers' Workshop at www.mhhe.com/lucas09).

- *Pause occasionally.* This simple yet dramatic technique can sometimes affect the course of a conversation. By pausing after you make a statement or ask a question, you give yourself time to breathe and think. You also give your customer an opportunity to reflect on what you have said or to ask questions. This practice can greatly aid in reducing tension when you are speaking with an upset customer or one who does not speak your language fluently.

- *Smile as you speak.* By smiling, you project an upbeat, warm, and sincere attitude through the phone. This can often cheer the customer, diffuse irritation, and help build rapport. A technique some telephone professionals use to remind themselves to smile when placing or answering a call is to put a small mirror or a picture of a "smiling face" in front of them or next to their telephone. This reminds them to smile as they talk.

- *Project a positive image and attitude.* All the tips related to using your voice that were presented in earlier chapters contribute to how people envision you. Customers generally do not want to hear what you cannot do for them or about the bad day you're having. They want a timely, affirmative answer to their questions or solution of their problems. Giving anything less is likely to discourage or annoy them and result in a service breakdown.

- *Wait to speak.* Many people tend to interrupt a customer to add information or ask a question. As you read in Chapter 5, this is not only rude but can cause a breakdown in communication and possibly anger the customer. If you ask a question or if the customer is speaking, allow him or her to respond or to finish speaking before interjecting your thoughts or comments.
- *Listen actively.* Just as with face-to-face communication, effective listening is a crucial telephone skill for the customer service provider. The need to focus is even more important when you are speaking on the phone, since you do not have nonverbal cues or visual contact to help in message delivery or interpretation. Information on active listening was covered in Chapter 5.

TIPS FOR CREATING A POSITIVE TELEPHONE IMAGE

People form an opinion of you and your organization quickly. The message they receive often determines how they interact with you during the conversation and in your future relationship. Keep in mind that when you answer your organization's telephone, or call someone else as part of your job, you represent yourself and the organization. Since many telephone calls are short, you have limited opportunity to make a positive impression.

When you feel good about yourself, you normally project a naturally confident and pleasant image. On days when things aren't going so well for you, your self-image may tend to suffer. Here are some suggestions to help serve your customers effectively and leave them thinking well of you and your organization.

- *Continually evaluate yourself.* You are your own best critic. From time to time, think about your conversation—what went well, what could have been improved. If possible, occasionally tape-record your conversations and evaluate your voice qualities and message delivery. Have someone else listen to the tape and provide objective feedback. To help in your self-assessment, you may want to make copies of Worksheet 9.1 (see www.mhhe.com/lucas09) and evaluate all your calls for a specific period of time (for example, a couple of hours or a day).
- *Use proper body posture.* The following can negatively affect the sound and quality of your voice:

  Slouching in your chair.

  Sitting with your feet on a desk with your arms behind your head as you rock back and forth in your chair.

  Looking down, with your chin on your chest, to read or search through drawers.

  Resting the telephone handset between your cheek and shoulder as you do other work (e.g., type data into a computer, look for something, write, or doodle).

  Strive to sit or stand upright and speak clearly into the mouthpiece whether you are using a headset or handheld receiver. If you are using a handheld receiver, make sure that the earpiece is placed firmly against your ear and the mouthpiece is directly in front of your mouth.
- *Be prepared.* Answer a ringing phone promptly and use a standard greeting as outlined later in this chapter.
- *Speak naturally.* Whether you are calling someone or providing information to a caller, speak in a conversational voice. Don't use a "canned" or mechanical presentation, and don't read from a prepared script, unless you are required to do so by your company. If

ethical dilemma 9.1

You are on your break in the break room and can hear the telephone ringing on an administrative assistant's desk. You know that the temp who is filling in for the administrative assistant just went to take an important document to the Executive Office. Your CEO does not like voicemail and will not allow it to be used during working hours.

1. What would you do in this situation, if anything? Explain.
1. From a procedural standpoint, what should the administrative assistant have done in this situation? Explain.

you must read from a script, *practice, practice, practice.* Before you connect with a customer, become very comfortable with your presentation so that you can deliver it in a fluid, warm, and sincere manner. Nothing sends a more negative message than a service provider who mispronounces a customer's name, stumbles through opening comments, and seems disorganized.

- *Be time-conscious.* Customers appreciate prompt, courteous service. Be aware that time is money—yours, your organization's, and the customer's. Have your thoughts organized when you call a customer. It is a good idea to have a list of questions or key points ready before calling (see Worksheet 9.2 at www.mhhe.com/lucas09 as an example). If a customer calls you and you don't have an answer or information readily available, offer to do some research and call back instead of putting the customer on hold. Respect your customer's time. Chances are that customers will prefer to hold if they will be waiting only a short time, but give them the option. In addition to helping better organize your calls, a written call-planning sheet will provide a good record of the call.

- *Be proactive with service.* If you must say no to a customer, do so in a positive manner without quoting policy. Tell the customer what you can do. For example, if your policy prohibits refunds on one-of-a-kind or closeout items, you might make an offer such as this (depending on your level of authority or empowerment):

    "Mr. Targowski, I see that the computer you ordered from our website was a closeout item. I understand that you have decided that you need more RAM. Although I cannot give refunds on a closeout item, I can give you a voucher good at any of our retail locations for a $50 discount on a memory chip upgrade or free installation, whichever you prefer."

- Doing more than the customer expects after a breakdown (this is called *service recovery* and is discussed in Chapter 7) is important, especially if you or your company made an error. When you or your company is not responsible for the error, but you want to maintain a positive customer-provider relationship, going out of your way to help make it better is just good business practice.

- *Conclude calls professionally.* Ending a call on an upbeat note, using the caller's name, and summarizing key actions to be taken by both parties are all recommended practices. For example, you might say, "All right, Ms. Herrick, let me confirm what we've discussed. I'll get _____ by the 23rd, and call you to confirm _____ . You'll take care of _____ . Is that correct?" Once agreement has been reached, thank the customer for calling, ask what other questions he or she has or what else you can assist with, and then let the customer hang up first. By following this type of format, you can reduce misunderstandings and elicit any last-minute questions or comments the customer might have. If you fail to bring the conversation to a formal close and hang up abruptly, the customer may feel you are in a hurry to finish servicing him or her (regardless of the fact that you have just spent 15 minutes talking with him or her!). Think of this final step as wrapping a gift: it looks fine, but adding a nice ribbon and bow makes it look even better. The thank-you and polite sign off are your ribbon and bow.

EFFECTIVE TELEPHONE USAGE

One basic strategy for successfully providing effective customer service over the telephone is to thoroughly understand all phone features and use them effectively. This may seem to be a logical and simple concept, but think about times when you called a company and someone attempted to transfer you, or put you on hold, or did not communicate clearly. If the transfer was successful, you were lucky (Figure 9.7 gives tips for effectively using the

FIGURE 9.7

Transfer Calls and Use the Hold Function Properly

Be sure you understand how the telephone transfer (sometimes called the *link*) and hold functions work. Nothing is more frustrating or irritating for callers than to be shuffled from one person to the next or to be placed on what seems to be an endless hold. Here are some suggestions that can help to increase your effectiveness in these areas:

Always request permission before transferring a caller. This shows respect for the caller and psychologically gives the caller a feeling of control over the conversation. You can also offer options (you can ask the caller to allow a transfer or let you take a message). This is especially helpful when the customer is already irritated or has a problem. Before transferring the call, explain why you need to do so. You might say, "The person who handles billing questions is Shashandra Philips at extension 4739. May I transfer you, or would you rather I take a message and pass it along to her?" This saves you and the caller time and effort, and you have provided professional, courteous service. If the caller says, "Yes, please transfer me," follow by saying something like, "I'd be happy to connect you. Again, if you are accidentally disconnected, I'll be calling Shashandra Philips at extension 4739."

Once you have successfully reached the intended person, announce the call by saying, "Shashandra, this is (your name), from (your department). I have (customer's name) on the phone. She has a (question, problem). Are you the right person to handle that?" If Shashandra answers yes, connect the caller and announce, "(Customer's name), I have Shashandra Philips on the line. She will be happy to assist you. Thanks for calling (or some similar positive disconnect phrase)." You can then hang up, knowing that you did your part in delivering quality customer service.

If the call taker is not available or is not the appropriate person, reconnect with the customer and explain the situation. Then offer to take a message rather than trying to transfer to different people while keeping the customer on hold. You would make an exception if the call taker informed you of the appropriate person to whom you should transfer, or if the customer insisted on staying on the line while you tried to transfer to the right person.

You should avoid making a blind transfer. This practice is ineffective, rude, and not customer-focused. A **blind transfer** happens when a service provider asks a caller, "May I transfer you to Cathy in Billing?" or may even say, without permission, "Let me transfer you to Tom in Shipping." Once the intended transfer party answers, the person transferring the call hangs up. Always announce your caller by waiting for the phone to be picked up and saying, "This is (your name) in (your department). I have (customer's name) on the line. Can you take the call?" Failure to do this could result in a confrontation between the two people. If the calling customer is already upset, you have just set up a situation that could lead to a lost customer and/or angry coworker.

If you place someone on hold, it is a good idea to go back on the line every 20 to 30 seconds to let the person know that you have not forgotten the call. This action becomes more important if the phone system you are using does not offer information or music that the customer hears during the holding time.

One final word about holds. Once you return to the phone to take the call, thank the caller for waiting.

blind transfer
The practice of transferring an incoming caller to another telephone number and hanging up once someone answers without announcing who is calling.

hold and transfer features). If not, you probably couldn't understand what happened, got disconnected, were connected to the wrong party, or heard the original person come back on the telephone to apologize and say something like, "The call didn't go through. Let me try again." Sound familiar? If so, use the following strategies to ensure that you do not deliver similar poor service.

• *Eliminate distractions.* Don't eat food, chew gum, drink, talk to others, read (unless for the purpose of providing the customer with information), or handle other office tasks (filing, stapling, stamping, sealing envelopes, etc.) while on the phone. Your voice quality will alert the customer to the fact that you are otherwise occupied.

- *Answer promptly.* A lot is communicated by the way a phone call is handled. One tip for success is to always answer by the third or fourth ring. This sends a nonverbal message to your customers of your availability to serve them. It also reduces the irritating ringing that you, coworkers, or customers have to hear.

- *Use titles with names.* It has been said that there is nothing sweeter than hearing one's own name. However, until you are told otherwise, use a person's title (e.g., Mr., Mrs., Ms., or Dr.) and last name. Do not assume that it is all right to use first names. Some people regard the use of their first name as insolent or rude. This may especially be true of older customers and people from other cultures where respect and use of titles are valued. When you are speaking with customers, it is also a good idea to use their name frequently (don't overdo it, though, or you'll sound mechanical). Repeat the name directly after the greeting (e.g., "Yes, Dr. Carmine, how may I help you?"), during the conversation (e.g., "One idea I have, Mr. Perrier, is to . . ."), and at the end of the call (e.g., "Thanks for calling, Mrs. Needham. I'll get that information right out to you. Is there anything else I can do to assist you today?").

- *Ask questions.* You read about the use of questions earlier in the book. Use them on the telephone to get information or clarify points made by the customer. Ask open-end questions; then listen to the response carefully. To clarify or verify information, use closed-end questions.

- *Use speakerphones with caution.* Speakerphones make sense for people who have certain disabilities and in some environments (where you need free hands or are doing something else while you are on hold or are waiting for a phone to be answered). From a customer service standpoint, they can send a cold or impersonal message, and their use should be minimal. Many callers do not like them and even think that speakerphone users are rude. Also, depending on the equipment used and how far you are from the telephone, the message received by your customer could be distorted, or it might seem as though you are in an echo chamber. Before using a speakerphone, ask yourself whether there is a valid reason for not using a headset or handheld phone.

  When you are using a speakerphone, make sure that your conversation will not be overheard if you are discussing personal, proprietary, or confidential information. Also, if someone is listening in on the customer's conversation, make sure that you inform the customer of that fact and explain who the listener is and why he or she is listening. As you read earlier, some people are very protective of their privacy and their feelings should be respected.

- *Use call waiting.* A useful feature offered by many phone systems is call waiting. While you are on the phone, a signal (usually a beep) indicates that there is an incoming call. When you hear the signal, you have a couple of options: Excuse yourself from your current call, by getting permission to place the person on hold, or ignore the second caller. If you have a voice mail system, the system makes the choice for you by transferring incoming calls to your message system. Both options have advantages and disadvantages.

  By taking the second call, you may irritate your current caller, who might hang up. This results in lost business. On the other hand, by not taking the second call, you might miss an important message and/or irritate that caller.

  By ignoring the signal, you might offend the second caller. Research indicates that many customers forget to or decide against placing later calls to busy numbers, especially if they have already made several attempts. Customers may feel that you're too busy to properly serve them.

So, how do you handle the dilemma? Make a judgment about how the customer to whom you are speaking might react and then act accordingly. In some instances, company policies tell you what to do, so you don't have to decide.

VOICE MAIL AND ANSWERING MACHINES OR SERVICES

Although voice mail is hailed by many people as a time-saver and vehicle for delivering messages when an intended recipient is unavailable, many other people have difficulty dealing with this technology (including answering machines) or simply refuse to interact with a machine. Let's take a look at some ways to use voice mail.

• *Managing incoming calls.* To effectively use voice mail, you must first understand how your system works. Check the manuals delivered with your system or speak with your supervisor and/or the technical expert responsible for its maintenance.

A key to using voice mail effectively is to keep your outgoing message current, indicating your availability, the type of information the caller should leave, and when the caller can expect a return call. If your system allows the caller the option of accessing an operator or another person, you should indicate this early in your outgoing message to save the caller from having to listen to unnecessary information. Figure 9.8 provides a sample outgoing message. Also, Work It Out 9.1 can be used to evaluate the voice mail messages of others when you call them. Another key to effective voice mail usage is to retrieve your calls and return them as soon as possible. Usually 24 hours, or by the next working day, is a good guideline for returning calls. Doing so sends a positive customer service message.

• *Placing calls to voice mail.* Many normally articulate people cannot speak coherently when they encounter an answering machine or voice mail. One technique for success is to plan your call before picking up the phone. Have a 30-second or less "sales" presentation in mind that you can deliver whether you get a person or machine. For example, if you get a person, try, "This is (your first and last name) from (company) calling (or returning a call) for Wilhelm Tackes. Is he available?" Also, have available a written list of the key points you want to discuss so you don't forget them as you talk.

If you get a machine, try "This is (first and last name) from (company) calling (returning a call) for Inez Montoya. My number is _____. I will be available from _____ to _____." If you are calling to get or give information, you may

FIGURE 9.8

Sample Outgoing Message

• "Hello. This is (your name) of (company and department).
• I'm unavailable to take your call at the moment, but if you leave your name, number, and a brief message, I'll call you as soon as possible.
• Thanks for calling."

If you know when you will be returning calls (e.g., at the end of the workday), tell the caller so. If your voice mail system offers callers the option to press a number to speak with someone else, let them know this right after you tell them whose voice mail they have reached. This avoids requiring them to listen to a lengthy message before they can select an option.

Evaluating Voice Mail

To HELP INCREASE YOUR AWARENESS OF THE EFFECT OF VOICE MAIL MESSAGES, MAKE NOTE OF THE FOLLOWING QUESTIONS DURING THE COMING WEEK. As you call people or organizations, consider the outgoing messages that they leave on their voice mail or answering machines and evaluate them, using the following questions.

1. Was the call answered by the fourth ring?
2. Did the announcement contain the following:

   Greeting (hello, good morning, or good afternoon)

   Organization's name

Departmental name

A statement of when the person will return

An early announcement of an option to press a number for assistance

Instructions for leaving a message

When calls will be returned

want to add, "The reason I am calling is to _____." This allows the return caller to leave information on your voice mail or with someone else and thus avoid the game of telephone tag.

- *Avoiding telephone tag.* You have probably played telephone tag. The game starts when the intended call receiver is not available and a message is left. The game continues when the call is returned, the original caller is not available, a return message is left, and so on.

     Telephone tag is frustrating and a waste of valuable time. It results in a loss of efficiency, money, and in some cases, customers. To avoid telephone tag, plan your calls and make your messages effective by giving your name, company name, phone number, time and date of your call, and a succinct message, and by indicating when you can be reached. If appropriate, emphasize that it is all right to leave the information you have requested on your voice mail or with someone else. Also, you may suggest that your message recipient tell you a time when you can call or meet with him or her face-to-face. By doing this, you end the game and get what you need. Use Worksheet 9-3 (see www.mhhe.com/lucas09) to help plan your calls effectively.

TAKING MESSAGES PROFESSIONALLY

If you have ever received an incomplete or undecipherable telephone message, you can appreciate the need for practice in this area. At a minimum, when you take a message you should get the following information from the caller:

Name (correctly spelled-ask caller for spelling)

Company name

Phone number (with area code and country code, if appropriate)

Brief message

When call should be returned

Time and date of the call and your name (in case a question about the message arises)

If you are answering someone's phone while he or she is away, let the caller know right away. This can be done by using a statement such as, "Hello, (person's name) line. This is (your name). How may I assist you?" In addition, be cautious of statements you make

FIGURE 9.9

**Communicating
Messages**

Message	Possible Interpretation	Alternative
"I'm not sure where he is" or "He's out roaming around the building somewhere."	"Don't they have any control or structure at this company?"	"He's not available. May I take a message?"
"I'm sorry. She is *still* at lunch."	(Depending on the time of the call.) "Must be nice to have two-hour lunch breaks!"	Same as above or "I'm sorry, She is at lunch or is unavailable. May I assist you or take a message?"
"We *should* have that problem taken care of soon."	"Don't you know for sure?"	"I apologize for the inconvenience. We'll attempt to resolve this by _____."
"He isn't available right now. He's taking care of a crisis."	"Is there a problem there?"	"He isn't available right now. May I assist you or take a message?"
"She's not in today. I'm not sure when she'll be back."	Same as above.	"She's not in today. May I assist you or take a message?"
"He left early today."	"Obviously, you people are not very customer-focused or he would be there during normal business hours to assist me."	"He is out of the office. May I assist you or take a message?"
"I don't know where she is. I was just walking by and heard the phone ringing."	"Nice that you're so conscientious. Too bad others are not."	"She isn't available right now, but I'd be happy to take a message."
"I'll give him the message and try to get him to call you back."	"So there's a 50-50 chance I'll be served."	"I'll give him the message when he returns and ask him to call you back."
"Hang on a second while I find something to take a message with."	"Doesn't sound as if people at this company are very prepared to serve customers."	"Would you mind holding while I get a pen and paper?"

regarding the intended recipient's availability. Sometimes, well-meant comments can send a negative message to customers. See Figure 9.9 for typical problem messages and better alternatives.

GENERAL ADVICE FOR COMMUNICATING BY TELEPHONE

Don't communicate personal information (someone is at the doctor's, on sick leave, etc.), belittle yourself (e.g. "I don't know", "I'm only . . .") or the company (e.g. "Nobody knows"), or use weak or negative language (i.e., "I think," "I can't"). Instead, simply state "Malik is unavailable. May I take a message?" or if appropriate, "I'd be happy to assist you." After you have taken the message, thank the caller before hanging up and then deliver the message to the intended receiver in a timely manner. If you discover that the receiver will not be available within a 24-hour period, you may want to call the customer and convey this information. If you do so, again offer to assist or suggest some other alternative, if one is available.

SUMMARY

Delivering customer service via technology can be an effective and efficient approach to use to achieve total customer satisfaction. However, you must continually upgrade your personal technology knowledge and skills, practice their application, and consciously evaluate the approach and techniques you use to provide service.

In the quality-oriented cultures now developing in the United States and in many other countries, service will make the difference between survival and failure for individuals and organizations. You are the front line, and you are often the first and only contact a customer will have with your company. Strive to use technology to its fullest potential, but do not forget that you and your peers ultimately determine whether expectations are met in the eyes of your customer.

KEY TERMS

automated attendants 223
automatic call distribution (ACD) system 223
automatic number identification (ANI) system 223
blind transfer 237
computer telephony integration (CIT) 223
customer contact center 221
electronic mail (e-mail) 225
emoticons (emotional icons) 231
facsimile (fax) machine 225
fax on demand 225
fee-based 900 numbers 222
help desk 222

interactive voice response (IVR) system 225
Internet callback 225
Internet telephony 225
iPod 224
media blending 225
offshoring 221
online information fulfillment system 226
predictive dialing system 226
screen pop-ups 226
spamming or spam 225
teletype system (TTY) 226
voice response unit (VRU) 225

REVIEW QUESTIONS

1 In what ways can technology play a role in the delivery of effective customer service? Explain.

2 What are some advantages of using technology for service delivery?

3 What are some disadvantages of using technology for service delivery?

4 What are some of the communication skills for success?

5 How can you project a more positive image over the telephone?

6 What information should you always get when taking telephone messages?

7 When transferring calls, what should you avoid and why?

8 When you leave a message on voice mail, what information should you give?

9 What is telephone tag, and how can it be avoided or reduced?

SEARCH IT OUT

Search the Internet for Customer Service Technology

1 Log onto the Internet and search for sites that deal with customer service and the technology used to deliver quality customer service. Also, look for the websites and organizations that focus on the technology and people involved in the delivery of customer service.

2 Log onto the Internet to search for books and other publications that focus on customer service and technology. Develop a bibliographic listing of at least seven to ten publications, make copies of the list, and share it with your classmates.

Practice Customer Service with Your Team Members

Get together in teams of three members each. One person will take the role of a customer service provider, one will be a customer, and one will be the observer. Use the following scenarios to practice the skills you have learned in this chapter. Incorporate other communication skills covered in previous chapters as you deal with your "customer." Use three of the four scenarios so that each person in a group has a chance to play each of the three roles. Depending on the scenario, you might use copies of Worksheet 9-2 (see www.mhhe.com/lucas09) to plan your call.

Scenario 1:

You are a customer service representative in a customer contact center that provides service to customers who have purchased small appliances from your company. A customer is calling to complain that she purchased a waffle iron from one of your outlet stores two weeks ago and it no longer works. She is upset because her in-laws and family are arriving in two days for an extended visit and they love her "special" waffles.

Scenario 2:

You are a customer care specialist for a company that provides answers to travel-related questions for a national membership warehouse retail store. A customer calls to find out about the types of travel-related discounts for which he qualifies through his membership.

Scenario 3:

You are a telemarketing sales representative for a company that sells water filtration systems. You are calling current customers who purchased a filtration system seven to ten years ago to inform them of your new Oasis line of filters, which is better than any other system on the market. You can offer them:

A 30-day money-back guarantee.

Billing by all major credit cards or invoice.

A one-year limited warranty on the system that replaces all defective parts but does not cover labor.

If they find a less expensive offer for the same product, a refund for the difference and an additional 50 percent of the difference.

Scenario 4:

This scenario has two parts. In Part 1, you are a mechanic in an automotive repair shop. You answer a phone call from an irate customer calling to complain about what he perceives is an inflated billing charge for a recent air-conditioner repair. He is asking for your manager, who is at lunch and won't be back for 45 minutes. You take the incoming call, using the message-taking format covered in this chapter. In Part 2, you are the manager. You have just returned from lunch and find a message from the irate customer described in Part 1 and must call the customer. Use Worksheet 9.3 (see www.mhhe.com/lucas09) to plan your return call based on the message you received.

Telephone Techniques at Staff-Temps

Background

Staff-Temps International is a temporary employment agency based in Chicago, Illinois. It has six full-time and three part-time employment counselors. The office is part of a national chain owned by Yamaguchi Enterprises Ltd., headquartered in Tokyo. The chain annually places over 100,000 temporary employees in a variety of businesses and offices.

Most of Staff-Temps' contacts are made by telephone; therefore, greater emphasis is placed on selecting and training employees who have a good phone presence. Each employee is required to meet certain standards of quality in dealing with customers on the telephone. To ensure that these standards are applied uniformly, an outside quality control company (Morrison and Lewis) is used to make "phantom calls" to staff members. In these calls, Morrison and Lewis staff pretend to be potential clients seeking information. Employee-customer calls are also randomly taped. Through the calls and tapes, levels of customer service are measured.

Your role

Your name is Chris Walker. As an employment counselor with Staff-Temps, you are aware of the customer service standards, which include the following:

Answer a ringing telephone within three rings.

Smile as you speak.

Use a standard salutation (good morning, afternoon, or evening).

Give your name and the name of your department and company.

Offer to assist the customer ("How may I assist you?").

On the way back to the office after lunch, you were involved in a minor automobile accident. Even though it was not your fault, you are concerned that your insurance may be canceled since you had another accident and got a speeding ticket earlier this year. Because of the accident, you were an hour late in returning from lunch. Upon your arrival, the receptionist handed you six messages from vendors and customers. Two of the messages were from Aretha Washington, human resources director for an electronics manufacturing firm that has been a good client for over two years. The two of you had spoken earlier in the day.

As you walked into your office, the telephone started to ring. By the time you took your coat off and got to your desk, the phone had rung five or six times.

When you answered, you heard Aretha's voice on the line. Her tone told you that she was upset. This was the conversation:

You: "Staff-Temps. Chris speaking."

Aretha: "Chris, what's going on? You told me when I called first thing this morning that you would find out why my temp didn't show up today and would call me back. I've left messages all day and haven't heard a thing! We've got a major deadline to meet for a very important client, and I can't get the work done. My boss has been in here every half hour checking on this. What is going on?"

You: Aretha, I'm sorry. I just got in from lunch and haven't been able to get back to you."

Aretha: "Just got back from lunch! It's after 2:30! It must be nice to have the luxury of a long lunch break. I didn't even get to eat lunch today!"

You: "Listen, Aretha, I couldn't help . . ." Obviously anxious and raising your voice.

Aretha: "Don't you 'listen' me. I'm the customer, and if you can't handle my needs, I know someone else who can. If I don't hear from you within the next half hour, I don't ever want to hear from you again! Goodbye!" [Slamming receiver down.]

Critical Thinking Questions

1 How well was this customer call handled? Explain.

2 What should you have done differently?

3 Do you believe that Aretha was justified in how she treated you? Explain.

4 How do personal problems or priorities sometimes affect customer service?

To get a better idea of how well your own organization uses technology to serve customers, use the following checklist to ensure that you and the organization are delivering the best possible service to customers, using technology effectively, and sending a positive image to others.

Call your own organizational (office) telephone number to determine:

- How many times the telephone rings before being routed to another person or voice mail. (Four rings should be the maximum unless your organization has another standard.)

- If the "O" (operator) option is chosen, does the call go to a live person at another number? In other words, do you have service coverage when you are away from your telephone?

If you choose the voice mail option, is your outgoing message:

- Upbeat and friendly?

- Concise?

- In compliance with organizational guidelines for voice messages? If no standards exist, does your message comply with the suggested message format in this chapter?

E-mail yourself to determine:

- If the message is delivered properly to your mailbox.

- If your "out of office" message is sent automatically (assuming that you have this option on your system and have activated it). For example, a response might be generated that tells correspondents that "I'll be out of the office from (date) until (date) but I will be checking my e-mail during that period and will respond as soon as possible."

Examine your fax cover sheets (if used) to ensure that excessive information and graphics (e.g., bulky logos or icons) have been removed and that your name and phone number are provided.

TECHNOLOGY-eBay Inc.

1 From your personal experiences, what you read at the beginning of the chapter, and what you found on eBay's website, what do you feel are the strengths of the company from a customer perspective? Explain.

2 What factors in society do you feel have allowed eBay to attain such phenomenal growth and have such an impact on the Internet environment in a relatively short time period? Explain the relationship of these factors to eBay's growth.

3 What do you think are eBay's future opportunities for growth related to customer service? Explain.

4 As a consumer, are you a fan of eBay and what it has accomplished? Why or why not?

QUICK PREVIEW ANSWERS

1	T	6	T	11	F
2	F	7	T	12	T
3	T	8	T	13	T
4	F	9	F	14	T
5	T	10	T		

Ethical Dilemma 9.1

1   What would you do in this situation, if anything? Explain.

Whether there was a temporary employee filling in or not should not matter. Anyone calling in should be professionally greeted and the call handled effectively, as outlined In this chapter. You or someone should make an effort to answer the telephone and if necessary, take a message and make sure that the administrative assistant's replacement gets it when she returns to her desk. Remember that customers do not care and should not have to deal with internal issues or policies. They should be able to expect fast, effective, and efficient service. Otherwise, they may take their business elsewhere.

2   From a procedural standpoint, what should the administrative assistant have done in this situation? Explain.

She should have made sure that someone else was covering her phone when she was away from her desk, either by getting someone to stay and monitor calls or by forwarding calls to another employee's telephone who can answer incoming calls and take messages.

Encouraging Customer Loyalty

Being on par in terms of price and quality only gets you into the game. Service wins the game.

—Tony Alessandra

learning objectives

After completing this chapter, you will be able to:

1 Establish and maintain trust with customers.

2 Explain customer relationship management and explain its importance to quality service.

3 Develop the service provider characteristics that will enhance customer loyalty.

4 Describe the provider's responsibility for establishing and maintaining positive customer relationships.

5 Identify strategies that can be used to make customers feel like they are number one.

6 Discuss strategies that can enhance customer satisfaction.

7 Define quality service.

In the Real World   Service-7-Eleven Inc.

7-Eleven is a household name for many people in North America and around the world. No matter where you travel you are likely to come across one of the 7,100 stores located in the United States. In all, there are over 30,000 licensees and franchise-owned operations throughout the world. 7-Eleven sets the standard for convenience stores. Currently a subsidiary of Japanese-based Seven & I Holdings Company, stores are located in North America, Japan, Australia,

Mexico, Taiwan, Singapore, Canada, the Philippines, Sweden, Denmark, South Korea, Thailand, Norway, Turkey, Malaysia, China, and the U.S. territory of Puerto Rico.

7-Eleven started in 1927 as the Southland Ice Company in Dallas, Texas, when an employee began selling eggs, milk, and bread to ice customers as a convenience when grocery stores were closed on Sundays and evenings. The idea caught on and the rest is retail history. Many other convenience chains have copied the 7-Eleven model, but have not reached the level of success accomplished by the original.

Originally called Totem stores because people "toted" merchandise away in paper bags, the company changed to 7-Eleven in 1946 to celebrate its new hours of operation—7 A.M. until 11 P.M., seven days a week. The concept obviously paid off, since sales figures in 2005 reached $43 billion.

7-Eleven continues to look for new and innovative products and practices and is known internationally for Big Gulp® fountain soft drinks, Big Bite® hot dogs, Slurpee® beverages, and Café Select® fresh brewed coffee. In addition, the stores regularly add to their food service deli and baked good items. According to their website, the company sells over 30 million gallons of fountain soft drinks per year—enough to fill 59 Olympic-sized swimming pools—and 41 million gallons of milk each year.

7-Eleven also focuses on changing customer needs by offering convenient services based on each neighborhood's individual needs, including gas sales, automated money orders, copiers, fax and automatic teller machines, long-distance phone cards, and lottery tickets, where available.

For more information about this organization, visit www.7-eleven.com/about/about.asp. See activity related to this section on page 275.

Quick Preview

Before reviewing the chapter content, respond to the following questions by placing a "T" for true or an "F" for false on the rules. Use any questions you miss as a checklist of material to which you will pay particular attention as you read through the chapter. For those you get right, congratulate yourself, but review the sections they address in order to learn additional details about the topic.

_____ **1.** Customer satisfaction and loyalty are the result of effective product and service delivery, resolution of problems, and elimination of dissatisfaction.

_____ **2.** The number of customers with major problems who continue to do business with an organization if their complaint is resolved is about 9 percent.

_____ **3.** One way to take responsibility for customer relationships is to personalize your approach when dealing with customers.

_____ **4.** Customers usually decide to purchase or repurchase from a supplier on the basis of the quality and performance of the products and services.

_____ **5.** Many customers return to organizations because of relationships established with employees even though comparable products and services are available elsewhere.

_____ **6.** As customers develop long-term relationships with an organization, they tend to become more tolerant of poor service.

_____ **7.** Projecting an enthusiastic "I'm happy to serve you attitude" is one way to have a positive effect on customer relationships.

_____ **8.** Customers usually exhibit six common needs that must be addressed by service providers in order to ensure customer loyalty.

___ **9.** Using a customer's name is a good way to personalize your relationship with a customer.

___ **10.** Trust is not a major concern for most customers.

___ **11.** Handling complaints quickly and effectively is a good strategy for aiding customer retention.

___ **12.** An important step often overlooked in dealing with customers is follow-up.

Answers to Quick Preview can be found at the end of the chapter.

 1 **THE ROLE OF TRUST**

Concept: Trust is the most important criterion for a relationship. Trust depends on many factors. Communicating effectively, keeping your word, caring, and trusting your customers are some of these factors.

customer loyalty
Term used to describe the tendency of customers to return to a product or organization regularly because of the service and satisfaction they receive.

trust
Key element in cementing interpersonal relationships.

touch point
Any instance in which a service provider or organization (e.g., face to face, in writing, through technology) comes in contact with a customer; it is an opportunity to influence customer loyalty and enhance the customer relationship.

Customer loyalty is an *emotional* rather than a *rational* thing. Tied to commitment, loyalty is typically based on customer interest in maintaining a relationship with your organization. Often, customer interest is created and maintained through one or more positive experiences that lead to a relationship.

Relationships are built on **trust**! The most important thing to remember about trust is that, without it, you have no relationship. This applies to all human situations, not just the customer service environment. For customers to continue doing business with you, they must trust you and your organization. Trust has to be earned, and it does not happen overnight. Only through continued positive efforts on the part of everyone in your organization can you demonstrate to customers that you are worthy of their trust and thereby positively affect customer retention. Through actions and deeds, you must deliver quality products, services, and information that satisfy the needs of your customers. Every **touch point** with a customer is an opportunity for you and your organization to influence customer loyalty. Even when you win trust and achieve customer satisfaction, the customer relationship is very fragile. It is easy to destroy trust quickly: an inappropriate tone, a missed appointment, failure to follow through on a promise, a lie, or a misleading statement to a customer are just some of the ways you can sabotage this relationship. The good news for North American businesses is that according to a 2007 report by the University of Michigan's American Customer Satisfaction Index (ACSI), "customer satisfaction with the goods and services that Americans buy reached an all-time high in the fourth quarter of 2006."[1]

In a June 2001 poll[2] by Harris Interactive, five dimensions of trust were identified that help explain why customers trust one organization over others. These types of trust can be used by organizations to create systems and staffing strategies that foster trust. The dimensions are:

- Personal experience
- Organizational knowledge (of the company)
- Deference (trust of companies in general)
- Reference (what one learns about a company from others)
- Glitz (advertising, packaging, and high pricing)

[1]Consumer Spending Growth Likely to Remain Strong as Customer Satisfaction Hits All-Time High, www.theacsi.org/index.php?option=com_content&task=view&id=165&Itemid=161.

[2]Humphrey Taylor, "Why Some Companies Are Trusted and Others Are Not: Personal Experience and Knowledge of Company More Important Than Glitz." June 20, 2001, www.harrisinteractive.com.

To gain and maintain trust, you and the organization must actively work toward incorporating the values and beliefs you read about in other chapters into daily actions. Failure to do so can send a message that you are not trustworthy or that you act according to a double standard of saying one thing but doing another. You must exhibit trustworthiness in words and actions, for although it takes a long time to gain trust, it can be lost in seconds. Once trust is gone, if you do not react quickly to correct the situation, you may never regain total customer confidence. An example of how customer trust can erode was found in a 2007 Harris Interactive poll related to ongoing recalls in the pet and food product markets. The poll found that, " . . . consumers are concerned about the incidence of recalls among manufacturers and suppliers of food and pet food products. More than four in five (86 percent) mentioned at least some concern with three in ten (29 percent) indicating that these recalls are a serious concern for them."[3] These continued recalls, and those of many consumer products in the past (e.g., toys, tire, car, and dishwasher manufacturers that produce products that cause death, injury, and product loss to users), are causing a lot of uneasiness and distrust of many manufacturers.

Displaying caring and respect for customers is essential. *What are some ways you can go "above and beyond" when providing customer service?*

Communicate Effectively and Convincingly If you cannot articulate or clearly explain (verbally and in writing) information that customers can comprehend and act upon, they will not believe in you. You must provide more than facts and figures; you must send a message of sincerity, knowledge, and honesty.

As you communicate, project your feelings and emotions by being positive and enthusiastic. Let customers know that you are human and approachable. Also, communicate frequently and keep customers informed. This is especially important when they are awaiting a product or service that has been delayed. If you fail to update them regularly, they may become frustrated and could cancel their order, complain, take their business elsewhere, and tell others about their disappointing experience.

Display Caring Emphasize to your customers that you have their best interests at heart. Work to demonstrate that you are willing to assist in satisfying their needs. Asking questions that uncover their needs and then taking positive action to satisfy them can do this. It can also be accomplished through passionate efforts to solve problems. Remember that their problem is your problem. Too often, service providers send a message that customers are not really that important. This can happen when service providers adopt a "next" mentality and treat customers as if they were numbers, not people. For example, think about the difference wording can make. Which of the following sends a more caring message to a group of customers standing in line as they wait for service?

1. A provider calls out "Next."
2. A provider looks over to the next person in line, smiles, and motions the person over with a waving hand gesture while saying, "May I help the next person in line?"

If you chose No. 2, you are on your way to providing caring service.

[3]*The Harris Poll*® No. 53, June 12, 2007, Consumer Concern Over Product Recalls High. www.harrisinteractive.com/harris_poll/index.asp?PID=769.

Be Fair   Make sure that you treat all customers (internal and external) with respect and consistency. If you give special discounts to established or return customers, do so discreetly. Failure to exercise discretion in these cases could cause other customers to be offended and take their business elsewhere. People like to feel that they are special. If a customer believes that another customer is getting special treatment, you could have problems. Such perceptions might even lead to legal action if customers perceive they are being discriminated against.

Admit Errors or Lack of Knowledge   You are human and are expected to make mistakes. The key is to recover from errors by apologizing, accepting responsibility, and then quickly and appropriately solving the problem or getting the necessary information. One of the biggest mistakes a service provider can make is to deny accountability in dealing with a customer. When you or your organization, or the products or services it sells, cause customer inconvenience or dissatisfaction, take responsibility and work toward an acceptable resolution with the customer. To do otherwise is courting disaster. In some cases, even if a customer incorrectly perceives that you contributed to his or her dissatisfaction, it may be wise to take responsibility.

A story about the power of such action has been circulated for years. It involves the highly successful department store Nordstrom. As the story goes, a disgruntled customer brought a used car tire into a Nordstrom's store and complained that it was defective. After some discussion, the manager cheerfully accepted the tire and refunded the customer's money. This may not seem too unusual, except that Nordstrom does not sell automobile tires! So, why would the manager take such an extreme action? Think about the word-of-mouth publicity (how many people in your class now know this story from just reading it?) and the customer loyalty that likely resulted from it. Whether the event actually took place or someone made it up is irrelevant. The point is that taking unusual actions to solve ordinary customer problems can pay dividends long into the future.

In another classic example of taking responsibility for a problem, in 1982 an unknown person or group contaminated bottles of Extra-Strength Tylenol with cyanide. Seven people used the product and died. Upon finding out about the situation, the parent company (Johnson and Johnson) immediately called a press conference to announce the total recall of the product from store shelves (approximately 264,000 bottles). Johnson & Johnson started a major media campaign to reassure the public that its other products were safe. The company also helped lead the way in developing tamper-resistant packaging. The cost—millions. The result—walk into any store that sells over-the-counter drug products and look for Extra-Strength Tylenol. Tylenol is right there with all its competitors and is a strong seller. How did Johnson & Johnson pull this off? The actions of the company in taking responsibility for a situation that was not of its making communicated strong values and concern for public safety, and the public remained loyal as a result.

Other companies have not fared so well in the face of adversity. For example, think about the Exxon oil tanker *Valdez*, which spilled more than 200,000 gallons of crude oil along the Alaska coastline in 1989. This disaster caused major environmental as well as financial losses in the millions of dollars. This does not include the almost $3 billion Exxon has spent cleaning up the environmental damage and paying legal settlements. The company was slow to react, however, and did not, at first, take responsibility. As a result, it is still the object of litigation and jokes. From a trust standpoint, people harbor resentment over the incident, and, in protest, many people will still not patronize Exxon gas stations.

In light of the costs associated with procuring new customers, a 2007 customer loss study of over 500 sales, marketing, and corporate buying executives found that "A massive 62% of buyers surveyed who recently dismissed a key supplier reported choosing

---

another supplier that offered basically the same product or service. This finding indicates that the lost account's needs have not changed and can still be filled by the dismissed supplier. Importantly, buyers also report their dismissed suppliers do not even attempt to win them back. Only 25% reported the dismissed supplier offered an apology and only 14% of buyers said dismissed suppliers adopted a keep-in-touch strategy with them."[4]

In an era of strong competition from competitors worldwide, the policy identified in the study above makes little fiscal sense and does nothing to stimulate and maintain customer loyalty.

Trust Your Customers   Most customers are not out to cheat or "rip you (or your organization) off." They do want the best value and service for their money and expect you to provide it. Make a good-faith effort to accomplish this and deal effectively with customers by communicating openly, listening objectively to their questions and concerns, providing service to the best of your ability, showing compassion for their needs, and demonstrating that you are their advocate when things go wrong (if appropriate).

One of the most common mistakes service providers make in dealing with customers who have a complaint or problem is to verbally acknowledge and agree but nonverbally send a message of skepticism. For example, suppose a customer comes in to complain about a defective product she purchased. As she is describing the symptoms of the problem, you use some of the paralanguage discussed in earlier chapters (e.g., "Uh huh," "I see," "Hmmm"); however, the inflection you use or your tone of voice communicates questioning or doubt (e.g., "I seeee?" or "Hmmm?"). How do you think the customer might feel or perceive you at that point?

If you seek trust, communicate it.

Keep Your Word   Customers have many choices in selecting a service provider. If they feel you cannot be depended upon to take action, they simply leave, often without complaint or comment. When you tell customers you will do something, do it. Do not promise what you cannot deliver; many people take your word as your bond. Break the bond, and you risk destroying the relationship. If feasible after providing service, contact your customer to make sure that he or she was satisfied and that your service met expectations. This follow-up can be an informal call or a more formal questionnaire. Always strive to *under*promise and *over*deliver. An example of this concept in action would be for you to suppose that a customer drops off film to be processed at your store on Tuesday. The store guarantees that the photos will be ready on Saturday. If possible, develop the film before Saturday, and call to tell the customer it's ready. When he or she comes to pick it up, give a coupon for a discount on the next roll of film. Such actions help secure customer loyalty.

Provide Peace of Mind   Be positive and assertive. Assure customers through your words and actions that you are confident, have their best interests at heart, and are in control of the situation. Let them know that their calls or messages, questions, and needs will be addressed professionally and in a timely manner. Reassure them that what they purchase is the best quality, has a solid warranty, will be backed by the organization, and will address their needs while providing many benefits. Also, assure them that their requests and information will be processed rapidly and promises will be met. All of these things can lead them to the belief that they made the right decision in selecting you and your organization and that you will take care of their needs.

---

[4] Lost Customers Are Ripe for Win-back, www.customersat.com/News/PressRelease_68.asp.

⚫ 2 THE IMPORTANCE OF CUSTOMER RELATIONSHIP MANAGEMENT (CRM)

Concept: Long-term relationships are the ones that sustain organizations.

Why bother building relationships with customers? The answer would seem obvious —so that you can stay in business. However, when you examine the question further, you may find that there are more reasons than you think. This is where the customer relationship management (CRM) concept comes in. There are actually several components of the CRM process: operational (involving sales and service representatives), collaborative (involving Interaction with customers through such means as e-mail, Web pages and automated voice response, or AVR, systems), and analytical (involving analyzing customer data for efforts like marketing and financial forecasting). Through CRM, organizations and employees get to better know their customers and project needs that can be satisfied through appropriate products and services.

At one point in history, business owners knew their customers personally. They knew their customers' families, what their religious affiliation was, and what was happening in their lives. That was then, and this is now. Our current society is more mobile; people live in large metropolitan areas where relationships are distant, and families live miles apart from one another in many instances. Large multinational organizations provide the products and services once provided by the neighborhood store. All this does not mean, however, that the customer-provider relationship can no longer exist.

Additionally, with B2B (business-to-business), customers are often companies. This makes managing **customer relationships** more difficult because of the number of contacts you might have in an organization and the varying requirements or needs each might have. Also, much of business-to-business service is delivered through technology. Many service organizations use customer **relationship management** software to better keep track of customer needs and to record service provided. CRM is a crucial element of customer loyalty.

customer relationships
The practice of building and maintaining ongoing friendships with customers in an effort to make them feel comfortable with an organization and its service providers and to enhance customer loyalty.

relationship management
The process of continually monitoring interactions with a customer in order to strengthen ties and retain the customer.

Relationships are a crucial part of customer service. By working to build trust and getting to know customer needs, service providers increase their effectiveness. *What techniques do you use to build rapport and trust with customers?*

Typically, many service providers look at customer interactions from a short-term perspective. They figure that a customer calls or comes in (or they go to the customer), they provide service, and then the customer (or the service provider) goes away. This is a shortsighted viewpoint in that it does not consider the long-term implications. This is not the way to gain and sustain customer loyalty.

A more customer-focused approach is to view customers from a relationship standpoint. That does not mean that you have to become intimate friends with all your customers; it simply means that you should strive to employ as many of the positive relationship-building skills that you have learned as possible. By treating both internal and external customers in a manner that leads them to believe that you care for them and have their best interests at heart, you can start to generate reciprocal feelings. Using the interpersonal communication skills you have learned throughout this book is a great way to begin doing this. People usually gravitate toward organizations and people with whom they have developed rapport, respect, and trust, and who treat them as if they are valued as a person. Relationships are developed and enhanced through one-on-one human interaction. This does not mean that people who provide service via technology cannot develop relationships. Those relationships develop on a different level, using the nonverbal skills addressed in Chapters 4, 6, 8, and 9.

Remember that long-term customer relationships (**customer retention**) are the ones that sustain organizations. Seeking out new or replacement customers through advertising and other means is a very costly proposition. This is because in addition to having to find new customers, you and your organization have to educate and win them over. You have to prove yourself to newly acquired customers. More than likely, new customers are also going to be more apprehensive, skeptical, and critical than customers who have previous experience with your organization. For these reasons, it is imperative that you and every other member of your organization work to develop loyalty on the part of those customers with whom you have an existing relationship.

> **customer retention**
> The ongoing effort by an organization to meet customer needs and desires in an effort to build long-term relationships and keep them for life.

Many organizations and industries seem to forget the value of fostering solid customer relationships. They often treat existing customers poorly or not as well as newly acquired ones. Examples of this can be found in:

High maintenance and transaction fees charged by financial institutions.

High fees charged by hotels for local calls.

Exorbitant fees charged by airlines for ticket changes.

Inability for existing cell phone customers locked into contracts to get the same deals as new customers.

Cancellation fees by doctors' and dentists' offices.

Restocking fees charged by many online retailers.

One way that organizations try to cement relationships and elicit customer loyalty is through loyalty or rewards programs. In many cases this strategy seems to be working. Maritz Loyalty Marketing in a 2006 study of 2,178 shoppers who had made purchases in the past six months found that "In an increasingly fragmented retail landscape, customer loyalty programs are an important tool to help retailers maximize their 'share of wallet' among consumers . . . . [R]ewards program members are more likely to have spent a greater amount of money in the past six months across the 11 retail categories examined in the study, including home improvement, electronics, grocery and book stores."[5]

Benefits of Customer Relationship Management

- Less need to obtain new customers through marketing, since current customers are aware of offerings and take advantage of them.
- Reduced marketing costs, since direct mail, follow-up, and other customer recruitment activities are reduced.
- Increased return on investment (ROI), since marketing can target specific customer needs.
- Enhanced customer loyalty due to pricing and product service offerings that meet current customer needs.
- Elevated profitability due to increased sales, customer referrals, and longer customer retention during life cycle.
- Targeted marketing based on statistics on which customers buy more and on high-ticket item sales.

[5]The Face of Loyalty Programs: Who Has What Cards in Their Wallet, August 2006,www.maritzresearch.com/release.asp?rc=297&p=2&T=P.

Effective product/service delivery

+ Proactive relationship building

+ Elimination of dissatisfiers

+ Resolution of problems

+ Follow-up

= Customer satisfaction and loyalty

By providing excellent customer service and dealing with dissatisfaction as soon it is identified, you can help ensure that customers remain loyal and keep coming back. Figure 10.1 shows an equation that conveys the loyalty concept.

Traditionally, customers will remain loyal to a product, service, or organization that they believe meets their needs. Even when there is an actual or perceived breakdown in quality, many customers will return to an organization that they believe sincerely attempts to solve a problem or make restitution for an error. According to the **Technical Assistance Research Program (TARP),** many organizations have found that, when complaints were acted upon and resolved quickly, most customers returned to the organization (see Figure 10.2).

The bottom line is that you and other employees must realize that customer service is everyone's business and that relationships are the basis of that business.

Technical Assistance Research Program (TARP)

An Arlington, Virginia, based firm specializing in customer service research studies for call centers and many other industries.

cost of dissatisfied customers

Phrase that refers to any formula used to calculate the cost of acquiring a new customer or replacing a current one as a result of having a dissatisfied customer leave an organization.

COST OF DISSATISFIED CUSTOMERS

Many research studies have been conducted to try to determine the **cost of dissatisfied customers.** Too often, service providers look at the loss of a sale when a customer is dissatisfied as a single event. However, as you saw in the last section, one dissatisfied customer can cost your organization a lot.

FIGURE 10.2

The Importance of Customer Loyalty

For almost three decades, the research firm TARP has conducted various studies to determine the effects of customer service. The research has revealed the following:

- It will cost an organization at least five times more to acquire a new customer as it will to keep an existing one.

- On average, 50 percent of consumers will complain about a problem to a front-line person. In business-to-business environments, this figure jumps to 75 percent.

- For small-ticket items, 96 percent of consumers do not complain or they complain to the retailer from whom they bought an item. For large-ticket items, 50 percent complain to front-line employees, and 5 to 10 percent escalate the problem to local managers or corporate headquarters.

- At least 50 percent of your customers who experience problems will not complain or contact your organization for help; they will simply go elsewhere.

- Customers who are dissatisfied will tell as many as 16 friends about a negative experience with your organization.

- The average business loses 10 to 15 percent of its customers per year because of bad service.

Source: Technical Assistance Research Program (TARP), 1300 Wilson Boulevard, Suite 950, Arlington, Virginia 22209.

Personal Customer Relationship Experiences

THINK ABOUT A SERVICE PROVIDER WITH WHOM YOU DEAL FREQUENTLY AND WITH WHOM YOU HAVE ESTABLISHED A BETTER-THAN-AVERAGE CUSTOMER-PROVIDER RELATIONSHIP. Perhaps you have been dealing with the organization for a long period of time or visit frequently.

Reflect on the relationship and make a list of positive customer service behaviors exhibited by this person. Then review the list and make it a personal goal to replicate as many of these behaviors as possible when dealing with your own customers.

To get an idea of what one negative customer experience can cost your organization over a 10-year period, consider the following example:

Ms. Ling comes in to return a product that she paid $22 for over a month ago. She explains that the product did not fit her needs and that she had been meaning to return it since the date she purchased it, but kept forgetting. She also explains that she comes in at least once a week to make purchases. Your company has a three-day return policy, your manager is out to lunch and you do not have the authority to override the policy. Ms. Ling is in a hurry and is upset by your inability to resolve the issue. She leaves after saying, "You just lost a good customer!"

Let's assume that Ms. Ling spends at least $22 a week in your store and calculate the potential loss to your organization.

$22 × 52 (number of weeks in a year) = $1,144

10 (number of years) × $1,144 = $11,440

16 (number of people statistically told of a negative experience) × $11,440 = **$183,040**

These numbers are the bad news. The good news is that you and every other employee in your organization can reduce a large percentage of customer defections by providing quality service.

3   PROVIDER CHARACTERISTICS AFFECTING CUSTOMER LOYALTY

Concept: Personal characteristics of a service provider may affect customer loyalty, positively or negatively.

According to the 2006 J. D. Power and Associates Sales Satisfaction Index (SSI) study, a leading cause of lost sales at new-vehicle dealerships is poor customer treatment. Nearly one-half of all shoppers who walk away from a dealership cite poor treatment as a reason."[6]

Many of your personal characteristics affect your relationships with customers. In customer service, some circumstances are beyond your control; however, your personal characteristics are not. Some of the most common qualities of service providers that affect customers are described in the next sections.

[6]Customer Satisfaction with the New-Vehicle Sales Process Reaches Record Levels as Dealers Strive to Be in Better Sync with the Needs of Their Customers, 15 November 2006, www.jdpower.com/corporate/news/releases/pressrelease.aspx?ID=2006250.

THINK OF HOW YOU WOULD EXPECT TO BE TREATED IF YOU WERE A CUSTOMER OF THE COMPANY YOU WORK FOR CURRENTLY. List behaviors that you would expect to encounter from customer service employees.

RESPONSIVENESS

Customers typically like to feel that they are the most important person in the world when they come in contact with an organization (see Figure 10.3). This is a human need. If customers feel that they are not appreciated or not welcome by you or another service provider, they will likely take their business elsewhere. However, they will often first complain to management and will tell anyone who will listen about the poor quality of service they received.

A simple way to demonstrate responsiveness is to attend to customer needs promptly. If you get an e-mail or voice mail message, respond to it immediately, if possible. If that is not possible, try to respond within 4 hours, or certainly within 24 hours. If you have face-to-face customer contact, greet customers quickly (within 10 to 15 seconds), even if you are busy with someone else. If nothing else, at least smile and gesture that you will be with them momentarily.

Once you do get to serve the customer, and before getting to the business at hand, greet the customer with a smile and start the interaction on a friendly note in one or more of the following ways:

Be enthusiastic. Use open body language, vocal cues, and gestures that you have read about previously in this book, coupled with some of the techniques described below to let your customers know that you are glad they have chosen you and/or

FIGURE 10.3

Addressing Customer Needs

Everyone has needs that must be met in some fashion. Here are six common customer needs, along with strategies to satisfy them.

Customer Need	Strategies for Satisfying the Need
To feel welcome	Use an enthusiastic greeting, smile, use the customer's name, thank the customer, be positive
To be understood	Listen actively, paraphrase, ask key questions, give positive feedback, empathize
To feel comfortable	Use an enthusiastic welcome, relieve anxiety through friendly communication, explain your actions calmly, ensure physical comfort (e.g., seats, refreshments)
To feel appreciated	Thank the customer, follow up, go beyond service expectations, provide "special" offers, remember special details about the customer (e.g., birthdays, favorite colors, facts about their families)
To feel important	Use the customer's name, personalize service, give special treatment when possible, elicit opinions, remember details about him or her (e.g., last purchase made, last visit, preferred styles or foods)
To be respected	Listen, don't interrupt, acknowledge the customer's emotions and concerns, take time to serve, ask advice, elicit feedback

your organization. *Use the customer's title and name.* If you know the customer's name, use it. Remember, though, not to assume familiarity and start using the customer's first name unless you are given permission to do so.

Show appreciation. "Thank you for coming to (organization)." "It's nice to see you this morning." "You have been very patient while I assisted the previous customer. Thank you."*Engage in small talk.* "Isn't this weather terrible?" "Is this your first visit to our store?" "Didn't I see you in here last week?" (Say this only if you recognize the customer. If he or she answers yes, thank the person for returning to the store.)

Compliment. "You look like you're having a good day" (assuming the customer is smiling and does look happy). "That color really looks nice on you," "That's a beautiful necktie," or other appropriate compliment.

ADAPTABILITY

In a continually evolving world, you will undoubtedly have many opportunities to deal with customers who have different beliefs, values, perceptions, needs, and expectations. You will also encounter people whose personality styles differ from yours. Each of these meetings will provide an opportunity for you to adapt your approach in dealing with others. By doing so, you increase the likelihood of a successful interaction as well as a satisfied customer emerging from the encounter. Taking measures to adapt your personality style to that of your customers in order to communicate with and serve them effectively is a smart move. Keep in mind that you cannot change the customers; however, you can adapt to them and their approach to a situation.

Another, more subtle way to show your ability to adapt relates to technology. By quickly learning and mastering new technology systems provided to you by the organization, you can respond faster and more efficiently to customer needs. This is especially true, since many of your customers will likely be very technology-literate. If you cannot match their expectations, or at least demonstrate knowledge and effectiveness in using technology, you might frustrate them and drive them away. In turn, you might create negative word-of-mouth publicity about your organization and its employees.

COMMUNICATION SKILLS

As you have read earlier in this book, your ability to obtain and give information, listen, write, and speak effectively, and deal with emotional situations are keys to successful customer service. By using a variety of effective interpersonal techniques, you can determine customer needs. The most successful service providers are the ones who have learned to interact positively and build rapport with customers. To help ensure the most effective service possible, you should continually strive to improve your ability to interact and communicate with a variety of people. The better your skills are, the more likely you will be able to address different situations that arise in the workplace.

CUSTOMER SERVICE SUCCESS TIP

Trust is gained though listening to your customer and addressing his or her needs; not just talking about yourself, your organization, products, and services.

DECISIVENESS

Decisiveness relates to being able and willing to make a decision and take necessary actions to fulfill customer needs. Taking a wait-and-see approach to customer service often leads to customer dissatisfaction. Just as you probably do, customers value their time. By keeping them waiting while you run to someone else for a decision or answer can be frustrating. Granted, such a situation is sometimes created by a management style that makes it necessary to get certain approvals (e.g., for checks, returns or refunds, or discounts). However, these are internal issues that should be resolved *before* the customer encounters them. If you face such barriers, think of alternative ways of handling them, and then approach your supervisor with suggestions for improvement. Your ideas may make your life easier by reducing the chances of a frustrating and unproductive service encounter.

Once you have supportive systems in place, gather information effectively by using the listening techniques discussed in Chapter 5, carefully and quickly analyze the situation, and then make a decision on how to solve the problem.

ENTHUSIASM

As discussed earlier, attaining and maintaining a level of excitement about your customers, products, services, organization, and job that says "I'm happy to help you" is an important step toward establishing a relationship.

If you are enthusiastic about serving your customers, they will often respond by loyally supporting you and the organization. People typically react positively to enthusiastic employees who appear to be enjoying themselves as they work. This should not be interpreted as meaning that providers should act unprofessionally or create an environment in which they have fun at the expense of customer service or attention to their customers. Find a good balance between fun and professionalism. Southwest Airlines has succeeded in finding the right mix. Employees dress casually, are recruited partially on the basis of their personality, and often use jokes and games on flights to reduce some of the stress of air travel in a security-conscious industry. They have been rewarded with continued corporate profits while other airlines often report losses.

The long-term benefit is that if you and your organization can generate return customers through enthusiasm, the potential for organizational growth and prosperity exists. This in turn sets the stage for better benefits, salary, and workplace modifications that lead to higher employee enthusiasm. Once all the elements are connected, all contribute to successful customer service.

As a side note, many employees and employers are trying to find ways to make the workplace less stressful and more enjoyable for themselves and customers. Several resources listed in the Bibliography will help in this quest.

ETHICAL BEHAVIOR

With a heightened incidence of actual or alleged corporate wrongdoing (e.g., Enron and Martha Stewart), customers have been sensitized and made wary of organizations, their leaders, and practices. Many organizations have formed ethics committees made up of employees from across their organization. They have also adopted a **code of ethics** or codes of conduct that are taught to all employees, new and old, and to which they are held accountable. Even if the organization for which you work does not have such a code, it is crucial that you and your peers guard against any words or actions that might raise scrutiny or customer skepticism.

Establishing (and maintaining) high legal, social, and ethical standards in all interactions with customers is imperative. Failure to do so can lead to loss of reputation and business, and/or legal liability. Some positive examples of **ethical behavior** are the following:

- Before someone complains, companies voluntarily recall a product that it discovered was defective or potentially dangerous.
- A manager who notifies a customer when he or she finds out that an employee has lied to or deceived the customer.
- An employee who reports a theft carried out by another employee.
- A truck driver who tracks down the owner of a parked car at a mall to identify herself as the person who accidentally scraped a bumper while making a delivery.
- A cab driver who finds a wallet in his taxi and turns it in.

Some negative examples are:

- Providing or substituting an inferior or more expensive product for an advertised name brand item.
- Providing inferior or nonstandard parts or repairs on a service call but charging for factory parts.
- Misleading a customer about what is covered on an extended home warranty in order to sell a policy and make a commission.
- Failing to adhere to local, state, or federal regulations (e.g., dumping hazardous waste, such as petroleum or pesticide products, in unauthorized areas or collecting sales taxes but failing to report the taxes).
- Lying to a patient about why they have to wait so long before being seen by a technician, nurse, doctor (e.g., the medical professional came in late or returned late from lunch).

code of ethics
A set of standards, often developed by employees, which guide the conduct of all employees.

ethical behavior
Expected performance that sends a message of being trustworthy and honest, and having the intent to provide quality service.

INITIATIVE

Taking an action related to your job or customer service without having to receive instructions from others is a sign of initiative. Such actions also help to ensure that your customer's needs are identified and met in a timely fashion. Too many service providers take the "It's not my job" or "I can't do that" approach to dealing with customer situations. This can lead to customer dissatisfaction because the provider seems to be lazy or uncaring. To counter such impressions, you should take responsibility when a problem arises. By building a strong knowledge base (as described in the next section) and using the skills discussed in this book, you will have the tools you need to deal effectively with various situations without having to turn to others for assistance. This can expedite service and enhance your reputation in the eyes of your customers, peers, and supervisors.

KNOWLEDGE

Your customers expect you to know what business your organization is in. With all the products and service variations available to customers, the high level of technology, deregulation of industries, and innovations coming on the market daily, customers depend on service providers to educate and guide them in making purchases and decisions.

Training is usually provided by most organizations to increase employee knowledge and effectiveness with customers. *What training do you think would be useful to you in a new position in customer service?*

Taking time to learn about policies, procedures, resources, products, services, and other information can help you provide total customer satisfaction in an efficient and timely manner.

If the organization you work for does not provide training or resources, take the initiative to ask supervisors or team leaders for materials and information. Also develop a network with other employees throughout the organization and use that network to gain access to information. Network in other ways as well: organizations involved in your particular product or service can provide general training to you; service organizations can lead you to mentors and other individuals who can help your career; and networking with others in your line of work outside of your company can also help in many ways. Joining an organization whose membership includes people who do what you do for a living can give you different perspectives and add to your knowledge base. You, your organization, and your customers will ultimately benefit from your initiatives.

PERCEPTIVENESS

Recognizing the need to pay close attention to verbal and nonverbal cues, cultural factors, and the feelings or concerns of others is important. If necessary, you may want to review these topics in Chapters 4 and 8. By staying focused on customers and the signals they send, you can often recognize hesitancy, interest in a product or adamant rejection, irritation, anxiety, and a multitude of other unspoken messages. Once you have identified customers' signals, you can react appropriately and address their needs.

One way you can address customer needs is to anticipate them. Suppose that a customer makes a comment like "Man, is it hot outside. My lips are parched." You might offer a cold drink or direct the customer to a cafeteria or soft drink machine. You might offer a blanket to a family member staying with someone in the emergency room in the middle of the night when it is very cold. Or you might offer a chair to someone who is accompanying a customer while he or she shops and tries on clothing. Such small gestures show that you are astute in noticing their needs and nonverbal cues. Remember, sometimes the little things mean a lot. Moreover, in both of these examples, by taking care of the customer's basic needs, you might encourage him or her to shop longer.

PLANNING ABILITY

Planning is a crucial skill to possess when operating in today's fast-paced, changing customer service environment, especially in technology-based environments. To prepare for all types of customer situations, you and your organization must have a strategy. This often involves assessing various factors related to your organization, industry, products, services, policies and procedures, resources, and customer base. By being proactive and in thinking about such factors, you will be able to provide better service to your customers.

Also, you should consider alternative strategies for dealing with unusual situations (**contingency plans**). Such alternatives are helpful when things do not go as originally

contingency plans
Backup systems or procedures that are implemented when regular ones break down or fail to function as intended.

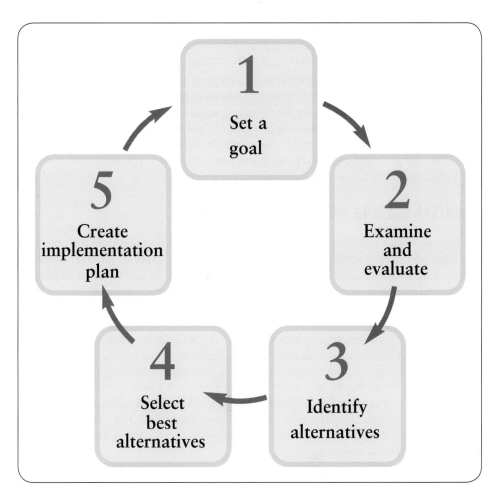

FIGURE 10.4   Planning Process Model

planned (e.g., a computer database fails, service is not delivered as promised, or products that were ordered from another organization for a customer do not arrive as promised).

Figure 10.4 shows the **Planning Process Model,** the basic steps of which are:

Set a goal. In a customer service situation, the obvious goal is to prevent problems from occurring. You also want to successfully address customers' needs, have them leave the service experience satisfied, spread positive word-of- mouth advertising, and return in the future.

Examine and evaluate the situation. In this phase of planning, you should look at all possible factors that could affect a customer interaction (e.g., the environment, policies, procedures, your skills and authority level, management support, and the customer). With these factors in mind, work with your peers and supervisor or team leader to establish criteria for selecting acceptable actions. For example, it might be acceptable to use voice mail if you are dealing with a customer; however, it is not proper to forward incoming messages to voice mail so that you can meet with a peer on a non-work-related issue.

Identify alternatives. Meet with peers and supervisors or team leaders to develop a list of alternatives for dealing with various customer situations. Consider the advantages and disadvantages of each option.

Planning Process Model
Five-step process for creating contingency or backup plans to better serve customers when problems arise or things do not go as expected.

Select the best alternative. After reviewing all the options, select the one (or more) that best addresses the targeted goal of providing quality service to customers. Do not forget to measure this choice against the criteria you established earlier.

Create an implementation plan. Working with peers and supervisors or team leaders, decide which resources (human and otherwise) will be needed to deliver effective service. Also, develop a system for evaluating success. For example, a customer wants two items, but you have only one in stock. You apologize for not being able to fulfill the customer's needs. Is this "success"? Or, would you be successful if, in addition to the apology, you called other stores, located another item, and had it delivered to the customer's house at no cost?

PROBLEM-SOLVING ABILITY

If a customer has a problem, you have a problem. Remembering this simple concept can go a long way in reminding you of your purpose for being a service provider. Your primary job function is to address the needs of your customer. To do this when a customer is dissatisfied or has a concern, you should take responsibility for the problem instead of trying to place blame and defer the issue to someone else. What or who created the problem (e.g., the weather, you, the customer, and the manufacturer) doesn't matter. Your goal is to identify and implement appropriate solutions to the extent that you are authorized to do so. Otherwise, you should seek assistance from the appropriate person according to your organization's policy. To accomplish sound problem solving, you will need a process for gathering and analyzing information. As with the planning process discussed earlier, you should take some specific steps in finding a solution to a customer problem. These steps are described in the following sections. The Problem-Solving Model discussed in Chapter 7 can also be applied when you are trying to encourage and maintain customer loyalty.

Problem resolution is not difficult if it is approached systematically. If you have done the planning described earlier and know what options are available and what authority you have, it becomes much easier.

PROFESSIONALISM

As you have read in previous chapters, projecting a positive personal image, through manner of dress, knowledge, appearance of your work area, and your mental attitude, is a crucial element in communicating an "I care" image to customers and potential customers. By paying close attention to such factors, you better position yourself to establish and maintain a strong customer relationship. This is especially true where attitude is concerned. Attitude can mean success or failure when dealing with customers and can be communicated through the various verbal and nonverbal cues you have read about in other chapters.

 4   BE RESPONSIBLE FOR YOUR CUSTOMER RELATIONSHIPS

Concept: Take responsibility for good customer relationship management by personalizing your service, listening, keeping an open mind, and respecting your customers. Ask for input from your customers.

Taking a concerned, one-on-one approach to working with customers helps satisfy immediate needs while building a basis for long-lasting relationships. Customers tend to

WORK IT OUT 10.4

Problem Solving

WORKING IN TEAMS OF THREE OR FOUR MEMBERS, DECIDE ON A COURSE OF ACTION TO RESOLVE THE PROBLEM POSED IN THE FOLLOWING SCENARIO:

You have been a cashier at Gifts Galore for a little over two months. A customer comes into your gift shop and wants to return a lamp that she says she purchased from your store as a gift for a wedding. Apparently, she discovered later that the recipient already had a lamp exactly like the one she bought. She tells you that she remembers the salesperson, Brittney, because her daughter's name is spelled the same way. You know that Brittney used to work at the gift shop, but quit about the time you started. The customer has no receipt, and you do not recognize the product as one that your store sells. You are empowered to make exchanges and give refunds up to a product value of $50. The customer says the lamp was $49.95 before tax. Store policy says that the customer must have a receipt if a refund is to be made. What questions would you ask to clarify the situation? How would you handle the problem?

enjoy dealing more with people whom they believe are caring and have their best interests at heart. To interact with someone they like is a pleasant experience. Take the time to personalize your customer interactions and to make each customer feel special. This can lead to enhanced trust and helps ensure that the customer returns.

You have reviewed some of the following points in other chapters. They are reviewed and expanded here because they are solid skills and go a long way toward building customer loyalty and, ultimately, customer retention. Take the actions described in the next sections to make your customers feel special.

PERSONALIZE YOUR APPROACH

Think of the theme song for the television show *Cheers*. The idea of the theme song was that *Cheers* was a great place to go because "everyone knows your name." For the most part, people are a social species and need to be around others to grow and flourish. Helping your customers feel accepted can create a bond that will keep them coming back.

To create a social bond with customers, you will need to take time to get to know your regular customers and serve them individually. Recognizing them and using their names while interacting goes a long way toward creating that bond. For new customers, immediately start using the positive interpersonal communication skills you have learned. Treating customers as individuals and not as a number or one in a series is a very important step in building rapport and loyalty.

LISTEN ACTIVELY

In Chapter 5 you learned specific strategies for effective listening. By practicing active listening skills and avoiding distractions while determining customer needs and providing service, you can send the "I care" message discussed earlier. At the same time, you can discover the customer's needs and work toward satisfying them.

KEEP AN OPEN MIND

To develop and maintain an open mind, make it a habit to assess your attitude about your job, customers, products, and services before making contact with your customers. Make sure that you are positive, objective, prepared, and focused. Don't let negative attitudes block good service. Many service providers, even the more seasoned ones, go through slumps during which they feel down about themselves, their job, supervisors, organizations, customers, and so on. This is normal. Customer service is a stressful job, and external and internal factors (e.g., circadian rhythm, workload, and personal problems) influence one's perceptions of people and the world in general; however, guard against pessimism.

If you are facing personal problems that seem overwhelming, contact your supervisor, human resources or personnel department, or any other appropriate resource [e.g., Employee Assistance Program (EAP) representative] to help you sort out your problems. Failure to do so could lead to poor customer service or a less-than-professional image.

INDIVIDUALIZE SERVICE

Each customer is unique and has his or her own desires and needs. For that reason, every situation you handle will be slightly different. As you read in Chapter 8, you should view each person as an individual and not deal with customers on the basis of preconceived ideas or the demographic group of which they are part. By addressing a customer as an individual, listening so that you can discover his or her needs and problems, and then working to satisfy the needs or solve the problems, you potentially create a loyal customer. A simple way of accomplishing individualized service is to ask what else the customer would like. For example, in the case of a restaurant server who uses such a question, a customer might respond, "Do you have any (item)?" If the item is available, the server could cheerfully reply, "We certainly do. I'll get it for you right away." If the item is not available, the server might reply, "I'm sorry we do not have (item) However, we do have (alternative item) Would that be acceptable?"

SHOW RESPECT

Even if you don't agree with a customer, respect his or her point of view or need and provide the best possible service. In return, the customer will probably respect and appreciate you and your efforts. A variation of an old adage may help put this concept into perspective: *The customer may not always be right, but he or she is still the customer.*

If you lose sight of the fact that it is the customer who supports the organization, pays your salary, provides for your benefits, and gives you a job, you may want to examine why you are working in your current position. By acknowledging the value of your customers and affording them the respect and service they deserve, you can greatly improve your chances of having a satisfied customer. Some easy ways to show respect to customers include:

- When addressing the customer, use his or her last name and title. (If you are on the telephone, write down the customer's name along with other pertinent information.)
- Stop talking when the customer begins to speak.
- Take time to address the customer's questions or concerns.
- Return calls or e-mail messages within reasonable amounts of time.
- Show up on time for scheduled meetings.
- Do what you promised to do, and do it right the first time, within the agreed-upon time frame.

ELICIT INPUT

Some people actually encourage rewarding customers who complain. Complaints provide feedback that can enable service providers and organizations to rapidly shift resources to fix things that are not working well in an effort to satisfy the customer. If you think about it, that makes sense. You cannot fix what you do not know is broken.

Many times, service providers do not take the time to ask for feedback because they are afraid that it may not be good. In other instances, they simply do not think of asking or care to do so. To increase your own effectiveness and that of your organization, actively and regularly seek input from your customers. No one knows better than the customer what he or she likes or needs. Take the time to ask the customer, and then listen and act upon what you are told. By asking customers questions, you give them an opportunity to express interest, concerns, emotion, and even complaints. There are many ways of gathering this information (e.g., customer satisfaction cards, written surveys, and service follow-up telephone calls). The key is to somehow ask the customer "How well did we do in meeting your needs?" or "What do you think?" If this is not a normal procedure in your place of business, you should consider bringing it up at a staff meeting. It will take extra effort on the part of the customer service employees, but the effort will be well-rewarded in the good will it will elicit from your customer base.

There are many ways to gather information about customer satisfaction levels. Some of the more common include:

- *Customer comment cards* are simple 5- $\times$ 7-inch (approximately) card stock questionnaires that quickly gather customer reactions to their service experiences. These cards are commonly found on restaurant tables and at point-of-sale locations (e.g., cash registers). They typically consist of four or five closed-end questions that can be answered with yes/no or short answers and have a space for general comments.
- *Toll-free numbers* are often used to obtain customer opinions after a service encounter. Customers are provided a toll-free number on their sales receipt and encouraged to call within 24 hours. As a reward, they are often given discount coupons, bonus frequent guest/user points, or other small incentives.
- *Verbal comments* can be elicited from customers and logged in by service providers. By asking customers for feedback on their experiences and paying heed to them, immediate service adjustments can be made.
- *Follow-up telephone surveys* can be done by employees or consultants using a written list of questions. The key is to be brief, not impose on customers, and ask questions that will gather pertinent information (e.g., open-end questions).
- *Service contact surveys* that are mailed or e-mailed (with permission) to people who have contacted an organization for information, to make a purchase, or use a service can gather more in-depth information.
- *Exit interviews* conducted by greeters, hosts, or hostesses as customers leave a facility. These are typically one or two quick questions (e.g., "How did you enjoy your stay?," "Were you able to find everything you needed?," or "What can we do to make your next visit more pleasurable?"). The key is to log in responses for future reference.
- *Shopper/customer surveys* that can yield a wealth of information. These are typically longer and more detailed than a comment card. They can be given to a customer as he or she leaves or can be sent to customers later (get names and addresses from checks written). Offer discount coupons or other incentives for returned surveys and provide self-addressed, stamped envelopes.
- *Focus groups* of six to eight internal or external customers can be formed to do in-depth, face-to-face or online (chat) surveys. Often organizations conducting these provide snacks and gifts (e.g., $50.00) for each participant. Ask open-end questions related to the organization and products and services provided. Often, trained marketing or other facilitators are used to conduct such sessions. They also analyze responses and provide reports to management along with recommendations for improvement.
- *Sales and service records* can provide a wealth of information. They can reflect whether customers are returning and what products and services are being used most, and can show patterns of purchases.

Showing Respect

Take a few minutes to think of other ways that you can show respect for a variety of customers (e.g., older, younger, people with disabilities, or of various cultural backgrounds). Discuss how these can positively influence service.

---

churn
The process of a customer switching between products or companies, often simply to get a better price, rebate, or warranty.

USE EFFECTIVE CLOSING STATEMENTS

Just as you would likely part company with a friend by saying goodbye, you should leave on a positive note with customers. After all, this is your final opportunity to convey your appreciation and show that you value the relationship you have established with them. Some typical approaches to accomplishing this are: "May I assist you with something else?" "If we may assist in the future, please let us know." "Please come again." "I look forward to serving you again, Ms. Ramirez. I'll see you at your next appointment."

5 MAKING THE CUSTOMER NUMBER ONE

moment of truth
A phrase popularized by Scandinavian Airline System President Jan Carlzon in his popular 1987 book of the same name. A moment of truth is defined as any instance when a customer comes into contact with any element or representative of an organization.

Concept: Make a good first impression by establishing rapport; then identify and satisfy your customers' needs. Follow up to obtain repeat business.

The days of a customer adopting one product or company for life are long gone. With easy access and global competitiveness, customers are often swayed by advertising and a chance at a "better deal." Quality levels and features between competing brands and organizations are often comparable. The thing that separates competitors is their level of service. It is not unusual for customers to switch back and forth between products or organizations simply because of pricing. This is sometimes referred to as service **churn.**

Most people like to feel that they are important and valued. By recognizing and acting on that fact, you can go a long way toward providing solid customer service, reducing churn, and building a strong relationship with customers. By being an "I care" person, you can generate much goodwill while meeting customer needs.

Every time you encounter a customer in person or over the phone, you have an opportunity to provide excellent service. Some companies call a service encounter the **moment of truth** or refer to them as **contact points,** in which the customer comes into contact with some facet of the organization. At this point you and other service providers have an opportunity to deliver "knock your socks off" service, as Kristin Anderson and Ron Zemke discussed in several of their books on customer service. Each customer encounter moves through the following stages, although

Customer loyalty is won by providing extra service for the customer. Organizations must assess individual needs and determine how to meet those needs better than the competition does. In this case, customers who have mobility impairments or limitations will keep coming back to this establishment because they have provided transportation for those with disabilities. *How can you provide extra service for customers with special needs?*

Personal Customer Experiences

REFLECT ON A RECENT INTERACTION YOU HAD WITH AN INTERNAL OR EXTERNAL CUSTOMER AS A PROVIDER (OVER THE TELEPHONE, IN PERSON, VIA E-MAIL, OR THROUGH ANY OTHER MEANS). Immediately after that interaction, if someone had handed the customer a piece of paper and asked him or her to write down impressions of the treatment received from you, what would he or she likely have said? Why do you believe the customer would have said this?

Note: If you do not deal with customers, think of a situation that you recently experienced as a customer and answer the questions based on your experience. Record your perspective of what your customer's comments would have been, along with anything you could have done differently to improve the situation. Be as objective as you can.

---

sometimes the order varies. At each step, you have another opportunity to provide excellent customer service.

MAKE POSITIVE INITIAL CONTACT

First impressions are crucial and often lasting. To ensure that you put your best effort forward, remember the basics of positive verbal and nonverbal communication—giving a professional salutation, projecting a positive attitude, and sincerely offering to assist. This is crucial because the average customer will come into an initial contact with certain expectations. If the expectations are not met, you and your organization can lose **relationship-rating points** that can ultimately cost the organization a customer. Such points are like the ones on performance appraisals used in many organizations to evaluate and rate employee performance (see Figure 10.5). Use this scale frequently to evaluate your rating as you deal with various customers.

ESTABLISH RAPPORT

Customers react to and deal effectively with employees whom they perceive as likable, helpful, and effective. Throughout your interaction, continue to be helpful, smile, listen, use the customer's name frequently, and attend to the customer's needs or concerns. Also, look for opportunities to generate small talk about non-business-related matters. When something goes wrong, people who feel a kinship with service providers typically give higher ratings on the **relationship-rating point scale** than people who do not feel this connection.

IDENTIFY AND SATISFY CUSTOMER NEEDS QUICKLY

Use the questioning, listening, observing, and feedback skills outlined in this book to focus on issues of concern to the customer. By effectively gathering information, you can then move to the next phase of customer service.

EXCEED EXPECTATIONS

As you can see on the relationship-rating point scale, customers typically expect that, if they pay a certain price for a product or service, they will receive a specific quality and quantity in return. This is not an unusual expectation. The average customer looks for

contact points
Instances in which a customer connects with a service provider or some other aspect of an organization.

relationship-rating points
Values mentally assigned by customers to a service provider and his or her organization. They are based on a number of factors starting with initial impressions and subsequently by the quality and level of service provided.

relationship-rating point scale
The mental rating system that customers apply to service and service providers. Ratings range from *exemplary* to *unsatisfactory*, with *average* being assigned when service occurs as expected.

FIGURE 10.5

**Relationship-Rating
Point Scale**

Exemplary (4) Service that is out of the ordinary and unexpected falls into this category. Examples: An auto repair shop details a customer's car after replacing a transmission. A beauty salon owner provides a free Swedish massage to a regular patron on her birthday. A restaurant server provides a complimentary meal and a coupon for a discount on a future visit to a customer who had to send her steak back twice to be cooked properly. A nurse visits one of his patients in the intensive care unit after his 12-hour shift ends to ensure that everything is okay and to ask the spouse if she needs anything.

Above Average (3) Service in this category goes beyond the normal and may pleasantly surprise the customer, but does not dazzle the customer. Example: A regular customer at a bar gets a free second drink from the bartender. A clerk at a bank gives a customer a free wall calendar at the end of the transaction. A customer's son, who just received his first haircut, is given a lollipop by the barber.

Average (2) Service at this level is what is expected by a customer. Examples: A customer drops off laundry and when it is picked up, his shirts are starched as requested, on hangers, and in a plastic garment bag. A grocery store bagger asks, "Paper or plastic?" and then proceeds to comply with the customer's request. An accountant finishes a client's tax return on time, as promised. A receptionist properly processes a new dental patient and gathers pertinent health and insurance information in a pleasant manner.

Below Average (1) Service provided at this level is not as expected and disappoints customers. Examples: A newspaper deliverer brings a replacement paper after a customer calls to complain, leaves it on the doorstep, rings the bell, and departs without apologizing. A patient waits in a doctor's waiting room 15 minutes or longer beyond her scheduled appointment, and when she is finally seen, no one apologizes. A call center representative gives a customer a $15 credit on service because the customer had to call back three times to have a problem resolved.

Unsatisfactory (0) Service at this level is unacceptable and typically leads to a breakdown in the customer-provider relationship. Examples: A customer's cat is neutered by a veterinarian when taken in for a flea dip. A plumbing company that advertises "immediate emergency service" takes over four hours to send a repair person to fix a leaking pipe in a wall; meanwhile, all carpeting in the living room is being saturated and one wall is crumbling. A contracted tree-trimming worker cuts a large section from a tree that crashes through the garage roof and onto a brand-new car. A doctor operates on the wrong leg of a patient.

value. As you read in Chapter 9, with the Internet and global competition, many products and services are only a mouse click away. If you and your organization fail to deliver as promised or expected, customers may simply go away. In earlier chapters, you also saw that today's customers tend to be better-educated consumers who recognize that if they cannot fulfill their needs in one place, they can easily access the same or similar products and services on the Internet or by visiting a competitor. Therefore, you need to exceed a customer's expectations. Many terms are used to describe the concept of exceeding expectations—knock-their-socks-off service, positive memorable customer experiences, E-plus service, customer delight, dazzling service, fabled service, and five diamond or five star service. All these phrases have in common the concept mentioned before of going above and beyond customer expectations—*under*promise and *over*deliver. By going out of your way not only to satisfy customers but also to "wow" them by doing, saying, or offering the unexpected related to high-quality service delivery, you can exceed expectations. The result could be the reward of continuing patronage by the customer.

An example of unexpected service or going the extra mile follows. A customer bought flooring tiles from a home product warehouse and took them home. Upon opening the box,

Strategies for Making Customers Number One

ON A SHEET OF PAPER, LIST EACH OF THE INITIATIVES FOR MAKING CUSTOMERS NO. 1 THAT YOU JUST READ ABOUT. Then, develop an action plan for addressing each of them in your customer contacts. Be specific about exactly what you will do or say to address each strategy. Use the following initiatives and specify your actions and the expected customer response.

Make positive initial contact.

Establish rapport.

Identify and satisfy customer needs quickly.

Exceed expectations.

Follow up.

Encourage customers to return.

he discovered that several tiles were broken. After the customer called the store, an employee delivered the replacement tiles and assisted the customer in laying them.

FOLLOW UP

Service professionals regrettably often overlook this important element of the service process, although it can be one of the most crucial in establishing long-term relationships. Follow-through is a major factor in obtaining repeat business. After you have satisfied a customer's needs, follow up with the customer on his or her next visit or via mail, e-mail, or telephone to ensure that he or she was satisfied. For external customers, this follow-up can be coupled with a small thank-you card, coupons for discounts on future purchases, small presents, or any other incentive to reward their patronage. You can follow up with internal customers by using voice mail or e-mail messages, leaving Post-it® notes on their desks, inviting them for coffee in the cafeteria, or any other of a number of ways. The prime objective is to let them know that you have not forgotten them and appreciate their business and support.

ENCOURAGE CUSTOMERS TO RETURN

Just as with your initial impression, you need to close on a high note. Smile, remind the customer you are available to help in the future, give an opportunity for last-minute questions, and invite the customer to return.

6 ENHANCING CUSTOMER SATISFACTION AS A STRATEGY FOR RETAINING CUSTOMERS

Concept: Do the unexpected; deal with one customer at a time; handle complaints efficiently. These are just some of the things you can do to enhance customer satisfaction.

Building good relationships in order to increase **customer satisfaction** is valuable because it can lead to repeat business—the key to keeping a business productive and profitable.

Satisfaction is a big factor for many customers in remaining loyal. According to a national customer satisfaction survey (the American Customer Satisfaction Index), by the University of Michigan, a recent review of customer satisfaction in the United States shows a slight rise in the level of general customer satisfaction. There had been a steady decline

customer satisfaction
The feeling of a person whose needs have been met by an organization.

that began in 1994 (when the numbers were first tracked) through 1997. Since then, there has been a slow increase to 75.2 percent in 2007.[7]

The University of Michigan study shows that there is definitely room for improvement in delivering customer service. In your own organization, your efforts could be a deciding factor in customer ratings for the quality of service rendered.

Keeping customers can be difficult in a competitive, global marketplace because so many companies have joined in the race for customers. By providing a personal, professional strategy, you can help ensure that customers return. Some tips that can help provide quality service to customers are given in the following sections.

PAY ATTENTION

As you listen, focus all your attention on the customer so that you can identify and address his or her needs. If you are serving in person, use positive nonverbal cues (e.g., face the customer, smile, use open gestures, make eye contact, stop doing other things, and focus attention on the customer) and language. Ask open-end questions to determine the customer's needs. Also, use the active listening techniques discussed in Chapter 5 to ensure that you get all the information you need to properly address the customer's needs or concerns.

DEAL WITH ONE CUSTOMER AT A TIME

You cannot effectively handle two people (on the phone or in person) simultaneously. When more than one call or customer comes in at the same time, seek assistance or ask one customer to wait (or ask whether you can get back to him or her at a later time). Then, give personalized attention to the other customer.

KNOW YOUR CUSTOMERS

This is crucial with long-term customers, but it is also important with everyone. You may see or talk to hundreds of customers a week; however, each customer has only one or two contacts with you. Although you might not recall the name of everyone you speak with during a day, your customers will likely remember what was said or agreed upon previously, and expect you to do the same. For that reason, use notes or your computer to keep a record of conversations with customers. You can review or refer to these notes in subsequent encounters. This avoids having customers repeat themselves, and they will feel "special" because you remembered them. Many professionals use database management programs or contact software (e.g., ACT or Maximizer) to log and catalog contacts and customers, as well as to keep detailed notes on each contact with a customer. Consider such programs to be your electronic "cheat sheet" to help you remember important details about all your customers, clients or patients (e.g., spouse names, favorite colors, birthdays, sizes, last purchase).

GIVE CUSTOMERS SPECIAL TREATMENT

As you read earlier, you should try to take the time for a little small talk once in a while. This will help you learn about your customers and what's important to them (potential

[7] Customer Satisfaction Growth Slows, Many Companies Struggle to Keep Up, www.theacsi.org/images/stories/images/news/0507q1.pdf.

needs). Occasionally, paying them compliments also helps (e.g., "That's an attractive tie," or "That perfume is very pleasing").

SERVICE EACH CUSTOMER AT LEAST ADEQUATELY

Take the necessary time to handle your customer's questions, complaints, or needs. If you have a number of customers on the phone or in person, service one at a time and either ask to get back to the others or get help from a coworker, if possible. You might also suggest alternative information resources to customers, such as fax-on-demand or your website, online information system, or interactive voice response. This may satisfy them and help reduce the calls or visits from customers, because they can now get the information they need from alternative sources.

DO THE UNEXPECTED

Do not just provide service; provide exceptional service. Provide additional information, offer suggestions that will aid the customer, send articles that may be of interest, follow up transactions with calls or letters to make sure that needs were met, or send cards for special occasions and to thank customers. These are the little things that mean a lot and can mean the difference between a rating of Average or Exemplary on the relationship-rating point scale. Read the example below to see this concept in action.

> **Give 'Em the Extra Pickle!**
>
> An example of doing the unexpected came when Bob Farrell, founder of Farrell's Ice Cream Parlor restaurants, responded to a customer complaint a number of years ago. Farrell received a letter from a regular customer of many years. The customer had been ordering hamburgers with an extra pickle since he started patronizing Farrell's. At some point, the man went to Farrell's and ordered a hamburger but was told by a new server that the extra pickle would cost an additional 25 cents. When the man protested, the server conferred with her manager and happily reported that the extra pickle would cost only 5 cents. At that point the man left and wrote Farrell, who wrote back enclosing a free coupon, apologizing, and inviting the customer back.
>
> The lesson to be learned here is that when you have a loyal customer whom you might lose because of enforcement of a trivial policy, you should be flexible. When policies inhibit good service and negatively affect customer relationships, they should be pointed out to management and examined for possible modification or elimination.

CUSTOMER SERVICE SUCCESS TIP

Whether someone is a new or existing customer should make no difference. Treat all customers as if they are crucial to the organization—they are!

HANDLE COMPLAINTS EFFECTIVELY

Treat complaints as opportunities to redeem missed service expectations, and handle them effectively. Acknowledge any error on your part, and do everything possible to resolve the problem quickly and to the customer's satisfaction. Thank the customer for bringing his or her concerns to your attention.

SELL BENEFITS, NOT FEATURES

An effective approach to increasing sales is used by most salespeople. They focus on benefits and not features of a product or service. A feature differs from a benefit in that it is a descriptive aspect of a product or service (e.g., has a shorter turn radius, has 27 options, comes in five different colors, has a remote control, and uses less energy than competing models).

Show each customer how your product, service, or information addressed his or her needs. What benefit will result? Stress that although other organizations may offer similar products and services, yours fit their needs best (if they do), and how. If your product or service doesn't fit their needs, admit it, and offer any available alternatives (such as referral to a competitor). Your customers will appreciate your honesty, and even if you can't help them, they will probably return in the future because you are trusted.

KNOW YOUR COMPETITION

Stay abreast of what other, similar organizations are offering in order to counter comments about them. This does not mean that you should criticize or belittle your competitors or their products and services. Such behavior is unprofessional, unethical, and will likely cause the customer to lose respect for you. And when respect goes, trust goes.

Staying aware of the competition has the additional benefit of helping you be sure that you can describe and offer the products, services, and features of your organization that are comparable to those being offered by others.

In 2003, the Marriott hotel chain recognized a need to compete with cheaper reservation rates being offered on the Internet. Marriott announced its "Look No Further Best Rate Guarantee" that matched reservation rates for the same hotel, room type, and reservation dates at all its hotel (excluding Ritz-Carlton) no matter where the customer found them. The chain states as part of its guarantee, "If the lower rate you found qualifies, we will adjust your room rate to reflect that rate, and give you an additional 25% off the lower rate."[8] The hotel chain did this to remain competitive and fill rooms.

7   STRIVE FOR QUALITY

Concept: A customer's perception of quality service is often one of the prime reasons for his or her return.

A final strategy for helping to increase customer loyalty relates to the quality of service you and your organization provide. So much is written these days about quality—how to measure it and its significance—that there is a temptation to think of it as a fad. In the areas of customer service and customer retention, thinking this way could be disastrous. A customer's perception of quality service is often one of the prime reasons for his or her return.

total quality management (TQM) and continuous quality improvement (CQI)
A systematic approach to identifying and quantifying best practices in an organization and/or industry in order to make improvements in effectiveness and efficiency.

Terms such as **total quality management (TQM)** and **continuous quality improvement (CQI)** are often used in many industries to label the goal of improvement. Basically, quality service involves efforts and activities that are done well and that meet or exceed customer needs and expectations. In an effort to achieve quality service, many organizations go to great lengths to test and measure the level of service provided to customers.

On a personal level, you can strive for quality service by working to achieve an Exemplary rating on the relationship-rating point scale. Your organization's ability to deliver quality service depends on you and the others who provide front-line service to customers. If you do not adopt a professional attitude and continually strive to improve your knowledge, skills, and efforts in dealing with customers, failure and customer dissatisfaction can result.

[8]www.marriott.com/hotel-rates/pop-up.mi.

Build enduring, strong customer relationships based on the principles of trust, responsibility, loyalty, and satisfying customer needs. These are all crucial elements of success in an increasingly competitive business world. Retaining current customers is less expensive and more effective than finding and developing new ones. The key is to provide courteous, professional service that addresses customer needs. Although many factors potentially affect your ability to deliver quality service, you can apply specific methods and strategies to keep your customers coming back.

Too often, service providers lose sight of the fact that they are the organization and that their actions determine the outcome of any customer-provider encounter. By employing the strategies outlined in this chapter, and those you read about previously, you can do much to ensure customer satisfaction and organizational success.

churn 266
code of ethics 259
contact points 267
contingency plans 260
cost of dissatisfied customers 254
customer loyalty 248
customer relationships 252
customer retention 253
customer satisfaction 269
ethical behavior 259

moment of truth 266
Planning Process Model 261
relationship management 252
relationship-rating points 267
relationship-rating point scale 267
Technical Assistance Research Program (TARP) 254
total quality management (TQM) and continuous quality
  improvement (CQI) 272
trust 248
touch point 248

1   How can you build customer trust?

2   What are some key reasons why customers remain loyal to a product, a service, or an organization?

3   What are some of the provider characteristics that affect customer loyalty?

4   What are the steps in the planning process model? Describe.

5   What are six common customer needs?

6   What are ways for service providers to take responsibility for customer relations?

7   What are some techniques for making the customer feel that he or she is No. 1?

Search the Web for Information on Loyalty

Log on to the Internet to search for additional information related to customer loyalty. Select one of the following projects:

1   Go to the websites of organizations that deal with customers and service. Identify research data, articles, bibliographies, and other reference sources (e.g., videotapes) related to customer loyalty and create a bibliography similar to the one at the end of this book. Here are a few sites to get you started:

www.ICSA.com
www.SOCAP.com
www.CSR.com

www.Amazon.com
www.Barnes&Noble.com
www.Borders.com

2   Go to various search engines to locate information and articles on *customer loyalty*. To find information, enter terms related to concepts covered in this chapter or locate websites dealing with such issues. Here are a few to get you started:

Customer loyalty
Customer satisfaction
Customer retention
Customer Service Review magazine
Total quality management in customer service
Cost of customer service

Building Loyalty

Here are two options for activities that you and others can use to reinforce the concepts of building loyalty that you read about in this chapter.

1   Working with a partner, think of times when you have both been frustrated or dissatisfied with service received from a provider. Make a list of characteristics the service provider(s) exhibited that had a negative impact on you. Once you have a list, discuss the items on the list, and then honestly say whether either (or both) of you exhibit any of these negative behaviors when dealing with others. For the ones you answered yes, jointly develop a list of strategies to improve each behavior.

2   Take a field trip around your town. Walk through and/or past as many establishments as possible. Look for example of actions that organizations are doing to encourage and discourage customer loyalty. List the examples on a sheet of paper and be prepared to discuss them in groups assigned by your instructor when you return to class. Some examples of encouragement might be free samples of a product being distributed at a food court, discount coupons, acceptance of competitor coupons, or free refills on drinks. Negative examples might be signs that say "Restrooms for customers only" or "No change given," and policies that allow discounts only on certain days and no refunds on purchases (exchanges only).

Assessing the Need for Reorganization at Get Away

Background

After over nine years in business, the Get Away travel agency in Des Moines, Iowa, is feeling the pinch of competition. During the past 14 months, the owners, Marsha Henry and Consuela (Connie) Gomez, have seen business profits dwindle by 18 percent. Employee attrition was also over 50 percent in the past 6 months. Neither Marsha nor Connie can figure out what has happened. Although travel reservationists have had to deal with airline fee caps, customers making more reservations on the Internet, and the fact that many industry travel providers are cutting back, competing agencies don't seem to be suffering as much as Get Away. The problem is especially worrisome because Marsha and Connie recently took out a second mortgage on their office building so that they could put more money into promotion and customer acquisition efforts. The more efforts they make at gaining exposure, the more customers they lose, it seems. Recently, they lost a major corporate client that accounted for over $100,000 in business a year. Out of desperation, they have decided to hire you, a seasoned travel agency manager, to try to stop their descent and turn the operation around.

Your Role

As the new manager at Get Away, you have been given the authority to do whatever is necessary to salvage the agency. By agreement with Marsha and Connie, they are delaying the announcement of your hiring to other agency employees. Your objective is to objectively assess the operation by acting as a customer.

Your first contact with the agency came on Thursday morning, when you placed a phone call to the office at 9:00 A.M.,

posing as a customer. The phone rang 12 times and was curtly answered with "Hello. Please hold (click)." After nearly five minutes, an agent, Sue, came on the line and stated, "Sorry for the wait, we're swamped. Can I get your name and number and call you right back?" Two-and-a-half hours later, you got a call from Tom. He said that Sue had gone home for the day because she was sick, and he was doing her callbacks. Sue would follow up when she came in the next day. You had asked a friend to make a similar call yesterday (Wednesday), and she had similar results.

On Thursday afternoon, you stopped by the office at 1:55 P.M. Of four agents who should have been there, only Claudia was present. Apparently Tom and Sue were still at lunch. Two customers were waiting as you arrived. Aisha greeted you with a small smile and asked you to "Take a number and have a seat." You looked around the office and saw desks piled high with materials, an overflowing trash can, and an empty coffeepot in the waiting area bearing the sign "Please have a cup on us." In talking to your fellow "customers," you learned that one had been there for over 45 minutes. Both were irritated at having to wait, and eventually, one left. You left after 30 minutes and passed Tom and Sue, who came in laughing. You thought you detected an odor of alcohol on Tom. Neither acknowledged you. From the office, you proceeded to a meeting with Marsha and Connie.

Critical Thinking Questions

1   What impressions of the travel agency did you have as a result of your initial phone call?
2   How did your office visit affect you?
3   What will you tell Marsha and Connie about employee professionalism?
4   What customer needs are being overlooked in this scenario?
5   In what ways can this situation be improved?

SERVICE-7-Eleven Inc.

From your experience, what you read at the beginning of the chapter, and what you found on 7-Eleven's website, what do you feel are the strengths of the company from a customer perspective? Explain.

From a customer perspective, what weaknesses do you think the company has, if any? Explain.

How do you think 7-Eleven has done keeping up with the changing needs of its customers since its inception back in 1927? Explain.

In your mind, what separates 7-Eleven from its competitors in the convenience store industry?

To help enhance customer retention and foster customer loyalty efforts of any organization, think about the following questions:

1   What are some strategies that can be used to show customers that their business is valued?

2   What obstacles exist to customer loyalty and how might they be removed?

3   What are some of the things that positively impact customer loyalty in many organizations?

4   What are some things that differentiate organizations and which can be accentuated to build customer retention and loyalty?

1 T	5 T	9 T
2 F	6 F	10 F
3 T	7 T	11 T
4 T	8 T	12 T

Ethical Dilemma 10.1

1   What are the ethical issues here and how would you deal with them? Explain.

This is certainly a very awkward, sensitive and serious issue with which to deal. If you fail to share your concerns and feelings about the way the situation is being handled with the pharmacist, it will possibly be repeated, and potentially have serious medical repercussions or worse. The pharmacist is not only acting unprofessionally, unethically, and potentially illegally, he is also potentially putting himself and the organization in a litigious situation and endangering the lives of patients. Granted, this may have been a legitimate mistake on the part of the pharmacist; however, that does not make it any less serious.

On the other hand, if you refuse to do as the pharmacist tells you, your job and future opportunities might be in

jeopardy. This could be a reality; however, remember that federal law protects whistleblowers from retaliation. Also, you have an option of going to the store manager to discuss the issue. The bottom line is that this is a very serious medical issue.

2   What would you say or do to the pharmacist?

Because of the serious nature of this incident, you should not become part in a potentially litigious and health-threatening situation. Tell the pharmacist that you do not feel comfortable not telling the patient the truth and ask him to handle it himself.

3   What do you do or say to the patient? Explain.

In the immediate instance, you should probably defer discussion of the matter and explain that the pharmacist or someone else will be right with the customer.

4   What else would you do in this situation?

Because of the serious nature of this event, you should definitely report it to the store manager and depending on the reaction that you get, you may want to consider whether this organization is really somewhere that you want to continue working. If the situation is not properly resolved with the disciplining and/or removal of the pharmacist, there are going to be major legal and other problems in the future. If it is not handled at a local level, you can always contact the regional store manager and if necessary corporate headquarters. If all else fails, each state has governmental agencies that license and oversee pharmacies and pharmacists. You can report the incident to them for investigation.

5 How do such instances potentially affect customer loyalty?

There have been many media reports of similar incidents in recent years and as a result consumers are very skeptical and leery about going to pharmacies. Typically, when these cases arise, there is an exodus from pharmacies to their competitors. The old adage of "buyer beware" is certainly the watchword for many patients these days. Also, there are many watchdog groups monitoring such cases.

Reader's Customer Service Survey

Name _____

Title _____

Organization/School _____

Address (where you want booklet mailed) _____

_____

City/State/ZIP _____

Phone (_____ **)** _____

Customer feedback is crucial for delivering effective service and addressing specific needs. For us to make necessary additions, deletions, or corrections to this book we need your help. Please take a few minutes to provide feedback in the following areas and return this questionnaire to the address noted. In exchange for your thoughts and time, we'll send you a free booklet, "Communicating One-to-One," on effective interpersonal communication techniques. (Photocopy the questionnaire if you prefer).

Thank you.

1. Describe yourself in terms of customer contact experience:
   _____ Entry level (up to 1 year) _____ Midlevel (2–5 years) _____ Senior (5+ years)

2. Are you currently working in a customer contact position in a business or organization?
   Yes _____ No _____

3. The information provided in this book was clearly written and easy to read.
   1 _____ 2 _____ 3 _____ 4 _____ 5 _____ 6 _____ 7 _____
   Strongly   Neutral   Strongly
   disagree   agree

4. The techniques outlined in this book are realistic and useful.
   1 _____ 2 _____ 3 _____ 4 _____ 5 _____ 6 _____ 7 _____
   Strongly   Neutral   Strongly
   disagree   agree

5. The supplemental materials (website materials, figures, role-play activities, questions, references) added value to the text.

1 _____ 2 _____ 3 _____ 4 _____ 5 _____ 6 _____ 7 _____
Strongly   Neutral   Strongly
disagree   agree

6. The design of this book was logical, efficient, effective, and easy to follow.

1 _____ 2 _____ 3 _____ 4 _____ 5 _____ 6 _____ 7 _____
Strongly   Neutral   Strongly
disagree   agree

7. The level of information was well targeted to entry to midlevel customer contact personnel.

1 _____ 2 _____ 3 _____ 4 _____ 5 _____ 6 _____ 7 _____
Strongly   Neutral   Strongly
disagree   agree

8. The text included real-world examples and scenarios that helped make chapter content more relevant to the workplace.

1 _____ 2 _____ 3 _____ 4 _____ 5 _____ 6 _____ 7 _____
Strongly   Neutral   Strongly
disagree   agree

9. I can apply information or ideas learned directly to my current or future job.

1 _____ 2 _____ 3 _____ 4 _____ 5 _____ 6 _____ 7 _____
Strongly   Neutral   Strongly
disagree   agree

10. I plan to use this book as a reference in the future.

1 _____ 2 _____ 3 _____ 4 _____ 5 _____ 6 _____ 7 _____
Strongly   Neutral   Strongly
disagree   agree

11. This book met my overall needs and expectations.

1 _____ 2 _____ 3 _____ 4 _____ 5 _____ 6 _____ 7 _____
Strongly   Neutral   Strongly
disagree   agree

12. I will recommend this book to others.

1 _____ 2 _____ 3 _____ 4 _____ 5 _____ 6 _____ 7 _____
Strongly   Neutral   Strongly
disagree   agree

13. What chapter was most valuable to you? Why? _____

_____

14. In your mind, what is the most critical issue facing customer service professionals today? Why?

_____

_____

15. If you rated any question below a 5 above, please explain why you did so.

_____

_____

16. What other topics related to customer service are of interest to you? Why?

_____

17. Did you use any of the supplemental website content created for this book, if so, what did you use?

_____

Send form to: Bob Lucas, President
Creative Presentation Resources Inc.
P.O. Box 180487
Casselberry, Florida 32718-0487
Phone: (800)308-0399/(407)695-5535
Fax: (407)695-7447
E-mail: blucas@presentationresources.net

Glossary

A

acknowledgment A communication technique for use with customers who have a complaint or are upset. It involves recognizing the customer's level of emotion before moving on to help resolve the issue.

Americans with Disabilities Act of 1990 A United States federal act signed into law in July of 1990 guaranteeing people with disabilities equal access to workplace and public opportunities.

angry customers Customers who become emotional because either their needs are not met or they are dissatisfied with the services or products purchased from an organization.

appearance and grooming Nonverbal characteristics exhibited by service providers that can send a variety of messages that range from being a professional to having a negative attitude.

articulation, enunciation, or pronunciation Refers to the manner or clarity in which verbal messages are delivered.

assertiveness Involves projecting a presence that is assured, confident, and capable without seeming to be aggressive or arrogant.

assigning meaning The phase of the listening process in which the brain attempts to match a received sound or message with other information stored in the brain in order to recognize or extract meaning from it.

attending The phase of the listening process in which a listener focuses attention on a specific sound or message being received from the environment.

attitudes Emotional responses to people, ideas, and objects. They are based on values, differ between individuals and cultures, and affect the way people deal with various issues and situations.

automated attendants Provide callers with a menu of options from which they can select by pressing a key on their telephone keypad.

automatic call distribution (ACD) system Telecommunications system used by many companies in their call centers and customer care facilities to capture incoming calls and route them to available service providers.

automatic number identification (ANI) system A form of caller identification system similar to home telephone caller ID systems. ANI allows incoming customers to be identified on a computer screen with background information so that they can be routed to an appropriate service representative for assistance.

B

baby boomer A term applied to anyone born between 1946 and 1964. People in this age group are called "boomers."

behavioral styles Descriptive term that identifies categories of human behavior identified by behavioral researchers. Many of the models used to group behaviors date back to those identified by Carl Jung.

beliefs Perceptions or assumptions that individuals or cultures maintain. These perceptions are based on past experiences, memories, and interpretations and influence how people act and interact with certain individuals or groups.

biases Beliefs or opinions that a person has about an individual or group. Often based on unreasonable distortions or prejudice.

blind transfer The practice of transferring an incoming caller to another telephone number and hanging up once someone answers without announcing who is calling.

blogs or weblogs Online journals or diaries that allow people to add content. Many organizational websites use them to post "what's new" sections and to receive feedback (good and bad) from customers and website visitors.

body language Nonverbal communication cues that send powerful messages through gestures, vocal qualities, manner of dress and grooming, and many other cues.

burnout A category of stress that encompasses personal exhaustion, lack of enthusiasm, reduced productivity, and apathy toward the job and customers.

business-to-business (B2B) Refers to a business-to-business customer service.

C

channel Term used to describe the method through which people communicate messages. Examples are face to face, telephone, e-mail, written correspondence, and facsimile.

Chicano culture Refers primarily to people with a heritage based in Mexico.

churn The process of a customer switching between products or companies, often simply to get a better price, rebate, or warranty.

circadian rhythm The physiological 24-hour cycle associated with the earth's rotation that affects metabolic and sleep patterns in humans as day displaces night.

closed-end questions Inquiries that typically start with a verb and solicit short one-syllable answers (e.g., yes, no, one word, or a number) and can be used for such purposes as clarifying, verifying information already given, controlling conversation, or affirming something.

clusters of nonverbal behavior Groupings of nonverbal behaviors that indicate a possible negative intent (e.g., crossed arms, closed body posturing, frowning, or turning away) while other behaviors (smiling, open gestures with arms and hands, and friendly touching) indicate positive message intent.

code of ethics A set of standards, often developed by employees, which guide the conduct of all employees.

Cold War A period of military, economic, and political tension and competition between the United States and the former Soviet Union that lasted from the 1940s through the 1990s.

collective cultures   Members of a group sharing common interests and values. They see themselves as an interdependent unit and conform and cooperate for the good of the group.

comprehending   The phase of the listening process in which the brain attempts to match a received sound or message with other information stored in the brain in order to recognize or extract meaning from it.

computer telephony integration (CTI)   A system that integrates a representative's computer and phone to facilitate the automatic retrieval of customer records and other information needed to satisfy a customer's needs and requests.

concept of time   Term used to describe how certain societies view time as either polychronic or monochronic.

conflict   Involves incompatible or opposing views and can result when a customer's needs, desires, or demands do not match service provider or organizational policies, procedures, and abilities.

conflict resolution style   The manner in which a person handles conflict. People typically use one of five approaches to resolving conflict—avoidance, compromise, competition, accommodation, or collaboration.

congruence   In communication, this relates to ensuring that verbal messages sent match or are in agreement with the nonverbal cues used.

contact points   Instances in which a customer connects with a service provider or some other aspect of an organization.

contingency plans   Backup systems or procedures that are implemented when regular ones break down or fail to function as intended.

cost of dissatisfied customers   Phrase that refers to any formula used to calculate the cost of acquiring a new customer or replacing a current one as a result of having a dissatisfied customer leave an organization.

cottage industries   Term adopted in the early days of customer service when many people started small businesses in their homes or cottages and bartered products or services with neighbors.

crisis manager   A person who waits until the last minute to address an issue or take an action. The result is that others are then inconvenienced and have to shift their priorities to help resolve the issue.

cultural diversity   Refers to the differences and similarities attributed to various groups of people within a culture.

customer-centric   A term used to describe service providers and organizations that put their customers first and spend time, effort, and money identifying and focusing on the needs of current and potential customers. Efforts are focused on building long-term relationships and customer loyalty rather than simply selling a product or service and moving on to the next customer.

customer contact center   A central point within an organization from which all customer service contacts are managed via various forms of technology.

customer defection   Customers often take their business to competitors when they feel that their needs or wants are not met or if they encounter breakdown in customer service or poor quality products.

customer expectations   The perceptions that customers have when they contact an organization or service provider about the kind and level and quality of products and services they should receive.

customer-focused organization   A company that spends energy and effort on satisfying internal and external customers by first identifying customer needs, then establishing policies, procedures, and management and reward systems to support excellence in service delivery.

customer-friendly systems   Refers to the processes in an organization that make service seamless to customers by ensuring that things work properly and the customer is satisfied.

customer loyalty   Term used to describe the tendency of customers to return to a product or organization regularly because of the service and satisfaction they receive.

customer needs   Motivators or drivers that cause customers to seek out specific types of products or services. These may be marketing-driven by advertising they have seen or may tie directly to Dr. Abraham Maslow's Hierarchy of Needs Theory.

customer relationship management (CRM)   Concept of identifying customer needs: understanding and influencing customer behavior through ongoing communication strategies in an effort to acquire, retain, and satisfy the customer. The ultimate goal is customer loyalty.

customer relationships   The practice of building and maintaining ongoing friendships with customers in an effort to make them feel comfortable with an organization and its service providers and to enhance customer loyalty.

customer retention   The ongoing effort by an organization to meet customer needs and desires in an effort to build long-term relationships and keep them for life.

customer satisfaction   The feeling of a person whose needs have been met by an organization.

customer service   The ability of knowledgeable, capable, and enthusiastic employees to deliver products and services to their internal and external customers in a manner that satisfies identified and unidentified needs and ultimately results in positive word-of-mouth publicity and return business.

customer service environment   An environment made up of and influenced by various elements of an organization. Examples are delivery systems, human resources, service, products, and organizational culture.

customers with disabilities   Descriptive phrase that refers to anyone with a physical or mental disability.

D

decisive style   One of four behavior style groupings characterized by a direct, no-nonsense approach to people and situations.

decoding   The stage in the interpersonal communication process in which messages received are analyzed by a receiver in an effort to determine the sender's intent.

deliverables   Products or services provided by an organization.

delivery system   The method(s) used by an organization to provide services and products to its customers.

demanding or domineering customers   Customers who have definite ideas about what they want and are unwilling to compromise or accept alternatives.

deregulation   Occurs when governments remove legislative or regulatory guidelines that inhibit and control an industry (e.g., transportation, natural gas, and telecommunications).

difficult customers   People who challenge a service provider's ability to deliver service and who require special skills and patience.

dissatisfied customers   Someone who either does not (or perceives that he or she does not) receive promised products or services.

distress   Pain or worry brought on by either internal or external physical or mental strain.

diversity   The characteristics, values, beliefs, and factors that make people different, yet similar.

downsizing   Term applied to the situation in which employees are terminated.

E

e-commerce   An entire spectrum of companies that market products and services on the Internet and through other technology, and the process of accessing them by consumers.

electronic mail (e-mail)   System used to transmit messages around the Internet.

e-mail management   System of providing organizational guidelines for effective use of e-mail systems.

emoticons (emotional icons)   Humorous characters that send visual messages such as smiling or frowning. They are created with various strokes of the computer keyboard characters and symbols.

emotional messages of color   Research-based use of color to send nonverbal messages through advertisements and other elements of the organization.

emotion-reducing model   Process for reducing customer emotion in situations when frustration or anger exists.

employee assistance program (EAP)   Benefit package offered to employees by many organizations that provide services to help employees deal with personal problems that might adversely affect their work performance (e.g., legal, financial, behavioral, and mental counseling services).

employee expectations   Perceptions about positive and negative aspects of the workplace.

employee roles   Task assignments that service providers assume.

empowerment   The word used to describe the giving of decision-making and problem-resolution authority to lower-level employees in an organization. This precludes having to get permission from higher levels in order to take an action or serve a customer.

encoding   The stage in the interpersonal communication process in which the sender decides what message will be sent and how it will be transmitted along with considerations about the receiver.

environmental cues   Any aspect of the workplace with which a customer comes into contact. Such things as the general appearance of an area, clutter, unsightly or offensive items, or general disorganization contribute to the perception of an environment.

environmental factors affecting stress   Refers to the workplace, organizational, and societal elements that impact a service provider's mental and physical state.

ethical behavior   Expected performance that sends a message of being trustworthy and honest, and having the intent to provide quality service.

etiquette and manners   Includes the acceptable rules, manners, and ceremonies for an organization, profession, or society.

eustress   A term coined by psychologist, Dr. Hans Seyle, to describe positive stress that people sometimes experience when they set goals or objectves and exhilaration that are essential for personal expansion and growth.

expectations of privacy   The belief that personal information provided to an organization will be safeguarded against inappropriate or unauthorized use or dissemination.

expressive style   One of four behavior groups characterized as being people-oriented, fun-loving, upbeat, and extroverted.

external customers   Those people outside the organization who purchase or lease products and services. This group includes vendors, suppliers, and people on the telephone, and others not from the organization.

external obstacles   Factors outside an organization or the sphere of one's influence that can cause challenges in delivering service.

F

face   Refers to the important concept of esteem in many Asian cultures. In such cultures one tries not to cause embarrassment or otherwise create a situation in which someone looks bad in the eyes of others.

facsimile (fax) machine   Equipment that converts printed words and graphics into electronic signals and allows them to be transmitted across telephone lines then reassembled into a facsimile of the words and graphics on the receiving end.

faulty assumptions   Service provider projections made about underlying customer message meanings based on past experiences.

fax on demand   Technology that allows information, such as a form, stored in a computer to be requested electronically via a telephone and transmitted to a customer.

fee-based 900 number   A premium telephone number provided by organizations and individuals that, when called, can provide information and services that are billed back to the caller's local telephone bill.

feedback   The stage of the interpersonal communication process in which a receiver responds to a sender's message.

feel, felt, found technique   A process for expressing empathy and concern for someone and for helping them understand that you can relate to their situation.

fight or flight syndrome   A term used by scientists to describe the body's reaction to stressors in which the heart starts pumping the chemical adrenaline into the blood stream and the lungs start taking in more oxygen. This provides the fuel needed to deal with the situation. (*See also* stressors.)

filters   Psychological barriers in the form or personal experiences, lessons learned, societal beliefs, and values through which people process and compare information received to determine its significance.

foreign-born people   Refers to people not born in a given country.

form of address   Title used to address people. Examples are Mister, Miss, and Doctor.

G

gender communication   Term used to refer to communication between genders.

gender roles   Behaviors attributed to or assigned by societal norms.

globalization   The term applied to an ongoing trend of information, knowledge, and resource sharing around the world. As a result of a more mobile society and easier access to transportation and technology, more people are traveling and accessing products and services from international sources than ever before.

global terms   Potentially inflammatory words or phrases used in conversation. They tend to inappropriately generalize behavior or group people or incidents together (e.g., always, never, everyone, everything, all the time).

H

hearing   A passive physiological process of gathering sound waves and transmitting them to the brain for analysis. It is the first phase of the listening process.

hearing disabilities   Conditions in which the ability to hear is diminished below established auditory standards.

help desk   Term used to describe a service provider trained and assigned to assist customers with questions, problems, or suggestions.

Hierarchy of Needs Theory   Developed by Dr. Abraham Maslow. In studies, Maslow identified five levels of needs that humans possess—physiological (basic), safety, social, esteem, and self-actualization.

Hispanic culture   Refers to people who were born in Mexico, Puerto Rico, Cuba, or Central or South America.

human resources   Refers to the employees of an organization.

hygiene   The healthy maintenance of the body through such practices as regular bathing, washing of hair, brushing of teeth, cleaning of fingernails, and using commercial products to eliminate or mask odors.

I

"I" or "we" messages   Messages that are potentially less offensive than the word "you," which is like nonverbal finger pointing when emotions are high.

impact of culture   Refers to the outcome of people from various countries or backgrounds coming into contact with one another and potentially experiencing misunderstandings or relationship breakdowns.

inclusive   The concept of ensuring that people of all races, genders, and religious and ethnic backgrounds, as well as a multitude of other diverse factors, are included in communications and activities in the workplace.

indecisive customers   People who have difficulty making a decision or making a selection when given choices of products or services.

individualistic cultures   Groups in which members value themselves as individuals who are separate from their group and are responsible for their own destiny.

inflection   The change in tone of the voice as one speaks. This quality is also called pitch and adds vocal variety and punctuation to verbal messages.

information overload   Refers to having too many messages coming together and causing confusion, frustration, or an inability to act.

inquisitive style   One of four behavioral groups characterized by being introverted, task-focused, and detail-oriented.

interactive voice response (IVR) system   Technology that allows customers to call an organization 24 hours a day, 7 days a week to get infor-

mation from recorded messages or a computer by keying a series of numbers on the telephone keypad in response to questions or prompts.

interferences   Noises that can interfere with messages being effectively communicated between two people.

internal customers   People within the organization who either require support and service or provide information, products, and services to service providers. Such customers include peers, coworkers, bosses, subordinates, and people from other areas of the organization.

Internet callback   Technology that allows someone browsing the Internet to key a prompt on a website and have a service representative call a phone number provided.

Internet telephony   Technology that allows people to talk to one another via the Internet as if they were on a regular telephone.

interpersonal relationship   Focuses on the need for service providers to build strong bonds with customers.

interpersonal skills   The skills used by people to relate to and communicate effectively with others. Examples are verbal and nonverbal communication skills and the ability to build trust, empathy, and compassion.

iPod   A brand of portable media player that has been manufactured and marketed by Apple® computer since 2001. It can play digital audio files and videos and can also function as an external data storage unit.

job factors affecting stress   Refers to the elements of a job that frustrate or pressure someone.

job stress   Term coined to describe the impact of the internal and external elements of the workplace that cause service providers to feel mentally and physically pressured or to become ill.

L

lag time   The term applied to the difference in the rate at which the human brain can receive and process information and at which most adults speak.

Latino culture   Refers to people of Hispanic descent.

learning organizations   A term used by Peter Senge in his book *The Fifth Discipline* to describe organizations that value knowledge, education, and employee training. They also learn from their competition, industry trends, and other sources, and they develop systems to support continued growth and development in order to remain competitive.

listening   An active, learned process consisting of four phases—receiving/hearing the message, attending, comprehending/assigning meaning, and responding.

listening gap   The difference in the speed at which the brain can comprehend communication and the speed at which the average adult speaks in the United States.

M

media blending   Technology that allows a service provider to communicate with a customer via telephone while at the same time displaying information to the customer over the computer.

memory   The ability to gain, store, retain and recall information In the brain for later application. Short-term memory stores small bits of information (7 items, plus or minus 2) for approximately 20 seconds while long-term memory can store much larger quantities of Information for potentially unlimited duration.

mentees   Typically less experienced recipients of the efforts of mentors.

mentors   Individuals who dedicate time and effort to befriend and assist others. In an organization, they are typically people with a lot of knowledge, experience, skills, and initiative, and have a large personal and professional network established.

message   A communication delivered through speech or signals, or in writing.

miscellaneous cues   Refers to factors used to send messages that impact a customer's perception or feelings about a service provider or organization. Examples are personal habits, etiquette, and manners.

mission   The direction or focus of an organization that supports day-to-day interactions with customers.

mobility or motion impairments   Physical limitations that some people have, requiring accommodation or special consideration to allow access to products or services.

modesty   Refers to the way that cultures view propriety of dress and conduct.

moment of truth   A phrase popularized by Scandinavian Airlines System President Jan Carlzon in his popular 1987 book of the same name. A moment of truth is defined as any instance when a customer comes into contact with any element or representative of an organization.

monochronic   Refers to the perception of time as being a central focus with deadlines being a crucial element of societal norms.

N

needs   Motivators or drivers that cause customers to seek out specific types of products or services. These may be marketing-driven, based on advertising they have seen, or may tie directly to Abraham Maslow's hierarchy of needs theory.

noise   Refers to physiological or psychological factors (physical characteristics, level of attention, message clarity, loudness of message, or environmental factors) that interfere with the accurate reception of information.

nonverbal feedback   Messages sent to someone through other than spoken means. Examples are gestures, appearance, and facial expressions.

nonverbal messages   Consist of such things as movements, gestures, body positions, vocal qualities, and a variety of unspoken signals sent by people, often in conjunction with verbal messages.

North American Free Trade Agreement (NAFTA)   A trade agreement entered into by the United States, Canada, and Mexico among other things to help eliminate barriers to trade, promote conditions of fair trade across borders, and increase investment opportunities, and promote and protect intellectual property rights.

O

objections   Reasons given by customers for not wanting to purchase a product or service during an interaction with a salesperson or service provider (e.g., "I don't need one," "I can't afford it," or "I already have one").

offshoring   Refers to the relocation of business services from one country to another (e.g. services, production, and manufacturing).

online information fulfillment system   Technology that allows a customer to access an organization's website and click on desired information without having to interact with a service provider.

open-end questions   Typically start with words like who, when, what, how, and why and are used to engage others in conversation or to gain input and ideas.

organizational culture   Includes an element of an organization that a customer encounters.

outsourcing   Refers to the practice of contracting with third-party companies or vendors outside the organization (usually in another country) to deliver products and services to customers or produce products.

ownership of property   Refers to how people of a given culture view property.

P

paralanguage   Consists of voice qualities (e.g., pitch, rate, tone, or other vocal qualities) or noises and vocalizations (e.g., "Hmmm" or "Ahhh") made as someone speaks, which let a speaker know that his or her message is being listened to and followed.

paraphrase   The practice of a message receiver giving back in his or her own words what he or she believes a sender said.

pauses   A verbal technique of delaying response in order to allow time to process information received, think of a response, or gain attention.

perception checking   The process of clarifying a nonverbal cue that was received by stating what behavior was observed, giving one or two possible interpretations, then asking the message sender for clarification.

perceptions   How someone views an item, situation, or others.

personal factors affecting stress   Refers to issues that someone has related to family, finances, or other elements of life that can create pressure or frustration.

personal obstacles   Factors that can limit performance or success in life. Examples are disabilities, lack of education, or biases.

pet peeves   Refers to factors, people, or situations that personally irritate or frustrate a service provider and which, left unchecked, can create a breakdown in effective service.

pitch   Refers to the change in tone of the voice as one speaks. This quality is also called inflection and adds vocal variety and punctuation to verbal messages.

planning process model   Five-step process for creating contingency or backup plans to better serve customers when problems arise or things do not go as expected.

Platinum Rule   Term coined by speaker and author Tony Alessandra related to going beyond the step of treating customers the way you want to be treated, to the next level of treating them the way they would like to be treated.

podcasts or podcasting   A word that is a derivative of Apple® computers iPod® media player and the term broadcasting. Through podcasts, websites can offer direct download or streaming of their content (e.g., music or video files) to customers or website users.

polychronic   Refers to the perception of time as a fluid commodity that does not interfere with relationships and elements of happiness.

posture Refers to how one sits or stands in order to project various nonverbal messages.

predictive dialing system Technology that automatically places outgoing calls and delivers incoming calls to the next available service representative in a call center.

primary behavior pattern Refers to a person's preferred style of dealing with others.

prioritizing time Relates to how someone decides the importance of various tasks and the order in which they are dealt with.

problem solving The system of identifying issues, determining alternatives for dealing with them, then selecting and monitoring a strategy for resolution.

problem-solving model The process used by a service provider to assist customers in determining and selecting appropriate solutions to their issues, concerns, or needs.

process improvement Refers to the process of continually evaluating products and services to ensure that maximum effectiveness, efficiency, and potential are being obtained from them.

product Something produced or an output by an individual or organization. In the service environment, products are created to satisfy customer needs or wants.

prohibitions Local, state, or federal regulations that prevent a service provider from satisfying a customer's request even though the provider would normally do so.

proxemics Relates to the invisible barrier surrounding people in which they feel comfortable interacting with others. This zone varies depending on the level of relationship a person has with someone else.

psychological distracters Refers to mental factors that can cause a shift in focus in interacting with others. Examples are state of health and personal issues.

R

rapport The silent bond built between two people as a result of sharing of common interests and issues and demonstration of a win-win, I care attitude.

rate of speech Refers to the number of words spoken per minute. Some research studies have found that the average rate of speech for adults in Western cultures is approximately 125–150 words per minute (wpm).

rational style One of four behavioral groups characterized by being quiet, reflective, task-focused, and systematic.

receiver One of the two primary elements of a two-way conversation. Gathers the sender's message and decides how to react to it.

recognition A process that occurs in thinking when a previously experienced pattern, event, process, image, or object that is stored in memory is encountered again.

relationship management The process of continually monitoring interactions with a customer in order to strengthen ties and retain the customer.

relationship-rating points Values mentally assigned by customers to a service provider and his or her organization. They are based on a number of factors starting with initial impressions and subsequently by the quality and level of service provided.

relationship-rating point scale The mental rating system that customers apply to service and service providers. Ratings range from *exemplary* to *unsatisfactory,* with *average* being assigned when service occurs as expected.

respect for elders A value held by people from many cultures.

responding Refers to sending back verbal and nonverbal messages to a message originator.

road rage A term used to describe the practice of a driver or passenger in a vehicle verbally and/or physically assaulting others as a result of the frustrations experienced while driving (e.g., driver failing to signal, cutting into a lane abruptly, or tailgating).

rude or inconsiderate customers People who seem to take pleasure in being obstinate and contrary when dealing with service providers and who seem to have their own agenda without concern for the feelings of others.

RUMBA An acronym for five criteria (realistic, understandable, measurable, believable, and attainable) used to establish and measure employee performance goals.

S

screen pop-ups Small screen images that are programmed to appear on someone's computer monitor when a website is accessed.

seamless service Service which is done in a manner that seems effortless and natural to the customer. Processes and systems are fully functional, effective, and efficient, service representatives are well-trained and proficient in delivering service, and there is no inconvenience to the customer.

semantics The scientific study of relationships between signs, symbols, and words and their meaning. The way words are used or stressed often affects their perceived meaning.

sender One of the two primary elements of a two-way conversation. Originates messages to a receiver.

service breakdowns Situations when customers have expectations of a certain type or level of service that are not met by a service provider.

service culture A service environment made up of various factors, including the values, beliefs, norms, rituals and practices of a group or organization.

service delivery systems The mechanisms or strategies used by an organization to provide service to customers.

service economy A term used to describe the trend in which businesses have shifted from primarily production and manufacturing to more service delivery. As part of this evolution, many organizations have developed specifically to provide services to customers.

service industry A term used to describe businesses and organizations that are engaged primarily in service delivery. Service sector is a more accurate term, since many organizations provide some form of service to their customers even though they are primarily engaged in research, development, and manufacture of products.

service measurement Techniques used by organizations to determine how customers perceive the value of services and products received.

service options Alternatives offered by service providers when an original request by a customer cannot be honored because of such restrictions as governmental statutory regulations, nonavailability of products, or inability to perform as requested.

service philosophy   The approach that an organization takes to providing service and addressing the needs of customers.

service recovery   The process of righting a wrong or correcting something that has gone wrong involving provision of a product or service to a customer. The concept involves not only replacing defective products, but also going the extra step of providing compensation for the customer's inconvenience.

service sector   Refers to organizations and individuals involved in delivering service as a primary product.

setting priorities   The process of deciding which factors or elements have greater importance and placing them in a hierarchy.

silence   Technique used to gain attention when speaking, to allow thought, or to process information received.

Small Business Administration (SBA)   United States governmental agency established to assist small business owners.

small talk   Dialogue used to enhance relationships, show civility, and build rapport.

spamming or spam   An abusive use of various electronic messaging systems and technology to send unsolicited and indiscriminant bulk messages to people (also used with instant messaging, Web search engines, blogs, and other formats).

spatial cues   Nonverbal messages sent on the basis of how close or far someone stands from another person.

stereotype   Generalization made about an individual or group and not based on reality. Similar people are often lumped together for ease in categorizing them.

strategies for preventing dissatisfaction   Techniques used to prevent a breakdown in needs fulfillment when you are dealing with customers.

strategies for reclaiming time   Techniques used to eliminate time wasters and to become more effective and efficient.

stressors   Factors in a person's life that cause them to react positively or negatively to a situation that caused the pressure. (*See also* fight or flight syndrome.)

T

talkative customers   Customers exhibiting extroverted behavior who are very people-oriented.

Technical Assistance Research Program (TARP)   An Arlington, Virginia, based firm specializing in customer service research studies for call centers and many other industries.

telecommuting   A trend seen in many congested metropolitan areas and government offices. To reduce traffic, pollution, and save resources (e.g., rent, telephone, and technology systems) many organizations allow employees to set up home offices and from there electronically communicate and forward information to their corporate offices.

teletype systems (TTY)   A typewriter-type device used by people with hearing disabilities for typing messages back and forth via telephone lines. [Also known as telephone device for the disabled (TDD).]

telephone management   Strategies for the effective use of the telephone and associated equipment in communicating.

thought speed   The rate at which the human brain processes information.

time allocation   Amount of attention given to a person or project.

time management   The systematic practice of categorizing daily activities, identifying and eliminating factors that interfere with efficiency, and developing effective strategies for getting the most out of the time available.

time management and technology   Refers to the ability to use technology to improve effectiveness and efficiency in a service environment.

time management face-to-face   Techniques for increasing time efficiency when dealing with customers.

time management on the run   Strategies for using downtime effectively to accomplish small tasks or be creative.

time perception   The manner in which time is viewed as being either polychronic or monochronic.

time reality   Acceptance of the fact that each person has only a finite amount of time each day to accomplish tasks and to enhance its usage.

time wasters   Events, people, items, and other factors that create unnecessary loss of time.

total quality management (TQM) and continous quality improvement (CQI)   A systematic approach to identifying and quantifying best practices in an organization and/or industry in order to make improvements in effectiveness and efficiency.

touch point   Any instance in which a service provider or organization (e.g., face to face, in writing, through technology) comes in contact with a customer; it is an opportunity to influence customer loyalty and enhance the customer relationship.

trust   Key element in cementing interpersonal relationships.

two-way communication   An active process in which two individuals apply all the elements of interpersonal communication (e.g., listening, feedback, positive language) in order to effectively exchange information and ideas.

U

underpromise and overdeliver   A service strategy in which service providers strive for excellent customer service and satisfaction by doing more than they say they will for the customer or exceeding customer expectations.

V

values   Long-term appraisals of the worth of an idea, person, place, thing, or practice held by individuals, groups, or cultures. They affect attitudes and behavior.

verbal feedback   The response given to a sender's message that allows both the sender and receiver to know that a message was received correctly.

verbal fillers   Verbal sounds, words, or utterances that break silence but add little to a conversation. Examples are uh, um, ah, and you know.

vision disabilities   Condition resulting from reduced or lost visual acuity or ability.

vocal cues   Qualities of the voice that send powerful nonverbal messages. Examples are rate, pitch, volume, and tone.

voice mail management   System for creating outgoing messages and leaving messages on an answering system effectively.

voice quality   Refers to the sound of one's voice. Terms often attributed to voice quality are raspy, nasal, hoarse, and gravelly.

voice response unit (VRU)   System that allows customers to call 24 hours a day, 7 days a week by keying a series of numbers on the telephone keypad in order to get information or answers to questions.

volume   Refers to loudness or softness of the voice when speaking.

W

wants   Things that customers typically desire but do not necessarily need.

what customers want   Things that customers typically desire but do not necessarily need.

Wiki   A form of server software that allows nontechnical personnel to create and edit website pages using any web browser and without complex programming knowledge.

win-win situation   An outcome to a disagreement in which both parties walk away feeling that they got what they wanted or needed.

workplace violence   A trend that has developed and escalated in the past decade. Spawned by many changes in the workplace, shifting societal values and beliefs, and a variety of other factors, violence is blossoming in the workplace.

Y

Y2K bug   The term applied to a programming error made in many software packages that would cause a computer to fail to recognize the year 2000 at midnight on December 31, 1999. In instances where the oversight occurred, computers would cease to function at that hour. Billions of dollars were spent to correct the error worldwide.

younger customers   Subjective term referring to anyone younger than the service provider. Sometimes used to describe members of generation X (born to baby boomers) or later.

Bibliography

Aguilar, Leslie, and Linda Stokes, *Multicultural Customer Service: Providing Outstanding Service Across Cultures,* McGraw-Hill/Irwin, Burr Ridge, IL., 1996.

Alessandra, Tony, and Michael J. O'Connor, *The Platinum Rule: Discover the Four Basic Business Personalities and How They Can Lead You to Success,* Grand Central Publishing, New York, NY, 1998.

Andersen, Peter A., *The Complete Idiot's Guide to Body Language,* Penguin Group, New York, NY, 2004.

Anderson, Kristin, and Carol Kerr, *Customer Relationship Management,* McGraw-Hill,

New York, NY, 2002.

Anderson, Kristin, and Ron Zemke, *Knock Their Socks Off Answers,* AMACOM, New York, NY, 1995.

Arredondo, Lani, *Communicating Effectively,* McGraw-Hill, New York, NY, 2000.

Axtell, Roger E., *Gestures: The Do's and Taboos of Body Language Around the World,* Wiley,

New York, NY, 1991.

Berko, Roy M., Lawrence B. Rosenfeld, and Larry A. Samovar, *Connecting: A Culture-Sensitive Approach to Interpersonal Communication Competency,* 2d ed., Harcourt Brace, Fort Worth, Tex., 1997. Bowman, Judith, *Don't Take the Last Donut: New Rules of Business Etiquette,* Career Press, Franklin Lakes, NJ, 2007.

Bosworth, Michael T. and Holland, John R., *Customer Centric Selling,* McGraw-Hill, New York, NY, 2004.

Calero, Henry H., *The Power of Nonverbal Communication: How You Act Is More Important Than What You Say,* Silver Lake Publishing, Los Angeles, CA, 2005.

Capodagli, Bill and Jackson, Lynn, *The Disney Way: Harnessing the Management Secrets of Disney in Your Company,* McGraw-Hill, New York, NY, 2007.

Disney Institute, *Be Our Guest: Perfecting the Art of Customer Service,* Disney Editions, New York, NY, 2001.

Ford, Lisa, McNair, David, and Perry, Bill, *Exceptional Customer Service: Going Beyond Your Good Service to Exceed the Customer's Expectation,* Adams Media, Avon, MA, 2001.

Gee, Val and Gee, Jeff, *Super Service: Seven Keys to Delivering Great Customer Service,* McGraw-Hill, New York, NY 1999.

Lebon, Paul, *Escape Voicemail Hell: Boost Your Productivity by Making Voicemail Work for You,*

Parleau, Highland Village, TX., 2000.

Lucas, Robert W., *How to Be a Great Call Center Representative,* American Management Association, Watertown, MA., 2001.

National Restaurant Association, *Customer Service Competency Guide,* Prentice Hall, Upper Saddle River, NJ, 2007.

Pease, Allan and Pease, Barbara, *The Definitive Book of Body Language,* Bantam Dell New York, NY, 2004.

Quinlan, Kathryn A., *Customer Service Representative,* Capstone Press, Mankato, Minn., 1999.

Richardson, Will, *Blogs, Wikis, Podcasts and Other Powerful Tools for Classrooms,* Corwin Press, Thousand Oaks, CA, 2006.

Satterwhite, Marilyn, and Judith Olson-Sutton, *Business Communication at Work,* Glencoe/

McGraw-Hill, New York, NY, 2000.

Sterne, Jim, *Customer Service on the Internet: Building Relationships, Increasing Loyalty, and Staying Competitive 2nd ed,* Wiley, New York, NY, 2000.

Stinnett, Bill, *Think Like Your Customer: A Winning Strategy to Maximize Sales by Understanding How and Why Your Customers Buy,* McGraw-Hill, New York, NY, 2005.

Swift, Ronald S., *Accelerating Customer Relationships: Using CRM and Relationship Technologies,* Prentice Hall, Upper Saddle River, NJ, 2001.

Timm, Paul R. and Jones, Christopher G., *Technology and Customer Service: Profitable Relationship Building,* Pearson Education, Upper Saddle River, NJ, 2005.

Wainwright, Gordon R., *Teach Yourself Body Language,* Contemporary Books, Chicago, IL, 2003.

Zemke, Ron and Chip Bell, *Service Magic: The Art of Amazing Your Customers,* Dearborn, MI., 2003.

Zemke, Ron, Claire Raines, and Bob Filipczak, *Generations at Work: Managing the Clash of Veterans, Boomers, Xers, and Nexters in Your Workplace,* AMACOM, New York, NY, 2000.

Zemke, Ron and Woods, John A., *Best Practices in Customer Service,* AMACOM, New York, NY, 1998.

Zimmerman, Scott, Finklestein, Ronald, and Alessandra, Tony, *The Platinum Rule for Small Business Mastery,* Morgan James Publishing, New York, NY, 2007.

Photo Credits

Index